Mega-events and Modernity

'This significant new book extends the boundaries of analysis on mega-events and is sure to make a contribution to their study.'

Michael Hall, Professor at the Centre for Tourism,
University of Otago, New Zealand.

'This book should be required reading for all those interested in mega-phenomena, such as expos and the Olympics, academics and practitioners alike.'

Professor Ian Henry, Director of the Institute for Sport and Leisure Policy
at Loughborough University.

This ground-breaking new analysis explores the social history and politics of 'mega-events' from the late nineteenth century to the present. Through case studies of mega-events such as the 1851 Crystal Palace expo, the 1936 Berlin Olympics and the 1992 Barcelona Olympics, Maurice Roche investigates the impact expos and Olympics have had on national identities, on the marking of public time and space, and on versions of national citizenship and international society in modern times.

Historical chapters deal with the production of expos by power elites, their impacts on mass culture, and the political uses and abuses of international sport and Olympic events. Contemporary chapters deal with the impact of Olympics on cities, the growth of Olympics as 'media events' and the current crisis of the Olympic movement in world politics and culture.

Roche argues that mega-events provide power elites with 'flagships' and catalysts to promote their visions of society and of the future, but that they also provide ordinary people with opportunities to connect with and affirm or contest collective identities.

Maurice Roche is Reader in Sociology at the University of Sheffield and Co-ordinator of the SEDEC European social research network. He has published widely on the themes of mega-events, popular culture and citizenship.

D0243134

Mega-events and Modernity

Olympics and expos in the growth of
global culture

Maurice Roche

London and New York

306 ROC

First published 2000
by Routledge
11 New Fetter Lane, London EC4P 4EE

Simultaneously published in the USA and Canada
by Routledge
29 West 35th Street, New York, NY 10001

Routledge is an imprint of the Taylor & Francis Group

Transferred to Digital Printing 2003

Typeset in Baskerville by Exe Valley Dataset Ltd, Exeter

British Library Cataloguing in Publication Data
A catalogue record for this book is available
from the British Library

Library of Congress Cataloguing in Publication Data
A catalogue record of this book has been requested

ISBN 0–415–15711–0 (hbk)
ISBN 0–415–15712–9 (pbk)

In memory of my mother, Frances Roche (1909–2000), for whom life was always the great event

Contents

Tables and illustrations

Preface

I first got interested in 'mega-events' in the late 1980s. My home city of Sheffield made a successful bid for the (ultimately not-so-very-'mega' and enduringly controversial) 'World Student Games 1991' event in 1986. I made a study of this event, looking at its social context and policy implications and identifying themes and issues for further research. Ultimately I started work on this book in the mid-1990s. Back in the late 1980s, and for a long time afterwards, my interest in mega-events – although it resonated with the interests of various specialist historians and other researchers, as I discuss in the book – was a perennial source of puzzlement to many of my sociological and academic colleagues. Thankfully this by no means applied to all of them (as is indicated in the Acknowledgements section). The colleagues who were puzzled seemed to regard mega-events as demonstrably trivial, populist cultural ephemera, irrelevant to 'the problems of the real world' and 'the big issues' of the day, such as struggles in the contemporary period against war, class inequality, sexism, racism and xenophobia, and, conversely, struggles to promote peace, social justice and citizenship and social inclusion. However their puzzlement was, in turn, a puzzle to me. How could they not see that these events were undeniably, even if only periodically, 'problems of the real world' for many citizens in modern societies, and that, as they always have done throughout the modern period, they continue to provide periodic focal points and symbolic expressions, and arenas of debate and struggle in relation to many 'big issues'?

In recent years the clouds of mutual incomprehension have begun to lift. This is particularly so as the notion of 'the Millennium', and of the apparent imperative need to mark and celebrate it, has crystallised in the plans of governments and the consciousness of publics around the world. The fact that this book is published in the year 2000 was not something that had figured in my original plans for this project. Nonetheless it is a fortunate coincidence. In the year of such 'official' events as Britain's 'Millennium' Expo, the World Expo in Hanover, the Olympic Games in Sydney and also numerous 'alternative' large-scale events, few people, even sociologists, can credibly continue to claim ignorance of, or indifference to, mega-events.

Mega-events have come to have a high political profile in the contemporary period. In 2000, at the turn of the twentieth century, they are beginning to assume, once again, the kind of high political and cultural profile they had in 1900, at the turn of the nineteenth century. The year of 1900 saw the staging in Paris of the biggest and arguably most impressive expo the world had ever seen, the high tide of the 'belle epoque', an event which also contained the second in the series of modern Olympic Games. This was followed in the early years of the new century by the staging of two great expos in the USA, at Buffalo (1901) and St.Louis (1904), the latter event also containing the third Olympic Games. As this book tries to show, this was more than just a passing flurry of national cultural assertiveness and international cultural diplomacy. The current high political and cultural profile of mega-events is similarly misunderstood if it is seen in this way. In the main body of this book I explore the historical developments in the main genres of international mega-events, the various reasons and forces behind their creation, and their various impacts. For the moment, however, it is useful to briefly illustrate the high contemporary political profile of mega-events both in this Millennium year and beyond, by noting the interest of nations in winning and staging them. Take the cases of Britain and South Africa, for example. In each of these countries a governing party's attempt to re-new its nation's political identity and re-orient its path of development is has come to be closely associated with its ambitions to host and organise global mega-events.

In Britain, the New Labour government came into power in 1997 aiming to re-orient British society and politics after nearly a generation of 'New Right' Conservative government. Early on it affirmed its commitment to the staging of the Millennium expo in London. The expo was a controversial project, initiated by the previous Conservative government, criticised as an unnecessary and costly extravagance by many New Labour supporters and poorly conceptualised in terms of aims and contents. Nevertheless its distinctive and monumental architectural centrepiece, the Millennium Dome, echoes the dome at the centre of the 1951 'Festival of Britain' event. It thus allows New Labour to symbolically reconnect itself with a well-regarded and memorable image of the 'old' Labour Party's found-ational role in the post-war reconstruction of Britain's society and state. Also, as the flagship of an armada of minor events nationwide, the expo event provides a high-profile, readily identifiable and potentially memorable platform for the celebration of New Labour's versions of contemporary Britain and its visions of a new nationalism.

The linking of the visions and fortunes of the New Labour government to mega-events does not stop with its support for the staging of the Millenium Expo. It has also committed itself actively to the current bidding processes for at least two international mega-events, namely the 2006 soccer World Cup and the 2008 or 2012 Olympic Games. Wembley Stadium – which was an inheritance from the 1924 imperial expo, and became a true and legendary 'theatre of dreams' and a site of national sport-event pilgrimage for the British public (albeit mainly the male part of it) throughout the twentieth century – is to be completely reconstructed to support the bids for both of these events. In addition, it is possible that the Millennium Dome could have a part to play in the staging of some aspects of any future Olympic Games to be held in London. Although not quite going as far as creating a Minister and a 'Ministry for Mega-Events', in 1999 the ex-Sports Minister, Tony Banks, was given the role of government representative in the British bid team for the 2006 World Cup. This is an indication of the seriousness with which major international event projects are now seen. One of the nations competing with Britain to win the right to host the 2006 World Cup event is South Africa.

One of the first international cultural actions of the newly democratised post-apartheid nation of South Africa was to host the Rugby Union World Cup in 1995. Its success in doing this, and also in becoming World Champions, and the positive impact of this on the image of the new South Africa both at home and abroad seemed to convince President Nelson Mandela of the importance of events such as this. Mandela has a credible claim to being one of the twentieth century's most historically important politicians and statesmen. Since his retirement in 1999 he has, among other things, been prepared to provide support and, where necessary, leadership in the courts of the international mega-event organisers, for South Africa's bids for the 2006 World Cup and the 2008 Olympics. The fact that a politician of this stature would choose to continue to serve his vision of his nation by being involved in such bids speaks eloquently for the importance of mega-events for nations in terms of their self-image and place in world society in the early twenty-first century.

These prefatory observations hopefully indicate some of the reasons why I regard the field of mega-events as being more worthy of study by sociology and generally by the social sciences and contemporary humanities (with some notable exceptions) than it has typically been regarded as being hitherto. For me the study of mega-events has opened up windows and perspectives into areas as diverse as social history, architecture and urban planning, media studies, and the political history of the twentieth century. Mega-events contain and condense within themselves, and within the processes of their production and consumption, much of interest and importance, from these and other disciplinary areas. They contain much about the construction of, and connections between, the cultural, the political and the economic in modern societies and in the contemporary world order. To understand something about their origins, nature and development in modernity is to throw light on phenomena and processes within modernity which continue to influence us even when the lights of any particular event have been switched off and when 'the show' appears to be over.

Acknowledgements

Although events are, if nothing else, displays of sociability, unfortunately the act of writing about them all too often is not. Nonetheless, since this project has been brewing for a number of years, and a lot of my friends and colleagues have had to put up with me 'going on' about it for a long time, I have accumulated a fair number of debts to people for their witting or unwitting encouragement and assistance.

Sheffield University colleagues in the late 1980s who shared my original interest in researching and publishing on Sheffield's 'World Student Games 1991' event, and who contributed to my understanding of it, included Roy Darke, Paul Foley and Pat Seyd; and Eddie Friel's diagnoses of the Games' problems from a Glaswegian perspective were also helpful. David Perrow in Sheffield University Library assisted with my research in this period.

From the late 1980s the work of Michael Hall on the politics of events and tourism and Ian Henry on the politics of leisure and sport policy has been particularly valuable. Their consistent support on this project is much appreciated. Also in this period, in the world of international research into events, colleagues connected with the journal *The Annals of Tourism Research* (such as Brent Ritchie, Donald Getz and Jafar Jafari) encouraged my initial interests and work on mega-events. In addition, in more recent years, in the course of my sometimes slow progress on this project, it has been helpful to periodically exchange ideas with colleagues such as Franco Bianchini, John Urry, Chris Rojek, Soledad Garcia, Michael Real, Garry Whannel, Alan Tomlinson, David Chaney and Claudino Ferreira. Ideas and papers related to the themes of this book have been presented and discussed at various international social science conferences and seminars in universities in London and Paris, also in Bilbao, Bielefeld, Loughborough, Leicester and Sheffield. I would like to thank Ian Henry, Franco Bianchini, Liana Giorgi, Alan Tomlinson, Garry Whannel and Peter Taylor for creating the opportunities to make these presentations.

I have always gained a lot from discussions with my doctoral students, particularly on the connections between events, tourism and citizenship, and the various studies of Drs. Alan France, John McColl and Ning Wang made helpful contributions to my thinking about mega-events. Departmental colleagues in the Department of Sociological Studies at Sheffield University who have shown an encouraging and knowledgable interest in event analysis include Sharon MacDonald, Richard Jenkins and my good friend Nick Stevenson. Elsewhere in Sheffield University Peter Jackson, Barrie Gunter, John Arundel, Donald Trelford, Lorna Woods, Peter Taylor and (from

Sheffield Hallam University) Chris Gratton have also been been sources of encouragement on this project. Finally, and in particular for their endurance 'beyond the call of duty' as interlocutors, over the years, in our discourses on mega-events and life in general, I would like to thank my good friends and colleagues Jackie Harrison and Neil Sellors.

Various archives and specialist collections were consulted in the course of work on this book. These include the Bureau of International Expositions (BIE, Paris), the International Olympic Committee, the New York Public Library, The British Library, the British Public Records Office, the Victoria and Albert Musem, the Royal Society of Arts, the British Olympic Association, the Weiner Library (London), Churchill College Library (Oxford), the Edinburgh International Festival office, and the National Fair Archive (Sheffield). Thanks are due in particular to Vincente Loscertales (Secretary General of BIE), Susan Bennett (Librarian of the RSA), Dr Vanessa Toulmin (Director of the National Fair Archive), and also the staff of the Sports Library (Sheffield City Library) for their assistance with the research for this project. Thanks are also due to my editors at Routledge, initially Chris Rojek but then, subsequently, and mainly, Mari Shullaw, for their encouragement of my work on this project.

Of course, none of the people mentioned here have responsibility for any inadequacies in the ideas and information contained in this book. Finally, I would like to thank Jan, Helen and Stephen Roche for their patience and support over the years on this and other research projects.

1   Mega-events and modernity

Perspectives and themes

'Everyone loves a parade', as the saying goes. At least, governments and the powerful often hope that we do. This book is about some of modern society's great 'parades' and 'shows' which can be called 'mega-events'. 'Mega-events' are large-scale cultural (including commercial and sporting) events which have a dramatic character, mass popular appeal and international significance. They are typically organised by variable combinations of national governmental and international non-governmental organisations and thus can be said to be important elements in 'official' versions of public culture. This book aims to explores the history and social significance of two key types of the genre, namely World Fairs (hereafter Expos)[1] and Olympic Games. Its interest is in the ways in which these kinds of events have contributed to the meaning and development of 'public culture' 'cultural citizenship' and 'cultural inclusion/exclusion' in modern societies, both at a national and an international level.

To do justice to these sociological and political interests makes it imperative to take a broad and historical perspective. Thus the book covers a long historical sweep from the mid/late nineteenth-century origins of expo and Olympic events, through the inter-war period to the contemporary period. Along the way it looks at the role of these mega-events in relation to such issues as nationalism, civil society and empire-building in Britain and the USA, the development of authoritarian political cultures in Nazi Germany in the inter-war period, and urban politics and global media empires in the contemporary period. In addition to the expo and Olympic mega-events, it also takes a look at the popular cultures of cities, sport, tourism and the media, particularly the event-related aspects of these cultural spheres. Later in this chapter (section 4) an overview is provided of these themes and issues together with an outline of how they apply to the various studies and chapters which make up the book. This is followed by a final section in which the content of the chapters is summarised.

To prepare the way for the thematic overview we need to consider some basic questions about mega-events, namely what they are, and why and how they should be studied. The first two of these questions are considered in the first section of this chapter, and it is worth noting that general points raised here are picked up again in the theoretical reflections which make up the final chapter. The second section below addresses the third of our questions, namely how to study mega-events. It outlines some of the strengths and weaknesses of the main perspectives in existing research on mega-events together with some of the main features of the general approach taken in this book. To begin with, however, we need to get a broad picture of the nature of mega-events and of their potential significance in understanding our society and our times.

The nature and significance of mega-events

In this section we first consider some examples of the presence of mega-events in modern culture. Second, we consider some of the rationales for studying mega-events in terms of their personal, historical and sociological significance. Finally we consider some of their main characteristics.

The mega-event phenomenon

Some key examples of world-level mega-events in the contemporary period (1980–2012) period are indicated in Table 1.1. We discuss some of these, and their role in helping to structure international public culture, in more detail in Part 2 of this book.

Table 1.1 Structuring international public culture: key mega-events 1980–2012

Periods	City/nation	Mega-event
1980–1989 period		
1980	Moscow	Olympics
1982	Spain (Final in Madrid)	World Cup (FIFA)
1984a	Los Angeles	Olympics
1984b	New Orleans	Expo
1986a	Mexico (Final in Mexico City)	World Cup
1986b	Vancouver	Expo
1988	Seoul	Olympics
1990–2000 period		
1990	Italy (Final in Rome)	Word Cup
1992a	Barcelona	Olympics
1992b	Seville	Expo
1994	USA (Final in New York)	World Cup
1996	Atlanta	Olympics
1998a	France (Final in Paris)	Word Cup
1998b	Lisbon	Expo
2000a	Sydney	Olympics
2000b	London	Expo (Millennium)
2000c	Hanover	Expo (International)
Early 21st century		
2002	Japan and Korea	World Cup
	Salt Lake City	Winter Olympics
2004	Athens	Summer Olympics
2006	(venue to be decided)	World Cup
	Turin	Winter olympics
2008	(venue to be decided)	Summer Olympics
2010	(venue to be decided)	World Cup
	(venue to be decided)	Winter Olympics
1012	(venue to be decided)	Summer Olympics

Before we begin to consider the characteristics of events such as these, it is important to point out that the Olympics and expos are only the most visible and spectacular examples of a dense social eco-system and social calendar of public cultural events in modern societies. This thriving 'event ecology' or 'performance complex' includes a vast range of more specialist forms of great international events which have developed in the late twentieth century. For instance, the contemporary heirs to the Expo-event type include specialist world-level international trade fairs for a vast range of technologies and industries (e.g. aircraft, cars, computers, books etc.). The contemporary heirs to the Olympic event type include specialist world-level international sports competitions (e.g. the World Cup competitions in soccer, athletics, rugby, etc. and Grand Prix events for horseracing and motor-racing, etc.). The World Cup in soccer is particularly important in this context as it has grown, through television and the global diffusion of sport culture, to the same scale as the Olympics in terms of attracting unprecedentedly vast global television audiences.[2] Specialist world-level international arts and cultural events (such as the Edinburgh Festival, the Cannes Film Festival, etc.) derive from both of the main mega-event types. In addition, there are also the 'world regional'-level versions of these events. In the case of sports, these may be connected to either the multi-sport Olympics (such as the Asian Games, the Pan-America Games, the African Games, etc.) or to the world-level specialist events (e.g. the European zone qualifying competition for the soccer World Cup).

Below the international level the national level has traditionally been the main site for the development and staging of public events. While the kind of international mega-events we focus on in this book occur on a multi-annual cycle, such as the Olympic and World Cup four-yearly cycle, they can be argued to structure time in international public culture in a similar way to the more usual annual calendar of national-level public events. The nature and significance of the cultural and political symbolism attached to the annual cycles of public events, such as commemorative parades and sport events, within and between nations can be illustrated in various ways. For instance, Table 1.2 juxtaposes the contrasting public event calendars constructed to maintain the edifice of Soviet and Nazi power in the interwar period in the USSR and Germany, along with the contrasting quasi-national event calendars, within contemporary Britain, of the English middle and upper classes, Ulster loyalists and Irish Republicans in Ulster.

Below the national level, the notion of 'event ecology' reaches down to and incorporates urban and community-level events. Of course, there is always, in any case, a local-level urban dimension to international-level mega-events as we discuss later (Chapter 5). In addition, the level at which public events are experienced and have their effects, whether global, national or local, is to a significant degree affected by the kind of media coverage they can attract and the degree to which they can become national or international 'media events' as we also discuss later (Chapter 6). Table 1.3 suggests a preliminary overview of some the main types, levels and dimensions of public events in terms of which 'mega-events' can be situated and with which we are concerned in the course of this book.

So far we have attempted to indicate something of the characteristics and richness of public cultural events eco-systems and 'performance complexes'. While these systems are sociologically important in characterising and understanding modern societies at national and local level as well as at the international level it

Table 1.2 National public event calendars: contrasting contemporary and inter-war examples

Period of year	UK–1: England	UK–2: Ulster loyalism	UK–2: Ulster republicanism	USSR	Nazi Germany
Winter	• Int. Rugby Twickenham • Cruft's Dog Show	• Derry Apprentice Boys March	• Bloody Sunday Commem.	• Soviet Army & Navy Day • Engineers' Day	• Power Seizure Day • Nazi Party Day
Spring	• The Grand National • Ox-Camb Boat Race	• Derry Apprentice Boys March	• St Patrick Day Parade • Easter Rising 1916 Commem.	• Paris Commune Day • Lenin's Birthday • May Day	• Hitler's Birthday • Labour Day
Summer	• The Derby • Ascot Races • Wimbledon • Henley • Int. Cricket	• Orange Parades • Drumcree • Somme Commem.	• Wolfe Tone Commem.	• Metal WD* • Railway WD • Mine WD	• Summer Solstice Day • Nuremberg Party Rally
Autumn	• Horse Show • Mayor's Show (City) • RAC Rally	• Reformation Day		• Revolution Day • Ricket Forces Day • Agric. WD	• Munich Putsch Day

Sources: For Britain see Debrett's Social Calendar information presented in Rojek 1993, p. 43; for Northern Ireland see Jarman 1997; for USSR see Lane 1981; and for Nazi Germany see Grunberger 1974. *WD stands for 'Workers' Day'.

Table 1.3 Public events: types and dimensions[1]

Type of event	Example of event	Target attendance/market	Type of media interest
Mega-Event	Expos Olympics World Cup (Soccer)	Global	Global TV
Special Event	Grand Prix (F1) World Regional Sport (e.g. Pan-Am Games)	World Regional/ National	International/ National TV
Hallmark Event	National sport event (e.g. Australian Games) Big City Sport/Festival	National Regional	National TV Local TV
Community Event	Rural Town Event Local Community Event	Regional/Local Local	Local TV/Press Local Press

[1]Adapted from Hall 1989; IOC 1996a, p. 50.

should be noted that, understandably, and not least for reasons of space, in this book we do not attempt to provide a comprehensive sociology of their full range and complexity. We do indeed touch on such events as national mass rituals, urban festivals and media events in the course of our exploration of mega-events. However this is particularly to the extent that they help to throw light on the evolution and development of the Olympics and expos, which are the paradigmatic mega-event types with which we are mainly concerned here.

The significance of mega-events in modernity

Mega-events have attracted relatively little research attention. This may be because as a cultural phenomenon they appear to fall within and between a number of distinct and unrelated disciplines and areas. These include, in the case of Expos and Olympic games, the social histories of science, art and technology on the one hand and of sport on the other, and in the case of both of them, practical management-oriented studies as opposed to more searching social scientific literatures. Also, precisely because of their 'one-off' event characteristics, and thus because of the unique story which needed to be told about each of them, the generalizing social sciences have perhaps tended to assume that they belonged to the subject-matter of history and that there was little of a general kind to say about them. Thus it can be difficult to bring them into focus as an admittedly complex but long-lasting popular cultural genre and an influential cultural movement. However, the effort is worth making for a number of reasons. Mega-events like Olympic Games (particularly in the post-war period) and expos (particularly in the late nineteenth century and inter-war years) have been and continue to be important phenomena at many levels and in many respects. There are at least four sets of reasons which underwrite a social scientific interest in the genre, namely personal, national historical, cultural historical and general sociological reasons. In the rest of this section the first three of these reasons are considered. The fourth reason is considered in the following section on the approach to understanding mega-events taken in this book. All of these issues are reconsidered in the final chapter.

The personal level

It is a common observation that people in all societies periodise their lives in terms of 'life events' and their community's 'rites de passages' (Van Gennep 1960). It is also a common observation in modern large-scale complex societies that people reflect on and periodise their biographies in relation to the readily identifiable and memorable great public events which affected them during the course of their lives. This is evidently the case with people's responses to major wars and revolutions. But it is also the case with cultural events of various kinds, not least in, for instance, the 'fashion revolutions' in music or dress which have become mass phenomenona in succesive generations in the post-war period. But in addition to reflecting on and periodising their biographies in terms of the fashions specific to particular decades, people do the same sort of identity-work using mega-events as temporal and cultural markers. This is true in relation both to expos and expo-type events, and also to Olympic and major sport events in general.[3]

The national historical level

At this level the development of international mega-events parallels the growth and spread of 'modernity' and nation-state consciousness. The staging of international mega-events was and remains important in the 'story of a country', a people, a nation. They represented and continue to represent key occasions in which nations could construct and present images of themselves for recognition in relation to other nations and 'in the eyes of the world'. They represented and continue to represent key occasions in which national 'tradition' and 'community', including a national past, present and future (national 'progress', potential and 'destiny'), could be invented and imagined not just by and for leaders and citizens of the host nation, but also by and for the publics of other nations.[4] Their national historical importance can be gauged by the fact that, as we will see later, mega-events have occurred in all periods of modern nations' histories, from the good times to the bad times (e.g. 1870s Depression, 1930s Depression, post-World War reconstruction periods) and usually have been heavily subsidised by national governments.

The history of culture in modernity

Mega-events – particularly, initially, expos – were important and influential forces in the history of modern international culture in general. Part 1 of the book reviews their role and impact in some detail. However, for the moment we can summarise their importance and influence by briefly noting here their interdisciplinarity, their popularity, their institutional effects, and their attitudinal effects. In terms of interdisciplinarity the late nineteenth-century expo genre involved a series of unique exhibitions of some of the greatest contemporary achievements in most of the main 'high cultural' forms of Western civilisation, including science, technology, art and architecture, simultaneously and together as parts of a single event on a single site. Furthermore, these high cultural displays were extremely popular and attracted domestic and international visitors on a previously unprecedented scale. This event-based process of popularisation of high culture had institutional effects in the boost it provided to the creation of permanent cultural exhibitions in the form of publicly accessible museums and art galleries, department stores and theme parks, and also more generally in the form of post-primary public education. Finally, expos had important attitudinal effects in terms of the cultivation of mass interest in consumer culture and tourism culture, and the Olympics in due course had the same effect in terms of the cultivation of mass interest in sport culture.

On the sociology of mega-events

A multi-perspectival approach

We now need to introduce the general approach to the analysis of mega-events taken in this book in outline terms. This approach is reflected on in more detail in Chapter 8. The discussion in this section proceeds in three main steps. Firstly the general social significance of mega-events is indicated. Second, and addressing the multi-dimensional nature of mega-events, the main characteristics which need to be taken into account in any serious analysis of them are mapped out. Finally, a multi-perspectival approach to the sociology of mega-events, which proposes the need for a combination of 'dramatological' and 'contextual' perspectives in any analysis, is outlined. In the following section alternative approaches to the sociology of mega-events are reviewed and the way they relate to the approach taken here is considered.

The general sociological significance of mega-events

This book argues that mega-events are important both substantively and more formally in understanding structure, change and agency in modern society. Substantively, mega-events have been and remain important elements in the orientation of national societies to international or global society and in the theory and practice of public culture and civil society at this level. They have been important points of reference for processes of change and modernisation within and between nation-states, and for globalisation processes more generally. Mega-events, event movements and their networks remain of considerable importance in terms of the exchange, transfer and diffusion of information, values and technologies. In the pre-television era they were one of the main vehicles of cultural globalisation. Now, while secondary to the routine international flows of people and images in contemporary tourist culture and television culture, they still retain a distinctive influence, not least in terms of the space-time structures of global society.

The national and international 'ecology of great public events' – festivals which are simultaneously charismatic spectacles, products of rational calculation, and 'functional' social rituals – has helped to structure the (social) space and time dimensions of modernity at the national and the international levels. Spatially, mega-events uniquely, if transiently, identify particular urban and national places in the national, international and global spaces of media and tourist markets and the gaze of their consumers. Temporally, mega-events operate within event calendars and planning processes spanning generations. In a world of 'flows' they provide symbolic and real channels, junctions and termini. In a world in which space-time is said to becoming increasingly 'compressed', their calendars and periodicities create distance and space. In a world which is arguably becoming culturally homogenised and in which places are becoming interchangeable, they create transitory uniqueness, difference and localisation in space and time. Sociologically they offer concrete, if transient, versions and visions of symbolic and participatory community.

Interpreting their more general significance for modernity we can observe that international mega-events like the Olympic Games – along with the event-based aspects of other genres in contemporary popular culture, such as film, pop music, professional sport, and so on – offer national and international publics the experience of something unique, dramatic and literally extra-ordinary. That is, they promise modernity the occurrence (and, ironically, also the control) of charisma and aura in a world often appearing as excessively rationalistic and as lacking any dimensions beyond the everyday lifeworld and its mundanity.[5] Also, in their calendar and cycles mega-events offer modernity a vision of predictability and control over time, over the pace and direction of change, in a world where social, technological, ecological and other changes can often appear 'out of control' – unpredictable, too fast to adapt to, purposeless and generally anomic.[6]

More formally and abstractly the study of mega-events provides food for thought on the apparently intractable problem for social theory of understanding the relation between structure and agency in the social world, and understanding also how structures change. Theorists have often considered how social structures get enacted and conversely how actions generate structure. For instance, in his seminal critical analysis of modern capitalism, Marx tried to apply the principle that 'men make history, but not in conditions of their own making' and struggled, with varying degrees of success, to avoid the Scylla of structural determinism and the Charybdis of voluntarism.[7] Others have given up the struggle and opted for one-dimensional perspectives which focus on one and effectively ignore the other. Mega-events certainly require at least a two-dimensional analysis which recognises the nature and relevance of both structure and agency. But, in addition, they have an ambiguous and fluid character as social phenomena in their own right, occupying an intermediary position between structures and actions.

They are actions which contain a reflection on structures within them and which carry the potential either to reaffirm structure or to begin to mark a transformation in it. They are structurally-relevant phenomena which, nonetheless, exist as complex and variously unpredictable action processes over time. It is not the aim of this particular study of mega-events to attempt to resolve theoretical problems of structure–agency relationships. The approach to mega-event analysis which is taken in this book, as with any relatively concrete account of social phenomena, inevitably tends to draw upon, rather than to problematise and reflect on, its own assumptions about the structure–agency relation. In general, at this stage it is worth noting the distinctively intermediary character of mega-events as social phenomena and the potential theoretical significance of this. We touch on these assumptions again later in this chapter, and we also return to relevant theoretical issues in the final chapter.

Mega-events as multi-dimensional social processes

From the sociological perspective taken in this book, mega-events can be defined and analysed as complexes of three sets of characteristics. Each of the sets contains an axis and/or oppositional poles. Mega-events are thus, with respect to these axes at least, systematically dualistic and thus ambiguous phenomena. Mega-events simultaneously exhibit three main sets of characteristics. They are 'modern'/'non-modern', 'national'/'non-national', and 'local'/'non-local' (or 'urban'/'mediated'). The first set of characteristics is explored as a recurrent theme throughout the book. Three chapters are devoted to the second set (Chapters 2, 3 and 4), and two chapters are devoted to the third set (Chapters 5 and 6). Mega-events are a complex of these three sets of characteristics. Each set can be analysed in relative isolation, but all of them need to be considered and discussed together in a full and contextual analysis.

The modern/non-modern dimension of mega-events

As 'modern' cultural events, mega-events are 'progressive'. That is they typically involve non-religious/secular values, ideologies and principles of organisation connected with 'Western civilisation' including 'techno-rationalism' (positive roles for science and technology), capitalism, universalistic humanism, urbanism and transnational levels of organisation of communications and transport. However, precisely because of their 'modernity', and because of the reflexivity this implies, mega-events also necessarily contain and/or refer to some non-modern ('pre' and 'post' modern) dimensions. That is they contain implicit or explicit references to modernity's changing versions of its past and the future. In addition, they can at times contribute to social change and thus to the process of modernisation in which preceding periods become seen as 'traditional' and pre-modern, and in which the leading edge of change is seen as being beyond and qualitatively different from the present, effectively 'post-' modern.

As modern *cultural* events, mega-events are a genre which comprises a mix of two major sub-genres, namely 'exhibition' and 'performance'.[8] As performances they are eclectic forms and involve a mix of some or all of the following performance genres: ritual, ceremony, drama, theatre, festival, carnival, celebration, spectacle. Also these events are 'complexes' in other respects. In particular the paradigmatic forms of mega-events I am focusing on, the Olympics and expos, are 'universal' events in their field, which is to say that they try to represent and display a substantial range and mix of types of cultural phenomena (i.e. information and/or products and/or perfomance disciplines).

The national/non-national dimension of mega-events

As 'national' events, mega-events are nationally-based involving national power elites in the 'host nation' in their production, the official 'invented traditions' of host-state nationalism, and official versions of the host-state 'public sphere' (public spaces, publics, 'citizenship', etc.) and populist 'inclusion' strategies in this public sphere (which nonetheless typically contain important and distinctive divisive and exclusionary features and dynamics in relation to class, gender and ethnicity). Mega-events are thus ambiguous. On the one hand they provide powerful media and occasions for elites both to network amongst themselves and with international elites, and to project and disseminate old and new hegemonic and 'official' ideologies to 'the masses'. On the other hand, they also create opportunities – through information overload, mixed messages, selective readings, message failures, creative responses by sections of the crowds which gather for the event, and also through some of the divisive and exclusionary dynamics – for the development of 'popular cultural' and occasionally 'resistant' responses by members of the public.

As 'inter-national' events mega-events are variously multinational, cosmopolitan, supernational and global. They are multinational in that they involve the presence and 'recognition' of the representatives of many foreign nations in the host nation's event-site (the host's 'peer group'). They are cosmopolitan in that they involve the development of 'touristic consumerist' attitudes and values amongst the public of the host nation in relation to the representatives and exhibitions/performances of the 'foreign' nations.

Finally in various ways they are supernational. That is, typically, the host nation plays a significantly more powerful role than guest nations. The host nation can attempt to use the mega-event to emphasise its claims to having a leading status, mission and destiny in the world international order and world history. The host nation's special status could be claimed in terms of its imperial, or quasi-imperial or 'super-power' role, or through some special characteristic of its political ideology, political culture and organization (e.g. fascist or communist totalitarianism).

Because of these factors mega-events are distinctively large-scale (hence 'mega'), and opportunities to play the host-nation role circulate inter-nationally, a process organised by various international event movements and their organisations.[9] The distinctive international scale and character of mega-events can, in the contemporary period, and given the development of global media systems, allow mega-events to be seen as 'global events' in world society and global culture.

The local/non-local dimension of mega-events

As local events, the localism of mega-events consists in the fact that they are about concrete embodied spectatorship and participation, and they are about the particularity of place (a city's 'place' image). In relation to the implications of mega-events for issues of place and identity we can say the following. While mega-events are national and also importantly inter-national (even global), as events they are also localised in space as well as time. Mega-events are localised also in terms of being analysable as urban events, having important and distinctive 'urban' level characteristics (see Roche 1992a,b, 1994, 1999d, and Chapter 5).

These urban-level characteristics of mega-events are as follows. They provide a model of cities in their architecture, habitation areas, public functions and services, etc. They are usually intended to physically transform some strategically important area in cities (this is so even for temporary expos, and is particularly so for Olympics, where, as we see later the concept of an 'Olympic city' is effectively written into the Olympic Charter and the IOC's contract with candidate cities; see Chapter 5). They project the image and status of the local power elite which produced the event for the city's public.

Finally, they project the city to the world (in particular the city's image for tourism and inward investment) and they re-position the city in the world of global inter-city comparisons and economic competition.

By contrast, to call mega-events 'non-local' is to refer to the idea that mega-events are mediated. They were always at least 'news', but in the late twentieth century they have become 'more than news', they are 'media events'.[10] They developed from the late nineteenth century in parallel with, and indeed in a kind of symbiotic interaction with, the development of different forms of mass media, from the mass press, including mass distribution of photographs in the late nineteenth century, through radio and film in the early twentieth century, to TV in the post-war period. This parallel development had two aspects. On the one hand, event organisers were evidently extremely interested in connecting up with the latest mass communications technologies in order to promote their event publicity and also the commercial advertising and/or political propaganda connected with the event. So from this point of view the media helped disseminate the events. On the other hand, mega-events, particulary expos, often provided a platform for the first public display and use of some of these technologies. So from this point of view the events helped to disseminate the media. We consider this media dimension of mega-events further in Part 2, particularly Chapter 6.

An approach to the sociology of mega-events: three dimensions and perspectives

So far it has been suggested that mega-events can be characterised in terms of their modern/non-modern, national/non-national, local/non-local sets of features. In addition their study can be justified in terms of their pervasive presence and significance in modernity in personal (biographical), historical (national and cultural history), and sociological (substantive and abstract) terms. We now need to outline the overall approach to the study of mega-events which is taken in this book. This approach is generally a political sociological one which is intended to be sensitive to the three sets of sociological characteristics of mega-events outlined above. In the following section we then relate this approach to a brief review of some of the strengths and weaknesses, debates and gaps in the perspectives available in the interdisciplinary research literature on mega-events and public culture.

In relation to any given mega-event the approach taken in this book is multi-perspectival because of the need to do justice to what are evidently – (in terms of the discussions earlier in this section) complex (multi-dimensional), fluid and often ambiguous social phenomena. It addresses and attempts to relate together three distinct levels of analysis. These levels of analysis are suggested by the essential temporal characteristics of any event seen as a process over time. These are the event-related time periods of the present (and immediate past and future) (the 'event core' zone), the medium term pre-event and post-event processes producing the event (the intermediate zone), and the long-term (pre-event) causes/motivations and (post-event) effects of the event (the zone of the 'event horizon'). See Table 1.4 for a comparison of the approach taken in this book with alternative perspectives, discussed later in this chapter.

Table 1.4 Event analysis perspectives

A multi-dimensional event analysis perspective	*Alternative event analysis perspectives*
The dramatological dimension:	Ethnographic
Priority given to: • 'Event core' • Experiences and meanings • Agency	Textualist Cultural functionalist
The (intermediate) contextual dimension:	
Priority given to: • 'Intermediate' event zone • Event production and consumption processes • Critical political sociological analysis	
	Economic functionalist
	Political instrumentalist Critical functionalist
The macro-context dimension:	
Priority given to: • 'Event horizon' • Structural change • Historical periodisation	

The 'event core' zone

Understanding what we can call the 'event core' zone calls for a perspective which addresses the meanings of the event as a drama, a performance complex and an action arena for those participating in it (whether as event workers or event consumers, exhibitors or flaneurs, players or spectators) as a 'live' and 'lived' event. An important concern within this zone is the potential use of particular events as occasions for particular symbolic political actions and communications, whether by powerful elites or by sectors of the public or by both. In this political light the event core zone of particular mega-events can sometimes be usefully interpreted as arenas for debate or symbolic struggle over the nature and meaning of contemporary versions of cultural citizenship or the lack of it, and versions of cultural inclusion or exclusion. The various ritualistic and theatrical features which contribute to the charisma, aura and popular attraction of mega-events suggest that it would be useful to refer to this perspective as a 'dramatological' perspective.[11]

The 'intermediate' event zone

Understanding what we can call the 'intermediate' event zone calls for various forms of analysis concerned with the political and economic uses and functions, aims and impacts of the event for elites, social groups (classes, genders, ethnic groups, etc.) and publics (national and international) generally. A core concern in the intermediate event zone is the relationship between events and their medium-term production and impact cycles, on the one hand, and the development of forms and institutions of cultural citizenship and cultural inclusion, on the other. We can call this a(n) (intermediate) contextualist perspective, or a 'critical political sociological' perspective.

The 'event horizon'

Understanding what we can call the 'event horizon' zone calls for a historically informed and internationally/globally oriented analysis of the long-term structural and change-based causal/motivational preconditions and implications of inter-mediate event processes and of the core event. We can refer to this perspective as a 'general sociology of modernity' perspective.

The analyses generated by these three perspectives are intrinsically connected by the temporal flow of event-related processes and actions through the three time periods. Some of the connections within a multi-perspectival study of mega-events are as follows. To be sociologically defensible event analysis must be at least contextually adequate and not de-contextualised. Understanding event analysis as requiring consideration of the pre-event and post-event flows of event-related processes and actions from horizon to event and on to horizon again is a helpful guard against leaving a dramatological analysis of the event core sociologically de-contextualised. The perspectives can also be related by considering the contin-uities and discontinuities, within and between each of the time periods, of event-related collective actors (e.g. organisational interests and popular movements and interests such as the International Olympic Committee, nation–states and their governments, mass sport movements, high cultural professions, networks and movements such as those of the sciences and arts, etc.), and of the changing power struggles and alliances between them. Finally, the perspectives can be related together to the extent that each of them also helps to illuminate aspects of the development and politics of particular national and international 'public cultures' and 'cultural policies' and, relatedly, forms of cultural 'citizenship', cultural 'inclusion' and 'exclusion', and 'civil society' in and between the nation–states staging and/or participating in mega-events.

Given these interconnections the studies in this book use these three perspectives in the sociology of mega-events, and more broadly the 'public culture' forms and dynamics they represent and crystallise, in various combinations. However the primary concern in most of the studies represented in the chapters is with intermediate event zones. Thus the primary perspective is that of a contextual analysis, a critical political sociology of particular mega-events or series of mega-events, or mega-event movements. This typically involves giving an account of the intermediate political and economic processes, the actions involved in the production, and the impacts of these mega-events, which helps to provide a contextual understanding of them and of their implications for public culture and aspects of cultural citizenship. In addition the connections of the dramatological and horizonal perspectives on mega-events and public culture with the contextual perspective – the connections of aspects of both the lived and also the long-term horizonal event zones to processes at work in the intermediate zone analyses – are also discussed in each of the chapters and throughout the book. This is particularly so given the book's concentration on Olympic Games events which are, simultaneously, dramatic lived experiences for organisers, host cities, participants, visiting spectators and, in the contemporary period, television audiences worldwide; major medium-term political, cultural and economic projects for cities and nations with powerful impacts; and elements in the long-term evolution in the modern period both of an international cultural movement and also of international public culture more broadly understood.

To adequately grasp the sociological character and significance for modernity of the Olympic Games as a paradigmatic mega-event genre and also to understand any particular games event it is necessary to give due consideration to all three perspectives. Priority needs to be given to the 'critical political sociology contextual perspective' (Roche 1994). But appropriate weight also needs to be given, on the one hand, to the 'dramatological perspective' and, on the other hand, to the horizonal contextual understanding contained in a general 'sociology of modernity perspective' (Roche 1992a). Concerning these two (for the pragmatic purposes of this book) more secondary perspectives, it is necessary, on the one hand, to appreciate the ritual and dramatic character of Olympic events in general and in particular cases. Also, on the other hand, it is necessary to appreciate the changing nature and role of the Olympic movement, particularly the International Olympic Committee, in international cultural politics over the course of the century. The dramatological perspective on mega-events in this book is thus mainly carried in the various detailed case studies of Olympics, expos and other major cultural events we discuss throughout the book. By contrast the horizonal perspective in my discussion is mainly carried in the historical scope of the book and in its thematic structure. Thus the historical perspective is carried in the discussion of the development of mega-events – their origins, their particularities, their genres, their movements and their roles in public culture – from late nineteenth-century 'international society' through forms of 'supernational society' in the inter-war period (Part 1), to 'global society' in the contemporary period (Part 2).

The application of the three perspectives, particularly the critical political sociology and general sociology of modernity perspectives, to the discussion in this book, is considered in the overview section later. First, however, it is useful to briefly relate the multi-perspectival approach adopted in the book to other related and alternative approaches relevant to the sociology of mega-events and public culture.

Understanding mega-events: alternative approaches

Mega-events are multi-dimensional social phenenomena and require a multi-perspectival approach of the kind outlined above. This is also reflected in the research literature on cultural events and mega-events. Studies have been generated from a range of disciplines and perspectives. Such studies have various theoretical and methodological strengths and weaknesses, and as such can be used both positively and critically as models and resources for developing a multi-perspectival approach. To review them, and to briefly indicate their general utility, we can discuss them in terms of the perspectives indicated above, simplifying the categorisation into dramatological and contextual perspectives (the latter combining the intermediate and horizonal zone perspectives). The main types of dramatological event research can, in turn, be divided into 'ethnography', 'textualism', and 'cultural functionalism', together with mixtures of these types. The main types of contextual event research can be divided into 'economic functionalism', 'political instrumentalism' and 'critical functionalism', together with mixtures of these types.

Dramatological perspectives

Ethnography

Participation in events can involve instrumentally rational and also non-rational experiential attitudes by event attenders. Ethnographic approaches attempt to capture and map these attitudes and experiences. Event organisation requires at least the appearance of instrumentally rational attitudes by the politicians and professionals involved (see 'Contextual approaches' below). But similar attitudes are also evident in the uses of major cultural events made by various communities and social categories among the general public, such as ethnic minorities and youth sub-cultures, to express their own cultural identities or further their own collective interests. Rational instrumentalism applied to individuals explores the variety of personal reasons people have for 'using', 'consuming' or otherwise participating in great public events, reasons which may relate to such things as the pleasure, leisure or tourism interests of individuals, families or groups of friends. This latter concern is evident, for instance, in Ley and Olds' notable study of the 1986 Vancouver Expo (Ley and Olds 1988).

Non-rational experiential uses of event participation, by different social classes and by groups such as ethnic minorities and youth sub-cultures, range from the emotionally expressive to the aesthetic and even to the an-aesthetic. Connectedly the perspectives of individual spectators and crowd participants on their participation in great public events have been explored in accounts of individual attitudes and experiences ranging from a temporary 'aestheticisation' even 'sacralisation' of life to the anaesthesia of ecstacy, drunkenness or exhaustion. To a certain extent, some of the kinds of ethnographic and cultural studies influenced by anthropology noted later contribute to this approach by exploring participants' experiences of the special dramatic or extraordinary character of great public rituals, ceremonies and festivities. Qualitative and ethnographic studies attempt to preserve 'voice' and agency in modern popular cultural forms. Research along these lines in the field of great public events attempts to re-present and analyse event producers' and event participants' voice and agency from their documents (in the case of event producers in particular), speech and attitudes. This ethnographic form of textualism is in turn compatible with, and indeed could be argued to be a necessary descriptive precursor to, the various contextualist and political approaches to event analysis discussed later. Examples of the overlap between these interests can be found in the work of emerging fields of cultural geography and urban cultural studies.[12]

Examples of studies exploring these dimensions in relation to popular participation Worlds Fairs include Pred's studies of the 1897 Stockholm International Exhibition, which elaborates on the spectacular, the consumerist and also the 'dreamworld' character of the Exhibition, and de Cauter's account of the 'ecstasy' and 'disintegration of experience' promoted by such late nineteenth-century fairs and exhibitions (Pred 1991; de Cauter 1993; Gunning 1994). The analysis in each of these historical interpretations of the experience of participants in Worlds Fairs can be strongly influenced by post-modern thinking and can overlap with textualist approaches.

Textualism

Textual approaches refer to studies of culture which treat cultural phenomena as communications and which focus on the interpretation of their explicit and implicit meanings (that is their meaning both in their own terms and also in terms of generalisations about the society which the analyst can attribute to them on the basis of some theory of meaning–social structure relationship). Meanings are available in written 'texts' such as the press and fiction, and, by analogy, in various forms of human communication and expression, such as dramatic performance, visual symbols, and also speech, attitudes, and behaviour, the stuff of qualitative and ethnographic research. Forms of textualism can overlap and be connected up variously with approaches which emphasise functionalism, instrumentalism and context, and we can briefly outline these forms and relationships as they appear in the field of event analysis.

Great public events involve many kinds of texts and meanings. Traditional forms of textualism derive from the theory and ethnography of anthropology. Theoretical anthropological perspectives such as 'structuralism' involve re-presenting the texts of tribal collective meanings and myths as a theoretical system, and are sometimes connected with 'cultural functionalism'. Ethnographic anthropological perspectives explore tribal or traditional ritual and festival as actions and as forms of self-understanding, and also in line with cultural functionalism, as ways of actively making and remaking cognitive and social order (e.g. Handelman, see below).

In contemporary cultural studies approaches to the analysis of modern societies 'textualism' has a critical character. It typically involves the identification of various forms or 'genres' of popular culture and analyses the explicit and implicit contents (the meanings, codes and communications), and the often oppositional and subversive potential contained within them. Examples of this sort of approach can be found in Bakhtin's influential celebration of the pre-modern carnival and of the carnivalesque in modern culture, and in the work of cultural analysts inspired by Bakhtin (Bakhtin 1984, Morris 1994). A leading example of the latter is Stallybrass and White's cultural history of 'the politics and poetics of transgression' in eighteenth-century English fairs, markets and urban life (Stallybrass and White 1986). Critical textualist work relevant to event analysis includes Fiske's critical populist readings of contemporary popular and media culture (Fiske 1989a,b), Chaney's sociology of the drama and spectacle in modern public life (Chaney 1986,1993) and McGuigan's diagnoses of cultural policy discourses (McGuigan 1992, 1995). In related critical and 'post-modernist' versions of textualism the nature and role of authority, authorship and narrative form in high culture and official culture texts and genres is criticised and deconstructed into assemblies of forms and meaning possibilities available for plural readings and popular oppositional readings. This is sometimes connected with broader theories of self and modernity which emphasise the importance of play, ritual and drama in human affairs.[13]

Cultural functionalism

This analytic strategy is most evident in analyses based in an anthropological approach or in neo-Durkheimian sociology. Benedict, in his collection of studies of Worlds Fairs, argues that they 'are rituals of the kind often studied by anthropologists. . . . [Each one] is a collective representation that symbolizes an entire community in a massive display of prestige vis-à-vis other communities. . . . They are about power and economics, but they are also about culture.'[14] Classical anthropology addressed small-scale pre-modern societies, often tribal or tradition-based societies, as self-reproducing cultural systems. A heavy emphasis was usually placed in anthropological studies on the role of ritual, ceremonial and festival events of a great variety of kinds, in understanding the social world and the reproduction of particular tribal and traditional social systems.

Event analysts influenced by anthropology tend to view modern mega-events, with their 'invented traditions' and self-conscious rituals and ceremonies, as an analogy to tribal and traditional events.[15] Examples of the use of the anthropological analogy of pre-modern rituals, ceremonies and festivals for understanding public events in modernity can be found in a number of notable studies.[16] Handelman, for instance, provides a notable analysis of 'public events', stressing their continuities and analogies as between events in pre-modern and modern forms of society. He attempts to limit functionalism and keep it in its place by the simultaneous use of textualist and instrumentalist approaches. Nonetheless, in his view, public events are 'dense concentrations of symbols', 'locations of communication that convey participants into versions of social order'. In modernity as much as in pre-modernity 'Their mandate is to engage in the ordering of ideas, people and things. . . . Public events are constructs that make order' (Handelman 1998: 9, 15, 16).

Durkheim's sociology distinguished between the scale of pre-modern and modern societies and the nature of the social solidarity and cohesion they display, stressing the distinctive role in modernity of the individual (albeit the socialised individual together with the collective ideology of individualism), knowledge (science and education), urbanism, legalism and the division of labour. Nevertheless he viewed modern societies as self-reproducing systems of normative and cognitive order, and variously presented these structures and processes as comprehensible in terms of their analogy with such things as biological organisms and the 'primitive' tribal societies from which they could be assumed to have evolved. Durkheim's influence, along with that of anthropology, can be seen in event analysis which emphasises the ritual and ceremonial nature and functions of events, and also which explores the experience and structures of event meanings and the cognitive and symbolic world they imply and reproduce. The relevance of neo-Durkheimian thinking to the study of mega-events – whether in a conventional functionalist 'status quo'-endorsing form or in forms more critical of modernity – is clear in contemporary media studies approaches to the media-event characteristics of mega-events (as is noted later in Chapter 6).[17]

Contextual approaches

Economic functionalism

This analytic strategy is most often evident in the applied economic analysis of 'hallmark' events and mega-events in terms of their costs and benefits for local (urban and regional) economies, seen as self-reproducing and equilibrating systems. Ironically, they are also often connected with power-elite versions of rational and non-rational instrumentalism, which we will also consider later. Economic functionalist analysis of events in terms of the local economic system is often a common accompaniment of instrumentalist 'boosterist' campaigns to win support for the staging of a mega-event. This is particularly so in the case of the Summer and Winter Olympic Games – but it is often the case more generally with international mega-events – where cities which have to compete with each other for the right to host the event, and where the continued support of local citizens is needed over an often long drawn-out and expensive bidding process. The 'boost' which the staging of the event is claimed will deliver to the local economy is often calculated as an exogenous input to a local self-reproducing economic system in which the 'multiplier' conversion ratios of new income to job creation and additions to local spending power are assumed to be discoverable, predictable and (crucially) controllable variables (see Roche 1992a, 1999d and Chapter 5 below).[18]

Political instrumentalism

Political instrumentalism takes two forms, rational and non-rational. Rational political instrumentalism is connected with the economic functionalist approaches noted above. Applied to powerful groups it takes in the policy-making, planning and management of great events according to the nominally 'rational' criteria typically associated with economic (e.g. cost-benefit) and/or political means–ends calculations. Examples of nominally rational economistic approaches to great events as a means of economic growth and employment are plentiful in the planning and management literature (e.g. Ritchie 1984; Getz 1991). While the growing journalistic and social scientific literature on the Olympics and other mega-event movements, such as World Cup soccer, as spheres of political action, intrigue and conflict speaks in part to the relevance of appreciating political calculation in the understanding of mega-events.[19]

'Non-rational' variants of political instrumentalism emphasise more the extra-ordinary sensations, emotions and symbolic meanings connected with great public events, their spectacular, dramatic and charismatic character. Focusing on powerful groups this variant suggests the need to explore power-elites' and planners' willingness, in the course of nominally rational event projects, to commit them-selves to uncalculated risks, intuitive judgements and 'visions' of the future, which might (or might not) be brought about by their production of a great public event.[20] Various event analysts argue that mega-events and hallmark events, as Hall observes, 'are not the result of rational decision-making process. [They] grow out of a political process [which involves] a struggle for power' (Hall 1989b: 219; also Roche 1994). This is supported in Armstrong's notable comparative study of the policy and planning processes involved in thirty prestige projects and mega-events in major cities around the world. He concluded that 'decisions to go ahead were most often made before any data collection, analysis, evaluation, or constraint determination. Extra-rational factors such as whim, influence, creativity, intuition, vision and experience played large roles in the planning and/or decision to undertake the projects' (Armstrong 1984: 298).

Critical functionalism

This analytic strategy for understanding mega-events is most evident in neo-Marxist and critical theory approaches. Such approaches interpret mega-events as processes which have been called into existence by the capitalist system's require-ments, its needs to reproduce itself, and generally by the 'logic of capital' and of capital accumulation. Such analyses can either emphasise the economic role of commercialism and profit-seeking in mega-events, or their ideological role in legitimating capitalist consumerism and commercialism, or their ideological role in legitimating the nation-state and inter-state systems used by the capitalist system, or a mixture of these. Examples of these sorts of positions can be found in studies of dominant class power and ideology in the production of public events, the 'invention of traditions' and the formation of an official 'public culture' in general,[21] in studies of the role of public events in authoritarian states,[22] and in critical analyses of the contemporary Olympics.[23]

The critical character of accounts which argue for the political (and political economic) functionality of great public events can be illustrated briefly in Byrne's analysis of the 1936 Berlin Olympics and Gruneau's analysis of the 1984 Los Angeles Olympics. Byrne argues that:

> The Nazi Olympics were part of an ongoing ... reality of mass pageantry
> and festivity. . . . The organizers of the 1936 Nazi spectacle were
> concerned with fashioning a persuasive image of Nazi Germany and
> projecting it as much as possible in concurrence with the internationally
> sanctioned image of the Olympic festival. . . . [They] apparently succeeded

in their aim to make of the event a vehicle for the image of a powerful but peace-loving Germany. But this image was a mask

(Byrne 1987: 113, 117, 120)

We consider this important case of the political use of a mega-event in greater detail in Chapter 4 below. In comparable vein, Gruneau argues about the post-War period that 'Sport policies in most capitalist countries (and many socialist ones as well) are so tied into the bloc of vested interests supporting the Olympic movement that they cannot be easily opposed'. He suggests that the 1984 Los Angeles Olympics 'are best understood as a more fully developed expression of the incorporation of sporting practice into the ever-expanding marketplace of international capitalism.' (Gruneau 1984: 2, 15).

Many critical political functionalist accounts also include admixtures of some of the other approaches. That is, on the one hand they can often include, in particular, instrumentalism, by allowing some room for ruling classes' and elites' power of initiative and the play of political conflict around the exercise of this power. While, on the other hand, they can also include a concern for historical and structural change as well as their more characteristic concerns for reproduction of the societal 'status quo'. Bennett's mixture of neo-Marxist and Foucaultian critical analysis in his study of the 1851 London Exhibition and the British Museum, Rydell's study of 'visions of empire' in nineteenth-century and inter-war American International Expositions and Worlds Fairs, and Whannel's analysis of the Olympics as a media phenomenon, are among the more interesting and substantial examples of event research involving mixed approaches which, nonetheless, can for some purposes be categorised as taking a broadly critical functionalist approach to the analysis of media-events.

Lukes, reviewing sociological studies of great public events and 'political rituals' from the 1950s and 1960s (e.g. the Coronation of Elizabeth II in Britain, President Kennedy's Inauguration, his assassination and funeral, and so on), criticises the simple Durkheimianism of their assumption that these events functioned to reproduce social order and social integration. His own view is more critical of the potential dominant-class and ideological role of such events. Nevertheless, Lukes argues for the continued relevance of Durkheim's thinking to the analysis of great public events in modern societies, particularly the idea that rituals have a cognitive as well as a behavioural dimension. Applying a critical Durkheimian view, he believes that 'political ritual should be seen as reinforcing, recreating and organizing collective representations, i.e. models or political paradigms of society and how it functions' (Lukes 1975).

Some implications of alternative approaches

The sociological approach to mega-events developed in this book, as indicated earlier, is multi-perspectival. It principally explores the critical political sociology of intermediate-level processes and dynamics, but it also considers the dramatological and horizonal levels. There is evidently much to draw on and to guide such an approach in the varied event research literature we have outlined so far. However, equally there are weaknesses to be avoided and there are debates to contribute to. Dramatological-level analyses can either, on the one hand, sometimes be indifferent to the need for further sociological contextualisation of cultural events in terms of the politics and structure of modernity, or, on the other hand, they can provide this contextualisation in overly abstract and simplistic ways. The influence of anthropological description and theory is evident in both the former and the latter weakness, while the influence of post-modern theory is particularly evident in the latter. Contextual approaches, on their part, can sometimes lose touch with the dramatological level, interpreting mega-event production either in overly political or economic instrumental terms. Intermediate-level contextual analysis can also lose touch with the horizonal level and with the broader picture of structural social change. This is particularly true for approaches such as economic and critical functionalism, and also cultural functionalism, which see mega-events as effectively contributing to the reproduction of social systems. To address the horizonal- and intermediate-level contexts more adequately the discussion in this book attempts to take a long-range historical perspective. The aim of this is to enable the origins and changes in the dramatological character of mega-events themselves to be brought into view, together with their developing relationship to their contexts, in particular the contexts provided by long-term changes in the structure and politics of nation-states and international society. With these themes in mind we can now turn to an overview of the themes of the book.

Book themes: an overview

The book consists of six main chapters containing a range of studies of historical and contemporary mega-events in the modern period. In addition, some theoretical reflections on the relationship between mega-events, personal identity and modernity suggested by the preceding discussion are outlined in the concluding chapter. The main chapters are arranged into two parts. The first part is concerned with the role of mega-events in the late nineteenth-century origins and early/mid-twentieth-century development of national and international public culture, cultural citizenship and cultural inclusion. The second part is concerned with contemporary dimensions and problems of mega-events in relation to global society and their attendant implications for public culture and citizenship in the late twentieth century. In this section we first outline some background themes of the discussion in each of these parts, particularly in relation to the horizonal dimension of long-term structural change. Then the thematic concerns of each of the Parts and their chapters is outlined. In the final section a brief summary is provided of the content of the chapters.

Structural change and forms of international society

Throughout the accounts and analyses of mega-events presented in the two parts, the main perspective adopted is that of a critical political sociology of events in a medium-term time frame, but reference is also made to the dramatological and the horizonal dimensions. Our main explicit concerns are with the political sociology and dramatology of mega-events, whereas macro-contextual analysis of the mega-event phenomenon is implicit in, and is carried by, the long-term historical reach and periodisation of the account. This macro-context provided, and continues to provide, the motivation, opportunities and resources for the production and consumption of large-scale international popular cultural events. Given these points, it is useful at this juncture to make explicit some elements of the macro-context of long-term social change within modernity since the nineteenth century which provide the terms of reference for historically-based structure of chapters and Parts in the book. These and other related macro-contexual issues are reviewed in the final chapter.

This book is concerned with the contribution of mega-events to the construction of public culture in modernity, and this requires an historical dimension to the analysis. It focuses, in particular, on the international dimension of public culture, the construction of world views which relate to 'international society', including popular understandings of 'a world of nations' and 'universal human experiences and interests'. It suggests that there are three forms of internationalism (or from another perspective, forms of globalism) which have occured over time since the nineteenth century and which mega-events have been strongly connected up with and expressed. These are 'liberal-imperial' international society, supernationalist international society and global society. The three forms of internationalisation can be conceived as successive waves or layers, with the contemporary period being mainly influenced by the growth of global society, but also continuing to be influenced by liberal-imperialism which was dominant in the late nineteenth century and pre-First World War periods, and also by supernationalism, particularly the totalitarian forms of fascism and communism dominant in the inter-war period, and also, in altered form, continuing to be very influential for much of the post-war period. These three waves and periods are the underlying macro-context and 'structural change' themes of the two main Parts of the book.

Part 1: 'Mega-events and international culture: origins and developments'

International public culture

The concept of 'international public culture' can be taken to refer to four related phenomena. First, there are the public images of divers subordinate nationalities, ethnicities or religious groups (which may include immigrant/diaspora groups and/or membership in transnational religious communities, hence the inter-nationalism) held within any given nation. Second, there are national publics' images of and attitudes to 'other nations' ('foreigners', difference, etc.). Third, there are the images of 'international society' and transnational universalistic principles and practices (such as human rights) held by the members of any given national public as part of their conception of their own civil society and public sphere. Fourth, there is the sphere in which national governments' foreign policies, inter-governmental organisations, international non-governmental organisations (INGOs) and multinational capitalist corporations (MNCs) operate, particularly with respect to culture and comunications, a sphere of minimal (although slowly crystallising) governance (see Chapter 7).

International mega-events, in the forms of expos and international sport events, particularly the Olympics, played an important role in the development of both national and international politics and culture in the West from the late nineteenth century. International and supernational cultural events helped to create a fragile space, something of an 'international public culture', in which 'official' versions of collective identities, particularly but not exclusively national identities, were asserted and recognised in a (usually, at best, hierarchic and exclusionary; at worst, hate-filled and warring) international 'world of nations'.

This version and level of public culture was institutionalised in the early and mid-twentieth century in equally fragile ways by the development of elements of global-level governance from the League of Nations to the United Nations, and various regulatory networks and INGOs necessary to coordinate international trade, travel communications, etc. In the period of industrially-based economic and military internationalisation, running from the late nineteenth century up to the early post-war period, cultural internationalisation developed along with the other forms of internationalisation, but tended to lag behind them. In this period, prior both to mass national television and also to mass international television (via satellite technology), mega-events were among the main means for developing and promoting national culture and international cultural communication and exchange.

Mega-events can be argued to have helped to develop 'international public culture' in a number of ways. Organisationally they provided aims and rationales, resources and status, for internationally-based cultural event movements such as the Olympic movement. Substantively, they created internationally recognised calendars and cycles of these events and their convening of many national representatives and international tourists and visitors in a specific place and time. Intra-nationally they helped to create and concretise a specific 'transnational' and 'international' zone or dimension *within* the public cultures of most national societies.[24]

The origins of internationalism and the 'archaeology of post-modern culture'

Contemporary perspectives and debates in cultural studies and the sociology of popular culture, including those relating to mega-events, are typically concerned with the 'post-modern', 'global' and 'consumer' characteristics of current popular culture. They are typically critical of 'grand narratives' in socio-cultural analysis of the kind exemplified in this book in terms of processes of modernisation, the development of industrial capitalism, globalisation and so on. Occasionally their proponents are willing to acknowledge that post-modern culture did not emerged fully formed from the womb of the present, that it has precedents, and that the allegedly 'depthless present' may even have origins (deep) in history.[25] In post-modernists' occasional recognition of history and of the fact that 'We've been here before', the 'here' in question tends to be identified as the late nineteenth and early twentieth centuries, the 'fin de siecle' or, in France, the 'belle époque' – the period of rapid social change in Western modernity preceding the apocalypse of the First World War. This period is a focus of much of my discussion in Chapters 2 and 3. On this basis, the work undertaken in these chapters can be relevantly, if somewhat portentously, tagged as aiming at making a contribution to the, in my view, long overdue 'archaeology of post-modernity'.

However, post-modern concessions to history can also be overly selective, and there is a problem of 'the missing link' in these recognitions of the relevance of history in cultural studies accounts. For instance, there are the political and cultural consequences of the First World War (the first great wave of military globalisation), the political economic crises leading to the second great wave of military globalisation in the Second World War, and the consequences of this for the post-war period. These connections – the history linking the post-war present to the late nineteenth century – can be underplayed and even overlooked entirely in post-modern accounts. So, to contribute to current concerns and debates – and in particular to contribute to the understanding of the origins and characteristics of contemporary mega-events such as the Olympic Games (Chapters 3 and 4) – Part 1 focuses on the development of international public culture and international cultural events, in particular expositions and Olympic Games, in the late nineteenth century and early twentieth century.[26]

In Chapters 2 and 3 we consider respectively production and consumption aspects of Expos in particular, and in each chapter, issues of citizenship, inclusionary and exclusionary aspects. We consider the role of power elites in the production of expos and, in spite of their inclusionary messages and effects, the consequently exclusionary aspects of expos in relation to classism, sexism and racism, in their consumption as early forms of popular 'info-tainment'. These aspects were particularly notable in the imperialist version of the expo genre in this and later periods. Imperialism had been a foundational theme in the approach of Britain and France to the early international expos of the 1850s and 1860s. In addition it rapidly became an even more important theme in the expos of the 1880s and 1890s and thereafter, connected with the European nations' 'scramble for Africa' and America's extension of its influence in the Pacific via Hawaii and the Philippines. The imperial version of the expo genre, which continued well into the inter-war period, is reviewed in Chapter 2.

Internationalism as supernationalism: the inter-war 'missing link'

As noted above, Part 1 considers the issue of the nineteenth-century origins of the late twentieth-century complex of 'post-modern', consumerist and global culture, and also of the 'the missing link' between the late nineteenth century and the present provided by the aestheticisation of everyday life in the interwar period. It does so by developing the implications of the theme of the nationalist and imperialist character of the 'international society' developed in the late nineteenth century. It addresses the neo-imperialism of early twentieth-century authoritarian states using the notion that, in this period, we see the development of the concept of a 'supernational' wave and dimension of international society.

The supernationalist theme was most clearly and floridly developed in the neo-imperialism of inter-war totalitarianism: on the one hand, that of Stalinist Russia (neo-imperial in relation to the numerous other 'soviet republics' which made up the 'union' in the 1930s and the Eastern European communist states in much of the post-war period), and, on the other hand, fascist countries, particularly Nazi Germany in the 1930s (explicitly committed to aggressively expansionist neo-imperialism). These political and cultural developments were intertwined, in this period, with two others.

First, in this period a wave of new communication and transport technologies, cultural industries and institutions connected with, for instance, radio, film, and cars developed. Each of these technologies and their promised 'progressive' social impacts was either 'launched' at expos in this period or heavily popularised and propogated at them. They began to have a major impact on the structures and processes of modern societies in the social, economic and political reconstruction after the First World War. This wave of cultural technology offered supernational states new forms and levels of propaganda and surveillance. But it also opened up new cultural areas potentially beyond the control of government and dependent on international communications and trade. This left an impact on the mega-events of the period which we consider in relation to the media aspects of events in Chapter 6.

Second, supernationalism was both cause and effect of the two 'world wars'. These two nightmarish periods of warfare, slaughter and destruction in the supposedly 'progressive' and 'advanced' civilisation of Europe on an historically unprecedented scale of technological effectiveness and barbarism also left an impact on the mega-events of the period. In terms of all of these influences, political, cultural and military, supernationalism influenced international mega-events substantively and negatively. They influenced these public cultural events substantively by attempting to use them and take them over for propaganda purposes and also by providing them with models of address to mass publics. They influenced these public cultural events negatively by providing processes and arenas for the expression of political and cultural conflict, and also by making the pursuit and achievement of peaceful international communication through cultural events a matter of historic consequence for the future of modernity and of enduring concern and interest, both for elites and for mass publics.

The growth of twentieth-century supernationalism involved an address to mass publics, the use and promotion of emotionality and aestheticisation in politics and culture, involving a heavy emphasis on symbols and myths, and on the cultural forms of mass collective rituals, theatre and festival. The theatricalisation and ritualisation of politics and of events in the supernationalist period both had a direct impact on, and also provided a model for, the development of the sport movement in general and the Olympics in particular. Olympic symbols and rituals were developed and institutionalised in both the pre-1914 and inter-war periods. Chapter 3 discusses the impact of expos on this process in the pre-1914 period, and Chapter 4 discusses the impact of supernational mass festivals and rituals on this process in the inter-war period. Furthermore the Olympic movement was directly influenced by inter-war supernationalism and by the threat that the latter posed to its independence and integrity as an international cultural movement and institution. Olympism was influenced to invest much further than it had previously done in creating a distinctive and identifiable set of ideals, symbols and rituals. These needed to be *trans*-national as well as international, not least in order to act as counterweight to supernational influences. The alternative was to risk being taken over, used and abused by supernationalist powers and their versions of nationalism and internationalism. This risk undoubtedly threatened the Olympic movement in the 1930s in relation to Nazi Germany. We discuss the development of Olympism and international sport culture under the influence of supernationalism in the inter-war period in Chapter 4.

It is worth bearing in mind that inter-war supernationalism, this 'missing link' period and theme in many cultural analysis and 'post-modern' perspectives, continues to be of relevance in a number of respects for understanding the development of public culture and events in the contemporary period. First. in the late twentieth century we are supposed to be in a 'post-colonial' period. However, this means, both by definition and in real political experience, that the nature of contemporary nations, their independence and self-image, is in part defined by their image of the 'otherness' of Empire. That is, it is defined in relation to their previous identities from the historically recent (i.e. inter-war) past, identities that they ostensibly and actively seek *not* to become again, namely neither colonised or coloniser. Second, nations and the international system continue nonetheless to be affected by the heritage of imperialism through patterns and flows of migration and in many other ways. Third, powerful new forms of 'de facto' imperialism developed in the post-war period connected with the emergence of the two 'world superpowers' of the USA and USSR each holding potential dominion over the very existence of all other nations through the threat of world-scale nuclear war, the 'cold war' between them, and their zones of influence and client-states. Finally, in the post-communist period there are undeclared forms of de facto neo-imperialism present in the continued 'superpower' role of the USA, and in the emergence of a multi-polar global economy with actual or potential new world and/or 'world regional' 'superpowers' such as Japan and China.

Part 2: 'Mega-events and global culture: contemporary dimensions and problems'

In the late twentieth century and early twenty-first century, the importance of the national base, the nature of the international world as a 'world of nations', and also the supernationalism to which it gives rise, has not disappeared and will not be disappearing. This is, not least, given the new pre-eminence of the USA as the sole genuine 'superpower' and also the rapid emergence of China as a 'supernation'. However, in the post-Second World War and the late twentieth-century periods the long-term trends towards internationalisation and trans-nationalisation have grown qualitatively stronger. These trends relate to developments in economic, in cultural and, to a certain extent, in political spheres, which have long been implied in modern nation-statism and capitalism, which have been visible since the late nineteenth century and through the two world wars, and which we are now familiar with as processes of 'globalisation'. The role of mega-events in the construction of international public culture in the contemporary period is in large part most relevantly understood in relation to the idea that a global consumer culture is emerging (a key theme in chapters 5 and 6). Also, to a lesser extent, this role can be understood in relation to the idea that we are beginning to witness the emergence of embryonic spheres and forms of global global governance which will become qualitatively more important as the twenty-first century progresses (a key theme in Chapter 7).

In the late twentieth century, developments have occured, based on new communications and transport technologies, which make it more credible than ever before in human history to conceive of the human world as 'one world' in theory and as being firmly set on the road to 'one world' in practice. Fast efficient mass international transport systems for people and materials have developed since the 1960s together with satellite television and computerisation since the early 1980s. On the basis of these and other techno-economic infrastructures, the capitalist economy has been integrating (albeit in a multi-polar way and through the activities of large-scale multinational companies) and 'globalising' at a rapid rate.[27]

In this developing 'global society' context, 'core-periphery' international relations become renegotiable, nations can appear as if they are merely (world-) regional or local entities, and, ironically, the genuinely local (sub-national) level, particularly the urban level, can achieve a new social importance.

Global consumer culture

Global consumer culture is made possible by qualitative developments in transport and communications technologies in the late twentieth century which provide the material basis for the world-wide mass movement of people, images and commodities. It is driven, on the one hand, by the market-making dynamics of powerful American, Japanese and European multinational corporations producing, distributing and advertising personal lifestyle-relevant goods (such as fast food and drink, cigarettes, sport clothing, personal computers, cars, etc.), bringing these relatively standardised commodities and images of them to people in a vast range of societies around the world in an effective and routine way. On the other hand it is driven by tourism and touristic consumerism, in which mass publics in the advanced societies both routinely travel the world in search of escapist pleasure and (occasionally) exotic difference, and also, when not touring, consume media images and goods and services evocative of touristic hedonism.

Mega-events have had, and continue to have, an important role to play in the development of this global consumer culture through their long-established promotion of what I refer to in this book as 'touristic consumerism' (Chapters 3 and 5). They also contribute to understandings and experiences of 'one world' through their capacity to carry universalistic meanings and ideals. These include those associated with the benefits of peaceful cultural exchange between nations, ethnic and ideological communities (expos and Olympics), scientific and technological 'progress' (expos), human 'progress' and the value of personal and national achievement and recognition through rule-governed competition (Olympics and sport) (see Chapter 7).

In terms of the globalising culture of touristic consumerism it is important to bear in mind the degree to which this culture consists of meanings and values which have both a 'mediatised' and a 'localised' character. To say that global culture is mediatised is merely to point to the evident fact that it is propagated by media corporations, particularly through television, and that it is experienced as part of people's general experience of the pervasive presence and power of media in modern life. We explore the role of mega-events in this mediatised aspect of global culture in Chapter 6.

To say that global culture, in addition to being 'mediatised', is also in important respects 'localised', might initially appear paradoxical. However this simply refers to the idea that we, as touristic consumers, typically desire and address ourselves to the specificity of particular places, times and related experiences. While global culture clearly can and does have homogenising characteristics in the spread of general consumerist lifestyles and the technological support of them, it nonetheless also has another dimension which is about the preservation and/or construction of *distinctiveness*.[28]

This connects very well with mega-events since, whatever their often standardised features, they nonetheless offer three forms of distinctiveness to the touristic consumer. First, there is the specificity of *when* they occur (the year, their capacity to mark international public time and history). Second, there is the specificity of *what* uniquely dramatic and memorable activities and experiences occur when people attend them in person. Finally, there is the specificity of *where* they occur, namely the city that staged and 'hosted' them. Global culture, then, particularly the touristic consumerist aspect of it, consists of localised as well as mediatised images and experiences. Mega-events contribute to, and are constituted by, localisation processes as well as mediatisation processes. We explore this localised aspect of global culture in Chapter 5.

Mega-events and global culture: cities, the media and global governance

Cities' public cultures have always been complex and ambiguous. They have always contained the national as a dimension (particularly in their state-based institutions and functions, and particularly in capital cities). However, in the late twentieth century they have also come to contain the international, multicultural and cosmopolitan to a degree that they rarely did before. Late twentieth-century mega-events have tended to reflect this new balance of power between cities and states, and between both of them and the international/global level (just as they reflected the rise of the nation-state and 'a world of nation-states' in the nineteenth century). Now they reflect not only 'a world of nations' but also 'a world of cities' (a world of localities and different identities) together with versions of a 'one world' (an evolving singular and interconnected 'global society') worldview. Globalisation processes make 'the local' newly important in contemporary social formations. Mega-events are an important element in the propagation of globalisation processes in general and in the promotion of their associated 'localisation' aspects in particular.

Mega-events can be seen as having at least a two-dimensional character as tourist events (in the realm of global tourist culture and the global tourist industry/cultural economy) and also as media events (in the realm of global media culture and the global media industry/cultural economy). From each of these perspectives mega-events represent temporal and spatial 'localisations' of potentially globally relevant cultural economic activity and flows (of people, information and images). The main flows are distinctive in each case, and allowing for some oversimplification we can draw the following picture. The tourism industry operates by selling specific places to consumers and getting them and their money to flow into and around these places. By contrast the media industry operates, in significant part, by taking what are often extremely locally-based events (e.g. in news and sport programmes respectively) and generating flows of information and images from these locations out to broader non-local, national and/or global audiences. We consider this theme in Chapter 6. Since mega-events with few exceptions require a city to 'host' and 'stage' them, it is necessary to recognise the urban tourism background of contemporary mega-events if both their general global cultural (and global cultural economic) character and also their local significance is to be adequately understoood.

In Chapter 5 we consider the way Olympics and expo mega-events generate and propagate the global cultural forms of tourism and media culture. We consider the idea that mega-events, particularly dramatic 'performance'-oriented genres like the Olympics, operate to 'localise' global culture. They do so, first, by spatially locating (constructing a 'stage' for and 'producing'/directing) an event of much-more-than-local (historic, global) significance and interest. Second, they attract and accommodate international visitors and tourists connected with the event. Third, they are required to provide the necessary technical facilities to allow television to transmit the event as a 'media event' to 'the watching world' (allowing 'the watching world' to be co-present in important ways at the event along with local and visiting spectators). We consider these dramatological and contextual aspects of Olympics as urban events through discussion and illustrations of 'expo cities', 'Olympic cities' and 'Olympic media cities'.

In Chapter 6 we explore the 'media event' dimension of the mega-event in more detail. Just as the national and international dimensions were two sides of the same mega-event coin in the pre-television era, so (in addition to these axes) the urban and the media, the local and the global, are two sides of the same mega-event coin and important new axes in the late twentieth century. In Chapter 6 we consider the media event character of sport culture in general and of the Olympics in particular. We consider the increasingly important role of 'media sport' for multinational media and product organisations concerned with the global distribution and marketing of images and goods. Mega-sport events as global media events are important elements in these processes of cultural globalisation. We consider various dramatological and contextual perspectives on the Olympics as media event, together with case studies of the media aspects of particular Olympic mega-events.

Finally, beyond the consumer culture aspects of global culture there is also the slowly emerging sphere of global governance. In Chapter 7 we consider various problems in the contemporary Olympic movement in relation to this sphere of global governance. These problems stem from the powerful impacts of the Olympic movement on cities worldwide and on global media organisations, and they threaten to destroy the charisma of its mega-events and to disempower the movement in its potentially positive role in contemporary global civil society.

Book contents: summary

We are now in a position to briefly recap and summarise the content of the chapters in Parts 1 and 2. The chapters in Part 1 are concerned with the following. In Chapter 2 the first waves of events in the 'international' and 'imperial' versions of the expo mega-event genre are reviewed in terms of the power relationships they embody both within and between the advanced industrial capitalist societies. Key perspectives on the history and analysis of popular culture and events in the work of Eric Hobsbawm and Tony Bennett are discussed in this chapter. In Chapter 3 the nature and limits of the cultural citizenship and inclusion offered by expos, particularly in relation to problems of classism, sexism and racism, are explored together with the expo-based origins of the Olympic mega-event genre. In Chapter 4 the development of Olympism and the internationalisation of sport culture in the inter-war period is reviewed. To illustrate the discussion, these chapters contain accounts of a range of expos and also brief case studies of the 1851 Crystal Palace international expo, the 1924 Wembley imperial expo, and the 1936 Berlin Olympics.

The chapters in Part 2 relate to the contemporary period and are concerned with the following. While the expo genre is considered in Chapter 5, the main focus throughout Part 2 is on sport culture and the Olympic event genre and movement. Issues about the implications of mega-events for public culture and cultural citizenship are argued to arise in each of these spheres addressed by the chapters, namely in relation to civil society and membership in urban society, media(ted) society and global society. Chapter 5 deals with expo and Olympic mega-events understood as urban events promoting urban tourism and connected with the key late twentieth-century touristic cultural form of the theme park. It also discusses the implications of mega-events for urban cultural citizenship. Chapter 6 deals with Olympic mega-events understood as global media events and with the mediatisation of sport culture more generally. It also discusses the connection of mediatised mega-sport events with national and transnational forms of cultural citizenship. Key perspectives on the analysis of media and sport events in the work of Daniel Dayan and Elihu Katz, John MacAloon and Michael Real are discussed in this chapter. To illustrate the discussion these chapters, 5 and 6, contain case studies of, among other examples, the urban and the media dimensions of the Barcelona Olympics. Chapter 7 addresses the potential role and current problems of the world's leading cultural mega-event producer, namely the Olympic movement. It also discusses the notion of global cultural citizenship in relation to the Olympic movement.

Finally, in Chapter 8, we conclude with some general reflections on the meaning and social role of mega-events in modernity which arise both in this Introductory chapter and also in the reviews and analyses of events in Parts 1 and 2. It is argued that international mega-events are important aspects both of personal identity formation in late modernity and also of social structural processes in global society.

Part 1

Mega-events and the growth of international culture

2 Expos and cultural power
Capitalism, nationalism and imperialism

Introduction

This chapter reviews international and imperial expos in the period 1851–1939 and the discussion falls into four sections. Section 2 provides a brief overview of the origins and development of international expos in general, and section 4 provides a comparable overview of imperial expos over the same period. In the course of these accounts two case studies of each of these types of expo are considered in particular, namely the 1851 Crystal Palace expo in London, to illustrate the international genre, and the 1924/5 Wembley expo also in London, to illustrate the imperial genre. In section 3 we consider issues of power and the production of expos, looking briefly at diplomatic and political networks, event-planning groups and cultural professions. In section 1, as a prelude to these accounts and inquiries, and to help develop the conceptual framework for the discussion, we consider two notable and relevant analyses of late nineteenth-century and early twentieth-century public culture and events, namely Eric Hobsbawm's account of 'mass-produced traditions' and Tony Bennett's account of 'the exhibitionary complex'.

Perspectives on public culture: late nineteenth century and early twentieth century

Great events like the international expositions we discuss in this chapter were both products of and contributed to the growth of popular national public cultures which began to develop dynamically in the late nineteenth century. To help understand both the dramatological and contextual dimensions of these developments it is useful to take stock of two notable analyses of them, namely Hobsbawm and others' exploration of 'the invention of tradition' in the Victorian period (Hobsbawm and Ranger 1992), and Bennett's discussion of the Victorian 'exhibitionary complex' (Bennett 1988). In various ways these analyses have contributed to and improved on mainstream historical and sociological concepts of 'national culture', including influential interpretations of national culture such as those in terms of notions of the 'imagined community' (Anderson) and 'the public sphere' (Habermas).[1] Habermas and Anderson in their analyses tend to over-privilege the upper- and middle-class rationalistic cultural institutions of, respectively, eighteenth-century rational orality (e.g. coffee-house discussion) and nineteenth-century literacy. By contrast, as we will see in this section, Hobsbawm and Bennett give an interesting and relevant priority, in their analyses, to popular cultural events and movements involving the middle and working classes in both rationalistic and dramatological ways.

However, that being said, my discussion in this section also aims to go beyond their analyses in a number of ways. Hobsbawm is mainly concerned with the 'invention' of *national* traditions and Bennett with the *national* 'exhibitionary complex'. Thus both underplay the international dimension which is a key theme in this book. Also I will suggest that Bennett's conceptualisation underplays the dramatological or 'performance' aspects of producing and consuming in 'the exhibitionary complex' and, relatedly, misses the connection between the development of expo and sport/Olympic versions of great popular cultural events in this period. In relation to these perspectives my discussion suggests the need for a concept of late nineteenth-century and early twentieth-century mega-events and event movements as forming a 'performative complex' in modernity in which both national and international-level traditions and 'public culture' are produced by elites through the media of dramatic and large-scale events with the active involvement and participation of mass publics.[2]

Hobsbawm, nineteenth-century public culture and 'invented traditions'

Hobsbawm's influential account of the 'invention of traditions', indeed their 'mass-production' in the late nineteenth century, from the point of view of the concerns of this book is effectively an account of the social construction of public culture. One of its many strengths is that, unlike many nationally-based histories, it is comparative, surveying Britain, France, Germany and the USA. Thus, while it does not aim to provide a systematic social theory of these construction processes it is relevant to broad sociological concerns about the nature of Western 'modernity', 'modernisation' and social dynamics in this period. It is sociologically relevant firstly by drawing on and applying neo-Marxist analysis of the relevance of capitalist dynamics and state-building for class relations, particularly between the new middle classes and the working class, to the sphere of culture, and secondly through the comparative historical information it provides.

Allowing for many national historical differences, particularly in Europe, related to the uneven development of industrialisation and/or nationhood, Hobsbawm's account shows the development of similar patterns of popular and public cultural institution-creation by governmental and middle-class elites in late nineteenth-century Europe and the USA. These patterns emerged in response to the new political situation created by democratisation, the often fraught process of extending citizenship and voting rights first to men and (much) later to women in the USA and Europe from the 1870s onwards. Western governments and their states in general, from then onwards, needed to be legitimised by popular consent. This in turn created powerful interests on the part of national 'establishments', ruling elites and middle classes concerned with attempting to channel and control the development of working-class consciousness, demands and behaviour by means other than coercion. There was a need to win the 'hearts and minds' of newly enfranchised working-class 'citizens' for projects of economic growth and nation-building (Gellner 1983; Smith 1998).

This led to a variety of what we would now call 'cultural policies', and in particular 'cultural inclusion' policies and initiatives, by political and economic elites to involve the mass of the people in new cultural institutions and cultural industries. The most tangible and institutionalised of these from the 1870s was probably the development of universal compulsory primary, and later secondary, schooling in a nationally determined and characterised curriculum of the skills and knowledge, attitudes and behaviour appropriate for new 'citizens' (Bowles and Gintis 1976). In addition, the new citizens could be attracted to participate, on the one hand, in new forms of official/national culture and 'civil religion', appealing to public interests in collective identity, meaning and purpose. On the other hand, they could be attracted to participate in new civil society-based forms of popular culture and cultural industries, appealing to workers' growing interests in re-creation, escape from work, entertainment and consumption. Hobsbawm's concept of 'invented traditions' refers to this new generation of cultural inclusion policies. Of these cultural policies he observes:

> To establish the clustering of 'invented traditions' in western countries between 1870 and 1914 is relatively easy'. Examples include 'old school ties and jubilees, Bastille Day and the Daughters of the American Revolution, May Day, the Internationale and the Olympic Games, . . . the Cup Final and Tour de France as popular rites, and the institution of flag worship in the USA.
>
> (Hobsbawm 1992: 303)

While Hobsbawm focuses on official and elite-inspired 'popular cultural' policy he also recognises that there was a variable reception of 'invented traditions' by national publics, and thus that some of them failed. Further, new traditions were also created by class-based rather than nation-based popular movements, for instance the revival or invention of 'folk' costume among the peasantry, class-specific festivals such as May Day (created in 1890) (ibid pp.283–8) and migrant sub-cultures among the working class, and exclusive class-specific sports among the middle class (ibid pp. 305–6).[3] The account of the history of national and inter-national public culture and public events which I develop in this chapter and the next one emphasises the importance of two main categories of mass spectacle and their interconnection – namely mass sport events including the Olympics, and mass participation in expositions. It also touches on mass rituals and festivals *en passant* (see Roche 1999c, d). Since Hobsbawm's survey covers each of these three key categories, from the perspective of the themes in this book it is worth, at this point, taking a brief look at what he has to say about them.

First, Hobsbawm touches on expositions in the context of a discussion of official cultural policy in France in the 1870–1914 period. Coming out of the crises of 1870, a national defeat in the Franco-Prussian War and what was effectively a civil war in the Paris Commune, the new Third Republic embarked on a major series of cultural policies to consolidate itself with the public. Three policies in particular are worth noting. First, there was the creation of primary education 'a secular equivalent to the church . . . imbued with revolutionary and republican principles and content, and conducted by the secular equivalent of the priesthood . . . to turn peasants into Frenchmen and . . . Frenchmen into good Republicans'. Second, there was 'the mass production of public monuments', particularly of the female figure 'Marianne', symbol of the French Revolution, and local politicians, which virtually amounted to 'statue mania' (ibid. p. 272) and which became focal points for official ceremonies. Finally there was 'the invention of public ceremonies' including official and unofficial festivities connected with special holidays in the national calendar such as Bastille Day, created in 1880. On this and other similar uses of the symbols and heritage of the French Revolution for the purposes of a new wave of nation-building, Hobsbawm observes that the general tendency of this kind of policy 'was to transform the heritage of the Revolution into a combined expression of state pomp and power and the citizens' pleasure'. In this connection, then, it is worth noting that the Third Republic was responsible for three of the biggest and most important of the late nineteenth-century series of International expositions, namely those staged in Paris in 1878, 1889 and 1900, and we consider these at greater length later in this chapter. In this regard Hobsbawm notes in passing: 'A less permanent form of public celebration were the occasional world expositions which gave the Republic the legitimacy of prosperity, technical progress – the Eiffel Tower – and the global colonial conquest they took care to emphasize' (ibid. p. 271). Taking Hobsbawm's points further, it is worth noting an important and symbolic international effect of French Republicanism's 'statue mania' and its commitment to expos and monuments, particularly the Statue of Liberty. This was donated to the young American republic in 1886, parts of it having been displayed previously at American and French expos (the torch at the 1876 Philadelphia expo, and the head at the 1878 Paris expo (Bond 1996, ch. 2).

Second, regarding sport, Hobsbawm notes that among the entertainment-oriented newly 'invented' cultural forms in the 1870–1914 period, sport was undoubtedly 'the most significant of the new social practices' (ibid. p.298). In the case of Germany, mass gymnastic movements, and their events and festivals, had throughout the nineteenth century been associated with nationalism, and particularly so in the nation-building period following German unification in 1870.[4] However, British-originated elite and mass sport forms, movements and events, complemented by American and French developments of both nationally-specific (American football and baseball, French mass cycling) and international (Olympic) sports rapidly became very important in all of the societies surveyed. They provided important cultural institutions for promoting national identity whether through national specificity or through international competition, as well as providing the opportunity for the creation of more exclusive and divisive class-specific cultures and identities.[5]

Third, there is the issue of the development of mass rituals and festivals. Here Hobsbawm notes in relation to late nineteenth-century public culture and invented traditions, that one particular 'idiom of public symbolic discourse', namely 'the theatrical', in the form of 'Public ceremonies, parades and ritualized mass gatherings' had a lasting influence on early and mid-twentieth-century politics and history (Mosse 1975; Roche 1999c). While recognising that such events were 'far from new' he observes that:

> their extension for official purposes and for unofficial secular purposes (mass demonstrations, football matches, and the like) in this period is rather striking. [They were connected with] the construction of formal ritual spaces [and] this appears to have been systematically undertaken even in countries which had hitherto paid little attention to it. [This

period saw] the invention . . . of substantially new constructions for spectacle and de facto mass ritual such as sports stadia, outdoor and indoor.

(Hobsbawm 1992: 305)

The use of these constructions 'anticipate[d] the development of formal spaces for public mass ritual (the Red Square from 1918) which was to be systematically fostered by fascist regimes' and (as he implicitly acknowledges in the reference to Red Square) also by communist regimes, in the inter-war period.[6]

In summary, then, Hobsbawm's analysis is comparative and thematic so it does help to illuminate the international dimension of public culture in the late nineteenth century. However, that being said, it is mainly concerned with juxta-posing national traditions and national class relations. So, inevitably, the picture of the development of international public culture which it provides is limited. Also as a general historical survey it does not aim to provide a detailed focus on particular institutions and genres. These latter points do not apply to Bennett's studies which precisely concern themselves with such cultural institutions, genres and cases, and we can now turn to consider them. However, as we will see, his otherwise useful analysis of late nineteenth-century public culture is ultimately as limited as Hobsbawm's is in terms of addressing the international level.

Bennett, nineteenth-century public culture and 'the exhibitionary complex'

Bennett is concerned with understanding the nature and role of museums and exhibitions in late nineteenth-century society, Britain in particular. He develops his analysis through a constructive critique of Michel Foucault's influential accounts of the development of power and knowledge relations in the nineteenth century and their embodiement in forms of both institutional 'surveillance' and 'disciplinary' knowledge, represented respectively by the institutions of mental asylums and prisons, on the one hand, and social and human sciences on the other. In prisons and asylums, inmates are controlled in large part by being confined away from the gaze of the public and being made objects of institutional surveillance (by nurses or warders) and of disciplinary knowedge (by medical, psychological or other such professionals).

Bennett acknowledges that the institutional histories of museums and exhibitions and their correlative disciplines of art history, archaeology, etc. developed on parallel time-tracks to those of prisons and asylums, and that they all served the same general purposes of social control of the new urban working class and generally 'ordering the public'. However he argues that Foucault's account, while adequate as far as it goes, is limited and open to being mistakenly over-generalised, particularly if it implies that other sorts of institutions, such as museums and exhibitions, operated in the same way as 'surveillance' institutions did.

Bennett's thesis is that in fact they operated in almost the reverse way. That is they operated by attracting the public to participate in an 'exhibitionary' culture, in which they would be enabled to survey a vast range of ordered and valued information and objects, and ultimately also other 'different' human beings. Furthermore, control, order and influence in relation to the working class and the public was achieved through entertainment, that is through pleasure rather than anything resembling the pain of confinement and treatment or punishment. For Bennett, this form of power and ideological influence is best understood using Antonio Gramsci's concept of 'hegemony' which provides for the exercise of power through popular consent through the 'ethical and educative function of the modern state' and its enabling of 'civil society' (Bennett 1988: 76,85). He illustrates this thesis through a study which focuses on the British Museum and the Great Exhibition of 1851. In the following section, Bennett's concept of 'the exhibition-ary complex' is considered further and from a more critical perspective.

At this stage in the discussion, and on the basis of this brief account of Hobsbawm's and Bennett's analyses of late nineteenth-century public culture, we can confirm the importance that many cultural and social analysts attribute to this period. The changes that occurred in western societies in this period were of great significance, both intrinsically and in terms of their lasting implications for late twentieth-century modernity. Hobsbawm's account of invented tradition and the social construction of public culture in the late nineteenth century, as we saw earlier, involves a survey of a number of countries and thus some, albeit limited, reference to the international dimension. It involves a survey of a range of forms of popular public culture, ranging from official governmental and middle-class forms to non-governmental and working-class forms including sport and mass rituals as well as expositions. Finally, it involves a capitalist and class-based conception of power and the state, which sees them as used by elite and middle-class groupings to control the working class by consent. This control, however, was uneven, capable of failing and of co-existing with movements of critique and resistance. By comparison, while Bennett's account of 'the exhibitionary complex' is convincing and important, like the Foucaultian 'disciplinary and surveillance complex' it was developed to complement, it remains limited and institution-specific. While it is helpful in understanding exposition culture and events it tells nothing about the popular culture of sport, which developed in the same 1870–1914 period and which was at least as important, if not more important in forming collective identities.

'Exhibition' and 'performance complexes' in the development of public culture in modernity

My line of analysis in this chapter and in the book more generally is that the development of great public events in the late nineteenth century, particularly the international expos and, arising out of them, the Olympic Games, together with the event movements and networks and cycles connected with them, decisively influenced and helped create a new level and form of international public culture. However, expos need to be themselves understood as contextualised in a broader set of cultural and political cultural movements and developments in national cultural policy in the late nineteenth century. This has already been indicated in my discussion of Hobsbawm. In terms of political culture the background of all other movements in the late nineteenth century consisted of movements connected with the various versions of nationalism and nation-state-building in Europe, North America and South America (Anderson 1991) in particular, together with the various versions of imperialism and supernationalism often associated with them. These nationalist movements were an important background and resource for the cultural movements we are mainly concerned with. Evidently, nationalism was closely intertwined with the developing power structures of states and governments and greatly influenced the sphere of culture. But we should also bear in mind that other socio-political movements, without comparable direct access to state power, were also important elements and actors in the political environment, both nationally and internationally. In particular these included trade union and socialist movements which also had some presence and influence in the arenas of public culture and in the history and construction of public culture.

The late nineteenth-century cultural movements we are mainly concerned with here were 'rational recreation' movements concerned in large part, although not exclusively, with sport (including physical education and training, mass gymnastics and Olympics, as well as British-originated sports and other national sports) (Bailey 1978; Cunningham 1980). To a lesser extent, 'rational recreation' was also connected with the development of tourism as a form of education as well as entertainment. These cultural movements were also connected with religious and religiously-related movements, such as 'muscular Christianity' and 'temperance'.

Given the importance of sport culture in the developlment of late nineteenth-century popular culture I believe that it is necessary to complement Bennett's concept of the 'exhibitionary complex' if the development of a middle-class defined and dominated public sphere and public culture in the late nineteenth century is to be fully characterised and properly understood,. This is particularly so if we are to understand the 'spectacle' character of this culture as Bennett claims to aim to do. What is decisively missing from his account is any consideration of sport and its role in social change and cultural and political development in modernity.[7] This is understandable in a way, since sport, while it could involve the masses as spectators and rapidly generated the capacity to produce compelling spectacles, nonetheless cannot be properly understood through the language and logic of 'exhibition'. Consider the meaning of 'an exhibition match' for instance. It indicates something other than and less than the drama of sport. Also sport involves people in ways and to degrees that exhibitions cannot. Anybody can, in principle, learn a game, practice it and play it to some level or another. They can, thus, participate in it in a way which makes spectatorship of elite and professional sport events capable of being distinctively informed, active and engaging.

I prefer to see both sport participation and active spectatorship as a 'culture of the body' and in particular a 'culture of (bodily) performance'. This undoubtedly has connections with the 'exhibitionary complex' and overlaps with it in various ways and to various extents, but is nonetheless substantially very different from it and independent of it. Interestingly, sport and the 'performance complex' reconnects the analysis of culture, and possibly also elements of the exhibitionary complex, with commonsense (and even Foucaultian) notions of 'surveillance' and 'discipline', which Bennett otherwise would encourage us to see as irrelevant to the understanding of popular culture. We can explore the overlap between exhibition and performance in a number of ways. First, we can ask what it might be that sport events could be said to exhibit (e.g. about the nature, potential and limit of human bodies and. arguably, also their (universal) human character, as in the Olympic movement's 'worldview'). Second, we can consider the behavioural requirements of participating in spectacles. Bennett refers to this, but he seems to assume that it can be accommodated within the language and logic of 'exhibition'; in my view it cannot. As he points out, in the view of late nineteenth-century public culture constructors, in order to participate in mass spectacles, people must be not be an unruly violent, drunken 'mob'; they must at least be peaceful, sober and orderly in their behaviour. If, as Bennett rightly argues, part of the spectacle that Expos provided was the awesome scale and character of the peaceful orderly mass of people – the crowd looking at itself – then this is just better captured by the idea of people performing for each other and for the event, rather by the idea of the crowd being a special kind of object to be exhibited. [8]

Finally, we can see the overlap in the controversial area of 'human displays' at expos, which we will discuss further in this chapter when we consider them as carriers of the political culture of imperialism, and in more detail in Chapter 3 when we consider the racist and also the touristic dimensions of expos. These 'human displays' involved bringing mainly African and Asian tribespeople to live in 'native villages' allegedly representing their 'natural' style of life and living conditions. Evidently, this objectified the people involved, making them objects of racist Social Darwinist theory for nineteenth-century 'educated' public opinion, and objects of pity or racism for the masses. Without going in to it further at the moment once again it could be argued that what is going on here is more a complex of cultural performance and a performance of power relations rather than an exhibition of objects or 'people-as-objects'.

The tribespeople had to 'perform', that is they had to act out various rituals, dances, songs and the activities of everyday life. This was a precursor of the kind of 'staged authenticity' of 'exotically different' cultures with which we now so familiar in the tourist industry (MacCannell 1989). The crowds of Western spectators were precisely interested in the performative character of these 'displays'. It was through the performances that the supposed civilisational difference between themselves and the tribespeople could be best be visualised and grasped. Perfomance re-presented the idea that 'this is how they *live*', 'this is what they *do*'; it did not merely present the fact that 'this is what they *are*'. All of this speaks to the need to see these human displays as part of the exposition seen as a 'performance complex' as much as an 'exhibitionary complex'. These issues of overlap between the two complexes are relevant to understanding the origins of the Olympics and the influence of the expos on this, and we will discuss them further in the final section of this chapter.

International public culture and events

The discussion of the strengths and limits of Hobsbawm's and Bennett's analyses of the history of popular culture points to the need to explore the international dimension of public culture. It also points to the need to explore this dimension in terms of the 'performance complex' and thus through the world of international events. The international dimension of public culture can be defined as consisting of, on the one hand, people's 'imagined community' of world nations and of mankind[9] and, on the other, the international sphere of communication and interaction (through agencies such as nations, international institutions, non-governmental organisations (NGOs), and multinational corporations (MNCs)) particularly relating to 'cultural' matters. The rest of this chapter explores and illustrates these features of the international dimension of public culture and their emergence in the late nineteenth century, as a concomitant of nation-building and the construction of national public cultures. We explore them in particular through the specifically 'international' and 'performance' cultural event forms of international and imperial expos. The analysis outlined here is later extended to the world of international sport movements and events, and particularly to the early twentieth-century sport and Olympic movements (in Chapters 3 and 4).

The theme of the exercise of power through cultural events in these contexts is picked up throughout the chapters in Part 1, including this one. In Chapter 3 it is addressed in terms of the exclusionary aspects of expos, in spite of their typically inclusionary appearance, their construction of standard, second-class and non-forms of citizenship and citizen identities. In Chapter 4 it is addressed in terms of the Nazi attempt to use the Olympic Games and the Olympic movement more generally for propaganda and ideological purposes. In this chapter, to contribute to these analyses, we begin, in sections 3 and 4, to explore the all too evident character of international events as often successful attempts at the exercises of national elite power and hegemony through symbolic and cultural means – as forms of 'cultural policy'. However, in additon to this theme of power, and in the course of discussing it, I also aim to point up the way in which these mega-events provided opportunities and arenas for the display and exercise of 'civil society' in addition to 'the state', both at national and international levels.[10]

Civil society here means that, alongside state-based and funded agencies, non-governmental organizations (NGOs), including capitalist corporations, cultural professions and institutions, organised at national and international levels, were usually actively involved in the production and the presentation of expos. These were mainly middle-class groupings. But even with this class bias they contributed a divers and pluralistic 'civil society' appearance to the production of many expos. In addition, they often involved the formal and/or informal participation of social and political movements such as socialism and feminism drawn from the middle and working classes. In general the mixing of a range of social classes and nationalities in the crowd provided for the possibility of unpredictable cultural responses and even political conflict. We will consider this further in Chapter 3. In the following sections, then, we explore different forms of elite participation in the '*production*' of international and imperial events and event movements. The general nature of mass public participation in the '*consumption*' of these events will be explored more directly in Chapter 3. The responses of internationally-informed social movements to the production of international cultural mega-events and to their inclusionary and exclusionary social and political dynamics will be considered later, in Chapter 3 and Chapter 5. For the moment we must now turn to give an outline descriptive picture, together with some examples, of the main form of mega-event we are concerned with in this chapter, namely the late nineteenth-century and early twentieth-century international expos.

International cultural events and event movements: the origin and development of expos

An overview of expos in the late nineteenth and early twentieth centuries

This section aims to provide some basic information about international expos in the 1850–1914 period, together with some assessment of their general significance and social role. In the following section we explore themes connected mainly with the 'production' aspect of international expos, in particular the role of power elites and their networks in producing them, and also the role of expos in the construction and reconstruction of ideologies of empire. In the following chapter, in addition, we consider issues relating more to the 'consumption' aspect of expos, in particular the touristic and consumerist character of the public's experience of them, and also the socially divisive and contested aspects lying behind their culturally inclusive appearance. Each of these themes is relevant to the question of the nature of the international public culture, as well as the national public cultures, that expos helped to construct. They throw light, on the one hand, on inter-nationalisation processes at elite level among event-production groups, and on the other, on internationalisation processes at the level of mass publics, in terms of their increasing openness to touristic and consumerist forms of public culture. The purpose of this section is to provide a summary review of the expo tradition which will serve as a background and a basis for the more detailed thematic analyses in the following sections and in Chapter 3 (also see Burke 1994).

International expos were a very significant cultural institution both for the host cities and nations that played 'host' to them, and also for the international community, throughout the period 1851 to 1939 (see Table 2.1). They were held every few years, barring periods of major war, in one nation or another in Europe or in the USA throughout this period. Allowing for ambiguities in the definition of an international expo, roughly 15–20 major events were staged in the 1850–1914 period, and 5–10 were staged in the 1918–39 inter-war period. In addition, numerous more specialised or smaller-scale international and national events of a similar general type occurred in nations around the world. There was no particular planned temporal cycle or circulation of sites for the major events, but, because of their scale and costs, they were rarely staged more frequently than 5 to 10 years in each of the major countries, namely Britain, France and the USA. We can now briefly review these three major countries.

The British, who created the genre in 1851 (see below) had planned to hold one every decade, but after their 1862 expo, their approach to these events changed and the French, and later the Americans, effectively took over the leadership of the expo genre. In the 1870s the British staged specialist exhibitions virtually every year (Greenhalgh 1988 pp. 2, 23, 24, 113). From the 1880s to the first World War, besides the two Victoria Jubilee festivals (1887 and 1897), they held a number of Imperial expos and festivals (e.g. in London 1886, 1899 and the 1908–14 period; in Glasgow 1888, 1901, 1911), and re-animated this imperial version of the inter-national expo genre in the inter-war year with big events at Wembley in 1924/5 and Glasgow in 1938. The French, in particular the city of Paris, took the leadership of the genre over from the 1850s through to 1900 with five major events in Paris, one in each decade (1855, 1867, 1878, 1889, 1900). Interestingly the French and Parisian elites appear to have been exhausted and jaded by their monumental 1900 expo. Aside from various smaller-scale events, they did not stage another expo for a generation, until the series in the inter-war period (i.e. Marseilles 1922, Paris 1925, 1931, 1937). The Americans were preoccupied with the Civil War in the 1860s and with reconstruction thereafter. Setting aside their small-scale copy of the 1851 event in New York in 1853, understandably they did little in terms of major exhibitions in the 1850s and 1860s. However, they then produced a series of five major events from the 1870s to the First World War

Table 2.1 Expos 1850–1970: attendances and profitability

Periods	City	Visits (millions)	Profit–Loss
Late nineteenth century			
1851	London	6.0	Profit
1855	Paris	5.2	Profit
1862	London	6.2	Loss
1867	Paris	6.8	Profit
1873	Vienna	7.2	Loss
1876	Philadelphia	9.9	Loss
1878	Paris	6.0	Loss
1889	Paris	32.0	Profit
1893 profit	Chicago	27.5	Profit
Pre-1914			
1900	Paris	48.0	Loss
1901	Buffalo	8.1	Profit
1904	St Louis	19.7	Loss
1908	London	8.4	Profit
1910	Brussels	13.0	Loss
1911	Glasgow	11.5	Profit
1915	San Francisco	18.8	Profit
Inter-war			
1924/5	London	27.0	Loss
1926	Philadelphia	6.4	Loss
1927	Paris	(no data)	(no data)
1929	Barcelona	(no data)	(no data)
1931	Paris	33.5	Profit
1933/4	Chicago	48.7	Profit
1937	Paris	34.0	Loss
1938	Glasgow	2.6	(no data)
1939	San Francisco	17.0	Profit
1939/40	New York	45.0	Loss
Early post-war			
1958	Brussels	41.5	Profit
1964/5	New York	51.0	Loss
1967	Montreal	51.0	Loss
1970	Osaka	64.2	Profit

Sources: Allwood 1977; Schroeder-Gudehus and Rasmussen 1992; Knight 1978, p. 47; Mattie 1998.

(Philadelphia 1876, Chicago 1893, St Louis 1904, San Francisco 1915) and four in the inter-war period (Philadelphia 1926, Chicago 1933, San Francisco 1939 and New York 1939/40) together with a mass of USA regional and state-based national-level events throughout these periods.

National governments were always significantly involved in the organisation of these events. They were also always involved, to a greater or lesser extent, in the financing of these events, which often made considerable losses. In spite of that fact, and whatever the state of the economic cycle, whether boom or slump, national governments continued to encourage and sponsor these official forms of grand public spectacle and theatre, for reasons we will explore later.[11] National governments understood that expos, if successful, offered a platform for the international projection of positive images of their nation. Success could be better assured if nations copied successful models and attempted to improve on them in terms of the quantity or quality of previously succesful elements. This inter-country and inter-city competitiveness and 'leap-frogging' was clear in the relations between the London and Paris expos of the 1850s and 1860s, and again in the relation between the Paris and American expos in the 1889 to 1904 period, which we consider again later.

The expo cultural event genre: origins and developments

The 1851 'Crystal Palace' international expo in London, which we discuss as a case study later, was particularly influential on the whole of the expo tradition, and particularly on expos held in the 1850s and 1860s. Nonetheless, there were some significant developments of the genre in subsequent expos, particularly those held in France and the USA. Key elements of the genre had been developed over a long period of time, at least since the late eighteenth century, particularly in France, but also in Britain. The special contribution of Britain's 1851 event was more that it combined these elements and took them to a new level in an innovative institutional context and an awe-inspiring architectural context. In this section we should briefly consider the pre-1851 origins and post-1851 development of the genre.

Origins

Prior to Britain's 1851 expo the early modern origins of the international expo genre mainly lie in France. In the Napoleonic period the French government sponsored exhibitions of goods in Paris, produced at, among other places, the Royal Manufactories (including Sevres porcelain), in 1798 and 1801. Although the original intention had been to make these exhibitions an annual event, political circumstances made this impossible. However, French National Exhibitions were subsequently held on an irregular basis in places such as the courtyard and interior of the Louvre. Altogether, another nine such national exhibitions were held after the 1801 event in the period running through to the British 1851 expo. There were efforts over the same period to stage comparable exhibitions in England. But, in spite of Britain's lead over France in industrialised production, there was, at this time, little interest from producers or the public in such events, in spite of the efforts of such institutions as the Society of Arts and the Mechanics Institutes. The last in the series of French National Exhibitions was held in 1849. It was a very large-scale event involving a purpose-built building, 4,500 exhibitors, including international exhibitors, and it stayed open for a period of six months.This impressed British cultural and political elite groups and it effectively created both a model which could be used for reference in the planning of a British version, together with a competitive stimulus to do so (Luckhurst 1951, ch. 8; Allwood 1977, ch. 1).

Developments

The French series of five Exposition Universelles held in Paris from 1855 to 1900, were particularly important in giving new form, content and cultural character to the expo genre. The changes in form had to do, first, with the architecture and housing of the expos. This involved a shift away from the Crystal Palace and Paris 1867 models of using one single monumental building to house all of the various nations' exhibitions. Instead, following similar developments at the 1876 Philadelphia expo, the French expos provided nations with their own distinctive pavilions or the land on which to construct them. Thus the late nineteenth-century international expos came to take on an appearance of being self-contained and exotic 'cities' (see Chapters 3 and 5). Second, the form changes had to do with the creation of touristic entertainment sections in which a great range of shops, cafes and entertainments were presented in ways which identified them with distinctive ethnic and national cultures. Allied to this was the incorporation within the expo site of popular fairground developments which until then typically set up outside of the walls of the great expos. These innovations added to the official 'informational and educational' aims of the great expos a clear hedonistic, touristic and consumerist character (see discussion in Chapter 3). These changes occurred particularly at the Paris expos of 1878 and 1889, and the Chicago expo of 1893. The changes in content had to with the inclusion of fine arts, particularly painting (which occurred from the first Paris expo in 1855), and 'native villages' (at the Paris expo of 1889). The changes in the cultural character of the expos was connected with the wide-ranging and ultimately irreconcilable combinations of experiences increasingly presented in the late nineteenth-century expos, stemming from the form and content changes we have noted. The American series of three World's Fairs (Philadelphia 1876, Chicago 1893 and St Louis 1904) in the late nineteenth-century/pre-First World War period gave new scale and commercialism to the genre, and considerably amplified the entertainment and human display dimensions introduced by the French. Finally various British expo-type events held in London in the 1890s and also in the 1908–14 period gave a new imperial and theatrical caste to the genre, as we see later in this chapter.

The cultural significance and social role of late nineteenth-century expos

The expos were a new and powerful cultural medium for conveying information and values to a mass public. What Marshall McLuhan famously once said of television, that to a significant extent 'the medium is the message', could also be said about expos. A large part of the excitement, attraction and spectacle of expos derived from the medium itself, namely the main buildings and site architecture, together with the huge peaceful gatherings of people on an historically unprecedented scale outside of mass mobilisations for war. This was as important as the contents of the exhibition.[12] However, the contents were also spectacular, consisting of huge collections and exhibitions of, among other things, raw materials from around the world, new productive and communication technologies, new products and commodities, art objects and scientific information. They represented attempts to achieve both an encyclopaedic stock-taking of the current state of knowledge and practice among the advanced industrial societies and also an attempt to communicate and popularise this among mass publics, mainly in the host nation but also, through the press and later radio and film, in many nations. Expos were effectively mass theatres in which 'progress', particularly advances in the technologies which were transforming peoples' lifeworlds, were represented and dramatised as spectacle. This character of the international expo genre has continued from its inception in the nineteenth century throughout the twentieth century and up to the contemporary period (see Allwood 1977; Rydell 1984, 1993; Harvey 1996). Table 2.2 lists the various technologies launched and popularised at expos over the generations (for expos' roles in promoting media-related technologies, see Table 6.1 below).

An expo supporter, American President McKinley (who ironically was later shot at the Buffalo expo of 1901) optimistically and idealistically summed up the significance of Expostions as follows:

Table 2.2. Expos and technology 1851–2000

Period and year	City	Technologies
1851-1915 period:		
1851	London	Industrial machinery, mechanical grain thresher, Colt revolver
1853	New York	Elevator (Otis)
1862	London	Steel making innovation (Bessemer), steam locomotive innovation (Crampton)
1867	Paris	Aluminium, petroleum, gasoline engine (German), submarine electricity cables, hydraulic elevator
1876	Philadelphia	Monorail system, large scale steam engine (Corliss)
1878	Paris	Internal combustion engine, rubber tyres, refrigeration
1889	Paris	Electric light, Eiffel's tower
1893	Chicago	Alternating electrical current (Westinghouse), electric lightbulb , electric train
1900	Paris	Moving sidewalk, military technology (German)
1901	Buffalo	Electrical storage battery
1904	St Louis	Flying machines
1915	San Francisco	Mass production cars
Interwar period:		
1925	Paris	Modernist and 'Art Deco' design
1929	Barcelona	Modernist architecture (Mies van der Rohe)
1933	Chicago	Deco architecture and design, popularisation of technology's base in science
1939-40	New York	Rocketry, nylon, plastics, domestic air conditioning
Post-war period:		
1958	Brussels	Nuclear reactor, atomic clock, peaceful use of atomic energy
1962	Seattle	Electronic car, multi-car monorail
1967	Montreal	Lasers
1985	Tsukuba	Robots
1998	Lisbon	Marine technologies
2000	Hanover	Environmental technologies

Sources: Allwood 1977; Wachtel 1986; Rydell 1993; Nye 1994.

Note: The technologies noted here are do not include media technologies. For media-related technologies promoted by expos, see Table 6.1.

Expositions are the timekeepers of progress. They record the world's advancement. They stimulate the energy, enterprise, and intellect of the people and quicken human genius. They go into the home. They broaden and brighten the daily life of the people. They open mighty storehouses of information to the student. Every exposition, great or small, has helped this onward step.

(quoted in Rydell 1984: 4)

On the other hand, the Frankfurt School critical theorist Walter Benjamin, writing in 1935 and unfortunately without reference to the great expos of his own day (e.g. the Chicago expo 1933 and plans for the Paris expo 1937, of which he was almost certainly aware), observed about the late nineteenth-century Paris series that:

'World exhibitions were places of pilgrimage to the fetish Commodity. . . . Fashion prescribed the ritual by which the fetish Commodity wished to be worshipped. . . . The workers were to the fore as customers. The frame-work of the entertainment industry had not yet been formed. The public festival provided it. [Generally, the expos] opened up a phatasmagoria into which people entered in order to be distracted. The entertainment industry made that easier for them by lifting them to the level of the commodity. They yielded to its manipulations while enjoying their alienation from themselves and from others.

(Benjamin 1973: 165–6)

Benjamin also observes that the 1862 expo 'was of direct importance for Marx's foundation of the International Workingmen's Association' (Benjamin 1973: 166) a topic we return to in Chapter 3 below.

Two contemporary exposition historians, who acknowledge the real popularity, attraction and memorability of expos for ordinary people throughout the late nineteenth and early twentieth century (Greenhalgh 1988: 225; Rydell 1993: 2–3) nonetheless are equally as critical in their general assessments as Benjamin. Paul Greenhalgh observes: 'the genre became a self-perpetuating phenomenon, the extra-ordinary culture spawn of industry and empire'. Their purpose was 'to indicate civilization was advancing in some known direction' (in spite of the often chaotic changes produced by nineteenth-century industrialisation) and 'that "things would get better"'. Generally his view of expos is that, 'As cultural mani-festations, they revealed an expansive West in its most flamboyant and bombastic state; baroque, overblown expressions of societies that felt they ruled the material world absolutely.' (Greenhalgh 1988: 2, 23, 24). In particular Greenhalgh suggests that elites used expos to propagandise nationalism:

This [nationalist ideology] penetrated popular cultural forms in all sorts of ways, many of which Expo organisers also used. The exhibitions had to do more than simply whip up general verbal enthusiasm, they also had to give physical form to pavilions and palaces and to penetrate higher levels of cultural production with nationalist dogma. They had to cater for the educated as well as the ignorant, providing a formula and a rationale for national culture which was capable of being interpreted by a wide cross-section of the population.

(Greenhalgh 1988: 113)

In a related vein, Robert Rydell, focusing particularly on the American series of World's Fairs, observes that:

> Between 1876 and 1916 a network of international expositions spanned the nation, putting the world on display and shaping the world view of millions of Americans. Without exception, these expositions were upper-class creations initiated and controlled by locally or nationally prominent elites. . . . To alleviate the intense and widespread anxiety that pervaded the United States [in this period], the directors of the expositions offered millions of fairgoers an opportunity to reaffirm their collective national identity in an updated synthesis of progress and white supremacy that suffused the blueprints of future perfection offered by the fairs. . . . The influence of America's international expositions permeated the nation's arts, political system, and economic structure. Far from simply reflecting American culture, the expositions were intended to shape that culture. They left an enduring vision of empire.
>
> (Rydell 1984: 235, 4 and 237)

More generally, Rydell also observes that: 'the Victorian era fairs played . . . an important role in shaping the contours of the modern world'. They 'were part of what became, after the success of London's Crystal Palace Exhibition in 1851, a worldwide movement.'(Rydell 1984: 15, 8). So it is now appropriate to begin our analysis of Expos, their character as an event movement, and, ultimately (see Chapter 3), of their implications for the Olympics as an event movement, with a look at the founding 1851 event. This case presents in outline some of the main features of the form, content and heritage of the genre.

The 'Crystal Palace' expo 1851: a case study[13]

The international exposition as a new public cultural genre, distinct from national expositions, was really first created by the British in the Great International Exhibition of 1851 in London. This was organised by a Royal Commission, including four ex-Prime Ministers and headed by Prince Albert, and it was debated by Parliament which decided on the site. It was opened by Queen Victoria and attended by heads of state from all over Europe. These included Napoleon III of France, who reciprocated the invitation when France held its first expo in Paris in 1855. Around twenty-five nations and many colonial territories attended and exhibited. It attracted over 6 million visitors during the five months (May to October) that it ran. Prince Albert, who had originally determined that the event would have the innovative character of being 'international' rather than national, called it a 'peace festival' of nations. Queen Victoria whose view of the opening ceremony was that 'the sight . . . was magical, so vast, so glorious, so moving', believed that it 'united the industry of the nations of the earth' (quoted in Allwood 1977: 20). We can now briefly consider some of the main features of the content, form and heritage dimensions of this event.

Content

The 1851 expo exhibited products and produce from all over the world in four main categories, three of them in a logical sequence to demonstrate the power of industrial production, namely raw materials from around the world, machinery and manufactured products. The British elite's confidence to create an international exhibition came from Britain's evident power and world leadership in these three areas at the time, in raw materials through its Empire, and in machinery and manufactures through the energy and level of its industrialisation. It had little to fear from competition from other nations and it had everything to gain in terms of advertising the superiority and value of its wares, by inviting them to participate. Prizes were given to encourage exhibitors in each of the main categories. In addition, the fourth category was sculpture and plastic arts. Unlike later expos, particularly those organised by the French in Paris, fine arts such as paintings, were not exhibited as they were not deemed relevant to the industrial and economic themes of the exhibition.

Form

The event came to be known as the 'Crystal Palace' exhibition because of the impressiveness of the huge, innovative and spectacular, but essentially temporary building in which it was held in Hyde Park (see photo). The building was designed by Joseph Paxton, the Duke of Devonshire's head gardner, after many other designs, (including one by the eminent Victorian engineer, Isambard Kingdom Brunel) had been rejected. The innovative modular iron frame and glass panel design allowed the building to be rapidly assembled from mass-produced parts (e.g. over 3,000 iron columns and 300,000 panes of glass). As against traditional stone-based forms of architecture, it represented a triumph of the new power of engineering in the physical shaping of modern buildings and cities. This message, which continued to emerge after 1851 from the influence of industrialised contruction techniques in the building of the tracks, bridges and train sheds and station concourses for the railway boom, was reinforced in subsequent expos. This was most spectacularly demonstrated in Gustav Eiffel's great tower, an engineering *tour de force* built for the 1889 Paris expo. The Crystal Palace and the Eiffel Tower have left a permanent and pervasive mark on the physical look of modern cities and modernity. This is not least by the influence they had (together with American elevator design, first displayed by Elisha Otis at the 1853 New York expo), in showing American architects in the late nineteenth century in New York and Chicago what could be conceived and achieved by constructing monumental yet publicly accessible buildings, ultimately 'skyscrapers', based on assembled metal frames.[14]

The Crystal Palace building itself was eloquent testimony to Britain's industrial capacity and its level of development at the time. Paxton's gardening background helps to explain the simplicity and functionality of the design, since it was, in a sense, a monumental greenhouse. It was a building of unprecedented scale, enclosing 19 acres. It created new visions of the exterior appearance and the interior space of buildings, and new visions of their potential new functions in modern cities which exercised a profound and long-lasting influence on modern architecture. For instance the designs of contemporary mega-shopping malls in North America and Britain often contain echoes of the design of the Crystal Palace.

Figure 2.1 The 'Crystal Palace' built for the Great International Exhibition of 1851, in Hyde Park, London.

Figure 2.2 Crowds inside the 1851 'Crystal Palace' exhibition.

'Event Heritage'

One important aspect of 'the event heritage' in this case was the building itself. The Crystal Palace was subsequently disassembled and re-located to a site in Sydenham, south London, where it housed popular exhibitions and events for generations, including a Festival of Empire in 1911. This was one aspect of the 'event heritage' and long-term effect of the Great Exhibition. The building was destroyed by fire in 1936 and was not rebuilt. A more important aspect of the event heritage relates to the fact that, unusually for this sort of event, it made a very significant profit.[15] This was invested in 87 acres of land in the South Kensington area of central London, which provided a very substantial and long-lasting 'event heritage' from the 1851 expo. The site was used to stage two major international expos in 1862 and 1886. But, more importantly, a permanent 'exhibitionary complex' of institutions and buildings was developed on this site. This complex is now sometimes refered to as 'Albertopolis' in recognition of the role of Prince Albert in stimulating it. It includes the buildings now known as the Victoria and Albert Museum, the British Museum of Natural History, the Albert Hall, together with the Royal Colleges of Art and Music, and the Imperial College of Science and Technology. [16]

Producing international cultural events: expos and power

Expos and power networks

This chapter is interested in exploring the production of expos. Understanding the aims and rationales of their producers is relevant to this interest whether they are taken at face value, as in liberal approaches, or subjected to questioning and scepticism, as in critical approaches. However, expos were multidimensional phenomena which cannot easily be reduced to the terms of either the liberal or the critical interpretations. On the one hand even though political elites created these events and used them to try to communicate ideological messages to the masses in the form of 'popular education', nonetheless in doing so they also created a new form of public arena for exercising knowledge interests, personal freedoms and civil society. Further, the educational aspect co-existed with a vibrant entertainment and 'leisure-pleasure' aspect of these events. This made it more difficult to pre-determine their ideological contents and impacts, and the uses to which people put them. On the other hand – precisely because of the involvement of national governments and national prestige in these events, and because they were hugely ambitious in concept – they were always at least vulnerable and even risky political and ideological projects. Their long planning lead times and their inflexible timetables made them vulnerable to short-term political conflicts and crises both on the domestic front but also on the international front.[17] Finally, their basic two-dimensional structure, as both national and international events, simultaneously presenting a national face to the outside world and to the domestic public, could make them sometimes appear ambiguous and difficult to evaluate in terms of their significance, for instance sometimes claiming a significance in world terms that they could only really justify in national terms.

From the nineteenth century onwards, four sets of elite actors were usually in-volved in the production of international events, namely a core group of planners and organisers, a set of nationally-oriented political elite groups, together with internationally-oriented but nationally-based economic and cultural elite groups, and possibly also internationally-based event organisations. The original concept for an expo could come from econo-cultural elites, but usually came from political elites, which then created the core planning group.

The planning and organisation group usually came to constitute the focal point of a new tailor-made national power network in which interested elements of the nation's political and econo-cultural elites were formally and informally involved and used in the design, financing, organisation and marketing of the event. In the case of expos the typical pattern was a state-backed Commission consisting of a planning group, incorporating, among other things, leading political and financial figures to create the financial and political base for the event, and also an organisational group, headed by an event General Commissioner and comprising specialised Commissioners for the various sub-divisions and elements of the exhibition.

The 1851 expo provided a model for all of those that followed, not only in its concept, architecture, contents and popularity, but also in terms of its organisation and production. The original concept emerged from the cultural elite circles of the Society of Arts (later the Royal Society of Arts), and the British political and economic elite of the time was heavily involved, as we saw earlier. The general organisation and production model, then, was that of the creation of an alliance of elite political, cultural and economic groups to lobby for various forms of governmental and state legitimacy and support for an expo project. The aim of the lobbying would be to get the event legitimated as an 'official' event in which the lead group could claim to be acting as agents for 'the nation' and to which the nation (the public) as well as 'the world' could be invited. From country to country there were different balances in event organisation and finance, in the relation between the state (including different levels of the state from city to national) and civil society (including, for these purposes, the market or capitalist economy, along with voluntary and professional organisations). British and American expos tended to rely heavily on elements of civil society, while nonetheless incorporating them within a national state project, while French expos were always heavily state-dominated projects.

Internationalising the production of mega-events

The credibility and success of international expos, from the 1851 Great Exhibition and the late nineteenth-century series, was based on the degree of 'recognition' of the host nation given by the quality and quantity of nations agreeing to attend, to take a stand or construct a pavilion, and to display their wares. In order both to market the event as of compelling national significance for the national public and also to secure the maximum available international 'recognition' for the event, event organisers usually were able to associate the national government, political leaders and heads of state with the event through the organising committee and/or the opening and closing ceremonies.[18] Effectively this made the expo into a temporary and cultural arm of state foreign policy and diplomacy to which other states would feel obliged to respond as part of the expected reciprocities of international relations.

Event planning and organisation groups: international dimensions

To achieve a demonstrably 'international' (rather than purely national) event, the core planning group had to develop some kind of an international outlook and experience. While retaining overall control and responsibility, they usually attempted to 'internationalise' the production of the event to some significant degree. At the most basic level they usually felt the need to gather relevant international event experience and information in one or both of two ways. First, where possible, they consulted with and/or incorporated experienced fellow nationals who had been involved in previous international events staged in their country. Occasionally the same person might run the planning and organisation group of successive expos. For instance, Henry Cole played this role in both of the first two British international expos in 1851 and 1862.[19] Frederic Le Play took a leading role in the Paris 1855 expo and ran the Paris 1867 expo. William P. Blake contributed to the organisation of the Paris 1867 expo and was a leading figure in the Philadelphia 1876 expo. Alfred Picard wrote the official report on the Paris 1889 expo and ran the Paris 1900 expo. Imre Kiralfy took a leading role in the series of British imperial expos from 1899 to 1914. There was a comparable pattern of notable individuals, typically from the rapidly growing and institutionalising sphere of the US corporate business elite, taking leading roles in successive American expos both in the late nineteenth century and the inter-war period.[20]

Second, they learned from such events staged in other countries. As far as the latter goes, periodically inter-city and international comparison and competitiveness have assumed a great importance in the history of mega-events, as with Anglo-French competitiveness over expos in the 1850s and 1860s, and Franco-American competitiveness over expos in the 1870s to 1900s. Event production groups in these periods usually gathered intelligence on the successes of their competitors, in order to emulate and outdo them, by travelling to expos in other countries and liaising with their event organisers. For instance, Henry Cole, the main organiser of the London 1851 event gathered information on large-scale national events by travelling to the Paris 1849 event (Allwood 1977: 14). In turn he lent his expertise to the first international expo in Paris in 1855 and took intelligence on this back to Britain for the 1862 London expo. Imre Kiralfy was consultant to the Chicago 1893 expo and contributed to large-scale pageants in the USA in the 1890s before coming to London to develop his imperial expo series from 1899 to 1914. American organisers of Chicago 1893 attended and reported on Paris 1889.[21] The same is probably true of the Buffalo 1901 and St Louis 1904 expo organisers in relation to the Paris 1900 expo, and it was certainly true of the 1933 Chicago expo organisers in relation to the 1931 Paris expo (Rydell 1993: 72, 82).

In addition, event planning and organisation groups had to involve internationally-oriented national economic power elites and cultural establishments and their organisations. Also – although to a much lesser extent in the nineteenth and early twentieth centuries – they had to involve international event NGOs. Nationally-oriented organising groups and political elites could not have run successful international events without support from and partnership with these sorts of more internationally-oriented flanking elites, particularly, in this period, the economic and cultural elites. As far as the national econo-cultural elites go – the core organising groups, on the one hand, needed to be able to draw on the support of a full range of their nation's most internationally well-known and technologically advanced capitalist industries, to display their products at the event, and to help sponsor and finance it. On the other hand, they needed internationally-oriented and connected cultural NGOs such as intellectual and academic organisations in art and design, science and technology, and in the human and social sciences.

Expos and cultural organisations

Cultural organisations were needed to help directly in the production of expos, by designing the knowledge base of the exhibition programme, by supplying internationally notable exhibits (scientific, artistic, archaeological, anthropological, etc.), and by 'educating the public' (i.e. explaining and communicating the information and knowledge bases of the exhibition to the public in as popularly accessible and attractive a way as possible). In Britain, the Royal Society of Arts (RSA) – (the original Society of Arts received royal patronage and title as a consequence of the success of the 1851 exhibition) – and also the South Kensington 'exhibitionary complex' of institutions, particularly the museums, played this crucial role in relation to the 1851 and 1862 events and also subsequently.[22] In the USA, the Smithsonian Institute in Washington DC became the key institution to play this role, and was an important part of the federal government's commitment to expos from the Philadelphia 1876 expo onwards.[23]

Besides such direct input elite cultural organisations also helped international expos indirectly. That is, they legitimised the quality and status of such events by using them as venues for national and international scientific and professional conferences and meetings. Leading intellectuals in the late nineteenth and early twentieth centuries attended and contributed to conferences held in association with international expos. Besides Sigmund Freud, who visited the 1873 Vienna expo as an ordinary fairgoer, these included such figures as Emile Durkheim (Paris 1900), Henri Poincare and Max Weber (St Louis 1904), and also, later, Albert Einstein (New York 1939).[24] At Paris 1889 there was a Colonial Exhibition and Congress which involved USA Smithsonian personnel (who then went on to contribute to Chicago 1893). There were sixty-nine other conferences at this Paris expo (MacAloon 1981: 137). At Chicago 1893 a number of international congresses met, including congresses on Anthropology and on Education. In addition, there was a meeting of the American Historical Association. At St Louis 1904 there was an International Congress of Arts and Sciences and this was attended by Max Weber (Bendix 1962: 3). This international conferencing aspect of expos was also of some considerable importance in relation to the early development of the Olympic sport movement, as we discuss later.

In the sphere of expo events no coordinating and legitimating international agency evolved in the late nineteenth century, in spite of attempts to create one.[25] Rather, this developed later, in the 1930s, in the form of the Bureau International des Expositions (BIE) and we consider it further in Chapter 3. Sport and Olympic events were less important in the late nineteenth century period than expos. However, they developed international governing bodies quite substantially in the late nineteenth-century period and continued to do so in the inter-war years. From the inter-war period onwards, national elites increasingly had to negotiate with and accept guidance from these event-INGOs (international non-governmental organisations) – particularly the IOC (the International Olympic Committee), FIFA (the Federation Internationale des Football Association) and the BIE.

Expos and imperialism: the late nineteenth-century and inter-war periods

Background

The imperial theme had been part of national expos in France in the 1840s and was an important part of the first international expo in London in 1851. Britain was the world's leading industrial and imperial power in this period and used this expo to display its industrial achievements and its imperial possessions. Commenting on the fact that international expos were vehicles for nationalism, Paul Greenhalgh observes, about the specificity of English nationalism and its connection with Empire as follows: 'Empire was the vehicle for [British] nationalism, royalty the focus, making royal and imperial presences at the exhibitions imperative for them to have any real meaning. Thus, every major international exhibition held in Britain through to the First World War had extensive imperial sections and a member of the monarchy involved in the organization' (Greenhalgh 1988: 121). The same was true to a lesser extent, as we will see in a moment, of France and other countries staging international expos in this period.

It is important to recognise that the imperial dimension in international expos, and indeed imperial expos as a sub-genre of the international expo genre, were themes which, while they reached a high point in the 1880–1914 period, nonetheless continued through to the 1930s and the build-up to the Second World War. In the inter-war period, 'imperialism' is a theme which, both explicitly in the case of fascist Italy and Germany and also more implicitly in the internal and external neo-imperialist politics of the leadership of the USSR, links the capitalist democracies with the totalitarian states. We consider this connection further in Chapter 4. In this section we focus on the capitalist democracies, in particular Britain, the USA and France, and on some of the expos they staged in the period. The explicit commitment of these nations to the building and displaying of empires, in my terms 'supernationalism', was usually reflected in, and indeed was often the dominant theme in, many of these events.

Late nineteenth-century imperial expos tended to use and develop the form of the spectacular mass pageant, involving parades, choirs and drama with a variety of historical, contemporary, traditional or exotic themes. Comparable types of mass pageants and mass festivals also developed in the same period in the new Soviet communist state in the 1920s and in the Nazi state in Germany in the 1930s (Roche 1999b). Just as there is a connection between expos and Olympic Games in the turn of the century/pre-First World War period, so there is also a connection between expos, mass festivals and Olympics in the inter-war period. The 'theatres' of empire, power and revolution in the official ceremonials and mass festivals of the imperial and neo-imperial 'supernations' in the inter-war period influenced the ceremonies and rituals of the Olympic Games, particularly their opening and closing ceremonies.

The great importance and continuing legacy of this original development of the turn-of-the-century/early twentieth-century mass pageant form in great public events can be readily seen in the theatricality of major elements of the opening and closing ceremonies of the contemporary Olympic Games and other similar sorts of events. We should also note here that, in this period, another version of mass display, namely German and Soviet mass gymnastic displays, made at least an equally important contribution to the development of the spectacular and ritual aspects of Olympic event ceremonial, and we consider this contribution later (in Chapter 4).

In the inter-war period, in spite of the concurrent, massive and relentless growth and popularisation of spectator sport, the expo movement remained just as popular as it had been in the late nineteenth century. In this section we consider mainly the imperial expos, giving an overview of them and then an outline of some of their main characteristics. To illustrate the discussion we look in particular at the case of the 1924/5 British imperial expo at Wembley.

Imperial expos: an overview

One of the biggest, richest and most exotic of Britain's colonies, India, was prominently presented in the Crystal Palace 1851 expo. This was the beginning of a long tradition of British displays of India, both in the British-based expos and in the British-controlled sections of foreign expos, running through to the Second World War, effectively the end of Britain's Empire, and the beginning of the end of the imperial era more generally. The British East India Company took a leading role in organising the 1851 expo and, in particular, the creation of an 'Indian Court' within the Crystal Palace, which displayed Indian produce, textiles, tea, spices and so on. Subsequently, India was often displayed by means of the construction of a separate and architecturally distinctive 'Indian palace', including such things as Indian tea shops. These were staffed by Indians in traditional dress and helped create and popularise the (subsequently) 'typically English' habit of tea-drinking at all levels in British society in the Victorian period. The displays of India grew more extravagant over time from the 30,000 square feet Indian Court of the Crystal Palace expo to a three-acre palace in a five-acre site at the 1924/5 Wembley expo (Greenhalgh 1988: 59).

Along with other European nations, Britain committed itself to further imperial expansion in the late nineteenth century, including 'the scramble for Africa' which led to the Boer War in South Africa in 1898. The British elite, preoccupied with the growth of Empire and needing popular support, recurrently used the staging of great public expo events to communicate the imperial message to the public in a captivating, entertaining and attractive way. The monarch's jubilee festivals in 1887 and 1897 were used to promote the theme of Victoria as 'Empress of India', and numerous expos were staged, usually in London, to popularise Britain's 'imperial' identity and its current imperial projects (Mackenzie 1984; Richards 1990). Colonialism was an important theme in an expo series staged in the 1870s, and it was the dominating theme of significant expos in 1886 and 1899, and in a series from 1908 to 1914.

The 1908–14 event series was largely created by the expo impressario and producer Imre Kiralfy in collaboration with leading British imperialist politicians (MacKenzie 1984: 102–7). The series required the construction of a relatively permanent expo event site in London, including a large stadium which could be used both for imperial pageants and major sports events. Kiralfy labelled his site 'the White City' in recognition of the Chicago 1893 expo which was also popularly known by this name. One of the first uses of the White City stadium was to stage the fourth Olympic Games, the 1908 London Olympics. The White City stadium became the home of British national and international athletics for generations afterwards.[26] This connection between expos and major sport events was echoed later in British mega-event experience. Wembley stadium, the now legendary stage of generations of soccer and other major sport events, was built as part of facilities for the 1924/5 imperial expo event, and was subsequently used as the Olympic stadium, together with other ex-expo buildings on the site, when London staged the Olympic Games in 1948 (Abrahams 1976).

France began to include imperial themes relating to its North African colonies in its 1878 expo. This expo marked 'the beginning of the genre whereby imperial sections were presented as exotic cities of pavilions and palaces' (Greenhalgh 1988: 65). Reacting in part to the success of the first explicitly imperial expo, namely Britain's 'Colonial and Indian' in London in 1886, this theme was massively expanded in the great Paris expos of 1889 and 1900. The organisers of the 1889 expo devoted over 100 acres of the 1889 expo site around the newly constructed Eiffel Tower to the 'exotic city of pavilions and palaces' of imperial nations and their colonies, with their own buildings and displays prominent among them.[27]

Among the other European nations, the most committed to the concept of imperial expos was Belgium which colonised the huge Congo area of central Africa in the late nineteenth century from 1878.[28] This project amounted to a major claim for recognition as an imperial nation. To communicate and symbolise the project, Belgium staged four international expos with prominent colonial themes in the pre-First World War period (Antwerp 1894, Brussels 1897, Liege 1905, Brussels 1910). It is worth noting that the colonial expo genre, as a means of mass communication, was not restricted to circulation within the imperial heartlands. This form of expo was also cloned and reproduced within the colonised territories. MacKenzie observes that whereas in Europe

> they marked national self-confidence, and were occasionally a consolation for failure . . . Elsewhere they marked the coming of age of new States. ..In the Dominions exhibitions seemed to be a necessary rite of passage for pubescent responsible government, and were invariably held in the wake of notable economic advance.
>
> (Mackenzie 1984: 99–100)

Exhibitions of various kinds were staged in the British Empire to mark the development of dominions and colonies, including Australia (Sydney 1879–80, Melbourne 1880–1 and 1888–9, Adelaide 1887, Tasmania 1891–92 and 1894–5, Brisbane 1897), New Zealand (1865, Christchurch 1906–7, Dunedin 1924–6), South Africa (Cape Town 1877, Kimberley 1893, Johannesburg 1936–7), India (Calcutta 1883–4, Bombay 1910), Africa (Sierra Leone 1865, Zanzibar 1905), and Jamaica (Kingston 1891). MacKenzie observes that 'These colonial exhibitions were a celebration of the white man's successful transplantation to the farthest reaches of the globe, and his creation there of societies modelled on European lines' (ibid. p. 100).

In the USA, America's anti-colonial and democratic history and tradition constrained expo organisers from proclaiming imperial themes too explicitly.

However, the USA in practice rapidly extended its military power and presence in the Pacific, Caribbean and South American regions from the 1880s onwards, creating a de facto 'American empire' to rival those of the European powers. This expansionist and interventionist foreign policy was illustrated and legitimated at US international expos from Chicago's 1893 event onwards (Rydell 1984, 1993). For instance, this was conveyed through the concept of 'pan-Americanism' deployed in the 1901 Buffalo expo and the St Louis 1904 expo, together with displays of produce and people connected with such places as Hawaii and the Philippines. The importance attached to publicising and legitimating American control over the latter can be indicated by the fact that a site of 47 acres was given over to the Philippines display at the St.Louis expo (Greenhalgh: 77).

Major imperial expos were planned in Britain and France in the pre-1914 period. These plans were delayed by the war but were reactivated soon after it. France staged a colonial expo in Marseilles in 1922, and this was closely followed by the 'British Empire Exhibition' at Wembley in 1924/5, which attracted around 27 million visitors (see below). The inter-war period saw a number of other notable imperialism-oriented expos. These were interspersed with other major events on the traditional expo themes of technological, scientific and artistic 'progress', notably in Paris in 1925 and 1937, and New York in 1939/40. Belgium staged a two-city international expo with colonial themes in 1930 in Liege and Antwerp. In what was probably the high tide of this imperial expo genre, France staged a 'Colonial and International' expo in Paris in 1931 which attracted over 33 million visitors and is described by Rydell as providing a 'stunning imperial fantasyland' (Rydell 1993: 69; also Greenhalgh 1988: 69). The USA appeared to officially acknowledge the legitimacy of colonialism by accepting an invitation to exhibit at this event (Rydell 1993: 72). American expo organisers were by then less inhibited about using colonialism as an explicit theme and discourse in subsequent inter-war expos, notably the great Chicago expo of 1933, visited by over 47 million people, and the San Francisco expo of 1939/40. The Chicago planners were influenced by the Paris 1931 expo and also drew on the 1924/5 Wembley experience (ibid. p.82). As the inter-war period drew to a close, Britain returned to the imperial theme for the final time in the Glasgow expo of 1938 (MacArthur 1986).

The imperial expo genre

Typically the political elites and organisers of imperial expos in the late nineteenth and early twentieth centuries had three main aims. First, they aimed to assert, establish and if possible justify a nation's empire in the eyes of the imperial 'peer group', that is, the other empire-seeking nations which might, or might not, be willing to tolerate particular claims to territory or zones of power and influence. Second, they aimed to justify empire to the imperial nation's public which supplied the taxes to finance these projects and the men to fight and die in them. Finally they aimed to justify empire to elite groups among the colonised peoples, who would be invited to participate in expos, in order to assist with current imperial control but also to have a chance of influencing the shape of any independence movement and any future post-imperial nation which might emerge when 'the imperial mission', 'the civilizing mission', might be deemed to have been completed.

The imperial expo genre, as a variant of the international expo genre outlined earlier in this chapter, was sometimes contained as a theme within the latter, sometimes organised entirely independently. Typically, this imperial expo event sub-genre involved the use of a range of methods and approaches to achieve the three aims indicated above. First, relating to the first and third aim above, there was a great deal of flexibility about which other countries, if any, would be invited to participate. At one end of the continuum imperial expos could make a claim to being 'international', or at least 'quasi-international', even if they excluded all other imperial and major nations, by virtue of the presence of colonies and associated 'dominion' countries. An example of this most 'supernational' type of expos is the Wembley 1924/5 expo. At the other end of the continuum, explicitly imperial expos could also explicitly claim to be 'international', in which case invitations would be made to a range of major countries to participate. The Paris 1931 expo is an example of this type. In between these extremes, imperial nations in alliances with each other might stage a joint expo, and the Franco-British expo of 1908 is an example of this type. While all of these types of imperial expo were used to influence national publics and colonial elites, the closed type was also particularly aimed at colonial and dominion elites, while the more open type was particularly aimed at impressing other foreign powers.

Second, and particularly to impress national publics, imperial expos aimed to present the imperial power's colonies as constituting major reserves of economic resource for the nation. In this scenario the expo would show how the imperial nation's public benefited from the products created from colonial raw materials, or directly from exotic foodstuffs, etc. For instance, the 1851 London expo tended to take this approach. A later development on this theme was the promotion of the colonies as places in which to invest capital and to which to emigrate, as in some of the themes of Wembley 1924/5.

Finally, and most importantly, imperial expos were ideological vehicles used to impress national publics, and also to present an image to other imperialist powers. They typically displayed the cultures of their colonies as different, exotic and interesting, but also as flawed, inferior, stagnant or otherwise 'in need' of the imperial nation's intervention to control their destinies. Connected with this they typically developed and promoted a uniquely national 'civilising mission' ideology, involving notions of the imperial nations' scientific and technological superiority enabling them to create tangible improvements and 'progress' through transformations of land use, culture and people in the colonies. The British, French and Americans all had their own particular versions of this 'progress-bringing' 'civilising mission' as a thematic running through and connecting both their imperial expos and their more conventionally internationalist expos. The racism involved in this is considered at greater length in chapter 3. We can now illustrate some of these points about imperial expos in a little more detail with a look at the Wembley 1924/5 expo.

The Wembley imperial expo 1924/5: a case study

In his study of '*Propaganda and Empire: The Manipulation of British Public Opinion 1880 to 1960*', John MacKenzie argues that the British Empire Exhibition at Wembley 'was the greatest of all the imperial exhibitions – in area, cost, extent of participation, and, probably, popular impact' (MacKenzie 1984: 108). We consider this and other competing assessments of the significance of the Wembley expo later. First, we need to consider why it occurred, what its main features were and how it was received at the time.

Origins and production

The context of the production of this expo, as with so many other, was one of serious social, economic and political problems. British society was shocked and damaged by the horrors of the First World War, its massive loss of men, its indebtedness to the USA, the revelation of its relative economic and military decline vis-à-vis the new powers of the USA and Germany. There was unemployment among ex-servicemen, a portent of what was to come in the labour unrest of the late 1920s and the international economic depression of the 1930s. The value of the Empire, indeed Britain's dependency on it, had been made clear in the important contribution of the dominions and colonies to the Allied war effort. But Canada and Australia were effectively distinct and independent nations, the 'free state' of Eire would be conceded to the southern Irish in 1921, and there was restlessness for independence in the Caribbean and India. The Wembley expo project had originally been proposed in the pre-war period as an extension of the Kiralfy White City series. By 1919, to the pro-Empire politicians in the British government, the House of Lords and the British Empire Club, the time was right to revive the project of a major new British Empire expo, and to make it a bigger and better event than the pre-war White City imperial expos.

MacKenzie suggests that the main purpose of the Wembley expo was economic. A third of Britain's trade was with the Empire, and there was growing emigration to these countries. The purpose of the expo was to promote both of these forms of economic linkage and investment. Prime Ministers, High Commissioners and other leaders of colonial and dominion countries backed the project at a conference in 1919. The Liberal Prime Minister Lloyd George and the Prince of Wales actively supported the project. The government committed half the £2.2 million finance needed, the rest coming from public subscription. It acted as co-guarantor of the expo, [29] and it intervened to have its appointees on the organising committee. Parliament supported the project in 1920 on the grounds that the expo would 'benefit trade, provide employment and be a token of goodwill towards the dominions' (quoted in Stallard 1996: 7). Support for the project was widespread and reached across all of the parties. The Labour Party actively supported the expo when it took control of government in Britain for the first time in 1924.

The Wembley site, in what was then a greenfield site in the outer suburbs of London, was chosen partly because it had long been of interest to leisure industry developers. A commuter railway line had been built out to the suburb in the 1880s, and a pleasure park and the first stage of a grandiose Eiffel-type observation tower had been built. The pleasure park and the first stage of the tower had become a reasonably sucessful London visitor attraction (Varrasi 1997). But financial problems intervened, the project collapsed, the tower was dismantled in 1907/8, and some of the eventual 200-acre site was acquired by members of the expo project committee (Stallard 1996).

Figure 2.3 Aerial view of the 1924 British Imperial Exhibition at Wembley which included, as part of the expo, the newly built Wembley stadium.

Contents and reception

The expo was a success as a popular spectacle attracting over 17 million visitors in the first year and over 9 million in the second year it was open. It presented a wide variety of pavilions, produce and people from the many areas of the world controlled directly or indirectly by the British in this period, including, among others, India, Ceylon, Malaya, Burma, Hong Kong, South and West Africa, Guyana, as well as the self-governing dominions of Canada and Australia. The expo's official music was composed by Edward Elgar, and Rudyard Kipling provided names for the expo's streets. According to the exhibition's official guide:

> The grounds at Wembley will reproduce in miniature the entire resources of the British Empire. There the visitor will be able to inspect the empire from end to end. . . . From Canada it is but a stone's throw to Australia, from Australia a short step to India. . . . In a single day he will learn more geography than a year of hard study would teach him. And he will be able to see, in each case, the conditions of life in the country he is visiting. That is the importance of the British Empire Exhibition. It is a stock-taking of the whole resources of the Empire.
>
> (Quoted in Rydell 1993: 65)

Unlike most previous expos, which used temporary architecture, many of the buildings at Wembley were built as permanent structures with after-use in mind. The two main buildings housing the industrial exhibits were among the largest ever constructed for an expo (Stallard 1996). In addition, as noted earlier, the expo organisers associated the building of a major new 100,000-person capacity sport stadium on the expo site with the staging of this event. Wembley Stadium became legendary with the British public just prior to the opening of the expo when, in 1923, it provided the venue for its first FA Cup Final, attracting a crowd dangerously in excess of its designed capacity. The stadium staged the expo's opening and closing ceremonies, attended by members of the Royal Family. The radio broadcast of the the opening ceremony performed by King George V was the first time the British public as a whole had been gathered together to participate in a national event through the new medium. The expo was thus one of the first major 'media events' in modern British cultural history.

Whatever messages about empire were intended to be communicated would have been filtered through the strong entertainment, fairground and leisure character of the expo. During the expo, the stadium was the venue for the daily 'Pageant of Empire', involving 15,000 performers and hundreds of animals, and also for beauty pageants and various sporting events, including a colonial boxing tournament. The site contained an amusement park with the latest rides, including dodgems, river caves, water chutes, and rollercoaster (Stallard 1996: 14; Walthew 1981). The new mass medium of film, particularly travel film of Africa, was displayed to a mass public at the expo. The expo site also contained a number of dance halls, and popular music and dancing were strongly associated with the experience of visiting the expo. The expo was criticised by a certain section of London's cultural elite, including P.G. Wodehouse and Noel Coward. There was also a certain small amount of criticism by students from the colonies studying in London. But, among the popular press, the masses who visited it over two seasons, and more generally among the British public, the Wembley expo was undoubtedly a popular event.

Assessment and perspectives

Commentators on the Wembley expo generally concur that it appears to have been successful as a popular attraction. This is in spite of the facts that there were some financial and managerial problems in the production phase and that it initially made a loss in its first season. The loss was recouped by extending the expo into a second season (Stallard 1996). If there are differences of assessment here they are relatively marginal ones concerning whether the event was very popular (Walthew 1981) or merely reasonably popular (Rydell 1993, Stallard 1996). Rydell's assessment is that 'the British at Wembley had revitalized a national exhibition tradition without making that tradition seem sufficiently modern to appeal to the mass public. What was needed were new architectural designs to sell national imperial designs' (Rydell 1993 p.67). This seems strained to say the least. The expo patently did attract a mass public, and it did so through the use of familiar but nonetheless spectacular and monumental expo architecture. The idea that it might have been even more popular had it attempted to introduce the notoriously culturally conservative British public to avant garde modernist forms of architecture – of the kind previewed at expos in Paris in 1925 and Barcelona in 1929, and soon to be found at the Chicago 1933 expo – is unconvincing.

Conclusion

In this chapter introducing the expo genre of mega-events we have gone back to the mid-nineteenth century to explore its origins. We have traced the general development of the genre, in both its international and imperial versions, in Britain, France and the USA in the late nineteenth and early twentieth centuries, illustrating this process with more detailed looks at the two cases of the seminal 1851 Crystal Palace international expo and also the 1924/5 Wembley imperial expo. Throughout this discussion we have been concerened with the way that expos reflected the development of capitalism, nationalism and imperialism from generation to generation in the 1850 to 1939 period. The expos were recurrently popular and influential forms of national cultural policy periodically used by powerful national elite groups in each generation to symbolise and contribute to these underlying structures of their societies, and to influence national public culture. In addition, they were also important focal points in the emergence of an international dimension in public culture, not least through the processes of international communication, networking, and competitive imitation engaged in by the elite groups which produced them.

From this focus on power in the 'production' of mega-events we now need to consider the theme of power and social differences as it is reflected in the 'consumption' of mega-events in the 1850 to 1939 period. This involves looking more closely at both consumerist and citizenship-relevant forms of public experience at the expos, in particular (in relation to citizenship), experiences of classism, sexism and racism. In addition, we need to understand the early expansion of the field of international mega-events through the development of the sport culture and the Olympic movement, and the emergence of the Olympic mega-event genre from out of the expo tradition.

3   Mega-events and cultural citizenship

Consumerism, inclusion/exclusion and internationalism

This chapter explores the contribution of nineteenth- and early twentieth-century mega-events, particularly international expos, to the construction of modern public culture, looking in particular at the forms of cultural inclusion and internationalism they developed. The discussion proceeds in three main steps. The first section considers the role of expos in probably the most straightforwardly culturally inclusive dimension of expos, namely their propagation of popular experiences and attitudes of what can be called 'touristic consumerism'. I suggest that this represents the nineteenth-century origin – in, it should be emphasised, a process of modernisation – of the late twentieth-century consumer culture we sometimes like to regard as 'post'-modern.[1] Expos were arguably most apparently inclusive in relation to the emerging white male working class. The second section considers the exclusionary features which were built in to this attempted class inclusiveness, both for the working class, and also for women and for people of non-Western ethnic groups and 'races'. Finally in the third section we consider the development of cultural internationalism emanating from the development of the expo genre. Here we explore first the connections and differentiation of the Olympic movement in relation to expos, as international cultural forms, and then the institutionalisation of these forms in the development of international regulatory and governing bodies in the late nineteenth and early twentieth centuries.

Mega-events and cultural inclusion: expos and tourism culture

Modern culture, post-modern culture and expos

In 1873 Austria joined the developing international expo tradition with an expo staged in Vienna. Although this was a financial disaster it was the most popular expo to date recording over 7 million visits. Among the visitors was Sigmund Freud who summed up his reaction as follows: 'A great comprehensive panorama of human reality, as the newspapers profess to see, I don't find in it. . . . On the whole it is a display for the aesthetic and superficial world, which also for the most part visits it.' However, in spite of this elitist and negative judgement, Freud also notes that he visited the expo twice.[2] His observation at least has the merit of identifying the popular cultural nature of expos, and the mixture of information, entertainment, tourism and consumerism they represented.

In this section I suggest that it was in the rise of the expo as mass popular entertainment form that many of the institutions that we are familiar with in contemporary popular culture – a culture sometimes characterised as 'post-modern' – arguably had their origins. Contemporary popular culture can be conceptualised as a changing mixture of 'modern' and 'post-modern' forms and themes. The former relates to the processes of homogenisation and massification connected with the building of nation-states and nationally and imperially-based industrial capitalist economies as work-based societies, and it is most strongly connected with periods of initial 'modernisation'. The latter relates to the processes of individualisation and de-massification connected with the late twentieth-century reconstruction of the state and capitalism, towards multi-tiered political and regulatory institutions, information and services-based economies, oriented to consumption and animated by global and technological factors and forces. The contemporary combination of (among others) the national, imperial, industrial and 'work-driven' elements comprising 'modern culture' and (among others) the post-national, post-colonial, post-industrial and consumerist/leisure-oriented elements comprising 'post-modern culture', not to mention the dynamics and tensions between these formations, has its origins in a similar combination of formations in late nineteenth-century popular culture, which can be seen most clearly in the great expos of the period.

The 'modern' and 'post-modern' elements and formations of popular culture, in spite of their tensions and contradictions, since their development in the late nineteenth century, have typically been connected through various sets of cultural institutions and cultural industries. The development of schools, teaching professions, publicly funded schooling systems, national curriculum programmes and the progressive extension of obligatory attendance to older aged chidren and young people in the late nineteenth and early twentieth centuries was evidently connected with nation-building, 'modernisation' processes and the construction of 'modern' public culture. Something similar could be said about the initial developments of 'national' or 'public' broadcasting, first radio and then TV, in the 1920 to 1960 period. However, another set of cultural institutions and 'industries', arguably, has had as much societal impact and significance in modernity as national schooling and broadcasting systems.

This institutional set includes museums, art galleries, department stores, theme parks and large-scale fairs. Their development as aspects of popular culture was either anticipated, or given crucial boosts, by the late nineteenth-century series of international expos. Compared with the rigidities and relentlessly 'modern cultural' character of much of state-based schooling and broadcasting, they provided a flexibility – particularly in their interconnections with the international expo movement – which allowed them to be turned and used by people to engage in public culture in either, or (intermittently) in both, 'modern' and 'post-modern' ways. We consider this set of institutions again in a moment. First, however, we need to consider the main types of public behavioural and attitudinal styles and repertoires which influenced peoples' ways of orienting to and using these cultural forms and institutions in their visits to expos. These attitudes and practices can be characterised as, first, 'touristic consumerism' and, second, 'urban cosmopolitanism'. They are interconnected and they had as much to do with the international dimension of these events as with their national dimension. They are consistent with, and anticipate, many features of contemporary 'post-modern' culture that we often wrongly assume to be unique to, and characteristic of, our times.

Touristic consumerism and expos

The connection of expos with 'touristic consumerism' can be analysed into four main aspects. The first and most obvious aspect is that most visitors attending the expos had to become tourists in order to get to them. The relative minority of international visitors had to engage in the newly developing mass transport systems and technologies of steamship travel or long-distance railway travel, and a large proportion of domestic visitors had to become 'excursionists' and use the new railway systems.

The birth of the cultural industry of tourism, which has become so dominant nationally and globally, both as an industry and as a form of cultural experience in the late twentieth century, and which in many ways is virtually consonant with the concept of 'post-modern' times,[3] occurred in parallel with, and in close connection to, the development of international expos. The expos themselves provided powerful 'new age', if temporary, tourist attractions in the mid and late nineteenth century. Pre-eminently in the case of Paris, but also in other cities, they left an accumulation of 'event heritage' architecture which contributed to the permanent tourist attraction of major cities (see Chapter 5). Also they were occasionally used to promote tourism and even to attract and recruit migrants to major continental regions or imperial colonies, as in the 1915 and 1939 San Francisco expos in relation to California and the US West Coast and the 1924/5 London (Wembley) expo in relation to India, Canada and Australia.

To demonstrate the importance of expos for the development of the tourist industry both nationally and internationally in the mid/late nineteenth century, it is sufficient to point to the growth of the archetypal tourist company, Thomas Cook. It is true that the tourist industry – as led and illustrated by the growth of Thomas Cook's operation selling 'railway excursions' from his Midlands base in Leicester in the 1840s – grew on the back of the growth of steam-powered transport systems in the mid-nineteenth century, in particular the massively important growth of railways. Nevertheless, people needed motives as well as locomotives to travel, and the great expos helped to provide these motives and popularise these demands.

The press of the period called Thomas Cook the 'prince of tourists' and described him in very contemporary, even 'post-modern', terms as 'domiciled in ubiquity, the incarnation of perpetual motion' (Buzard 1993: 64). Given his fairly unique 1840s experience, the Midland Railways company asked Cook to organise excursions to the Great Exhibition in 1851. He publicised the idea in innovative ways. He created and distributed his own 'Excursionist' newspaper to advertise the attractions of the expo and his trips. He campaigned in numerous industrial towns, helping groups of workers who were eager to attend the expo to form 'Exhibition Clubs' which were savings clubs to generate the money for the trip. He helped persuade employers to give the workers time off to make the trip. Buzard reports that Cook argued that 'factory owners and managers owed it to their employees . . . to give them the chance to witness the marvellous productions of the industries in which they were engaged' (ibid. p. 53). In his newspaper, Cook asked 'Why Should Working Men Visit the Exhibition?'. He argued that they should go 'not as to a show or place of amusement, but a great School of Science, of Art, of Industry, of Peace and Universal Brotherhood' (quoted in ibid. p. 54). He

Figure 3.1 Crowds at the hugely successful 1900 Exposition Universelle in Paris showing 'tourist cultural' and 'event heritage' features such as the appearance of an exotic 'city in miniature', Eiffel's classic viewing tower (created for the 1889 Paris expo) and a Ferris wheel (invented for the 1893 Chicago expo).

ended up organising the travel of 165,000 of his mainly working-class excursionist visitors. Buzard notes that Cook 'was to play similar roles in many of the other grand cultural spectacles of the next two decades' (1853–73) (ibid. p.55). For instance he organised smaller-scale excursions to successive expos in Dublin in 1853, Paris in 1855, London in 1862 , and Paris in 1867.

The second main aspect of the connection of expos with the development of touristic consumerism is that all visitors to late nineteenth-century international expos, whether or not they actually bought anything substantial, were exposed to a powerful new consumerist world-view, that is to the concept and potential pleasures of a life filled with an endless variety and supply of buyable commodities. Typically, an unprecedented quantity and quality of goods were on display at international expos. Most of these products were for sale to the trade and to the public at a clearly indicated price, or could be bought or ordered from stocks. If these good were too expensive for the masses the new trade in cheap mass-produced 'souvenirs' (including postcards using the new technology of photography) ensured that everybody could buy at least something to take away with them. It is a profound mistake about the nature of popular culture in modernity, to imagine that 'consumer culture' and the 'post-modern culture' it is associated with somehow emerged 'ex nihilo' in the dying decades of the twentieth century. This ignores a century of growth of consumer institutions (department stores, advertising, etc.) which had been introduced in the late nineteenth century expos and which were continually developed and diffused in the early and mid twentieth century – before television took over this role in the post-war period – by the expo movement. Many analysts point to this late nineteenth-century precursor of contemporary consumerism in their studies.[4] For instance in his study of the development of the 'commodity culture' and advertising in Victorian Britain, Richards sums his view up as follows:

> The Crystal Palace was purported to be a place where everyone in England could rub shoulders democratically, a place where social distinction seemed to reside not in persons but in things. The Exhibition turned everyone who entered it into a leisured flaneur, while at the same time it transformed the meticulous flaneur of the Parisian arcades into a manageable consumer of manufactured objects. In a very real sense the Exhibition fashioned a phenomenology and a psychology for a new kind of being, the consumer, and a new strain of ideology, consumerism.
>
> (Richards 1990: 5)

A third aspect of the expo-touristic consumerism link is that usually what was most impressive to the new mass public visiting late nineteenth-century expos about the products on display, apart from their unprecedented quantity and quality, was the fact that most of them had been brought to the expo from all over the world. The actual or fantasy consumption of these unfamiliar 'foreign' and 'exotic' goods and/or of the images associated with them provided an early version of the kind of vicarious experience of touristic sensations through consumption that we are now very familiar with in contemporary culture.

Fourth, and finally, in a number of different ways the mass public of the expo host nation typically encountered an unprecedented range of foreigners and people from very different cultures. In his account of this aspect of expos, Greenhalgh suggests that there were a variety of ways in which 'others' were encountered at these events. These included diplomats, servants in exotic leisure and entertainment zones, and those appearing as 'educational'/'scientific' objects in racist 'human displays' of 'primitive cultures' (Greenhalgh 1988: 82). We discuss these issues at greater length in the following section in relation to the exclusionary and racist aspects of the expo genre. However for the moment we can suggest that this amounted to a kind of vicarious and virtual tourism, tourism-without-the-travel, in which the 'others' and their tourist sights and ways of life 'come to you' rather than 'you going to them' – a process mass publics became very familiar with in the early twentieth century through the impact of film on popular culture (Gunning 1996) and again in the late twentieth century through the pervasive influence of television.

All of these four aspects of expos taken together amounted to the promotion of a new kind of 'touristic consumerism' in popular consciousness and attitudes. This represented a 'popular cultural' version of internationalism comparable with the versions engaged in by the elites which produced the events. It is, of course, entirely consistent with this version of internationalism to observe that 'travel (vicarious or otherwise) does not necessarily broaden the mind' and that it created the space for competitive, militaristic, xenophobic and racist attitudes to grow, as much as for attitudes of tolerance, co-existence, peace between nations, and the brotherhood of man.

Connected with the propagation of popular attitudes and experiences of 'touristic consusmerism' oriented to the national and international spheres is the notion that this also had implications for how people living in big modern cities began to view their own urban environments. Obviously the quasi-touristic encounter at least with the sophisticated versions of 'foreigners' discussed above, contributed to a popular taste for participation in a cosmopolitan dimension of the public culture of the times. Indeed the relevance of cosmopolitanism to his times was a theme which Emile Durkheim lectured on at a conference held, appropriately enough, at the 1900 Paris expo (Lukes 1973: 350). Expos and their associated influx of foreign tourists and travellers, lent a periodic focus to the emerging cosmopolitanism of modern cities. The cosmopolitanism of the international expo event site was an exaggerated microcosm of the kind of cosmopolitanism characteristic of nineteenth- and twentieth-century urbanism, particularly the cultural mixtures present in most capital cities, but also in other large cities, especially those acting as trading and migrant centres. The expos themselves were designed and experienced as 'cities-in-miniature' and as 'ideal cities'. Hence the name for Chicago's 1893 site 'the White City'[5] which, as was noted in Chapter 1, was also used as the name for one of London's main sites for the series of virtually annual imperial expos held there in the 1908–14 period.

These public attitudes and practices propagated by expos interacted with a new set of popular cultural urban forms, institutions and 'industries' – namely museums, art galleries, department stores, theme parks and large-scale fairs.[6] Obviously museums, art galleries and fairs antedate nineteenth-century expos and have a long institutional history in Western Europe in particular. However, even these were qualitatively transformed by the international expo movement. This resulted, in the case of museums and art galleries, in a new level of popular recognition of, and access to, institutions which previously were effectively closed and elite-oriented. In the case of fairs it resulted in an increase in their scale, the techno-logical complexity of their infrastructures (through high tower elevator rides, cable car rides, Ferris wheels, and roller coasters among many other such innovations), and their capacity to create, control and sell 'excitement' and extreme emotional stimuli and experiences (de Cauter 1993).[7] In the other cases, notably department stores and theme parks, these quintessential consumerist and touristic forms and institutions were either effectively created as concepts by the international expo movement, or their development was rapidly accelerated and widely diffused by them. This set of institutions and industries provided the substantial settings and experiences within expos with which the public – understanding itself in terms of the entertainment frameworks of touristic consumerism and urban cosmopoli-tanism – interacted and which repeatedly attracted them to the events in huge numbers.

We explore this connection between expos and the modern urban experience further when we consider mega-events and cities (Chapter 5). For the moment, we can conclude that our discussion so far suggests some of the ways in which expos could be seen as culturally inclusive. We now need to consider the ways that this inclusiveness contained structures of social and cultural exclusion within it.

Mega-events and cultural inclusion/exclusion: expos and social divisions

Background

The nineteenth-century expo movement in general, as we have seen so far, was a product of nation-building and economy-building in modernising Western societies. They offered elites a form of popular cultural policy-making which could be used to promote among the mass of ordinary people an acceptance of, incorporation in, and positive attraction and loyalty to, the new political economic formations being constructed around them. Expos were a powerful method for promoting versions of citizenship, social membership and cultural inclusion, notably those we have characterised as touristic consumerism and urban cosmopolitanism. In this section, by contrast, we need to consider the exclusionary aspects and dynamics involved in these apparently positive and progressive developments, particularly in relation to the three major social divisions of class, gender and race.

First, however, some comparative comments need to be made about the inclu-sionary/exclusionary dynamics of the expo and Olympic mega-event genres before summarising the implications of the relationship of expos to the three social divisions overall. Then we can look at each social division separately in a little more detail. From a comparative perspective we can note that the main event-based movements we are concerned with in this book – namely the expo, Olympic and international-level sport movements, each of which began to develop in the 1880–1914 period, and which developed strongly in the inter-war period – also carried with them important implications for, and effects on, the dynamics of public cultural inclusion and exclusion. We discuss the Olympic and sport move-ments at greater length in relation to these issues in the next main section of this chapter (in terms of their nineteenth-century origins), and again in Chapter 4 (in terms of the interwar period). However, it is worth making some general points about them at this stage.

The Olympics and international sport were always in principle positively oriented towards cultural inclusion, in terms of the values of peaceful co-existence and the maximal representation of the diversity of nations. However, this orientation, until the post-Second World War and post-colonial periods, was always heavily skewed in practice towards the interests and perceptions of the 'advanced' Western nations and empires. Athletes and teams from colonised 'nations' were either excluded from international competitions, or only included as representatives of the colonial power. Up to and through the inter-war period, sport and the Olympics as movements in popular culture were profoundly and ideologically exclusionary in relation to the three social divisions we are concerned with here. In these periods they were initially systematically constructed and institutionalised as aristocratic and middle-class, white, male cultural preserves and on a basis of class, gender and ethnic prejudice, discrimination and exclusion.

The working class was excluded from the British version of sport and also from the Olympics by means of the ideology of 'amateurism'; women were excluded by means of pseudo-scientific theories of 'feminine' physical vulnerability; and blacks and Asians were excluded for reasons of imperialism and assumptions about their racial inferiority. These exclusions were struggled with as the sport forms became institutionalised and diffused internationally between 1880 and 1939. Progress was initially made by working-class males in terms of the development of participation in and spectatorship at mass professionalised sports, such as, in Europe, soccer and in the USA, baseball in the 1880s and 1890s. Concurrent with the achievement of female suffrage women lobbied increasingly successfully for equal rights to participate in national and international sport in the inter-war period, developing a platform from which to make further progress in the post-war period. Blacks and Asians gained rights to participate in international sport as a consequence of the success of independence movements in the post-colonial period and in national sport as a consequence of struggles for civil rights and recognition throught the post-war period. In each case, particularly for women, blacks and Asians, exclusionary problems have persisted and the struggles for inclusion have had to continue through to the contemporary period.

The expo movement's implications for the inclusion or exclusion of the working class, women, blacks and Asians developed along a similar general path. However, there were some differences in this case of this mega-event genre. Expos' contribution to the construction of public culture in modernity could be summarised in the following way. They accorded significant recognition, cultural inclusion and cultural citizenship to the white male working class, albeit circumscribed within the reproduction of class inequalities. This amounted to an incorporation of the middle and working classes within the evolving frameworks of 'organised' or 'Fordist' capitalism and 'national functionalism'.[8] However, this primary strategy of a conditional inclusion was bounded by the promotion of new version of various 'divisions of labour'. 'Internally' it was bounded by male elites' attempted uses of expos to construct a special 'private sphere' domestic status for women, a dependent form of inclusion. 'Externally' it was bounded by the attempt to legitimate imperial relations in racial terms, a clear strategy of ideological and cultural exclusion. Thus the expo genre accorded a second-class citizenship circumscribed by patriarchal power to women and it accorded to many members of non-white and non-Western ethnic cultures very little in the way of real membership or citizenship in modern nations, empires and humanity in general. However, that being said, in addition to the positive use that (white, male) working-class individuals and groups were able to make for themselves out of expos, women and ethnic groups and movements were also ocasionally able to make some positive use out of them to promote their own interests in and claims to autonomy, equality, inclusion and citizenship. Expos occasionally played a positive as well as a negative role in what, to adapt Raymond Williams' expression, we can refer to as the 'long revolutions' – still underway, and still a long way to go – to construct non-class divided, non-sexist and non-racist social relationships and public cultures in modern societies.

Like the Olympics, expos claimed to promote universalistic and humanistic ideals and world-views as well as internationalist and nationalistic ones. They thus appeared to promote notions of identity and inclusion in nation, the international order and the human race. However, in practice these were mainly aimed at a symbolic cultural inclusion of the white male working class who were, on the one hand, being politically empowered by gaining the new powers to vote and to organise trade unions, and, on the other hand, were facing the rigours of work and work discipline in rapidly changing, harsh and debilitating industrial and urban environments. In each of the major expo nations, whether a-political or politically aware, the huge numbers of white working-class males helping to make up the mass attendances at the expos indicated that they seemed generally persuaded of the educational and/or entertainment value of these events.

Women tended to be addressed mainly through their domestic and familial role and their dependent marriage relationship to men, and also to a certain extent as sex-object entertainment. With the growth of the women's movement, these exclusionary forms of inclusion were occasionally notably challenged. Non-white ethnic and 'racial' groups – other than those representing their national governments and in ambassadorial roles – were included in expos in various exclusionary ways, most of them in subordinate entertainment roles and some de-humanised as objects of racist pseudo-scientific presentations.

The women's movement and the movements of trade unionists and consumers each got positive benefits out of the expos, as well as being hegemonised in and by them. This cannot be said in relation to ethnic and racial divisions. Expos tended to be racist and exclusionary in many ways as we indicate later. However it is worth noting that wittingly or not they did provide a reference point and a rallying point for some more positive and inclusionary developments. First, movements in the Afro-American community were able to make some long-term use of the expos to challenge racism and discriminatory practices and to promote the case for full civil rights in the USA (Foner 1976, Rydell 1993). Second, the ancient Asian nations and cultures of Japan and China were able to use expos to project a relatively positive national identity at the numerous expos where they were represented. Finally, anti-imperialist national independence movements were able to use expos to learn about the forms and benefits of nationhood and international 'recognition' and, for good or ill, also about the cultural and ceremonial trappings of nationhood. We can now consider the implications of expos for people's inclusion and exclusion in each of the three social divisions we are concerned with in a little more detail.

Expos, class power and workers' movements

The implications of late nineteenth- and early twentieth-century expos for the growing and developing industrial working class in the capitalist societies which staged them can be summarised as follows. The expos accorded significant recognition, cultural inclusion and cultural citizenship to the white working class, albeit paternalistically, conditionally and from upper- and middle-class perspectives. In this sub-section we consider the nature of this attempted conditional inclusion further. First, strong and weak versions of the concept of class 'hegemony' at play in some of the main historians of expos are outlined. Second, the exclusion of the working class from expo production is reviewed. Third, the theme of 'social peace' in expos, and, fourth, the degree to which expos provided arenas which working-class movements could use to develop their own identities are discussed.

Expos as instruments of ruling-class hegemony

The concept of 'hegemony' refers to domination involving the consent of the dominated. It was first deployed in critical social analysis of class relationships in the modern capitalist state by the Italian Marxist Antonio Gramsci in the inter-war period and became a 'stock in trade' of critical social and cultural analysis in the post-war period. There are two general views about the class hegemonic character of expos at play in the social history of expos. We can refer to them as 'strong' and 'weak' hegemony perspectives (see Robertson 1992).

The view of the main historian of American expos, Robert Rydell, exemplifies a 'strong hegemony' or critical 'capital logic' perspective, and he outlines it with explicit reference to Gramsci. This perspective focuses on the interests of a presumptively unified capitalist ruling class, in this case the American capitalist class, and particularly the male and white dimensions of this class. His general position seems to be that international expos – however they were received (i.e. whether popular or not among the working class, women and ethnic minorities) and whatever they may have contained (i.e. whether containing simple or complex meaning and messages, whether explicitly promoting negative or positive attitudes and values) – are always ultimately and best explained as instruments of class control and vehicles of class propaganda. Rydell's presumption seems to be that, even if there was occasionally some criticism of, or resistance to, expos and their messages, nonetheless, on the whole they can be assessed as having operated as effective ideological weapons in the class struggle. They successfully served the defence of (American) capitalism in periods of socio-economic crisis and further-more they generally assisted it in making further advances. For instance he observes:

> If one function of the expositions was to make ther social world comprehensible, the directors of the fairs attempted to organize the direction of society from a particular class perspective. These events were triumphs of hegemony as well as symbolic edifices. By hegemony I mean the exercise of economic and political power in cultural terms by the established leaders of American society and 'the spontaneous consent [of the masses to this]. . . . World's fairs performed a hegemonic function precisely because they propogated the ideas and values of the country's

[i.e. the USA's] political, financial, corporate and intellectual leaders and offered these ideas as the proper interpretation of reality.

(Rydell 1984: 2,3)

There are alternative general views of the nature of expos, as we have seen in Chapter 2. Some are liberal views which avoid the issue posed by the concept of hegemony altogether. They tend to see expos as effectively politically innocuous and representative expressions of their host societies (Luckhurst 1951; Allwood 1977). Other analyses of expos engage with the issue of hegemony but deal with it differently than does Rydell. These analyses, while understanding expos critically and addressing their propagandist character, nonetheless also recognise their real complexity, ambiguities and contradictions. The perspective underlying these analyses generally tends to makes more out of the politics and agency involved in event production and reception than does the 'strong hegemony' view. We can refer to this as the 'weak hegemony' perspective, and it can be illustrated in the views of Greenhalgh, MacKenzie and Stallard in their studies of expos.

Greenhalgh argues, for instance, that expos were an 'absolute highlight for millions of people suffering the drudgery and alienation of working life in industrial society . . . Few who attended regretted the experience'. They were 'magnificent conceptions' although usually 'with such negative aims' (Greenhalgh 1988: 225). MacKenzie's general view is similar to this:

> The secret of their success was that they combined entertainment, education, and trade fair on a spectacular scale. . . . By the end of the century they were enormous funfairs, coupled with, in effect, museums of science, industry and natural history, anthropological and folk displays, emigration bureaux, musical festivals, and art galleries, together with examples of transport and media innovations, all on one large site. . . . They seemed perfect exemplars of rational recreation, combining pleasure and instruction, and millions attended them. Even if most went for the fun, some at least of the imperial propaganda cannot have failed to rub off.
>
> (MacKenzie 1984: 97)

Finally , drawing on Ley and Olds' study of the 1986 Vancouver expo, Stallard takes a similar view in his study of the 1924 Wembley imperial expo. He considers the relevance of Rydell's 'strong hegemony view' to the understanding of this particular expo and finds it wanting. He suggests that the organisation of the Wembley expo 'was a messy and chaotic affair' which can best be understood using 'a fractured and negotiated version of hegemony' (Stallard 1996: 1). The state sometimes pulled against the influence of the imperialist elite and represented the democratic interests of the mass of the working class, while there were real elements of class conciliation present in the popular leisure experience the expo provided.

Class exclusiveness in expo production

Expos, were organised on an exclusionary, elitist and paternalistic basis by power networks of leading politicians, aristocrats, corporate capitalists and professionals, as was noted in Chapter 2. In this respect they reflected, symbolised and reproduced the major class divisions, and thus the underlying social exclusionary character of their 'host' societies. The exclusionary manner in which they were decided on, produced and staged 'for', and rarely 'by', the people belied their apparently inclusionary, populist and loosely 'democratic' appearance and messages. This observation holds even if we take into account the apparent democratic legitimation for expos provided by debates and votes on funding which occasionally occurred at national and/or local city government levels.

As we have seen, political leaders and heads of state usually provided the ceremonial status for the opening ceremonies. In addition, they were sometimes involved more directly in the planning and organisation of expos. This was the case with Prince Albert and Napoleon III. It was also the case for a number of American Presidents. For instance, in their earlier careers Presidents Grover Cleveland and Herbert Hoover helped organise the expos of 1893 (Chicago) and 1926 (Philadelphia) respectively. President Teddy Roosevelt took a leading role in relation to the St Louis 1904 expo and also in decision-making in relation to the third Olympic Games which was held there. Finally, the inter-war American expos of the New Deal period are unthinkable without the enthusiasm of President Franklin D. Roosevelt, who in his earlier career had helped to organise the 1915 San Francisco expo.[9] In addition, expos required the participation of large corporations and corporate leaders. As Susman (1983) observes about American expos:

> It would be absurd not to see . . . the importance of bureaucratic and corporate structures in shaping the very institutions of the modern fair or to see what a serious business they were. Fair managers were, after all, major managers in corporate America.
>
> (Susman 1983: 7)

The involvement of these sorts of political and economic elites enabled decision-making to be decisive and effective, but it also meant that it was likely to be as closed, controlled and exclusionary as it would be within a private corporation.

'Class transcendence' themes in expos: drama and social peace

The main themes in expos which can be argued to have something of a 'class transcendent' character are those of drama (spectacle, awe, aura, etc.) and 'social peace'. First, there is the drama theme. Expos, particularly imperial expos, clearly involved the production of ideological and propagandist discourses by power elites intended to 'inform' and 'educate' (or, more cynically, dominate and/or hegemonise) the masses in general and the new urban industrial working and middle classes in particular. However, the messages themselves were often ideologically complex, were carried in spectacular symbolic and dramatic forms open to varied interpretations, and their effects on public attitudes were also complex and ambiguous.

As we saw earlier (Chapter 2), there was a lot of drama associated with attendance at expos – from the spectacular scale and design of the buildings, the quality of the technologies, the quality and quantity of the commodities, to the grandeur of the ceremonies, rituals and parades, etc. Rather than seeing this simply as ideological propaganda intended to fool the masses, it is more realistic to see much of this as expressing the perceptions, values and idealism of contemporary elites, authentically expressing the fact that they were as 'fooled' (if this is the language we must use) as the masses by the almost magical productivity and powers of the new capital–labour relationship they had constructed. Effectively, workers were invited, at expos, to join with capitalists in awe at the representation of industrial capitalism's power and potential.

This was an awe well understood and shared by Karl Marx, albeit in his characteristically critical and de-mystified way. The year before the large-scale (and effectively, although not nominally, 'international') Paris trade exhibition of 1849, the period in which the Crystal Palace expo was being conceived, Marx registered the unprecedented and awesome dynamism of mid-nineteenth-century capitalism in *The Communist Manifesto*, in terms which were entirely appropriate to the kind of message the international expo genre was about to begin popularising around Europe and the USA. He wrote:

> [The bourgeoisie] has been the first [class] to show what man's activities can bring about. It has accomplished wonders far surpassing Egyptian pyramids. . . . [D]uring its rule of scarce 100 years, [it] has created more massive and colossal productive forces than have all preceding generations together. Subjection of nature's forces to man, machinery, application of chemistry to industry and agriculture, steam navigation, railways, electric telegraphs, clearing of whole continents for cultivations, canalisation of rivers, whole populations conjured out of the ground – what earlier century had even a presentiment that such productive forces slumbered in the lap of social labour? . . . The bourgoisie, by the rapid improvement of all instruments of production, by the immensely facilitated means of communication, draws all, even the most barbarian, nations into civilisation.
>
> (Marx and Engels 1969: 53, 54)

Secondly there is the 'social peace' theme. Expos often carried explicitly instrumental and ideological 'class appeasement' themes aimed at promoting cooperation between the classes, by demonstrating to the working class the capacity of the market and state systems to raise the living standards of the masses and to resolve apparently endemic social problems by means of the further progress of science and technology, and their social applications.This theme of 'social peace' between labour and capital, rather than 'class war', was explicitly present in the organisation of the nineteenth-century French expo series, particularly those under the influence of the conservative republican social movement associated with Frederick Le Play (which we discuss further later) and the American inter-war series, particularly the 1939/40 New York expo which embodied President Franklin D. Roosevelt's 'New Deal' social policy thinking (Rydell 1993).

Expos as arenas for working-class movements

Expos were capable of presenting opportunities for working-class and trade-union movements to rally themselves. However, this did not usually extend to the working class and trade unionists actually involved in the construction of the expo site and facilities, and providing services during expos. There seem to have been relatively few strikes at the major expos.[10] Generally, expos occurred, in many of the leading capitalist nations, in the same era in which suffrage was extended, initially to the male working class, in which trade unions won legal recognition and formal rights in employment, and in which socialist parties and movements were created. Expos enhanced the visibility and status of industrial labour in direct and indirect ways; they acted as forms of public education, and thus they generally acted as progressive social forces. They played a role as arenas for the creation and rallying of the trade-union movement and the Socialist International movement. A few points are worth noting in support of this observation. Firstly the 1862 London expo played a role in the build-up to the First Socialist International, providing an occasion for a visit by French, German and English trade unionists, and also by Marx's contemporary, the influential German trade unionist and socialist Ferdinand Lasalle.[11] In the 1867 Paris expo the key theme was the productive power of human work and labour, which attracted visits by British workers and trade unionists (using the services of Thomas Cook's new tourism business). The 1889 Paris Expo provided an occasion for the conference which launched the Second Socialist International movement. Finally, possibly the only 'bourgeois' association Karl Marx ever joined for a period (1869–70) was the Royal Society of Arts, which, as we have seen in Chapter 1, was the 'think tank' probably most responsible for the creation and propagation of the international expo genre (Allan 1981).

Expos, sexism and women's movements

Expos presented a number of versions of women's identity and role in modern civil society and public culture, together with a series of opportunities for women's organisations and movements of various kinds to exhibit their work and ideas. One way or another, given the rate of change of the surrounding societies over the course of nearly a century from the 1851 Crystal Palace to the 1939/40 New York expo, a certain amount of real economic, social and to a lesser extent political progress in the position of women was inevitably registered in expo events over the course of the expo era. But, as in the wider society, the changes in women's situation symbolised in expos, were aspects of a series of all-too-long 'long revolutions' involving struggles, and defeats and misdirections as well as successes. Since expos were produced largely by elite groups of males, the overall frameworks and contents of expos were inevitably implicitly and explicitly highly gendered, and they emphasised male achievements. It is worth dwelling on this for a moment before we proceed to a brief review of women's participation in expos.

It is impossible to understand the development of women's identities and roles in expos or in wider society in modernity without reference to the male identities and roles in terms of which they were (and often continue to be) typically defined and differentiated, and against which women struggled. The dominant definitions have tended to be dualistic, emphasising difference, complementarity and notion-ally equal-but-different mutual dependencies rather than similarities and equality. Each gender has been constructed as the 'internal' Other to the other gender. The dominant dualities of male–female identities and differences, and thus of the male–female 'division of labour' in modern male-dominated culture were given powerful expression and popularisation at expos understood as a major new medium of mass communication.

These dominant dualities include the following set of assumptions, features, often presented as deriving from physical and 'natural' differences, associated with males and females respectively. First, there were assumptions about the natural character of male abilities at sciences, technologies, tasks requiring 'rationality' and the exercise of power as against female abilities at arts, crafts, tasks requiring 'non-rational' emotionality and the exercise of care. Second, there were assumptions about the natural character of male status in the public sphere, in the sphere of production in the formal economy, and in work in the outside world, as against (an albeit conditioned and dependent) female status in the private sphere, in consumption in the formal economy, and in work in the informal economy of the home. Finally, there were assumptions about the natural character of the male status of viewer-subject as against the female status of viewed-object. Males and females were expected to specialise in the 'appropriate' set of these dominant dualities, accepting that the loss of direct involvement in the opposite set could to some extent be compensated indirectly through gender relationships and particuarly through commitment to the institutions of marriage, the family, and family life centred on the private household.

These dominant dualities as features of modern civil society and mass public culture were constructed in the Victorian period and were registered as such in the expos. They remained largely unchanged into the post-war period and continue to be influential in contemporary society. They were, however, periodically adapted and renewed as economic growth increased labour market opportunities for female employment in low-skilled work but also in the professions, and as the women engaged in their long struggles to gain civil, political and social rights and to be recognised and heard in public culture. Some of these adaptations and renewals were also registered in the expo genre, particularly in the inter-war years. The longevity of the dualities relates to their functionality as key structures of the 'division of labour' in the 'modernising' social formation which emerged in the nineteenth century, namely dynamic urbanising and industrialising nations with expanding state sectors linked in a world system of empires and trade.[12] The expos enabled the male-dominated political and military cultures of nation and empire-building and statecraft, together with the male-dominated economic culture of the division of labour involved in science and technology-based industry to be celebrated. As such, expos could not completely avoid the issue of the sexual division of labour which helped to resource and reproduce the modern social system. For this reason, and also because of their claims to provide encyclopaedic coverage of human achievements, they could not avoid providing some explicit versions of the role of women in modernity and of women's contribution to 'Progress'.

Within the framework of the dominant dualities of gender identities and roles, and their main concern to showcase male cultural achievements, expos represented and addressed women in various ways, but largely as home-centred and family-centred wives and mothers. In addition, expos in general were comparatively 'woman-friendly' environments, secure and entertaining, and in the case of the French expos, in particular, imbued, in many aspects of their forms and contents, by an aristocratic and bourgeois 'feminine' aesthetic of art, beauty and luxury (Greenhalgh 1988, ch. 7). In these ways, at least, expos can be said to have promoted a circumscribed form of cultural inclusion. These women-oriented general aspects of expos were not inconsequential for the economics of expos and the subsequent consumerist evolution of popular culture in modern societies.

Women formed half of the visiting public and this economic contribution needed to be encouraged. In addition one of the main evolving mass markets addressed by large proportions of the industries on display at expos was the market for the vast variety of products which can be summed up in the concept of 'the home' (e.g. food, clothing, crockery and cutlery, textiles, decorations, furniture, 'labour-saving devices', etc.) (Scobey 1994). Among the upper and middle classes, women were the main consumers and drivers of the domestic products market. At expos and through the associated development of domestic product advertising, the mass of working-class women were provided with models of domestic lifestyle to aspire to through the work and income of their male partners and by developing their own interests, knowledge and skills as consumers. In these respects – as paying visitors to expos, and as consumers of many of the products for which expos effectively acted as huge advertisements – the address to women in their familial role was structurally and economically of considerable importance to the creation and sustenance of the expo genre, and to its vitality and longevity.

In addition, as the expo genre developed in the inter-war period, women were addressed in more explicitly ideological ways as objects of male technocratic culture, particularly so in the USA. Thus, on the one hand, they were addressed as mothers (or perhaps more accurately as breeders) by the eugenic movement and, on the other hand, as sex objects by the entertainment industry. The eugenic movement in the early decades of the twentieth century held pseudo-scientific and white racist doctrines about the importance of the family, and women's role within it, in reproducing the white race, 'improving' its 'stock' and preventing it from 'degenerating' whether through intermarriage with other 'races' or through tolerating the reproduction of people with physical or mental disabilities. They promoted their doctrines in explicit form at the San Francisco expo in 1915 and at subsequent US state- and regional-level expos and fairs, and also in more implicit forms of familist ideology at the 1939/40 New York expo (Rydell 1993, ch. 2).

Women as sex objects had been part of the expo genre since the introduction of the Midway fair zone at the Chicago 1893 expo with its shows involving erotic Egyptian dancers. All subsequent expos featured comparable erotic shows as part of their entertainment zones to enhance their attraction to male visitors. This element was added to by the emergence of males as mass market consumers for such things as films and cars in the 1930s, and by the awareness on the part of large corporations and advertising of the effectiveness of associating female sexuality with product images when marketing products to men. The big corporate sponsors involved in the 1933 Chicago expo and the 1939/40 New York expo were thus prepared to see suitably hyped and 'sophisticated' strip-shows added to the programmes of these expos (ibid. ch. 5).

Women, then, were in receipt of sometimes overlapping and discordant messages from expos about female identities and roles in modernity, ranging from being seen as home-making consumers to being seen as consumable sex-objects. In addition, some of these messages were discordant with developments in the situation of women in wider society, notably the growth of women's presence in both low-skilled and professional employment, and the eventual achievement of the vote. However, these more positive developments were also, to a limited extent, registered in expos, particularly in the early American expos at Philadelphia in 1876 and Chicago in 1893. With these two American expos particularly in mind, Greenhalgh suggests that 'International exhibitions were one of the first and most effective cultural arenas in which women expressed their misgivings with established patriarchy' (Greenhalgh 1988: 174). In these two events, at least, women – (specifically, it should be said, white upper- and middle-class women) – were part of the organising committees. They were responsible for the creation of exhibitions of women's work and achievements, centred, in the case of each expo, on special buildings created for the purpose. Similar specialised Women's Buildings, pavilions devoted to arts, crafts and technologies produced by women, subsequently became a feature of most international expos, including those in Europe, after they had been introduced at these two American expos. However, the impacts of the European versions of women's exhibitions were often compromised by the involvement of aristocratic women with little interest in either the reality of ordinary women's lives or in the struggle for suffrage.

The American women's suffrage movement opposed the women's exhibition at the 1876 expo, understandably suspecting it of being likely to promote sexist stereotyping and being diversionary from the wider struggles for women's full citizenship, for civil rights in relation to such things as divorce and property rights and for the political right to participate in democracy through the vote. However after Philadelphia the movement could see the publicity value of the platform provided by expos, and supported the women's exhibition and the Women's Building at the Chicago expo in 1893. In 1876, due to the novelty, complexity and pace of preparations for the expo, the Philadelphia women organisers had to make do with a male architect to design the Women's Building. However, at the 1893 expo, the Chicago women organisers were able to have the pavilion designed by a female architect. The exhibits in these pavilions were devoted exclusively to the work and achievements of women as examples of their skills and contribution to modern culture, and they developed in terms of quality and status between 1876 and 1893.

The Woman's pavilion at the 1876 Philadelphia expo presented a relatively predictable range of exhibits deriving largely from women's familial role and with the emphasis on textiles and domestic crafts. Scobey notes that the press at the time 'treated the building as a sort of shrine to the cults of republican motherhood and female benevolence' (Scobey 1994: 95). However, the background to the expo was that even in this period as many as one in five members of the US workforce were women, and the expo allowed this to be drawn to public attention. Dress designers raised the controversial issue of dress reform which was an important issue of personal health and liberation for women in this period. The exhibition also included new machines patented by women inventors, machinery operated by women engineers, and the work of women educators, medical professionals, writers and artists. In addition, as a practical demonstration of women's industrial and professional skills, a newspaper containing information and comment about the expo was produced on a daily basis by staff at the Women's pavilion.

At the 1893 Chicago expo the women involved on the organising committee, with the support of the suffrage movement, took a more ambitious internationalist view and aimed to produce an exhibition about the role of women as workers and breadwinners all over the world. The Woman's Building on this occasion was designed by a woman and aimed, among other things, to provide an educational service, containing a library on women's work from twenty-five nations in twenty languages. Textile arts and crafts were still dominant as at Philadelphia, but in addition there were large painting and sculpture sections. A greater quantity and quality of women's design skills and specialist industrial skills were displayed than had been the case in 1876. The US National Council for Women was formed in 1888 and held a conference at the Chicago expo on various contemporary social political issues of interest to women. The conference attracted over 300 speakers and huge attendances.

However, as was indicated earlier, the theme of women's role and interests as being mainly confined to work and consumerism in relation to the domestic sphere was reasserted in later expos both in Europe and in the USA. Greenhalgh's measured conclusion about these developments seems justified. He suggests that: 'the single real benefit the exhibition tradition bestowed on women [was] visibility'. We should probably add to this – particularly upper- and middle-class women, and particularly visibility in and for male-dominated culture. He continues: 'After the heady days of the Women's Buildings at Philadelphia and Chicago there was little in the treatment of women on exhibition sites that could be said to be objectively or intentionally beneficial apart from this one thing. They were seen. . . . Much in the way propaganda was generated to support and justify empire and the class system, women as an exploited race, were addressed and appeased' (Greenhalgh 1988: 191). However, he also makes the telling point that even this visibility was limited. Only small proportions of women artists and designers ever had their work exhibited, particularly in French expos, and that in these areas – i.e. exhibitions, museums etc. – the visibility of women's achievements continues to remains very poor (ibid. p.195).

Expos, 'Others' and racism

Displays of 'Others', people curiously different from host population, whether from intriguingly exotic foreign cultures (e.g. Arabia, China, Japan) or of unusual appearance (e.g. 'dwarfs', 'giants', deformities, etc.) or mixtures of exoticism and distinctive appearance (e.g. blacks in white societies), had been the stock in trade of fairs, circuses and popular shows for centuries in Europe before the advent of the large-scale international expo genre in the mid-nineteenth century (Altick 1978). These popular traditions continued in the shadow of the expo genre, not least in the travelling fairs and shows in the USA through to the mid-twentieth century.[13] However, the tastes in public culture these displays responded to and stimulated also made themselves felt in expos. Expo producers found that they could increase the dramatic impact and entertainment value of their events by including various kinds of displays of 'Others' on a new scale, in a new critical mass of diversity, and with new and more sophisticated rationales. Some of this ethnic imaging and stereotyping was relatively innocuous. For instance, at the diplomatic level of 'Others as Nations', visitors to most of the late nineteenth- and early twentieth-century expos could expect to see national pavilions and exhibits representing the achievements of the (albeit 'pre-modern') civilisations of Japan and

China and created by governments from those nations. In addition, many expos contained displays of European traditional peasant cultures now superceded by the advance of modernity, such as those of agricultural areas of Ireland or Scotland. However, other displays were much more objectionable, not only in retrospect but also, at the time, for some people, not least for African Americans and for Afro-Caribbeans in Britain

Greenhalgh observes that:

> Between 1889 and 1914, the exhibitions became a human showcase, when people from all over the world were brought to sites in order to be seen by others for their gratification and education . . . objects were seen to be less interesting than human beings, and through the medium of display, human beings were transformed into objects.
>
> (Greenhalgh 1988: 82)

He suggests that there were four types of human display at expos, namely ambassadorial, imperial, 'educational'/pseudo-scientific, and commercial (advertising), with all but the ambassadorial being variously stereotypical, objectifying and racist. As we saw in Chapter 2, the imperial type of display developed first in the British expos, because of the great extent and economic importance to Britain of its Empire, particularly India. It was taken on and developed by both Britain and France in particular, with the USA joining in later, from the 1880s through to the First World War and was revived in the inter-war period.

At imperial expos, and at imperial displays within international expos, ethnic groups were presented and paraded as defeated and colonised but exotically different peoples. Together with their land and raw materials, they were seen as providing valuable human and material resources for Western empires and as benefitting from the 'civilising' and 'modernising' effect of so doing. The main initial forms were (in the British expos) the Indian tea-house and (in the French expos) the Egyptian bazaar and 'Cairo Street'. The latter consisted of a reconstructed Egyptian street with traders, a multicultural mix of restaurants and various kinds of shows including erotic shows. These streets involved large numbers of Arabs and other ethnic groups as waiters and performers, and were a very popular feature of every major international expo from Paris 1889 to St Louis 1904.

The imperial theme in human displays was added to with a rather different 'educational' pseudo-scientific type of display in the form of the 'native village' from the Paris expo of 1889. This involved presenting groups of 'primitive' tribespeople from Africa or Asia living for the period of the expo in a reconstructed village, in native dress, putting their everyday lives and routines as well as their rituals and ceremonies on show for the public. In this context it is also worth noting about the 1889 expo that it included performances of 'Buffalo Bill' Cody's 'Wild West' show featuring recently defeated Plains Indian tribesmen (see photo). As Benedict observes: 'War dances, marriage ceremonies etc., were life cycle rituals in their cultures of origin, but at world's fairs they were presented theatrically. . . . [They] became rituals within a ritual' (Benedict 1994: 57) namely within the new expo ritual of Western representations of 'Otherness'.

The new 'science' of anthropology (through institutions such as the Smithsonian in Washington DC in relation to the American expos) (Rydell 1984, 1993) legitimated and contributed to these displays, contributing also Social Darwinian and other forms of 'scientific' racism in the interpretation of the displays for the public. The proximity of the displays to the entertainment-oriented aspects of the expos (particularly in the case of the French expos where these elements were often not relatively clearly separated as they were in the American expos) often turned the whole exercise into a bizarre cross between a zoo and a freak-show. Most expos typically presented a diverse range of representations of Others as more fundamentally 'pre-modern', even as 'uncivilised' and 'savage' humans and human communities, and they did so increasingly as the expo movement gathered steam from the 1880s onwards. These displays included such peoples as Pacific islanders (e.g. Fijians and Samoans), Arctic peoples (e.g. Lapps, Inuit), native Americans (e.g. Sioux, Apache), and tribal peoples of a variety of ethnic and linguistic groups from Africa (e.g. Senegalese, Dahomeans, Zulus, pygmies) and Asia (e.g. tribes from the Philippines). A number of these groups remained in Europe and North America, effectively becoming professional 'troupes', travelling from show to show and from expo to expo.

The two types of imperial and native village display fed off each other. They did so, in general, in that periodically in expos there would be assemblies and parades juxtaposing all of the 'Others' together for the benefit of the viewing public. They also did so particularly in relation to the bursts of colonial military struggle and projects to impose white domination (together with what we would now refer to as 'ethnic cleansing') on native peoples which periodically flared up concurrently with the expos. For instance, the 'taming of the West' in the the USA and the 'scramble for Africa' among the European powers were both domination projects which were reflected in the international expo genre.

In relation to the 'taming of the West' theme, it is worth noting that during the 1876 Philadelphia expo the Plains Indians put up one of their best-known, but nonetheless near-final, major acts of resistance to white domination by defeating US forces under General George Custer at the battle of the Little Bighorn river. The US government's and the white public's view of Indians as wild primitives impeding the march of progress was echoed in displays of Indian artifacts at the expo organised by two governmental organisations, the Smithsonian and the Indian Office. The US subsequently 'solved' 'the 'problem' of the Plains Indians in the 1880s through the use of force and the construction of 'reservations'.[14] Its success in this project was symbolised and propagandised by the incorporation of the defeated Indians in popular cultural shows, most notably those of the army scout and showman 'Buffalo Bill' Cody in the 1880s and 1890s.[15] Indians were also incorporated into the 1893 Chicago expo (outside the gates of which Cody staged one of his most successful shows) and into the 1904 St Louis expo. Representives and representations of fourteen Indian tribes were presented at the St Louis expo. European expo organisers undertook comparable displays to popularise and legitimate 'the scramble for Africa' and its benefits. In the 1897 Brussels expo pygmies from Belgian King Leopold's recently acquired Congolese colony were displayed (Hochschild 1999: 175–7). In the 1899 London imperial expo the expo impressario Kiralfy staged re-enactments of the Matabele War of 1893 and the Rhodesia revolt of 1896–7 and created 'Kaffir Kraal' and 'Savages of South Africa' displays. In Kaffir Kraal there were 174 Africans from various tribes, organised into four 'villages' together with cranes and giant turtles (MacKenzie 1984: 104). This display was re-staged in the 1904 St Louis expo.

As Greenhalgh observes, these displays were 'a powerful application of Social Darwinism to entertainment'. They were 'an extraordinary illustration of the imperial exhibition's capacity to chain and tame people who a (few) years earlier has been enemies, now sadly acting out their former resistance' (Greenhalgh 1988: 105). The overall effect of these human displays, by creating images of 'Otherness' as 'primitive' and 'savage', and thus, by implication and comparison, images of 'us' and who 'we' were as 'moderns', were probably as inclusionary for the host population and for visiting tourists from similar types of industrial society as they were profoundly and often racially exclusionary for the people displayed.

As in the case of the representation of women, American expos involved more complexities and tensions around the issue of race than did European expos. This is understandable given the difficulties in this period and subsequently in reconciling its anti-imperial, liberal and democratic political culture to its de facto genocide and 'ethnic cleansing' against American Indians, its de facto imperialism in places such as the Philippines, and the de facto and de jure racism involved in the condition endured by Afro-Americans since the period of slavery. The 1876 Philadelphia expo, 'The Centennial Exhibition', was presented as celebration of a century of progress for the new US nation, in a period of reconstruction after the Civil War. Afro-Americans had expected that their contribution, together with their new post-war notional status as citizens would be represented, but they were to be disappointed. Blacks were notably absent from the army of construction workers hired to put up the expo buildings, and were only offered service or entertainment jobs when it opened. Apart from the works of a few black writers, one statue on the liberation from slavery (sculpted by an Italian) (Scobey 1994: 93), and a stereo-typical 'band of minstrels', there was little evidence or symbolism of the presence of blacks in US society at this expo (Rydell 1984: 27–9). There was no special building for Afro-Americans as had been provided for women. Indeed, in spite of their fundraising contributions on behalf of it, black women and their work were not mentioned or represented in the Women's Building (Foner 1976).

In the 1893 Chicago expo the active disinterest of white America in including black America in a major international cultural event was again evident. As in 1876 there was effectively no black representation at organising committee level. In the pre-event period the black community was divided over whether to seek involvement in the expo and how to do so. Debates occurred in the Northern black press about whether or not to use the expo as an occasion to attempt to inform international politicians, tourists and media about the continuing extent of racism and discrimination in the USA. As to the form of any involvement, there was also a debate over the possibility of a separate Afro-American building which would have been open to mis-interpretation in segregationist terms, or involvement through state exhibits. Since the event directors banned segregated exhibits and since state exhibits were decided by all-white committees, the net result was to effectively exclude the black American contribution, as had happened at Philadelphia. Although a 'Coloured People's Day' was programmed, it was poorly attended.

Those blacks who did attend the expo would no doubt have been disturbed to have seen one of the 'native village' displays. This featured a group of Dahomeyan tribespeople. Dahomeyans were a warlike West African people with traditions of female as well as male soldiering and also of human sacrifice, and they were currently in the throes of being defeated and colonised by French forces. The

Dahomeyan village at the expo provided material and opportunity for a certain amount of racist press coverage which promoted stereotypes of both Africans in general and also Afro-Americans as 'primitives', and reproduced imperialistic rationales for the civilising effects of white colonial domination of blacks.[16] The contemporary black leader Frederick Douglass observed:

> as if to shame the negro, the Dahomeyans are also here to exhibit the negro as a repulsive savage . . . The degradation the Dahomey village brought on its own race was thus expanded to degrade all coloured peoples.

Pointedly he criticised the expo with its 'White City' architecture, as follows: 'to the coloured people of America, morally speaking, the World's Fair in progress is . . . a white sepulchre' (quoted in Greenhalgh 1988: 99).

The controversy surrounding the representation or lack of it of black Americans at Chicago led to the US government funding special 'Negro Buildings' at subsequent national-level and regional-level expos in the USA. Even with this minor concession the general justice of Douglass' judgement about expos in his own country and period, namely that they tended to promote racism and cultural exclusion – can be generalised also to the imperial expos in Europe in this period and onwards through the revival of the expo genre in the inter-war years.

This is clear in the record of the European imperial expos of the later period and is also clear in Rydell's research on the American expos of 1926 Philadelphia, 1933 Chicago and 1939/40 New York (Rydell 1993 ch.6). Afro-Americans were once again marginalised in the organising committees for these events, and also effectively excluded from the construction workforce and to a large extent from the events' sales and services workforces. Originally the planners of the 1926 expo approved a proposal from the Ku Klux Klan organisation of white racists to organise a meeting and burn a huge cross at the event. The plan was withdrawn following an outburst of protest from Afro-Americans who managed instead to get the black trade unionist and editor Philip Randolph on the platform of the opening ceremony. The ceremony was broadcast nationally on radio and Randolph was able to use it to call for full citizenship and civil rights for black Americans.

He subsequently organised a 'Negro Day' at the 1933 Chicago expo, which was more controversial (given the problems and segregationist implications noted earlier in relation to the 1893 Chicago expo). As in the earlier expo, the day was poorly attended. However, struggles during the Chicago 1933 expo against the racial discrimination in employment often practised at expos, led to improvements in the law in this field. After further trade union and Afro-American movement struggles, this led to some minor progress in black participation in the 1939/40 New York expo. In order, no doubt, to prepare black Americans for the sacrifices of conscription to the national war effort in the Second World War, a Negro Week was organised in the context of a multi-cultural cultural festival within the expo in 1940. Finally, albeit under pressure from extreme political conditions and far too late in the day, an expo had finally begun to envisage a multicultural concept of cultural inclusiveness and cultural citizenship which the expo genre in general had for so long denied.

Mega-events and cultural internationalism: expos and olympics

The aim of this final section is to consider the institutionalisation of popular forms of cultural internationalism and of the international dimension of public cultures. The general theme is that mega-events, initially specifically expos, were crucially important in this development which got under way in the late nineteenth century. The development gathered pace as the Olympics and international sport movements began to add new dimensions to the popular cultural internationalism opened up by the expo movement. After the First World War popular cultural internationalism resumed its growth in spite of the rising tides of aggressive supernationalism in the USSR, Germany, Italy and to a lesser extent in the imperialist nations. In addition to the renewal of the international and imperial expos genres which we have already considered, international sport event culture, with the Olympics at the centre of this, grew rapidly in the inter-war period. These developments are considered in more detail in Chapter 4.

However, to prepare the way for this we need to establish the historical and sociological connections which link our discussion, in Chapters 2 and 3 so far, of expos as the first great paradigmatic international mega-event genre and movement, with the Olympics as the other great paradigmatic international mega-event genre and movement. We tackle this in two steps. First, we review the ways in which expos provided a politico-cultural basis for the development of the Olympics. Second, we then move on to review the growth of institutionalisation of international mega-event genres, the building of international-level structures to govern or guide them. This process had its origins in the late nineteenth-century and pre-First World War period. However, it developed particularly in the inter-war period and continues to provide the regulatory frameworks and some of the key agencies involved in the mega-event-led and media-led cultural globalisation processes which characterise the post-war and contemporary periods, which we discuss in Chapters 5, 6 and 7.

Expos and Olympics: differentiation in international public cultural forms

In this sub-section we consider the way in which the first great mega-event genre in national and international culture, namely expos, helped to give birth to the other great genre, the Olympic Games. The Olympics in turn gave birth to a series of specialist international sport mega-event movements, including the soccer's World Cup event, whilst expos gave birth to other specialist international trade fairs and exhibitions. So to a certain extent what we are looking at here is a process of differentiation in the institutionalisation of international public culture. In the late twentieth century, in our 'post-modern' and globalised world, we are accustomed to living in highly complex and differentiated national and international public cultures. But the differentiation process has been a long-term one, and in this sub-section we consider the idea that some of its main origins lie in the late nineteenth century expo movement. First, then, we review some of the historical connections between expos and the Olympic movement, looking in particular at the three early expo-based Olympics of 1900, 1904 and 1908. This discussion of the influence of expos on Olympics relates to what we earlier termed the 'intermediate' context of mega-events (Chapter 1). Then we consider the argument that some of the key organisational, ceremonial and ritual aspects of the Olympics derive from the influence of Expos. This has been proposed in particular by the sport historian and cultural analyst John MacAloon and it relates to what we earlier termed the 'dramatological' dimension of mega-events (Chapter 1).

Contextual connections between expos and Olympics

The first of the modern series of Olympic Games was held as an independent multi-sport event in a purpose-built sport stadium in Athens in 1896. However, the second, third and fourth games events, in Paris 1900, St Louis 1904 and London 1908, were each held either within, or with the support of, an international expo event. After these early expo-based events, the Olympic Games event grew rapidly to be able to stand on its own two feet, and was normally staged as an independent sports event, usually in purpose-built facilities. However, periodically, the expo connection has recurred in the history of the games. We can first briefly review the three expo-based events and then consider the subsequent recurrence of the expo connection with the Olympics.

THE EARLY OLYMPICS IN RELATION TO EXPOS[17]

The second and third Olympic Games events were fairly chaotic and variously unsatisfactory events for athletes, organisers and spectators. After the 1896 Athens Olympics Baron Pierre de Coubertin, formalising the leading role he had played prior to this, formally became President of the IOC, a position he was to hold until 1925. Athens had been a great success and was a demonstration of what could be done given the support and resources of a national government. It had given a practical reality and credibility to the Olympic movement which otherwise risked being seen as the whim of an eccentric international group of aristocrats dreaming idle dreams of a revival of ancient Greek culture irrelevant to modern times. De Coubertin and the IOC had determined in 1894 that the Olympics were to be held on a four-yearly cycle, that after Athens the next was to be held in Paris, alongside the great international expo which was also to be staged in Paris in 1900, and the third was to be held in the USA possibly at Chicago.

Paris 1900   Because of his love of expos, but also with sport lacking a clear popular identity in France, and with no serious government support, de Coubertin had used his influence to ensure that the 1900 Olympics would be staged within the context of the expo and thus hopefully within the gaze of the national and international publics which would assemble at the expo. He hoped that the Olympics would be a dramatic sporting garland for the great expo. However, he was not able to properly prepare for it due to personal problems. In addition, the director of 1900 expo, Alfred Picard, disliked sport and saw it as a marginal cultural activity, but nonetheless assumed control of the Olympic programme. He effectively destroyed the identity and coherence of this programme. Particular events were distributed around a confusing variety of venues and the whole programme was stretched out over the full five months duration of the expo itself. Ultimately, only 3,000 people attended the high point of the programme, the athletics events (Meyer 1976). When it was clear that the expo organisers were going to make a mess of the Olympic Games event, de Coubertin tried unsuccessfully to regain control, and then tried, again unsuccessfully, to set up an alternative games event. Interestingly, the Paris experience in 1900 appeared to find an American echo the following year. Possibly assuming that the failure of the Olympic movement in Paris the previous year was terminal, but nonetheless impressed with the concept of an Olympics-type event as part of an expo, the organisers of the 1901 Buffalo international Expo tried to create an 'international athletics union' and to arrange an international athletics event as part of their expo event. They also failed (Meyer 1976).

St Louis 1904   In 1894 the IOC had decided that the third Olympic Games event would be staged in the USA. The previous year, de Coubertin had attended the great 1893 Chicago Expo, possibly in the capacity of a representative of the French government in the sphere of education.[18] He visited one of the millionaire financial backers of the expo and the head of Chicago University, key people in any prospective bid the city might mount to be the American venue for the third Olympic Games to be held in 1904. He convinced them of the importance and value of the event and informally appeared to promise that Chicago would be chosen as the venue for it. At the time this did not clash with plans for the next in the series of great American international expos, which was scheduled for 1903 in St Louis. In 1901 the IOC formally considered bids from Chicago and St Louis and confirmed de Coubertin's choice of Chicago. However, the St Louis event had to be delayed for a year because of financial problems, and this created the prospect of a clash between the expo event and the Olympic event. The Chicago group asked the IOC for a delay until 1905 to avoid this. For their part, the St Louis expo organisers pressured the IOC to transfer the games to St Louis, threatening to organise an alternative major athletics event which would have worsened the clash with the planned Chicago Olympics. Since the IOC required the head of the host state or their representative to open the games, they asked newly elected US President Teddy Roosevelt to arbitrate. He decided in favour of St Louis and the IOC agreed. This caused much resentment in Chicago and much embarrassment to de Coubertin. De Coubertin effectively boycotted his own games, interestingly (given later German involvement in the Olympic movement's fortunes, see Chapter 4 below) deciding instead to attend the annual dramatic festival of Wagner's music at Bayreuth in Germany.

The 1904 Olympic Games, while a large-scale event, was mainly a North American affair. Very few European or other nations participated, and the absentees notably included one of the world's strongest athletics nations, Britain, whose athletics authorities claimed not to be able to cover the costs of sending a team. The event organisation, the facilities at the University of Washington, and the performances were all of a reasonable standard, an improvement on Paris, although spectator numbers were as poor as at Paris. However in addition, as if to confuse the event's public and the watching press about the status of modern sports as a mark of 'civilisation' and 'progress', two 'anthropology days' were held in which various 'primitive' non-Western peoples were asked to learn and practice Western sports. These 'human displays' were controversial, resented by members of the Olympic movement and probably severed any residual interest de Coubertin and others may have had in maintaining an interest in communication between the Olympic movement and expo-planning groups as part of the long-term future of the Olympic Games.

London 1908[19]   With two Olympic Games disasters behind them, both of them involving expos, the Olympic movement and its key organisation, the IOC, was in difficulties. The IOC had awarded the fourth Olympic Games of 1908 to Rome. However, in 1906 Rome had to withdraw. The previous year, Britain had, after some delay, formally joined the Olympic movement. The British Olympic Association (BOA) was created in 1905 together with a British seat on the IOC. The IOC turned in desperation to Britain. As the originator of numerous sports and athletics events, and as the originator of amateurism in sport, Britain at the time was one of the strongest sporting nations in the world. In addition, through long-standing organisations like the Amateur Athletics Association (AAA), it was also one of the best organised. However, in spite of all this, Britain had no major athletics stadium of the kind necessary to stage the main athletics programme. Nonetheless, the IOC turned to Britain for assistance in this critical situation. It was a stroke of good fortune for them that, at this time, British and French event financiers and organisers were cooperating in the planning of an international expo, the Franco-British Exhibition of 1908. The expo organisers needed a venue for their own opening and closing ceremonies and other activities, and agreed to build a stadium to accommodate these together with the Olympic event. Although spectator numbers for the games were initially low, interest in the intense nationalistic clash between British and American athletes was picked up by the British media and this attracted the interest of the public. On the final day there were 90,000 spectators present together with the Royal Family to witness the legendary first modern Olympic marathon won by the Italian Dorando Petri. In this case, the association between an Olympic Games and an expo had paid off for the Olympic movement and had re-established the potential popularity of the Olympic event which had first been glimpsed at Athens. However, in spite of the success of this association betwen the two genres in 1908 the memories of the Paris and St Louis disasters were decisive in the Olympic movement and the Olympics were never again strongly associated with expos.

LATER OLYMPICS IN RELATION TO EXPOS

The period around the Second World War saw two notable connections between the Olympics and expos. First, in the mid-1930s the International Olympic Committee (IOC) decided to give the 1940 Summer Games event to Tokyo. However, in 1938 a fascist and warlike government came into power in Japan and forced the Japanese Olympic Committee to withdraw from staging the event. To enable the 1940 event to be salvaged and staged, elements in leading circles in the USA proposed to the IOC, before war swept international sport off the agenda, that they should relocate the event to New York, to be staged as part of the plans for extension of the 1939/40 New York expo into a second year (Mandell 1971: 290). Second, at the end of the war, resources for staging international sport were at a low level and the reputation of the Olympic movement was at a low ebb and in need of revival. The British were able to stage a low-cost Olympic Games event, in a context of austerity and national reconstruction, by using the stadium and buildings (for the media etc.) originally created for the 1924/5 imperial expo at Wembley in London (Anthony 1987; Abrahams 1976).

In the post-war period there were more, although even looser, connections between Olympics and expos. For instance, it is likely that the success of Montreal's staging of its 1967 international expo, together with the investment in transport and other infrastructure required for this event, encouraged the city to bid for what in fact turned out to be a much more problematic venture, namely the staging of the hugely expensive 1976 Olympics. In addition, in the mid-1980s the Spanish government committed itself to symbolising its emergence from the Franco era, its entry into the European Union and its economic development by funding the staging of two mega-events simultaneously in 1992, namely the Olympic Games in Barcelona and the international expo in Seville. Finally, cities have occasionally bid for the Games on the basis of adapting existing expo sites. For instance, Birmingham's unsuccessful bid for the 1992 Olympics was based on using what is effectively a permanent national-level expo site and complex (the National Exhibition Centre, NEC) (Anthony 1987, Howell 1990). Seville's similarly unsuccessful bid for the 2004 Olympics was based on the use of the site and facilities complex created by the 1992 international Expo that the city had staged. Finally, it is possible that London's bid for the 2008 or 2012 Olympics will involve a proposal to use the Millenium expo site, notably its architectural centrepiece the Millennium Dome, to stage some at least some of the Games programme.

DRAMATOLOGICAL CONNECTIONS BETWEEN EXPOS AND OLYMPICS:
THE MACALOON THESIS

The main research and analysis to suggest that the expo international mega-event genre was of crucial importance in the genesis of the international Olympic movement and its event has been provided by the sports historian and cultural analyst John MacAloon. His analysis suggests an analogy with the well-known Weber thesis which proposes the importance of the role of a religious movement (Protestantism) in the origins of 'the spirit of capitalism' in modernity. Comparably what we can refer to as the MacAloon thesis proposes the importance of a cultural movement (Expos) for understanding the origins of Olympism and the 'spirit of sport' in modernity.[20] The thesis is contained in MacAloon's history of Pierre de Coubertin and his founding of the modern Olympic Games. MacAloon argues for the influence of Expos on the development of de Coubertin's thinking in the 1880s and 1890s, particularly the 1878 and 1889 Paris expos, and to a limited extent also the 1893 Chicago expo, prior to the occurrence of the first modern games event in 1896.

As we saw in Chapter 2, the French series of late nineteenth-century international expos (1855, 1867, 1878, 1889 and 1900) were often vehicles for the promotion of contemporary French political and cultural ideologies, relating to the Second Empire in the pre-1870 period, and to republicanism and nationalism in the Third Republic, post-1870 period. Most of them also carried, as did the American expos, positive messages about the benefits of good relations between labour and capital, as we saw earlier in this chapter. A key figure in the development of this ideological theme in the French expo series was Frederick Le Play. Le Play was one of the first systematic empirical sociologists in his comparative and typological studies of family, work and community in European societies, and in addition he was also committed to conservative Catholic social philosophy.[21] His thinking influenced both Prince Albert and Napoleon III, respectively the political forces behind, on the one hand, the 1851 Crystal Palace expo and, on the other hand, the two Paris expos of 1855 and 1867. Le Play was in fact the main organiser of both of the Paris expos and was thus a leading figure in the development the expo genre and movement. He saw expos as opportunities to display the progress which was made possible by social cooperation between classes in the new division of labour being brought into existence by industrial capitalism. He organised the categorisation of exhibits in the 1855 expo, and indeed he designed the whole integrated structure of the 1867 expo to reflect the theme of types of work and production. Following the success of the 1855 expo, he founded two national associations which continued to be influential during the Third Republic, an academic social scientific association, the Society for Social Economy, and a political movement, the Union for Social Peace (MacAloon 1981: 87).

The founder of the modern Olympics, Pierre de Coubertin, was born into the French aristocracy, which gave him ready access to French and international elite circles throughout his life. However, he grew up and made his contribution to modern cultural history in the period of the anti-aristocratic Third French Republic. His interest in sport and Olympism could be said to effectively represent a renewal of the aristocratic ideal of 'nobility', but now 'secularised' in the form of the nobility of amateurism and competition, more appropriate versions of the ideal for a republican era (Hoberman 1986). He attended the 1878 Paris expo as a teenager and was profoundly influenced as a young man by Le Play and his followers who included leading republican politicians such as Jules Ferry. De Coubertin joined Le Play's Union in 1883 and joined his social scientific society in 1886. Through the influence of Jules Ferry who helped to organise it, the Le Play organisations were given a leading role in the design and preparation of the 1889 expo.

De Coubertin had become interested both in physical education and also in ancient Hellenic civilisation in the 1880s. In this period, in relation to the latter interest, the new discipline of archaeology had begun to make major breakthoughs in establishing the realities underlying the myths about ancient Greece, including the site of the ancient Olympic Games at Olympia. He proposed to the 1889 Paris expo organiser that Olympia should be a major theme of the expo, although this was rejected (Meyer 1976). However, de Coubertin was able to use the expo event as an occasion to organise an international conference on physical education, and to begin international networking and missionising in relation to the possibility of reviving the Olympic Games event (MacAloon 1981: 137, 132–8). Also, finds at the site of Olympia in the 1870s by the German archaeologist Ernst Curtius, had allowed a reconstruction of the ancient town and games area to be constructed and displayed at the expo. It is likely that de Coubertin saw this, and it would have helped fire his idealism for, in his words, 'the dream city'.[22] Also the expo organisers had arranged a few 'Olympic games' on the Champ de Mars during the expo. All of this meant that it is likely that it was the 1889 Expo which focused de Coubertin's mind on the idea of the Olympic Games and on the project of reviving them. MacAloon observes: 'the hour had struck' (MacAloon 1981: 138–9). The years immediately following the Paris expo and this particular conference were crucial in the crystallization both of the concept of the revival of the Olympic games and also of the international culltural and political networks which would, eventually, enable it to flourish.[23]

Dr William Penny Brookes, a leading British sports culture enthusiast and an important figure in the nineteenth-century project to revive the ancient Olympic

Games, visited de Coubertin in 1890. De Coubertin reciprocated, observing Brookes' small-scale Olympics event in the same year.[24] In 1892, de Coubertin persuaded the French President, Carnot, effectively patron of the 1889 expo, to act as patron to his next international physical education conference in Paris, which was concerned with the possibility of reviving the Olympic Games. Among other things, the 1892 conference envisaged the possibility that the first series of Olympic events would be held first in Athens, then in Paris (in connection with the expo which was being considered for 1900), and then in the USA. In 1893, de Coubertin, possibly supported by Jules Ferry, travelled to the Chicago expo as a formal or informal French representative, attending meetings on education and comparative religions. As we noted earlier, on this visit he appeared to offer Chicago city leaders the possibility of staging an Olympic Games after the first two at Athens and Paris. Finally, in 1894 he organised a further international conference on sport and Olympism, gaining support from the powerful British and American athletics associations, and also from the Greek King and government who indicated their willingness to stage the first event in 1896 in Athens. Although the Greeks planned to retain control of the Olympic Games and not allow their location to be varied de Coubertin and his IOC ignored them and committed themselves to making the next games the highlight of the great international expo planned for Paris in 1900, with the disasterous results we have already seen.

The basis for De Coubertin's misjudgement in this respect, and his trust in the expo tradition, which was derived from his experience of the 1878 and in particular the 1889 expo has been already been indicated. MacAloon observes that de Coubertin 'was seduced by the exposition tradition' . . . although 'in 1889, he could not have foreseen the incompatibility between these two great forms of nineteenth-century cultural expression' (MacAloon 1981: 138). The 1889 expo was particularly seductive not least because of its combination of a revival of classicism by means of the modernism of contemporary archaeology noted earlier, together with the awe-inspiring modernism of Eiffel's great tower. This provided a unique stage setting for the public theatre of the opening ceremony. In addition, the expo in general provided a unique public cultural stage for the first international appearance and recognition, as participating exhibitors, of new nations (in this case Mexico, Brazil and Argentina, ibid. p.136). MacAloon believes that:

> As in 1851, so in 1889: participants and thoughtful observers alike sensed that the universal exhibitions were unique, that they utterly confounded the familiar classifications . . . of cultural performance. The Olympic Games were to follow the exhibitions in this, . . . and very much of their cultural significance and mass appeal lies in this very thing.
> (MacAloon 1981: 134)

De Coubertin witnessed the procession of the French head of state, President Carnot, through the arches of the Eiffel Tower and into the main expo site, through crowds estimated to number 500,000, arriving at a statue of Marianne, symbol of the French Revolution and of the republican tradition. The current leader of the government, Prime Minister Pierre Tirard, 'presented' the expo to the President. Carnot dedicated the statue, the national anthem was sung, there was a military parade and review, and then Carnot declared the expo open. MacAloon notes that:

> Coubertin witnessed these rites and they impressed him mightily. Many of their elements were to reappear in the opening ceremonies of the modern Olympic Games, most notably the entry procession (though of athletes and athletic officials, not politicians and soldiers), the flag raising and anthems, and the declaration of opening by the head of state of the host nation. . . . The 1889 exposition provided Coubertin with his first experience of athletic games appended to an international festival/spectacle, devoted to the progress of science, art and industry, in which new symbols and rituals, for all of their 'inventedness', excited a sense of history such as no museum or book ever could.
>
> (MacAloon 1981: 137)

This experience undoubtedly led to de Coubertin's insistence on a range of Olympic rituals, not least those associated with the opening ceremony of the Games, which closely resemble or derive from those which were typically part of expo ceremonial. On the basis of this discussion, then, and concurrent with the MacAloon thesis, we can suggest that that the dramatological dimension of the modern Olympic Games event constituted by these rituals almost certainly derives from the influence of the expo tradition on their founder Pierre de Coubertin. Further analysis of this dramatological dimension, together with the development of Olympic rituals under the influence of such pressures as Nazi ideology in the inter-war period, and their translation into media events and media programmes in the contemporary period, will be explored at greater length in subsequent chapters.

Mega-events and the institutionalisation of International Public Culture

In the late nineteenth and early twentieth centuries, besides the developing calendars of national expo and sport events there also was a developing calendar of international expos and sport events. This calendar was abandoned twice during the great wars but, in spite of the destruction of these wars, the development of this calendar and of these events was picked up again surprisingly rapidly early in the reconstruction periods following each war. As fragile as they may often have appeared compared to the state powers surrounding them, particularly in the supernational period of the interwar years, these events and event movements outlasted the imperialist, fascist and communist states and movements of their day.

Mega-events in the 1900 to 1939 period: a review

In Chapter 2 we reviewed the main international expos and imperial expos in these periods. There was clearly an acceleration of cultural internationalisation around the turn of the century and in the pre-war period involving mega-events. There were two major international expos, Paris 1900 and St Louis 1904. In addition, a series of large-scale and virtually annual imperial expos was created in the 1908–1914 period in London. The Paris and St Louis expos in particular attracted vast numbers of visitors (see Table 2.1). In addition there were international expos in Buffalo 1901, Liege 1905, Milan 1906, Brussels 1910, Gent 1913, and San Francisco 1915. Each of these events also attracted huge numbers of visitors, from a minimum of 7 million to a maximum of 19 million visits. As we saw earlier the three expos of 1900 Paris, 1904 St Louis, and 1908 London also provided a basis for the staging of the 2nd, 3rd and 4th Olympic Games events. In the pre-war period there was one further Olympic Games event, in Stockholm 1912, the first (apart from Athens 1896) to be staged independently of an expo, and one at which, notably in terms of the themes we explore in Chapters 4 and 5 later) included participation by teams representing Russia and Germany. In addition, at Stockholm in 1912 the IOC awarded the soon-to-be-cancelled 1916 Olympics to Berlin, a commitment which was ultimately honoured, if that is the right expression, a generation later in the Berlin Olympics of 1936 (see discussion in Chapter 5 below). In the inter-war period there were four major international expos in the USA (Philadelphia 1926, Chicago 1933, San Francisco 1939 and New York 1939/40), two in Britain (Wembley 1924/5 and Glasgow 1938), and three in France (see Table 2.1).

In addition, there was the power of the sport movement as a force in cultural internationalization in general, and also of the Olympic idea of a calendar of international multi-sport events in particular. There were five Olympic Games events (Antwerp 1920, Paris 1924, Amsterdam 1928, LA 1932, Berlin 1936) in the inter-war period. Moreover, this period saw the creation of a number of Olympic-style multi-sport mega-events and event movements, which can be called 'alternative Olympics'. These included Western European Workers' Olympics and Womens' Olympics and also the Soviet 'Spartakiads'. There were at least three Workers' Olympics, two Soviet Olympics and four Women's Olympics (see Table 4.1). These were all large-scale and credible international events developed in part as responses and alternatives to the upper-class and middle-class-dominated and male-dominated Olympic movement. We will consider these in more detail in Chapter 5. These movements did not survive the Second World War, partly because the Olympic movement changed to accommodate women and to a lesser extent working-class men, and partly because the USSR joined the Olympic movement in the post-war period. Other Olympic-like or Olympic-relevant major sport events and related movements which were created in this period, but which, by contrast, did survive and prosper later in the post-war period, were the British Empire Games (subsequently renamed the Commonwealth Games) and the soccer World Cup competition. There were three British Empire Games and three soccer World Cups in the same years in the 1930s (1930, 1934, 1938) (see Table 4.1).

The institutionalisation of international expo and sport events

INTERNATIONAL EXPOS: BIE

As we noted earlier, in the field of international expositions no INGO developed in the late nineteenth century in spite of Franco-British attempts to create one in the 1860s.[25] Governments' perceptions of the need to bring some order to the organisation of the types and frequency of expos grew in the late nineteenth century. In 1907 the French government called for international agreement and in

1912 the German government convened an inter-governmental meeting in Berlin which drew up an international convenant. War intervened before it could be ratified but other governments took up the matter again in the early post-war period. In 1928 in Paris an international convention based on the Berlin agreement was signed. Besides rules governing the financing, types and frequency of expos this convention also created an executive agency, the International Bureau of Exhibitions (BIE), accountable to a General Assembly of national representatives meeting biennially (BIEa undated). It is claimed that 1928 'brought order to the world exhibitions situation by regulating their frequency and outlining the rights and obligations of the exhibitors and organisers' (BIEb undated p.2). There may be a reasonable degree of substance in this claim. But it is also worth noting that this system did not prevent the over-frequent, even over-lapping, series of major expos which occurred at the end of the 1930s (1937 Paris, 1939 San Francisco, and 1939/40 New York). Also throughout the post-war period the convention and the powers of the BIE have had to be upgraded to attempt to keep pace with, and to retain some influence and control on, the pace and scale of expo event creation around the world in the late twentieth century.

INTERNATIONAL SPORT IN GENERAL

Sport movement's national governing bodies (defining and standardising the aims, duration, space, players roles, and the rules of games and contests) were formed in the late nineteenth century and around the turn of the century, for instance in the two major sports of athletics and football.[26] These were, by then, already major spectator sports in Britain and elsewhere, attracting mass audiences and mass support. As we saw in relation to Hobsbawm's analysis of invented traditions and their role in nation-building and nationalising populations, sports had a powerful potential for popularising intra-national communication and national identity. I will refer to these governing bodies as cultural NGOs. At the turn of the century the situation had become ripe for a further step of international organisation, for the development of international competitions in which to parade the new sporting nationalisms, and for international governing bodies to regulate them. Through the concept of 'nationally representative' teams in team sports and/or multi-sport events, this was evidently consistent with the development of nation-building and nationalism. But it is a mistake to reduce this merely to nationalism.

This process also involved the building of popular assumptions and expectations about the interest and practicality of an international level of socio-cultural organisation through networks and organisations with the capacity to support essentially peaceable cultural competition, in which participation itself was worthy of recognition and respect, and in which 'losing' would be tolerated and not lead to exit or war. I will refer to these as cultural INGOs.[27] Even allowing for the destructive depths reached by supernationalism in the two world wars and the absence of any effective international peace-keeping system, these apparently fragile international networks and organisations, together with the popular interest in international competitions and events associated with them, while undoubtedly damaged by their association with supernational powers, nonetheless survived through this period and emerged to grow more strongly in the post-war period.

The creation of specialised international governing bodies (international federations, IFs) for each sport occurred in tandem with the development in the 1890s of a generalist and pluralist international sport movement, namely the Olympic movement, led by de Coubertin and the IOC and oriented to the promotion of its sport ideology and the development of its multi-sport games event. As we saw earlier, the Olympic model was important in the inter-war period, generating a number of alternative versions of international sport ideology, multi-sport movements and events, including those of Workers' Olympics, Women's Olympics and the British Empire Games (see also Chapter 4).

INTERNATIONAL SPORT GOVERNING BODIES : FIFA AND INTERNATIONAL SOCCER

Many IFs allied themselves with the Olympic movement and organised specialist world championships within the main Olympic Games event. The biggest and most important of these was the international governing body for football, FIFA, formed in Paris in 1904. FIFA helped the Olympic Games organisers (IOC, host NOC and host city) stage what were effectively international football world championships in each of the early Olympic Games until the 1920s. However, because of the growth of the game in general as a mass spectator sport, and because of the consequent growth of professionalism in the game and in international teams, there were conflicts with the, at that time, rigorously anti-professional sport ideology of the Olympic movement. The quality of the Olympic football event was rapidly becoming devalued in comparison with professional football and in 1928 FIFA took the decision to organise its own 'World Cup' competition on a four-year cycle intermediate to the Olympic four-year cycle and beginning in 1930 (Sugden and Tomlinson 1998, ch.1,2).

OLYMPIC INSTITUTIONS: RULES AND RITUALS

Cultural institutionalisation in the international sport area in particular involved processes of general formalisation ('rationalisation' and bureaucratisation), ritualisation (the developing and structuring of 'non-rational' – symbolic – aspects) and the specific formalisation of ritual aspects. These processes proceeded with different weightings as between the expo movement and the sport/Olympic movement. In this chapter we have seen how expo ceremonial structures and practices, practised by host nations but significantly standardised through competitive modelling and emulation, preceded and influenced the early Olympic movement in the 1890s. However, as we noted above the formalisation of expos through agreed rules of an international cultural organisation (INGO) – although practised informally among the leading expo host nations – was only achieved in 1928 through the formation of the BIE. Also, as we have seen above sport movements in general developed formalisation (standardised game rules etc.; Guttman 1978) and organisation more actively than the expo movement .

One of our main themes in the following chapters is the continued ritualisation of the Olympics in the inter-war years and the impact on this process of super-nationalist aestheticized political power – particularly, as we will see, through the influence of Nazi Germany during the preparation for and staging of the 1937 Berlin Olympics. However before we begin to address these issues we should note the formalisation of ritual in the Olympic movement. The main elements of ritual and symbolism in the modern Olympic tradition are bound up with the theatrical-religious stage or framework of the Olympic site itself, in particular the main stadium, which effectively becomes 'diplomatic territory' and a de facto 'sacred site' for the duration of the games. The stadium contains the Olympic flame, the Olympic flag, the flags of other nations and (ironically given the commercialisation of the contemporary Olympics) no advertising or commercial imagery to detract from the impact of the Olympic symbols. In terms of ceremonies, the opening and closing ceremonies and the victory ceremonies are particularly important and closely specified rituals. The opening ceremony includes the opening of the games by the head of state of the host nation, the entry and parade of the athletes with signs and flags representing their nations, the oath-taking by the assembled athletes and judges, the reception of the torch from the torch relay from Olympia, the lighting of the main stadium Olympic flame, and the peace symbolism of the release of doves. Also, the opening ceremony usually includes either some kind of mass pageant and/or some mass display of gymnastics.

These and other elements of the contemporary Olympic theatre were developed particularly in the the inter-war period. The five rings flag, the peace symbolic release of doves and the athletes' oath were introduced at the 1920 Antwerp games, the flame was introduced at the 1928 Amsterdam event, and the torch relay was introduced at the 1936 Berlin Olympics. These symbols and rituals went beyond the nationalist and internationalist ceremonial which the expo tradition had bequeathed to the Olympic movement. The pressure to develop specific trans-national symbols and rituals in the Olympics in the inter-war years derived from the supernationalist turn in world politics and the influence of supernationalism on mega-events in general in this period. This is one of the main themes explored in the next chapter.

Conclusion

In this chapter we looked at the 'consumption' of expos in terms of their embodiment and development of the popular cultural forms of touristic consumerism. We also looked at the implications of expos for cultural inclusion and exclusion, and generally for the development of citizenship. In this context we saw how problems of class, sexism and racism were intertwined with notions of social progress at expos. Finally we looked at the processes of differentiation and institutionalisation of international public culture which expos gave rise to, including the emergence of the new mega-event genre and public cultural form of the international sport event and in particular the Olympic Games.

We now need to consider the development of, particularly, international sport culture and Olympism in the inter-war period and consider some of its dynamics and conflicts. In this period the process of internationalisation in public culture and sport built up substantially. However, it did so in the new and threatening context of supernationalist power, ideology and conflict associated with the rise of German fascism and Soviet communism.

4 The Olympics, internationalism and supernationalism

International sports events and movements in the inter-war period

In order to understand the nature and role of international mega-events in late twentieth-century modernity we have suggested that it is necessary to understand their origins in the development of modern forms of national and international social order in the late nineteenth and early twentieth centuries. In particular, many features of the leading contemporary global mega-event, the Olympic Games, which is our main focus in Part 2, were formed by the political and cultural forces and conflicts connected with the growth of the various versions of early twentieth-century 'supernationalism', including imperialism and particularly communism and fascism. In this chapter, some of the main developments in the internationalisation of sport and its related large-scale events in the inter-war period are reviewed and we consider the influence of nationalism and super-nationalism on these developments. In particular, we focus on the growth of the Olympic movement and its cycle of sport mega-events, and the influence on the Olympics in this period, of 'supernational' (imperial, and totalitarian) and also 'alternative internationalist' versions of international sport.

This focus on major sport events and Olympic Games in the inter-war period should not be read as suggesting that the expo genre had no role to play as a stage for supernationalism in this period. On the contrary, as we have seen in Chapters 2 and 3, they performed just such a role for the imperialism of the major Western nations in this period, and increasingly so as time went by. In this context, and given the case study of the 1936 Berlin Olympics we consider later, it is worth noting that in the following year Nazi supernationalism found another international mega-event stage, namely at the 1937 Paris expo which recorded 34 million visits. The symbolic architecture of the pavilions of the competing supernationalisms of Nazi Germany and the USSR were deliberately positioned to face each other dramatically across the central space of the expo site (Speer 1970: 81, also see photo). However, the priorities of the French hosts to appease Germany at this time were evident in the fact that Albert Speer's grandiose planned designs for the Nazi Party Nuremberg Rally site (ibid. p.67) and Leni Reifenstahl's film of the Berlin Olympics both won prizes. Picasso's 'Guernica', painted to protest at the Nazi-backed destruction of Spanish democracy by Franco, was displayed in the pavilion of the soon-to-be-defeated Spanish republican government (Freedberg 1986). It was not painted to win prizes, but it is worth recording (and it is a comment on the political character of the expo) that it did not win any.

The discussion in this chapter proceeds in five main steps. The first section outlines the relationships between versions of supernationalism (particularly Soviet

Figure 4.1 Crowds at the 1937 Exposition International in Paris showing the symbolic conflict of the Nazi pavilion designed by Albert Speer, topped with the German eagle, on the left, and, on the right, the pavilion of the USSR, topped by the monumental image of a male worker holding a hammer and a female peasant holding a sickle.

communism and German fascism, but also including British imperialism), and international sport. Each of these versions of supernationalism generated Olympic-type sport mega-events. The second section outlines versions of what can be called 'alternative internationalism' in relation to international sport, in particular Western social democracy and feminism. Each of these movements also generated Olympic-type sport mega-events. The main examples of these events, and also, albeit implicitly, their structuring of international public culture, time and place in the inter-war period, are indicated in Table 4.1. The third section outlines the development of the Olympic movement, its ideology, rules and event rituals in this period, some of which were undoubtedly influenced by the supernationalist and alternative internationalist versions of international sport and sport events which were going on around the Olympic movement and which were often consciously created to challenge and change the nature of the movement and of its main games event. The fourth section looks at the case of the 1936 Berlin Olympics as an example of the influence of supernationalism, here Nazism, on the Olympics. Finally the fifth section reviews the general influence of fascism on the Olympic movement in the 1930s, a period in which, perhaps like the contemporary period, the movement seemed to seriously lose its way.

Table 4.1 Structuring inter-war public culture: major international sport events 1920–1938

Year	Olympic Games	World Cup	Empire Games	Worker's Olympics	Soviet Games	Women's Olympics
1920	Antwerp	–	–	–	–	–
1921	–	–	–	Prague	–	–
1922	–	–	–	–	–	Paris
1923	–	–	–	–	–	–
1924	Paris	–	–	–	–	–
1925	–	–	–	Frankfurt	–	–
1926	–	–	–	–	–	Gothenburg
1927	–	–	–	Prague	–	–
1928	Amsterdam	–	–	–	Moscow	–
1929	–	–	–	–	–	–
1930	–	Uruguay	Hamilton	–	–	Prague
1931	–	–	–	Vienna	–	–
1932	LA	–	–	–	Moscow	–
1933	–	–	–	–	–	–
1934	–	Italy	London	Prague	–	London
1935	–	–	–	–	–	–
1936	Berlin	–	–	(Barcelona)	–	–
1937	–	–	–	–	–	–
1938	–	France	Sydney	–	–	(Vienna)

Sources: Killanin and Rodda 1976; Phillips and Oldham 1994; Holt 1992; Jones 1988; Riordan 1994,1998; Hargreaves 1994.

Supernationalism and international sport: an overview

Imperial international sport

The British internationalised sport by exporting their cultural traditions and many of their games – old games (e.g. cricket) and new late nineteenth-century games (e.g. rugby, athletics, squash) – around the world to their colonies.[1] Initially this was done on a completely elitist and exclusionary basis to enable the ex-patriate British upper and middle classes, who controlled the administration, trade and military organisation of the Empire, to cohere and communicate among themselves. The classism, sexism and racism embedded in the organisation and development of sport culture in late nineteenth-century British society domestically was reproduced around the world.

However, even on the domestic front sport's exclusionary role began to mutate, in the late nineteenth century, into a more ambiguous hegemony role, particularly in relation to class, but also to a certain extent in relation to women. The English elitist 'amateur' version of sport was promoted as part of the attempt by upper- and middle-class 'rational recreationist' and 'muscular Christian' movements to 'civilise' and control the working class (Bailey 1978, Cunningham 1980). But while the working class were increasingly attracted to sport they resisted the amateur version. By the turn of the century the English working class began to adopt previously upper- and middle-class sports such as soccer and rugby (in the form of rugby league) and press for their adaptation into spectatorial and quasi-professional popular event forms, increasingly identifiable with and expressive of urban and industrial working-class communities and cultures (Dunning and Sheard 1979; Holt 1992).

Comparable developments occured in the colonies in relation to the elite British colonisers and the sports which both formed part of their cultural identity and also provided some of the content of their 'civilising mission' to control and change their colonial subject peoples. In the distant, white, self-governing dominions of Australia and New Zealand, cricket and rugby became 'national' games through which the people could identify with (and express their own developing identities against) the 'mother country'. However, in the Black and Asian colonies of the West Indies and India, cricket and other sports initially were used in relation to local ethnic elites, as were imperial expos, as vehicles both of limited inclusion in the culture of Empire and also of the reproduction of imperial hegemony and social control (Guttman 1994).

But, as the example of the English working class indicates, sports can play an ambiguous roles in socially divided societies, particularly if they become popularised as spectator events. In this form they can provide traditions of popular cultural participation and arenas in which social dominance and subordination can be symbolically expressed and challenged. Cricket, originally exported to the colonies in the eighteenth century, played some such role for local ethnic elites and their mass publics in India and the West Indies both in the development of national identity from the late nineteenth century and also in national liberation movements in the inter-war and early post-war years.[2] From the late nineteenth century, what were effectively international sport events, which often attracted mass audiences, began to be developed, in particular the 'Ashes' series of cricketr matches between England and Australia which began in 1882. This was the forerunner of similar inter-war and post-war events of England against colonies and ex-colonies, in particular involving Australia, India and the West Indies.

Influenced in part by the success of the the 1924 Wembley imperial expo, which contained some inter-imperial sport competitions, and no doubt also by the growth and example of the Olympic movement in its successful 1920, 1924, and 1928 events, the Olympic-style multi-sport Empire Games event was inaugurated in 1930, also on a four-year cycle, synchronised with the Olympic Games cycle. Before the Second World War the event was first held in Hamilton (near Toronto in Canada) in 1930, then in London in 1934 and Sydney in 1938 (Lovesey 1979). The idea for such intra-imperial games was initially raised in 1891, at the same time as de Coubertin was promoting his revival of the Olympic Games. The project was predictably connected with racist notions of the superiority of Anglo-Saxons and was focused on the white societies of Empire. Oddly, given America's Black minority and the waves of Italian immigration at the time, the project also proposed to include the USA in these games because of its presumed Anglo-Saxon heritage, and possibly to counter the appeal of de Coubertin's Olympic project for the English-speaking sport world.[3]

The revival of the idea in the 1920s was not explicitly racist in the way that the original 1890s version had been. Ironically, these Empire Games, unlike the Olympic Games in the same period, generally had a good reputation as providing for the non-discriminatory participation of different ethnic and 'racial' groups and also for promoting the participation of women. In the post-war twilight of British colonialism, this event was re-titled the Commonwealth Games in 1952. Until recent years, the event organisers have been able to present the Commonwealth Games as being – unlike the increasingly serious, and commercialised and high pressure Olympics – a relatively informal gathering of ex-British colonies ostensibly imbued with British sport traditions of fair play and sportsmanship.

Totalitarian international sport

As we have seen already, the commitment of both the Soviet communists and the Nazis to the cultural politics and mass theatre of festivals and rituals included a commitment to various forms of populist 'physical culture' including mass gymnastics and often also including competitive sports. In their different ways both revolutions promoted worldviews which claimed to celebrate the natural in man, through a 'body culture' (Brownell 1995) concerned with fitness, open-air activity and work, and dedicated to 'the creation of the new Nazi or Soviet man' (Hoberman 1984). There were voices in each of these revolutionary parties which were critical, on the one hand, of the undoubted elitist and exclusionary (aristocratic and 'bourgeois' class) character of modern sport (and its associated ideology of amateurism). On the other hand, they were also critical of the growth of professionalised and commercialised mass spectator sport among the working class, its superficial sensationalism for spectators and its rationalistic rule-dominated work-like character for players. These voices promoted versions of physical culture that, as against elitist sport, were populist and inclusionary, and as against spectator sport, were participatory and connected with wider cultural traditions and activities.

Allowing for some differences between them, and for some ambiguities, particularly among the Bolsheviks in the early years of their revolution, the Nazi and

Soviet state policies towards sport tended to proceed on both physical culture and sport fronts simultaneously. That is, they promoted mass participatory physical exercises and also tolerated the operation of competitive sports in the form of participatory clubs and also of spectator sport leagues and events. These usually tended to be seen as being equally useful, on the one hand, for mass training and fitness purposes and, on the other hand, also for reinforcing the people's commitment to the physical and mental disciplines required by industrial labour and military service in the totalitarian state. In both cases they were organised by what were effectively ministries of sport.[4]

Both the Soviets and the Nazis saw the staging of large-scale international sports events, together with their participation or non-participation in events held abroad, as significant resources in their conduct of foreign policy.[5] This is particularly evident in the case of the Nazis which we consider later in our discussion of the 1936 Berlin Olympics. In the case of the Soviet state, in the post-war Cold War period at least, sport evidently became an extremely important arena for the assertion of (super)national identity and power, and also for the gaining of prestige and the exercise of ideological influence around the world, particularly among Third World states. However, to a lesser extent, and in a more ambiguous way, this was also true in the inter-war period. Although the USSR was isolationist for much of this period, it maintained a commitment to the internationalisation of its revolution and to the exercise of international influence through the political and cultural activities of the Moscow-based Third International (Comintern) organisation (Riordan 1998). Although the Comintern did not initially create it the Moscow-based Red Sport International (RSI) organisation linked communist sport associations throughout Europe and effectively operated as an arm of Comintern. This was particularly so after 1925 when the Party formally decided that international sporting contact could be used to strengthen international cooperation between workers' organisations (Jones 1988: 169).

Tsarist Russia had competed in the 1912 Olympics and Tsarist aristocrats remained members of the IOC until the Second World War. For this reason, throughout the inter-war period, the USSR was not invited to take part in the Olympic Games when they resumed after the war in 1920. The USSR, in any case, committed itself for various ideological and practical reasons to non-participation throughout the 1920s and 1930s. Instead, throughout this period, usually more or less coinciding with the Olympics, a series of major Soviet sport-related events was staged (Riordan 1984, 1998).

In 1920 the first post-First World War Olympic Games event was held in Antwerp, a symbolic revival of the Olympic movement and its message from out of the killing fields of Flanders.[6] In the same year, possibly partly as a counterweights to this revival of 'bourgeois cultural internationalism', the USSR staged a number of notable large-scale cultural and sport events. For instance, a special mass dramatisation of the Bolshevik storming of the Winter Palace in 1917 was staged in Leningrad to celebrate the third anniversary of the Revolution (Von Geldern 1993). Also two major sport events were staged. First, a huge sport and gymnastic display, involving 18,000 athletes was performed for a packed house in the new Red Stadium in Moscow. Interestingly, the name of the event, the 'Pre-Olympiad', referenced the Olympics that the Soviets were not going to attend. This event was staged in part to impress the visiting international delegates at the congress of the

Third International. Second, an Olympic-type multi-sport event, the first Central Asian Games, was staged in Tashkent in the same year. It ran for ten days and involved 3,000 athletes, considerably more than took part in the Antwerp Olympics, although it is doubtful if the performances were comparable. This was an important gesture to the new Central Asian soviet republics and was the first time they had been convened together at a cultural and sporting event. It indicated the new relations being sought within the USSR by members of the Moscow power elite, with Stalin, who at the time was Commissar of the Nationalities, prominent among them.

In 1925, a year after the 1924 Paris Olympics, the Soviet trade unions staged a big multi-sport event (although, under the influence of the 'Hygenists', it omitted boxing and some other sports) (Riordan 1978). In 1928, the year of the Amsterdam Olympics, and also a year in which Stalin was climbing to absolute power, the USSR produced its own large-scale international Olympic-type multi-sport event in Moscow, the first 'Spartakiad' a combination of sport event and mass festival. The allegedly international character of the event was provided by the participation of communist athletes from fourteen Western countries, including Britain, through the RSI (Red Sport International), although non-communist socialist athletes refused to take part. The opening ceremony involved a parade from Red Square to the stadium by 30,000 athletes and participants carrying banners and torches. The 100,000-seat stadium was filled for most of the twelve days of the festival. Jones describes this event as a 'ritualised Marxist demonstration against the hypocrisy of the bourgeois Olympics, with their apparent discrimination against working-class athletes' (Jones 1988: 180). Another similarly huge and impressive sport festival event, the second Spartakiad, was held in Moscow in 1932. No doubt the year was carefully chosen. From the point of view of the use of sport in the international propaganda and ideological struggle, it is worth noting that 1932 was also the year in which Los Angeles, home of the booming new cultural industry of popular film, first staged the Olympic Games.

'Alternative internationalism' in sport: socialist and women's 'Olympics'

Socialist 'Olympics'

Before the First World War the strong socialist, social democratic and workers movements in various European countries, particularly Germany and the Czech territories of the Austro-Hungarian Empire, developed large sports organisations, but mainly on a national basis. However, after the disasters of the First World War European socialists became determinedly internationalist in outlook. An influential international socialist sport organisation was created in 1920, and later (1925) renamed as the Socialist Workers Sport International (SWSI). The emphasis in SWSI was on mass participatory and non-competitive activities like walking, rambling and gymnastic displays, and on retaining a connection between sport and wider political and cultural activities. The Left generally in the inter-war period were opposed to the elitism, nationalism and superficial sensationalism of much sport, and thereby was critical of the Olympic movement. Through its amateur rules, the Olympic movement tended to make sport inaccessible for working-class athletes. Its great games event also appeared to provide an international arena for competitive and aggressive nationalism, and through the pursuit of world records it appeared to promote superficial sensationalism (Hoberman 1984, ch. 7).

SWSI's political line was reformist and not revolutionary, which meant that – at least until the growth of the fascist military threat in the late 1930s made a united front necessary – it would have nothing to do with Bolshevism, the Comintern and the Red Sport International (RSI) organisation. This effectively split the Western European Left's sport movement and its theoretical and practical critique of modern sport. SWSI banned its members from participating in the RSI and the Spartakiads. As an alternative both to the bourgeois Olympics and to the Soviet Spartakiads it organised a series of large-scale workers' Olympic-type events during the inter-war period.

The main events here were SWSI's Workers Olympics in Frankfurt in 1925, in Vienna in 1931, and in Antwerp in 1937. These were interspersed with large-scale 'Olympiad'-type events, involving participants from SWSI and from many countries, organised by the Czech Worker's Gymnastic Federation in Prague in 1921, 1927 and 1934. The Prague events involved mass choirs and artistic displays as well as sports, and attracted crowds of up to 100,000 to the stadium.[7] The SWSI Worker's Olympics were even bigger events than this and often were comparable with the mainstream Olympic Games events in terms of scale, number of participating countries, and occasionally in quality of athletic performance. However, they went beyond the mainstream Olympics in their character as mass political festivals and in this respect were comparable to the kind of mass festivals held during the same period in Moscow and Leningrad (Riordan 1984: 103–4). For instance, SWSI's first Workers' Olympics in Frankfurt in 1925 was called a 'festival of peace', it had representation from nineteen countries and attracted an audience of 150,000 spectators. The quality of some of the athletics is indicated by the fact that the world record for the women's 100-metre relay was broken. But the emphasis overall was on mass participation and the experience of fellowship. Riordan states that the atmosphere at the Frankfurt event was 'festive and unashamedly political':

> The opening ceremonies and victory rituals dispensed with national flags and anthems, featuring instead red flags and revolutionary hymns like the 'Internationale'. The centrepiece was a mass artistic display accompanied by mass choirs, and featuring multiperson pyramids and tableaux, symbolising working- class solidarity and power in the class-struggle. The festival culminated in the dramatic presentation 'Struggle for the World' ... which used mass speaking and acting choruses to portray sport as a source of strength for the creation of a new world.
>
> (Riordan 1984: 104)

At the second SWSI Workers' Olympics in 1931, in 'Red' Vienna, 100,000 people watched the opening ceremony from a new purpose-built stadium, and 1,000 worker athletes took part from 26 countries. This was roughly comparable to the 1932 LA Olympics (which had 1,408 competitors, from 37 nations). Riordan states that there were '220 contests in all athletic disciplines, a children's sports festival, artistic exhibitions, dramatic performances and even fireworks' and that both the summer and winter games in Vienna 'far outdid in spectators, participants and pageantry the 1932 bourgeois Olympics at Lake Placid and Los Angeles' (ibid.

p.106). The third Workers' Olympics was planned to be staged in Barcelona in the new stadium on Mont Juic, built for the 1929 Barcelona expo. It was conceived as an international 'united front' demonstration against fascism, involving both SWSI and RSI. Unfortunately, fascism defeated the event. Franco launched his assault on the Spanish government and began the civil war on the morning of the opening ceremony. The event was relocated to Antwerp where it was successfully staged the following year (ibid. p.107).

In the 1920s, SWSI had a membership of over one million people drawn from many countries, although the great majority of members were in Germany, Austria and Czechoslovakia. Its membership peaked at two million in 1931 and included substantial numbers of women. However, it is also worth noting that working-class membership of nationally-based 'non-political' 'bourgeois' sport organisations in aggregate far outstripped SWSI, as also did the growth of working-class attendances at big spectator sport events. SWSI might have regarded itself as from the working class and as representing its best interests in sport. However, while it was undoubtedly a substantial and important cultural movement, it could not be said to be strictly representative of the bulk of working-class attitudes to and interests in national and international sport.

Women's 'Olympics'

Most of the groups of men who created and disseminated modern sport forms in Britain and elsewhere in the late nineteenth century tended to reproduce the sexist prejudices of their era and privileged the male physique and male sociability in their conception of sport culture. At best this forced, initially, middle-class women to develop their own forms of physical culture and physical education (McIntosh 1968; Mangan and Park 1987). At worst it left most working-class women with few opportunities in the realm of physical culture outside of possibly some participation as spectators in some sports events and also ad hoc recreations connected with family-centred holiday uses of urban parks and day-return railway excursions. The sexism embedded in the formation of modern sports in the West at national level was reproduced at international level. Women were never originally seen as equal partners, nor indeed as any kind of partners, in de Coubertin's project to revive the Olympic Games. They were banned from the inaugural Olympics in Athens in 1896, although they performed in a few unofficial exhibition events in the expo-related Olympics of 1900, 1904 and 1908. It is worth recalling that this pre-war period was one of rising demands from women in many Western countries to participate in political life and public culture through the vote. In principle sport offered a sphere of cultural liberation for women in terms of the social constraints of the Victorian dress code and 'body culture'. However, the IOC – for all of the much vaunted visionary and idealistic characteristic claims of their 'Olympic' values and world views – were at that time a profoundly sexist as well as class-ist organisation, and they formally banned women from participation in the Olympics in 1912 (Hargreaves 1994).

Women's response to this exclusionary attitude from the developing mainstream of international sport was similar to that of working-class and socialist organisations discussed earlier, namely they formed their own international association. Women from many countries who were, nonetheless, involved in physical culture, physical education and sport, formed the Federation Sportive Feminin International (FSFI) in 1921 and the Women's Amateur Athletics Association (WAAA) was formed in Britain in 1922 (Lovesey 1979: 66/7). It is also worth noting that women's participation in sport was encouraged in the national and international socialist sport movement and in the SWSI Worker's Olympics discussed above (Jones 1988; Hargreaves 1994: 140–1).

The FSFI staged their first Olympic-type international sport event in 1922 in Paris, although, because of the continued antagonism of the IOC who objected to their proposed use of the term 'Women's Olympics', they called the event the 'Women's World Games'. This was the first of a sequence of such events. The FSFI Women's World Games were held on a complementary four-year cycle to the mainstream Olympics, and national representation grew at each meeting. They were staged in Gothenberg in 1926 with representatives from ten nations, in Prague in 1930 with seventeen nations, and in London in 1934 with nineteen nations. The 1938 event planned for Vienna was cancelled because of the Nazi invasion of Austria. The FSFI events were well organised and well supported, and they acted as effective practical publicity for the cause of women's sport internationally (Hargreaves 1994).

Institutionalising international sport: the inter-war Olympics

The mass popularisation of sports both in participatory and high-performance spectator forms grew rapidly at national level in the West in the early decades of the twentieth century. The development of transport and communications systems, particularly radio in the 1920s, created the potential for a new level and frequency of organisation and mass communication of dramatic international sport events. And, as we have seen in the case of socialist internationalism, the First World War increased popular awareness of and interest in the need for international peace and cultural exchange. The disorganised character of nineteenth-century and pre-war international relations which had contributed to the disaster of the war was seen as inherently problematic. The creation of the League of Nations, however ineffective it was ultimately to prove to be in relation to the new wave of supernational neo-imperial and predatory states, acknowedged an objective need in the development of the world order at the time for more stable and institutionalised forms of international communication and cooperation. The universalism and humanism of the concepts and ideology of de Coubertin and the Olympic movement, even if much of it was rhetoric and undermined by the IOC's practices in this period, nonetheless made the movement's international institution-building appear compatible and convergent with broader processes of international institution-building. Thus the IOC in this period was interested in associating itself with the League of Nations.[8]

All of this fuelled both popular and elite interest in international-level sport events, in the early twentieth century. In international sport the fortunes of nationally representative individuals and teams would be at stake, and victory could enhance national pride and prestige in the newly salient international world order. These interests were initially, in the pre-war period, principally expressed through the Olympic movement and its events. But in the inter-war period they came to be expressed both within and outside of the Olympic movement, and through 'sport political' conflicts and struggles in relation to it, as we have already seen in relation to the socialist and women's sport movements. On the one hand the Olympic movement would ultimately have to recognise that it needed to change to accommodate the growth of popular interest in sport, particularly in relation to women. On the other hand, it also ultimately had to accept that many developments in popular sport, particularly the professionalisation and commercialisation of large-scale spectator sports such as soccer, would increasingly go on outside of its remit.

The Olympic movement itself had a certain degree of organisation, at least in principle if not always in practice in the early years.[9] On the one hand, there was the IOC (International Olympic Committee) which was self-recruiting and viewed its members as diplomatic representatives of the Olympic movement in their home coutries, rather than, conversely, as representatives of their nations. On the other, hand there were the national Olympic committees (NOCs) which organised national teams for the games event, and, where they were hosts of the event, which would also take a leading role in organising the event itself, but which were not formally represented on the IOC. However, given the fact that the Olympic event is multi-sport, in addition to this structure it was necessary to develop an international level of organisation in the constituent sports. This would connect together the various, often nationally powerful national-level governing bodies, and allow internationally standardised and trustworthy game rules and regulations for international events to be developed, recognised and diffused.

The need for this kind of development had become clear in the various weaknesses and conflicts over rules, regulations and decisions which had dogged the 'expo-Olympics' of 1900, 1904 and 1908, particularly the latter, where the British organisers, (the British Olympic Committee and the Amateur Athletic Association) in spite of their sport ideology of 'fair play', were accused of bias by the Americans. As we have seen, a number of important international sport governing bodies connected with the Olympic movement were formed in this period, including in soccer, FIFA in 1904, and in athletics, the IAAF (International Amateur Athletics Federation) in 1913 after the 1912 Stockholm Olympics (Lovesey 1979: 56). These organisations continue, nearly a century later, to play an important and relatively independent role both within and outside the contemporary Olympic movement.

FIFA initially assumed that the demand for an international soccer 'world championship' could be capable of being accommodated within the amateur soccer competition of the Olympic Games. However, professional soccer had already overtaken amateur soccer in England in terms of popularity and quality by the 1890s. An increasing number of nations took up the sport in the early twentieth century and it began to develop towards its contemporary position as the world's biggest single professionalised spectator sport. By the 1920s, with the increasing covert use professional soccer players at the Olympic event, it had evidently outgrown the Olympic framework. In 1930 FIFA staged its first World Cup event, an independent professional soccer world championship event entirely disconnected from the Olympic Games events, to run on a complementary four-year cycle, and which subsequently grew to equal the Olympics as the world's biggest sport and media-sport event.[10]

In the inter-war period the IOC established itself as the primary authority and actor concerned with international sport, its games event became the pre-eminent sport event and its four-year calendar structured world sport. The Olympic Games were initially reactivated after the destruction and demoralisation of war in 1920 in Antwerp. They grew strongly throughout the 1920s and 1930s, Germany was re-admitted to the movement in 1928, and increasingly impressive Olympic events were staged at Paris 1924, Amsterdam 1928, Los Angeles 1932 and Berlin 1936. However the movement and its events had retained class-ist, sexist and racist attitudes from its late nineteenth-century origins. The currents of national inter-national sport would have flown around and away from the Olympics if the movement had not accepted the need for some reform and change. As we have already noted the elitist and class-exclusionary aspects of the Olympics created opportunities and incentives for the growth of independent working-class-oriented socialist sport and professional spectator sport, and the sexist aspects led to the growth of independent women's sport. There was little equivalent pressure on the IOC in the inter-war period in respect of its attitudes to race.

The post-war and late twentieth-century Olympic movement, even given its many problems in recent years, which we discuss later (Chapter 7), has arguably, on balance, been a significant force in the promotion of a genuine universalistic humanistic ideology. Also, arguably, it has been a largely progressive force as far as working-class and women athletes are concerned. The same could be said about the Olympics, in the post-war period, in relation to racism. The post-war Olympic movement ultimately came to play an important role in the struggle against the apartheid regime in South Africa. It currently contains many Asians and Africans on the IOC, distributes finance for sport development in poor countries through its 'solidarity' fund, and helps to organise the African and Asian regional Olympic-type games events. However, up to and including the inter-war period the IOC's attitudes to race were closer to those of British and French imperial paternalism than to any real humanism.

De Coubertin believed that French imperialism in Africa constituted a 'sacred' 'civilising mission'. His 1923 IOC committee to study the possibility of a regional African games event recommended a version of sport apartheid by proposing a system of two concurrent biennial events, one for European colonisers and one for colonised 'natives'. However, this was one set of games too many for the colonisers and their lack of support made it ultimately impossible to arrange this event.[11] In terms of non-European 'racial' and ethnic groups, the Japanese were occasionally notably successful in inter-war Olympics, consistent with their impressive displays in expos in the same period, and generally consistent with the dynamics of their modernisation process. On the other hand while there was some occasional participation by African and Arab athletes on behalf of imperial nations, and also some occasional notable successes in early and inter-war Olympic Games, generally this could be regarded as tokenism (Guttman 1994). In addition, as we will discuss later, it is arguable that for a number of years in the late 1930s the IOC began to be influenced by the growth of fascist politics and political cultures in Europe with their in-built racist world views, which made it unlikely that it could act credibly as any kind of a cultural movement against racism. In the 1930s it is likely that even the avowedly imperialistic British Empire Games event was probably a more inclusionary international sport event in relation to non-European 'racial' and ethnic groups than was the Olympics.

However, throughout the twentieth century the Olympic movement has shown considerable resilience and capacity to adapt to pressures generated in its international political environment. In the post-war period this has involved many compromises, not least currently with the power of American and global media corporations and multinational corporate sponsors (which we consider later in Chapters 6 and 7). In the early post-war period the movement's adaptive and inclusive capacity was displayed in its recognition and involvement of newly de-colonised nations and in its taking a more proactive position in relation to racial discrimination than it had ever taken in the inter-war period.

On the other social exclusion problems, relating to class and sexism, the Olympic movement was somewhat more adaptive in an inclusionary direction in the interwar period. In relation to the problem of working-class exclusion, the Olympic movement, while reaffirming its commitment to the ideal of amateurism, nonetheless slightly eased its rules to tolerate 'broken time' payments to compensate workers for loss of earnings due to the time demands of training, travelling and competition.[12] In relation to its exclusion of women, the IOC's 1912 formal ban on women was publicly challenged in France in 1917 by Alice Milliatt . Also, as noted earlier, it was challenged generally in practical terms by the success in the 1920s of the FSFI events and also of national women's athletics associations such as the WAAA. De Coubertin and the IOC resisted pressure to include women in the 1924 Paris Olympics. But with de Coubertin's resignation as IOC President in 1925, and with the IAAF in favour, some women's athletic disciplines were included in the 1928 Amsterdam games for the first time. A full women's programme was included in the 1932 Los Angeles Olympic Games (Hargreaves 1994: 140–1).

In relation to the Games event itself, there were a number of changes in the inter-war period from early Olympic events. As we saw earlier, de Coubertin's attitude to the staging of the event was influenced by his understanding of the ritual and sacred aspects of the original ancient Greek Games and also by the ritual and ceremonial aspects of late nineteenth-century French international expos.[13] His original conception had been that the key aims of the Olympic movement and event, namely to promote and embody peace between nations, needed to be presented to the assembled athletes and public in an opening address, and that at least three other ceremonies were needed. First, as part of a broader opening ceremony in which the head of the host state, or their representative, formally declared the Games open, an oath would taken by the athletes, or their representative, modelled on the ancient Greek practice, in which the athletes agreed to abide by the rules and principles of the event. Second, there needed to be a victory ceremony in which special medals would be presented to winners, and third, there would need to be a closing ceremony.

In the inter-war period a number of innovations were introduced to increase the symbolic content and effect of the Games event. First, the flag with the five rings (symbolising the world's five continents), the flight of doves (symbolic of peace), and the representative athlete taking the athletes' oath were all introduced at Antwerp in 1920. Second, in 1928 at Amsterdam, given their return to the Games, German IOC members suggested introducing a permanently burning flame and a relay of torches to bring the flame from the original ancient Games site at Olympia in Greece. The flame was introduced at Amsterdam, was an important focal point at the following games in Los Angeles in 1932 and became an established part of Olympic ritual. The torch relay was not introduced in Amsterdam, and was deemed to be too impractical for Los Angeles. However, since German members of the Olympic movement had originally proposed it, they were able to introduce it at the Berlin Olympics in 1936 (Lekarska 1976).

Additional developments in the ceremonial and ritual aspects of the Olympics have been made in the post-war period. As with these inter-war innovations, they were probably necessary to maintain the public standing and charisma of the event, in conditions where alternative versions of mass public cultural assembly were becoming more prevalent and more competitive with the Olympics. In the post-war period the main competition has come from professional spectator sports and from the media. However, in the inter-war period, while these factors no doubt played a role, probably one of the main sources of competition in European countries was from the kind of mass festivals, rituals and physical culture displays noted earlier. Of particular importance in this context were the fascist countries, particularly Nazi Germany. Since Nazi Germany was responsible for the biggest and most impressive Olympic Games mega-event in the inter-war period, it is now useful to consider this case, together with its context and implications, in a little more detail.

Supernationalism and the Olympics: the 'Nazi Olympics'

In this section we consider the influence of one of the main forms of early twentieth-century supernationalism, namely German fascism, on the international sport movement and its mega-events, specifically the Olympic movement and the Games of its 11th Olympiad in 1936. It might argued that this case was unique and is only of passing historical interest. However, the perspective outlined here is that this case remains an object lesson in how an internationally-based cultural event movement can be manipulated by a powerful nation to project its image, ideology and influence internationally, and to reinforce its authority domestically. The fact that this kind of lesson has had to be learned on a number of occasions throughout the post-war period would indicate that this is a perennial weakness of international cultural institutions in the modern era. Comparable cases of supernational manipulation occured in the 'super-power' rivalry expressed throughout the post-war Olympic events, and particularly in the 1980 Moscow Olympics and in the 1984 Los Angeles Olympics. This vulnerability of the Olympic movement to supernational manipulation is of contemporary relevance not only because of the relatively recent replay of American image-projection in the 1996 Atlanta Olympics, it is also of relevance because an equally familiar, authoritarian, form of supernational superpower manipulation could recur in the future if an unreformed China was to win the right to stage the Olympics in the early twenty-first century.

In this section, then, we briefly consider some of the main features of the 1936 Olympics and we explore some of the background to the staging of the event in the 1933–6 period and its general significance in helping to legitimate the Nazi regime. Also, we consider the broader question of the influence of fascism on the Olympic movement beyond the Games in the 1936–40 and early post-war periods.

The 1936 Berlin Olympic Games event

Following the creation of the Olympic Winter Games in 1924 there were two Olympic events in Germany in 1936, the Summer Games in Berlin and the Winter Games in Garmisch. We focus here on the Summer Games. They are possibly best remembered for two things. First, there were the triumphs, in the sprints and long-jump competitions, of the incomparable black American athlete Jesse Owens. Second, there was 'Olympia', the classic film of the event made by the notable German film-maker and fascist fellow-traveller Leni Reifenstahl. Reifenstahl's film captured some of Owens' achievements and it also won international acclaim at the 1937 Paris expo and the 1938 Venice Film Festival (beating Walt Disney's cartoon 'Snow White' for the top award). The Berlin Olympics are probably also well remembered for the impressive character of their organisation and staging. On this front, the Berlin event far outstripped all previous Olympic events, including the preceding Los Angeles Games in 1932 in spite of that event's Hollywood flamboyance. The number of athletes attending was 3,000, which was equivalent to the previous maximum recorded at Paris in 1924. They were housed in a purpose-built high quality athletes' village located (and isolated) in an attractive woodland setting. The athletes came from an unprecedented 100 countries, more than double the international involvement in any previous Olympics (and, indeed, not matched again until over thirty years later at the 1968 Mexico City Games). This led to an equally unprecedented attendance by the world's media (3,000 journalists) and by foreign visitors (150,000).[14]

The Games took place in a completely renovated and extended modernist stadium holding 100,000, which had originally been constructed for the cancelled 1916 Berlin Olympics. The stadium was set in a modern sports and cultural facilities complex which also included a 16,000 seat 50-metre swimming pool, a huge fully equipped media centre, a sports science and research centre, a 25,000-seat ampitheatre and a mass festival area for performances in which the performers could number in the tens of thousands. The stadium was filled to capacity throughout most of the event period and certainly for the opening and closing ceremonies. At the opening ceremony the recorded voice of Baron de Coubertin was relayed, Hitler declared the games open, and the legendary winner of the first modern Olympic marathon, Spiridon Louis, who led the Greek team, presented him with a symbolic olive branch from Olympia, the site of the ancient Olympic Games in Greece. Hitler attended many of the competitions and the closing ceremony, and he also addresssed the IOC in private session. At the opening ceremony the symbolic Olympic flame was dramatically lit for the first time ever by a torch from a torch relay carrying a flame originally lit at Olympia (Hart-Davis 1986, ch. 9). The world's biggest ever aircraft, the 300-metre long Hindenburg airship, flew over the stadium and the city trailing huge flags (ibid. p. 154). At night Hitler's architect Albert Speer created impressive new dramatic 'light architecture' effects with powerful searchlights over the stadium, which echoed his similar 'theatre of power' effects at the 1934 Nuremberg rally (see photo). The city of Berlin was given over to the event and to the massive influx of foreign visitors, and it provided a festival context for the event and for them.

Finally the organisers were able to make use of the development of media technologies to make the Berlin Olympics a distinctive and notable 'media event'. First,y it was something of a minor TV event in the city of Berlin since, for the first time a major sport event was shown to the public by means of closed-circuit TV transmitted to over twenty viewing rooms around the city and seen by over 150,000 people over the course of the event. Second, and more importantly, it was

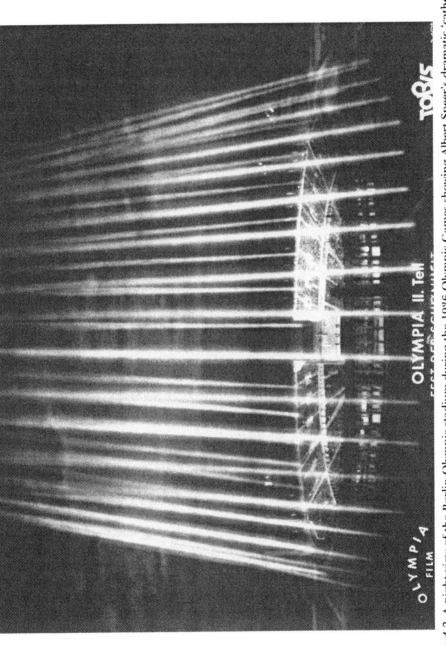

Figure 4.2 A night view of the Berlin Olympic stadium during the 1936 Olympic Games showing Albert Speer's dramatic 'cathedral of light' effect using 'light architecture' techniques he had pioneered at the infamous 1934 Nazi Party Nuremberg rally.

a major radio 'media event', being broadcast around the world to what was estimated to be the biggest ever international radio audience. However, in spite of all its achievements, a contemporary observer of the Berlin Olympics, Peter Wilson, a British journalist, felt that 'the prevailing air was . . . odiously chauvinistic and military' (Wilson 1976: 59). We now need to explore some of the background to the event which might have led to a judgement like this.

Contextualising the Berlin Olympic event

The nineteenth-century German nationalist movement was committed to mass festivals and rituals, and particularly so in popular 'physical culture' movements such the Turnen gymnastic associations. This connection between nationalism and event-oriented movements continued through the achievement of German unification in 1870 and the Bismarck era in the new German state. However, by the turn of the century the German version of nationalist traditions of events and 'body culture' was being challenged both in popular and official quarters by English competitive sport, particularly soccer, French Olympic internationalism, and also by the growth of sport associations particularly through the German and international workers and trade-union movements. The result of this in Germany was the creation of a state commission for festivals and for sport (Mosse 1975; Guttman 1994). The sport commission had the responsibility of promoting sport in the educational system in spite of opposition from the gymnastic associations. Two figures who were to be important in the Berlin Olympics were active in the promotion of sport in Germany in this pre-First World War period, namely Theodore Lewald and Carl Diem. Both were involved with the national German sport commission and with the Olympic movement at this time. Lewald helped organise the German teams for the 1904 and 1908 Olympics. Diem was a sport historian with a fascination for the ancient Greek Olympics and was also chairman of the national sport commission from 1910 to 1933. Both were members of the IOC.[15] Around the time of the 1912 Stockholm Olympics the IOC decided to give the 1916 games to Berlin. Lewald achieved the remarkable feat of organising the building of a new stadium, the Kaiserstadium, using mainly private rather than public finance. However, the war and the hostility of victors kept Germany out of the Olympics for nearly a generation.

Lewald and Diem remained leading figures in the both the German Olympic Committee and in the IOC and kept the case for a Berlin event alive, reviving it after the successful re-appearance of Germany at the Amsterdam Olympics in 1928. In awarding the 1936 Games to Berlin in 1932 the IOC was awarding it to the Weimar republic, which however, was almost immediately swept away by the Nazi's seizure of power in 1933.The planning and production of any large-scale public event is a long and complex process, particularly, as it typically does with Olympic events, if it requires the building of new event facilities and new accommodation, transport and communication infrastructures. The German National Olympic Committee's plans were already beginning to be implemented on these fronts when the Nazis came to power. Both the IOC and the Nazis faced the question of whether they should proceed. The IOC's attitudes we will consider in a moment. On their side, the Nazi view of the proposed Berlin event was ambivalent.[16]

On the one hand, the theory and practice of their movement gave a central place to the 'body culture' in terms of their racist conception of the German 'volk', and in terms of the need to ensure the fitness of the 'volk' for military service and for labour. The Nazi party's 'stormtrooper' organisation (politically controlled street thugs) and its Hitler Youth organisation both had sports divisions and sports leaders. Their 'Strength through Joy' physical culture movement provided formal instruction in sports throughout the Reich. Also, the Nazis gave a central place to the display of the collective will and the disciplined body in mass parades, festivals and rituals, the 'theatre of power', most strikingly exemplified by the Nuremberg rallies. However, on the other hand, Hitler and the Nazis were as critical of 'bourgeois' forms of culture as were the Bolsheviks, with the added force of their hypernationalism and racist paranoia against all things non-German. This meant that they were inevitably deeply suspicious in general about the Olympic movement. Since Hitler personally was not enthusiastic about sport culture and had his own dreams about the image and reconstruction of Berlin, he was initially cool about the Olympic project.

However, after representations by Lewald and Diem in 1933, Hitler became convinced of the potential propaganda value of the event, and the military and mass rally after-uses of the facilities. He became enthusiastic about it and gave it priority funding and considerable attention. Goebbels and his ministry of propaganda were given overall responsibility for the project. In addition to the involvement of the German Olympic Committee, the architect Albert Speer and the filmmaker Leni Reifenstahl were also assigned responsibilities respectively for stadium 'light architecture' and for filming the event. By the time of the event in 1936 they would be able to build on their achievements for Goebbels and his Nazi propaganda machine at the 1934 Nuremberg rally for which Speer had constructed spectacular searchlight 'architectures' and which Reifenstahl had publicised in her film of the rally, 'Triumph of the Will'.

In the early years of Hitler's dictatorship, 1933–6, the Nazi Party established an absolute ideological and cultural hegemony in Germany and appeared to be genuinely popular with, and attractive to, a majority of the German people. In these years, Hitler was building the Nazi state, popularising it through the event calendar of his 'theatre of power', and mapping out his 'vision' of Germany's 'world historical' 'civilising mission' in relation to Europe and the 'Thousand Year Reich'. The latter ideas echoed the periodicity of ancient European civilisations, particularly that of the Greeks, and resonated with the identification of late nineteenth- and early twentieth-century German intellectuals and European intellectuals more broadly with Hellenic civilisation.

It is not a mere coincidence that these early years were also the years in which Hitler, Goebbels, Diem and others were, both metaphorically and literally, building the Berlin Olympic project. The Olympic project allowed the Nazis to appeal to a number of different constituencies simultaneously. It enabled them to appeal to the popular culture of the German working class through the mega-event's spectacular, competitive and festival aspects. In addition, they could appeal to the 'high' cultural aspirations of the German upper and middle class through the event's Hellenic connections and resonance. German Hellenism, through the major projects and discoveries of its archaeologists in the late nineteenth century, had been a recognised and important feature of the Paris expo of 1889, as we saw earlier, and had influenced de Coubertin in his project to revive the Olympic Games in the 1890s. Finally, it could be assumed that the Olympic event would appeal to both classes through its theatrical and ritual aspects, and thus its resonance with Wagnerian culture and with the populist taste for these sorts of displays which had long been a part of German nationalistic culture and tradition.

Olympic organiser Carl Diem's innovation at Berlin was to add to the modern Olympic ceremony a highly symbolic connection between the modern Olympic event site and the ancient site of Olympia by means of a torch relay from Olympia. This was a product of Diem's long-standing and probably sincere sporting and Hellenic idealism. However, in this new Nazi context of the mid-1930s it inevitably carried with it some shadowy and suspect connotations and implications. Olympia had been used by ancient Greek cultures for their sacred games event for around a thousand years. It was a permanent site for what could be conceived of as having been a 'thousand year civilisation'.[17]

The idea of the 'thousand year' civilisation was evocative for Hitler for whom it contributed to his 'vision' of 'the Thousand Year Reich'. He also had a 'vision' for the future of the Olympic Games in a Nazi-dominated European and world order, as a key part of the international face and cultural apparatus of 'the Thousand Year Reich'. His plan for the Olympics was that they would be taken over by the Nazi movement and permanently based in the monumental 400,000-seat stadium he had commissioned Albert Speer to build in 1935 as part of the Nuremberg 'theatre of power' complex. Hitler, with a degree of diplomacy which was unusual for him – or perhaps merely with, more predictably, a considerable degree of political shrewdness, given the likely international boycott which would have resulted – did not express this plan publicly in the build-up to the Berlin Olympics. However, it was possibly known to some members of his inner circle, which, for Olympic project purposes, can be reasonably assumed to have included Germany's IOC members Lewald and Diem.[18]

All of this is to underscore the considerable importance ultimately accorded to the Olympic project by Hitler and the Nazi regime. In this regard it is a mistake to focus exclusively on the possibly short-term impacts of the 1936 event itself.[19] The build-up years 1933–6 also need to be taken into account, together with the long-term vision. In these crucial early years of the Nazi revolution, as with any revolution, the legitimacy and authority of the new state was vulnerable and conceivably it could have been short-lived. However, the coming of the Olympic event, when the eyes of the world would be on the new Germany, together with the production of the facilities, and preparation and rehearsal of its organisation, were significant factors in legitimising and popularising the regime internally and in legitimising and sanitising it internationally. In addition involvement in the Olympic project gave Hitler access to a symbolic discourse which was not only nationally and internationally prestigious and influential, but was also suggestive ideologically and politically about ways of conceptualising and expressing the world historical ambitions and significance of Nazism.

These sorts of issues were evident at the time to many concerned observers, both within and outside of the international Olympic movement, particularly those who called for a boycott of the Berlin Olympics. To appreciate the reasons for these calls and the debates around them, which we consider in a little more detail in a moment, we need first to add some relevant elements to our picture of the 1933–6 pre-event build-up period. From 1933 German sport, as much as every other aspect of social life, was 'Nazified' and was reorganised on a visibly and aggressively racist basis. In 1933 alone, Jewish teams were formally forbidden to play so-called 'Aryan' teams in any sport. Jews were formally banned from boxing, from swimming on all German beaches, from skiing at the key Garmisch site in preparation for the Winter Olympics which were to be held there, and so on.

In 1934 Propaganda Minister Goebbels recommended all party member to read a book called 'The Spirit of Sport in the National Socialist Ideology', and it is reasonable to assume, that it was, no doubt, widely read at the time within the movement. The book was written by Bruno Malitz, a so-called Sport Leader of the Berlin Stormtroopers. The book expressed the blatantly racist attitudes of both the Nazi leadership and its rank and file in crude language. For instance, Malitz claims: 'There is no room in our German land for Jewish sports leaders . . . for pacifists, political Catholics, pan-Europeans and the rest. They are worse than cholera and syphilis. . . .' (quoted in Hart-Davis 1986: 63–4, also see Mandell 1971: 59–60). Also, in 1935, popular sport textbooks were published by Kurt Munch, head of the Reichdiet organisation, which promoted the same sort of aggressively racist Nazi view of sport. In relation to the Olympic project, Malitz makes the Nazi perspective very clear: 'Frenchmen, Belgians, Polaks and Jew-Niggers [will] run on German tracks and swim in German pools. . . . Do we then want to have the Olympic Games in Germany? Yes, we must have them! . . . There could not be better propaganda for Germany. . . . The State will name the team' (quoted in Hart-Davis 1986: 70–1)

In 1935 a Reich Sport Federation took control over all sport associations. The Reich Sport Leader Tschammer und Osten publicly and crudely abused Jews in the official publications of his office and extended their exclusions from sport.[20] In addition, in 1935, during the rally season at Nuremberg, new German citizenship laws which had a clear racist and anti-Jewish aim and character were announced in a blaze of publicity. Concentration camps which treated innocent people as work slaves and brutalised them on a daily basis had already been established by the time of the Olympics. Indeed, one such concentration camp was clearly signposted as such and located not far from the Olympic stadium in the outskirts of north Berlin (ibid. p. 207).

There was thus clear evidence, for any reasonably objective observer, in the 1933–6 period of the blatant denial of basic humanitarian and Olympic values in Germany in general, in their sport policy and in their preparations for the Berlin Olympic event. There was also the evident cynicism of the Nazi's use of an Olympic event, notionally dedicated to the ideal of peace, as part of the build-up of their demonstrably aggressive foreign policy. Even as the Olympic event occured, the Nazis were actively supporting Franco's fascist assault on the elected government of Spain. In the face of these and other realities there were understandable calls, particularly from Jewish and Catholic groups in the USA, for a boycott of the 1936 German Olympic Winter and Summer Games. There were debates in the USA about the possibility of a boycott.[21] For instance, George Messersmith, USA Secretary of State, arguing against US involvement in the Berlin Olympics in November 1935, claimed that:

To the party and the youth of Germany, the holding of the Olympic games in Berlin in 1936 has become the symbol of the conquest of the world by National Socialist doctrine. Should the Games not be held in Berlin, it would be one of the most serious blows which National Socialist prestige could suffer.

(Quoted in Hart-Davis 1986: 76)

However, in the US debate about the isssue the boycott option was intransigently resisted by the American IOC member Avery Brundage, who later became the IOC's President throughout the early post-war period (1952–72). Brundage, together with the contemporary IOC President Baillet-Latour, visited Germany in 1934, allegedly to examine evidence of anti-Jewish racism. Amazingly both of these 'sports diplomats' pronounced themselves satisfied that if it did exist, any such racism was an internal and political matter for Germany and was none of the IOC's business, and that in any case the Nazi government had assured them (predictably falsely, as it turned out) that there would be no such behaviour at the Berlin Games. However, in 1935, American IOC member General Sherrill had a long interview with Hitler in which the latter made it perfectly clear that German Jews would be prohibited from representing Germany at the Olympics. Although this evidently breached 'Olympic ethics' it could be presented to the international public as being in accord with the rules of the Olympic system which allowed national Olympic committees discretion to select their own teams. On this basis, in the American boycott debate in 1935 Sherrill and Brundage campaigned for US participation in the Games. Unsurprisingly when it came to the event itself, there were effectively no German Jews in the German Olympic team.[22]

Fascism and the Olympic movement in the 1930s

The influence of fascism on the inter-war Olympics cannot be reduced simply to the short-term impacts of the 1936 Summer and Winter Games events. As we have seen, it extended throughout the 1933–6 build-up period to the games. The IOC collaborated with the Nazi government in allowing what was predictably a major Nazi propaganda exercise to be staged, an event which would use and abuse the good name and reputation of the Olympic movement. They refused to acknowledge and/or condemn Nazi sport policies, and they resisted boycotts and calls to relocate or cancel the event. Furthermore, in spite of much international criticism and condemnation of the Nazi Olympics after the event, they continued to refuse to recognise that collaboration with fascism was threatening to destroy the Olympic movement and its ideals. This can be indicated in the decisions they took in the 1936–40 period which we come to in a moment. Even contemporary pro-Olympic movement writers find it hard to understand what the IOC thought they were doing in the post-Berlin period. The noted British sports journalist and historian John Rodda remarks of IOC decisions in this period that they showed that the IOC was 'completely insulated from political events within Germany and the strong overtones produced at the Berlin Games' (Killanin and Rodda 1976: 60). The Olympic historian John Lucas regards the period as 'lost years' for the Olympic movement in which some of the decisions taken were 'bizarre' (Lucas 1980: 134/5) Other more critical commentators and analysts, including sport historian John Hoberman, regard the period as effectively one of at least fascist collaboration or at worst one of ideological 'capture' by fascism. Whereas for some commentators the degree of IOC collaboration with fascism is almost inexplicable for Hoberman it is all too explicable given the resonance between sport ideology and some elements of fascist aesthetics, and also given the (continuing) self-recruiting, hierarchic and secretive nature of the IOC. We can now briefly consider some factors which may have helped to open the IOC to the influence of fascism in the 1930s.

First, there were the background factors of the general political, ideological and sporting climate of the time. A number of major European national sports organisations, including national Olympic committeees in fascist countries such as Germany, Italy and Spain were directly controlled and put to the service of national versions of fascist ideology.[23] Also international sport organisations such as FIFA and the national sports organisations of non-fascist countries (such as the British Football Association, see Holt 1998a, Beck 1999) were prepared, for various reasons, to do business with fascist countries.

Second, the composition of the inter-war IOC included many aristocrats and big businessmen, and Russia continued to be 'represented' on it by exiled Tsarist aristocrats. It is reasonable to assume, given the Bolshevik revolution, Stalinism and the growth of the USSR as a world power, that the IOC, whatever other world-views and political sympathies its members may or may not have had, in general would have been profoundly anti-Bolshevik and generally anti-communist in this period. In this respect it would certainly have shared some common interests, and spoken a similar political language, with the inter-war fascist politicians and ruling parties in Germany, Italy, Spain and Portugal.

Third, a number of influential members of the IOC were openly fascists or were reasonably suspected to be so. These included the German members Carl Diem (a Nazi collaborator) and the acknowledged Nazi supporters Karl Ritter von Halt (IOC member 1929–64, IOC Executive 1957–63) and General Walter von Reichenau, together with the allegedly fascist aristocrats Count Paolo Thaon di Revel and the Duc de Mecklenberg-Schwerin (the latter was the Italian IOC member 1920–50).[24] In addition, in the 1930s, leading IOC figures such as President Henri Baillet-Latour and Avery Brundage, while not themselves fascists, were, for their own personal reasons prepared to cultivate positive relations with leading politicians and state officials in Nazi Germany.

Finally, it is of some relevance that the retired 'founding father' and presiding spirit of the modern Olympic movement, Baron de Coubertin, while not himself a fascist, periodically expressed positive views about the political leadership and state support for sport under Italian and German fascism in the 1930s. Prior to the Berlin Olympic event, in 1935, he accepted an invitation to visit Berlin where he was feted and gave support to the event's arrangements in a radio message.[25] In an interview conducted during the Berlin Games de Coubertin is reported as saying that: 'The imposing success of the Berlin Games has served the Olympic ideal magnificently', and he was reported as speaking positively of 'the fact that the Games of 1936 were illuminated by a Hitlerian force and discipline' (quoted in Hoberman 1986: 42–3). In 1936 the Nazi regime nominated de Coubertin for the Nobel Prize. Understandably with sponsors like these he was not awarded it, the prize instead being awarded to a German journalist, Carl von Ossietsky, a prisoner of conscience held at the time in a concentration camp by the Nazi regime (Hoberman 1986: 50). In addition, de Coubertin was also prepared, effectively, to be paid by the Nazi state. For the last few years of his life, until his death in 1937, he was rescued from penury and financed in his retirement in Switzerland by Nazi funds channelled through Carl Diem (Lucas 1980: 133; IOC 1994).

The IOC's willingness to collaborate with the supernationalistic politics of fascism was evident in a string of decisions they took about the staging of their great sport mega-event from 1936 onwards. Fortunately, from the point of view of the integrity and international reputation of the Olympic movement, the Second World War intervened to blot out these events and decisions. At Berlin in 1936 the IOC gave the 1940 games to Tokyo in the full awareness that Japan at the time was an aggressive corporatist state. In 1938 with war looming in Europe and in the Far East instead of cancelling their offer to Japan they asked the Japanese government, which was by now manifestly war-like and fascist, to confirm the 1940 Olympics.[26] In some respects it was fortunate for the IOC that the Japanese rebuffed them and refused to go ahead with the 1940 Olympics. They saw Olympism and its pacificist ideals as an effete form of European culture. They claimed that that they would hold their own Japanese national 'Olympics' involving sports connected with their warrior traditions. The IOC, having been rebuffed by a fascist state it was not very familiar with, then immediately returned to a fascist state it was very familiar with, namely Germany. At a meeting in 1938 – in spite of Nazi aggression against Austria and the build-up to war – the IOC planned to switch the 1940 Winter Games back to Garmisch and to run the Summer Games in Finland, in Helsinki. Perhaps to provide an appearance of political balance they also awarded the 1944 games to London.

In the context of this discussion it is also worth noting that in 1934 Italy's fascist leader Mussolini constructed a major new football and athletics stadium in Rome in which to stage the finals of the 1934 FIFA soccer World Cup. He was planning to host an international expo in the facilities complex around this stadium in 1942. Rome had not formally bid for the 1944 Olympic Games. However, it is likely that in the late 1930s Mussolini assumed that war in Europe against non-fascist nations was possible and that their defeat was probable. So he took practical steps to make sure that Rome would be available to host an Olympic Games in 1944 or whenever they might be possible in a post-war fascist future. It is likely that the IOC was kept informed of Mussolini's plans and ambitions through its Italian members throughout this period, as indeed it undoubtedly was through its Nazi-appointed German members.[27]

In 1940 the Olympic movement and its dubious dreams, along with the lives and dreams of the world, were consumed for the next five years by the fire of wars, wars that were instigated by the militaristic states that the IOC had courted throughout most of the 1930s. However, before this, at best, irresponsibly naive and, at worst, dishonourable chapter of the history of the Olympic movement was closed there would be one more strange episode. The IOC held a final meeting in 1940. Curiously indifferent to Nazi aggression and the outbreak of war, the IOC apparently still wanted to believe that the 1940 Helsinki games could be held. Ultimately, they reconciled themselves to the inevitable cancellation of the Helsinki games. However, in a final bizarre triumph of trust in ritual over belief in sport, they apparently continued to hope that, at the very least, the torch relay, the great ritual innovation at the Nazi Olympics, could nonetheless be staged on its own, as an independent event (Lucas 1980: 135). Predictably, given the wave of Nazi attacks on European countries in 1940, the torch relay had to be cancelled.

Conclusion

In this chapter we have looked at international sport culture and the Olympic movement in the inter-war period, a period which is too often ignored in understanding the sources of contemporary 'post-modern' and global culture. We began with an account of the impact of supernationalist imperial and totalitarian social systems on the internationalisation of sport. Sport for these systems was one of a number of popular dramatic forms, which also included such forms as mass festivals, parades and demonstrations, through which to propagandise ideology and to display power. As such sport culture became part of an 'aetheticisation of everyday life' and mega-events became elements in a 'theatre of power'. To illustrate this analysis we concluded with a discussion of the influence of fascism on the Olympics, both in the 1936 Berlin games and more generally in the 1930s.

In addition, in this chapter we considered two important forms of internationalism in sport, namely those generated by the democratic socialist movement and by the feminist movement. Each understood itself to be an alternative both to the by-now mainstream and 'bourgeois' Olympic movement and also to communist and fascist versions of sport. These two forms of sport internationalism and their mega-events were ultimately absorbed back into the mainstream forms. Nonetheless, they can be judged to have advanced the cause of working-class men and women in terms of cultural inclusion and citizenship and they exercised a progressive influence on the nature of participation in Olympic Games events, which slowly became more inclusive particularly in the early post-war period.

Building on the analysis of mega-events established in Part 1 we now need to bring our acount forward to address the nature and role of mega-events in the late twentieth-century period. Inevitably there are discontinuities between the late nineteenth- to mid-twentieth-century period and our own times. This is particularly so in terms of advances and mass diffusion of communication and transport technologies in the late twentieth century. These enable mega-events to be accessed worldwide by people either as televised 'media events' or as visitable touristic events in a way which was unknown in earlier periods. However, as we will see, alongside of the discontinuities there are also important continuities linking mega-events in the contemporary period with the developments we have discussed in Part 1. This is not least the case, for instance, in terms of the performative and ritual forms and contents of the main mega-event genres themselves, which, as we have seen, were substantially laid down in the 1850–1939 period.

Part 2

Mega-events and the growth of global culture

The discussion in Part 1 provides a basis from which to address three key dimensions of the two main contemporary mega-event genres, expos and Olympics. Thus Part 2 explores the urban, media and global dimensions of contemporary mega-events, particularly the Olympics. A connecting theme in this discussion, as in Part 1, is that of citizenship. Thus one of the main concerns of Part 2 is to begin to understand the implications of the three mega-event dimensions under scrutiny – the urban, the mediated and the global – for the theory and practice of cultural citizenship in the contemporary period. The three mega-event dimensions and their implications are discussed in succession in Chapters 5, 6 and 7 which deal, respectively, with urban, media and global aspects of the contemporary mega-event phenomenon.

Each of the mega-event dimensions has its origins in the periods and the factors considered in Part 1. So there are continuities as well as discontinuities to consider throughout Part 2. However, the combination of the urban and the media dimensions of the Olympic mega-event in the 1980s and 1990s has created a new, complex and uncertain situation for the Olympic movement involving both positive and negative dynamics and possibilities. We discuss some of the key city-based and media-based problems for the staging of Olympic Games events at the end of each of the relevant chapters, 5 and 6. In addition, the problems they pose, both independently and in combination, for the Olympic movement, as the leading mega-event movement of our period, are considered in Chapter 7 in relation to issues of 'global citizenship'.

5   Mega-events, cities and tourist culture

Olympics and expos

Introduction

In this chapter we begin to address the themes of Part 2 by considering the urban dimension and mega-events as local and touristic events the staging of which carries implications for urban politics and citizenship. However, before we proceed with this discussion, it is important to note that to begin with the local dimension of contemporary mega-events is not to begin from outside of the sphere and the problematic of 'global culture'. Contemporary global culture is not one-dimensionally 'global'. As was suggested in Chapter 1 it is better understood as the production and consumption of meanings and images in a dynamic 'global-local' process.

Meanings and images are carried and diffused, nationally and internationally, in the most internationalised and globalised sectors of contemporary popular culture, namely tourism and the media, particularly television. These are also among the most highly commercialised sectors of contemporary culture and its 'cultural industries', and constitute core elements in what we refer to in the concept of 'consumer culture' and its contemporary globalisation. Tourism and media cultural processes help to generate and operationalise the meanings, such as standardisation/sameness and uniqueness/difference, which we routinely attach to the 'global' and the 'local', and to global-level and local-level times, spaces/places and identities. As we have also suggested mega-events have been both a cause and effect of the development of the tourist and media cultures, and contain both a global and a local dimension.

In this chapter we are mainly looking at expos and Olympics as localised events in space and time, and thus as unique urban/local events. However, these events also carry and project global cultural meanings through their character as tourist and media events. These touristic and media aspects carry direct implications for the cities which host events like expos and particularly Olympic Games. We look at the general tourist cultural implications together with the particular urban tourism implications for cities involved in projects to stage expos and Olympics in this chapter, and we discuss the 'media event' character of contemporary Olympic Games events in the next chapter. As a link to the discussion of Olympic media events it is necessary to consider the urban level. There are major implications for cities' information and communication technology (ICT) infrastructures of winning the right to host an Olympic Games in the contemporary era. So, later, we consider the 'media city' and urban ICT policy aspects of Olympic cities.

The thrust of these discussions is to understand the impacts of mega-events on cities and their meaning for cities in general terms. In the course of this analysis it needs to be borne in mind that, whether their impacts are positive or negative, urban mega-events are typically conceived and produced by powerful elite groups with little democratic input to the policy-making process by local citizens. On the contrary, local citizens are typically expected to act as if they welcomed the event that is imposed upon them along with and the visitors it may attract. In addition, they are expected to provide the often large numbers of volunteer workers such events typically need (40,000 at the Atlanta Olympics), and also to contribute to their finances through paying to spectate it and paying towards local taxes or funds for it. In these and other ways, mega-events are often a very mixed blessing when interpreted in terms of their implications for urban citizenship. Positive and negative versions of these impications are readable in the various economic and tourism impact issues discussed in this chapter, and also in the political contexts and processes indicated in the case study of the Barcelona Olympics and the inter-city competition to win the right to host the Games. We touch on these citizenship issues again in the Conclusion to this chapter.[1]

The discussion in this chapter takes three main steps. In the first section we consider expos and theme parks in relation to the development of tourist culture in modernity. In the second section we consider Olympic cities in terms of the economic and tourism urban impacts of the Olympic mega-event, and we look at one case study in particular, namely Barcelona and its hosting of the 1992 Olympics. In the third section we consider the idea of the 'global Olympic city'. Here, we look first at Olympic cities as 'media cities' and at Seoul in 1988 and Barcelona in 1992 to exemplify this. We then consider the global inter-city bidding 'game' to get selected by the IOC as an Olympic city, and at some of the contemporary problems with this 'game'.

'Expo city': expos, tourist culture and theme parks

The role of nineteenth-century and inter-war expos in relation to the development of tourism was touched on in Chapter 2. Here, we look in particular at expos in the post-war period. As we saw earlier, expos played an important role, as tourist attractions, in stimulating domestic and international tourism and tourism as a cultural industry from the mid nineteenth century, and also in stimulating the allied popular cultural world-views of 'touristic consumerism' and 'urban cosmopolitanism'. As such they have left their imprint on the late twentieth-century tourist industry in particular, and its touristically permeated popular culture in general, not only through their continuing mega-event calendars and 'event heritages' in cities but also through their influence on and connection with an archetypal late twentieth-century form of tourist attraction, namely the 'theme park'. Expos were (and are) effectively temporary theme parks. The development of theme parks, particularly by the Disney organisation from the late 1950s, and later by many imitators across the world, was a development of what were, in certain respects, 'permanent expos' and of what could thus be thought of as 'permanent mega-events'. So, in this section we will first consider the relationships between expos and theme parks and then the relationships between both of them and cities.

Expos and theme parks

In the contemporary period the connection between expos and theme parks such as the Disney parks is fairly clear from the points of view of visitors, on the one hand, and organisers, on the other. From each perspective, expos are coming to be interpreted and/or modelled using theme parks as reference points; effectively they are being seen as temporary theme parks. In a moment, we will explore the other side of this relationship, namely the idea that initially it was the expo tradition which provided the model for theme parks, the latter effectively being permanent expo-type mega-events and 'cityscapes'. However, for the moment we can illustrate the two contemporary perspectives from two studies of recent expos.

On the one hand, the perspective of expo visitors can be illustrated from Harvey's study of the 1992 Seville international expo. She reports: 'When I asked two British visitors what they thought about the UK pavilion they said that it was better than the Welsh Garden Festival but not as good as Disney.'[2] On the other hand, the perspective of expo organisers can be illustrated from Ley and Old's study of the 1986 Vancouver international expo, Expo 86. They report that the person finally appointed to direct the expo (Michael Bartlett) was an 'experienced developer of theme amusement parks' who had presided over the construction of the 'Canada's Wonderland' theme park. Bartlett's view was that he knew 'how to build theme parks. There's not much difference between this [expo] and building those' (quoted in Ley and Olds 1988: 202). There were criticisms of his 'Disney-land model', and also there were labour problems connected with his theme park-based approach to labour discipline and labour relations.[3] Bartlett responded to comparisons of his plans for Expo 86 with Disneyland by saying:

> when you ask me about Disneyland I have to say that it's one of the highest quality theme park experiences around, and what we'd like see is that kind of operational quality applied to the product of a world's fair. . . . We are committed to high quality education and entertainment.
>
> (Quoted in Ley and Olds 1988: 202)

His informal comment to a colleague about his aims was considerably less pious, and more realistic: 'You get 'em on the site, you feed 'em, you make 'em dizzy, and you scare the —— out of 'em.'[4]

In a notable review of 'theme parks' from a political economic perspective Davis (1996) stresses their strategic importance in contemporary national and global cultural (tourism) and media industries. Thus she argues that theme parks are an 'omnipresent fixture in tourism's landscape', that they are 'a new kind of mass medium' and are 'important parts . . . of what is becoming a global media system'.[5] As she points out, contemporary theme parks evolved from fairs and amusement parks[6] and also, as we will see in a moment, from expos. Like fairs and amusement parks they sell excitement and sensory stimulation through a concentration of high technology-based rides and related experiences. Unlike fairs, but like amusement parks, they are fixed and walled-off from the outside world. Unlike many amusement parks they are only accessible through fee-paying; unlike fairs most rides are then 'free'. Theme parks make half of their money through entry fees and the rest from sales of goods (food and drink, souvenirs and merchandise, etc.) from companies which pay 'concession' fees to the theme park and/or directly owned sales operations. Davis observes that:

> unlike the rock concert and more like the shopping mall, the theme park depends on the construction of a landscape and the careful planning of human movement through space. The spatial rationale of the theme park is to cluster commercial opportunities – from hot dog stands to designer boutiques – around attractions which can range from rides to human or animal or robotic performances. Events, architecture and landscaping help move people through and past concessions at speeds and intervals that have been carefully determined to enhance sales per capita. Because of the overriding importance of concession sales...organisational and perceptual control is central to the park.[7]
>
> (Davis 1996: 403)

This organisational and environmental control and the thematic programming of visitor experiences it involves differentiates theme parks from the divers, often sleazy and carnivalesque atmosphere of fairs and amusement parks. The Disney corporation's concept of theme parks was innovative in a number of ways. First, it involved the total environmental control we have noted above. Davis observes: 'the theme park specializes in experiential homogeneity . . . the fully designed, highly coordinated 'land' with all services, performances and concessions designed and provided in house' (Davis 1996: 403). Second, it provided tangible, memorable and, crucially, buyable (and hence 'ownable' and personalisable) experiences of popular film and TV-based images, stories and fantasies. International expos always had a 'fantasy city' 'film set' quality to them, as we have already seen (for instance in Chapter 2). In theme parks controlled by corporations operating also in the media industry, like Disney, such fantasy architecture could be explicitly themed and connected with images, stories and characters from the massively popular world of inter-war and post-war film and then post-war TV. This gave a renewed lease of life to the concept of visiting and experiencing such 'fantasy cities' and 'fantasy lands'. This media-connection allows film and TV to be used to market the theme parks, and in more recent years has allowed the theme parks to be used to market new films and TV programmes.[8]

Finally, the Disney corporation innovated organisationally by involving a limited set of major multinational corporations from consumer and other industries to use their theme parks as selling and marketing sites. Corporations might buy franchises in the park to sell directly to the public, or they might sponsor special exhibits or rides. These corporations, such as Coca-Cola and many others, were already involved with inter-war mega-events such as expos and Olympics. And they have been even more heavily involved in post-war generations of such mega-events. These sorts of conceptual and organisational innovations were the Disney corporation's main contribution to what was to become an important new element of late twentieth-century popular culture and of the cultural industries which shape and supply this culture.

After much boardroom politics, Walt Disney got his way with his theme park concept and the Los Angeles Disneyland opened in 1955, the huge success of which effectively created a new industry (Eliot 1995, chs 14–16). The Disney corporation subsequently deployed the same concept in developing their theme parks in Orlando, Florida (Disney World, 1971), Tokyo (1983) and Paris (Euro Disney 1992). The Disney parks typically contain at least four themed zones or 'lands' within the overall park, namely the traditional ('Main Street USA'), the futuristic ('Tomorrowland'), and the escapist ('Adventure Land' and 'Fantasyland').[9] Each of the zones is linked back into the core Disney concept by being part of a clean, safe and controlled environment designed to stimulate special types of experiences and consumer behaviour, and by the regular appearance of staff in the costume of the familiar Disney cartoon characters. The parks provide an ideal marketing context for the Disney corporation and its merchandise, and enables brand reinforcement and development, and new film and product launches and campaigns, to be achieved with maximal effect.

The Disney theme parks have had many imitators and competitors usually exploiting some important film/TV link, particularly in the USA (e.g. the 'Sea-World' theme parks run by Anheuser-Busch, the 'Six Flags' theme parks run by Time-Warner, and theme parks run by Viacom (Paramount) and MCA), but also in Europe (e.g. Port Aventura, near Barcelona, Spain; Futuroscope, Poitiers, France, etc.) and around the world. Together with the retail and hotel businesses often connected with them, these tourist-attraction complexes are typically very successful and have been called the 'cash cows' of the organisations which own them (Davis 1996).

Disney theme parks' designed and controlled environments reflected Walt Disney's alleged dislike of the traditional amusement park and New York's Luna Park (Coney Island) in particular (Kasson 1978). On the other hand, it is claimed that he was positively impressed with the 1939/40 New York expo, and he also worked on exhibits for a number of big corporations for the 1964 New York expo.[10] The contemporary genre of theme parks to which he helped to give birth contain many expo features, and many commentators have noted the influence of the great international expo tradition on the concept of the post-war theme park. For instance, Davis observes: 'The roots of the theme park run deep in the history of popular and commercial culture. Its ancestors include the older amusement park and its peripatetic ancestors, the circus and the carnival, but also the industrial expositions and World Fairs of the 19th and 20th centuries' (Davis 1996: 400). Smoodin, in his collection of studies of Disney, notes: 'Disneyland, that homage to the possibilities of the future, really functioned as a further development of the last century's gigantic public spectacles – the Chicago Exposition of 1893, for instance' (Smoodin 1994: 12). This connection is generally visualisable in relation to Disney theme parks, and is particularly so in relation to the EPCOT Centre zone at Disney World in Orlando, Florida, which was opened in 1975. The EPCOT Centre is a distinct concept and area within Disney World. EPCOT is an acronym for Experimental Community of Tomorrow. The final realisation differs from Walt Disney's original concept in not being a 'new era' residential centre, nonetheless it provides a substantive demonstration of the continuity of the expo genre in the theme park industry. In particular, EPCOT contains a large geodesic sphere as a key architectural feature which is effectively copied from Buckminster Fuller's sphere at the 1967 Montreal expo and which echoes similar spheres and domes at the New York expos of 1939/40 and 1964. More generally, like international expos, EPCOT also claims to be dedicated to the concept of technological progress and aims to provide information and 'education' about this and its potential benefits for mankind in an accessible and entertaining way (Fjellman 1992, ch. 5,11; Wilson 1994). Like expos, it also has an international theme and contains a large range of national pavilions. Finally, and, once again like expos, it also contains large exhibits and related 'experiences' sponsored by major (usually American) multinational corporations.

Sharon Zukin, in her significant studies of contemporary urban culture observes: 'Disney World's imaginary landscape made dramatic improvements on its closest multimedia precedents' which were the 1893 Chicago expo and the 1939 New York expo. 'Both world's fairs featured the four kinds of attraction that Disney World would later integrate to perfection: amusement parks and rides, stage-set representations of vernacular architecture, state-of-the-art technology, and a special construction of the ideal community' (Zukin 1993: 225–7). She points out that the 1939 New York' expo's 'World of Tomorrow' theme anticipated EPCOT (also Fjellman 1992: 116–7, Wilson 1994), Zukin observes that the 1939 expo:

> shared three general motifs with Disney World: the high price of admission to separate exhibitions or theme parks, the blend of progress and consumerism in selling corporate image, and the landscape of 'a new fantasy world that could be enjoyed because it could be controlled'.
>
> (Zukin 1993: 227)

Finally, Zukin makes the telling point that 'Many of the technology exhibits represent the same corporate sponsors who built pavilions in 1939' (ibid. pp. 225–7) at the New York Expo. These included General Motors, Eastman Kodak, Bell Telephone, Exxon, and Kraft Foods. In addition, it should be noted that companies such as Kodak and Bell were connected with American expos from the very creation of the genre in the late nineteenth century. As Zukin and others indicate, over 60 years on from the great inter war expo mega-events, these companies continue their traditional use of this kind of expo-derived theme park context as a 'showcase' for their 'corporate strategy', effectively making a claim on the concepts of 'progress' and 'the future' as something producable and consumable by means of their technologies and products (Rydell 1993; Rydell and Gwinn 1994).

Expos, theme parks and cities

Expos as temporary mega-events and theme parks as permanent mega-events have had, and continue to have, a range of impacts on cities both from the short- and long-term perspectives. Expos have a more direct and obvious effect on cities since they are traditionally staged either in a prestigious central area of a city, as in the case of the great Paris nineteenth-century expos or, alternatively, in an urban area which the city leadership has zoned for economic development, as in the case of most of the post-war expos, and as has recently been the case for the 1998 Lisbon and 2000 London expos for instance. We will consider further these sorts of expo impacts on cities in a moment (see also section 2 below). First, we can briefly consider theme park impacts.

Theme park impacts on cities

Theme parks, like mega-shopping malls but unlike expos, are typically sited within a relatively short distance (e.g. one hour 'drive time') from one city or a cluster of cities. They need some proximity to cities and city regions because this is where their biggest national consumer markets are located. On the other hand, their space requirements also mean that they need a large supply of relatively inexpensive land to work with, which is usually unavailable in cities. Also it helps to be located so as to require at least some minimal travel effort, even from 'local' city dwellers, to get to them. This is for two reasons. First, it tends to pre-select the people who visit them, prioritising people from those social classes, from the upper working class upwards, who have resources such as a car and disposable time and income, and conversely limiting access from the poor, the unemployed and poorly resourced. In addition, this kind of location helps to inscribe the perception and memory of a visit as part of tourist culture. It helps contribute to their tourist image and status if they are seen as 'different' and 'special' destination places which require people to 'get away' and 'escape' from their own localities, to become trippers and travellers.

That being said, their basic accessibility from and proximity to cities combined with the long-term tendencies towards suburbanisation and satellite/dormitory town development in the advanced societies, means that they increasingly come to affect habitation, transportation and economic development in nearby cities. Either, as in the case of the Los Angeles–Disneyland or Paris–EuroDisney relationships, linear development along access routes and suburbanisation reaches out from the cities to establish new networks of connections between them and the theme parks which locate in their gravitational field, or, as in the Orlando–Disney World relationship, the gravitional pull of the theme park suburbanises the city's region, helps promote the city's image and regional tourism and lifts its economic profile and potential for inward investment, providing the city with a unique and powerful economic development dynamic.[11]

In addition to these concrete kinds of impacts it is also worth noting the more intangible kinds of impacts theme parks can have on cities through their capacity to provide working models of city-like environments and public places and spaces. Most of the visible, threatening and depressing problems of real city environments – the conventional depressing litany of urban problems in the advanced societies, of litter, vandalism, homelessness, drunkenness, theft, violence, prostitution, etc. – have somehow been removed, and are somehow kept at bay in these model and ideal city-scapes. How these working models actually function has no doubt provided food for thought for urban planners in the contemporary period. How their lessons in the creation of attractive, clean and secure quasi-public spaces and places, might be applied in real city contexts has provided even more food for thought, both for planners and also for city leaderships, grassroots area-based interest groups and the politicians who mediate between these two poles.[12]

Expo impacts on cities

Expos as temporary model cities and as event theme parks can be analysed as essentially 'ephemeral' phenomena, 'ephemeral vistas' (Greenhalgh 1988), leaving little trace on the cities which host them and having little impact beyond the short term. The analogy here might be with the traditional travelling fair or circus, a short-term local and visitor entertainment attraction (Toulmin 1994). In more contemporary experience, the temporary 'Big Top' circus arena has its analogy in the tours of international rock stars such as the Rolling Stones and Michael Jackson, 'on the road' with their huge theatrical stage sets and light shows. But this analogy would be misplaced and is misleading. While many expos have indeed left little architectural trace, as we saw in Part 1 (Chapter 2), a number of the nineteenth- and early twentieth-century expos left important and distinctive architectural and facilities heritages in their host cities, particularly expos held in the cities of London, Paris and Barcelona. In addition, their various social, economic and cultural impacts were often considerable and were experienced in the host cities at least in a medium-term historical time-frame. In this section we will briefly look at post-war expos and consider the issues of expo heritage and expo impacts.

The main post-war international expos in the early post-war period are indicated in Table 2.1 above. They include Brussels 1958, Seattle 1962, New York 1964, Montreal 1967 and Osaka 1970. After a dearth of expo creation in the 1970s, and some notable expo project failures in the early/mid 1980s,[13] the expo movement was reanimated by the successful 1986 Vancouver expo. The 1990s have seen a renewed interest in these mega-events as a cultural genre and a general reactivation of the expo movement. At least four major expos were held during the 1990s, in Seville 1992, Taejon (South Korea) 1993,[14] and Lisbon 1998, and at least two will mark the 'Millennium' in 2000, namely the expos in Hanover and London.

As we have seen, nineteenth-century and inter-war expos, as pre-television era mega-events, could and did reasonably claim the attention of 'the world' through the media of the day, whether national presses or national and international radio. Set against this, post-war expos have had to compete with the exhibitionary and entertainment power, and general consumer culture, of national and international television. Unlike the Olympics which has thrived through television, this has reduced the international status and impact of expos.[15] However, this has not necessarily reduced their international symbolic and touristic significance for the host nation and city. If anything, their local city and regional role and impacts have come to be seen as increasingly important. This is particularly so since it is in the post-war period that applied economics and other social scientific disciplines have claimed to be able to provide event impact analysis and information to event producers and managers, encouraging them to see positive impacts as readily predictable, producable and controllable.

As with earlier expos, most post-war expos have usually been expected to feature some unusual monumental architecture and related spectacular 'centrepiece' structures, 'event architecture', such as the spheres we noted earlier at the 1967 Montreal expo and at EPCOT. These may or may not be permanent and thus contribute to an urban event heritage. Two which did so contribute are in Brussels and Seattle. The centrepiece of the 1958 Brussels expo was the 'Atomium' structure built to commemorate the key theme of the expo, namely the advent of the atomic age and of peaceful uses of atomic energy. The 'Atomium' is a 70-metre high lattice of large steel spheres with connecting tubes and escalators, the spheres containing displays, viewing areas and a restaurant. This represents a permanent physical 'event heritage'. This also applies in Seattle to the 'Space Needle', a 185-

metre high viewing tower created for the city's 1962 expo to commemorate a theme of the expo, namely the advent of space flight and the space age. Relatedly in Britain, in the run-up to the Millennium 2000 expo, there was a public debate about the desirability of some permanent event heritage for the city and about the fact that the expo's spectacular, monumental and expensive centrepiece 'Dome' structure was, at least initially, conceived as an essentially temporary facility. On the other hand, the London Millenium expo mega-event project incorporates other forms of less visible and non-spectacular permanent physical event heritage, which have become an increasingly important aspect of post-war mega-events. These include transportation and infrastructure developments and the reclamation of industrially polluted and/or derelict inner-city land for urban regeneration uses, in this case an important but neglected riverside tract of land in the historic and relatively central London area of Greenwich.[16]

These kinds of often non-spectacular physical event heritages, through transport and infrastructure development and generally through urban reclamation and regeneration, have been evident and important aspects of many post-war expo plans and experiences. For instance, the 1967 Montreal expo involved the development of an island area in the St Lawrence river together with the architecturally innovative 'Habitat' high-density housing complex. Comparably, and more recently, the 1998 Lisbon expo involved the regeneration of a declining and derelict river-front area on the river Tagus.[17] We can now look in a little more detail at similar physical event heritages and also wider economic and related impacts in relation to the cases of the 1986 Vancouver expo and the 1992 Seville expo.

The 1986 Vancouver expo, although the subject of some controversy in its planning and building stages, was intended to have positive economic and related impacts on the city and the province of British Columbia more generally (Anderson and Wachtel 1986). It was largely successful in achieving these aims (Ley and Olds 1988). It generated 22 million visits and, in a contemporary context of high unemployment, it also generated 25,000–30,000 full-time jobs. The expo's stimulation to urban and provincial (British Columbian) tourism was substantial (i.e. a 25 per cent increase compared with previously stable tourist flows in the early 1980s) and it was lasting, also being connected with an increase in business immigration from Hong Kong and the Pacific Rim. One commentator observed: 'Expo is really a gigantic urban development project' (Gutstein 1986: 65) not just in the renovation of the previously derelict site of the expo itself but also more broadly in the city. He noted that among many other indirect impacts of the expo in the city of Vancouver, the development of a new light rail system, a major stadium, a bridge and a harbour-front trade and convention centre were all levered and catalysed by its creation. These amounted to around $1.5 billion (Canadian) of new development. The expo also generated an initially unanticipated and ultimately officially 'expected' deficit of $300 million, a cost the expo's public sector sponsors regarded as a price worth paying for the various economic benefits the expo succeeded in delivering to the city and the province. Despite concerns and conflicts about the expo in the pre-event phase, the expo was generally deemed to have been a success. Citizens were largely positive about it and re-elected the provincial government with a large majority soon after the expo ended (Ley and Olds 1988; see also Anderson and Wachtel 1986, and Wachtel 1986).

The Seville 1992 expo, whatever its broader internationalist aims, was planned by the Spanish and provincial governments as an instrument to reclaim and re-generate the site on which it was held, an historic but arid island in the Quadalquivir river, and to boost the Seville city economy and the economy of the relatively poor region of Andalusia more generally. The expo plan required a major new investment in transport and infrastructure in the site, the city and the region, including a number of new bridges over the river, new road systems and a site connection to the new high-speed rail system linking Seville and Madrid. Permanent physical expo-related heritages include a new opera house, an open-air venue for rock concerts, and a number of other theatres. The Seville expo was one of the biggest and most successful expos ever in attracting visits (42 million). In addition because of heavy public subsidies and expenditures both on it and the Andalusian economy in general, it appears to have been at least relatively successful, in a difficult economic climate, in encouraging inward investment and industrial location. However, post-event there have been delays and problems in maintaining critical mass and in building up the occupancy of the permanent expo site facilities. The 1992 event itself was less successful than hoped in terms of its employment creation (5,500 full-time jobs). Also, the tourist industry responded to the expo over-enthusiastically, over-expanding Seville's stock of hotel rooms, and it has since had to contract. So while the expo and associated cultural and infra-structural developments may well have had a positive impact on urban and regional tourism there have also been problems in this sector and in these impacts, together with other post-event land-valuation and land-use problems (Findling 1994b).

Significantly, the Seville expo plan also envisaged the creation of many permanent buildings and two permanent 'parks' on the expo site after the expo finished. One is effectively an 'industrial park' connected with a science and technology research and development centre and housing many of the multinational corporations which exhibited at the expo and which have been attracted to locate permanently in the area. Interestingly, in terms of our earlier discussion of theme parks, the other park is a technology-oriented theme park, the 'Cartuja Park of Discoveries', utilising some of the main pavilions and the site infrastructures and visitor attrac-tion features created for the expo. As we noted earlier, the temporary expo mega-event genre, particularly in the USA, played an important role in creating the concept and stimulating the creation, in the USA by Disney and others, of the permanent theme park genre. Whereas once this was a generalised process of influence, the case of the Seville expo indicates that it can now be part of more coordinated and planned policies for the cities' economic development in general and the development of their cultural industries sectors in particular. This theme is supported by the phenomena of sport, culture and event-led urban regeneration and the use of Olympic Games mega-events in these processes which we consider next.

'Olympic city'

This discussion of 'the Olympic city' proceeds in five main steps. In the first section we discuss the background to this idea and the concept of 'the Olympic city' as a kind of theme park. In the second section we review some of the main economic impacts and also the main physical impacts and heritages, and touristic impacts of Olympic events on their host cities. We then illustrate and explore some of these impacts, and the urban policy issues connected with them, in more detail in a case study of the city of Barcelona and its 1992 Olympic Games event. In section four, given that the next chapter is concerned with the media's power to transform 'local events' into 'global events', we consider the Olympic city as 'media city'. That is, we look at the local basis of the Olympic 'media event', namely the special communications organisation and investment in the host city which is often necessary to make the Olympics possible as a 'global' event. In this context we look at the ICT infrastructures and policies necessary to stage the Olympic Games and broadcast the event to the world in the cases of Seoul and Barcelona. Finally, we consider the inter-city bidding process which cities have to commit themselves to in order to gain the right to host the Games. This process connects the local with the global, re-images localities as global actors, and looms large in the policies of bid cities and their leaderships for long periods during bidding cycles. This process has recently revealed major problems in the operations of the Olympic movement as the main contemporary 'global mega-event' 'franchise' organisation, and we consider these in the final section of this discussion.

Background: the 'Olympic city theme park'

One of the many ambiguities and paradoxes of the modern Olympic Games is as follows. On the one hand, each Olympic Games is both utterly standardised, in that it is run according to IOC rules and the incorporated rules of the numerous governing bodies regulating the sports represented and on the standardised periodicity of its four-year calendar. On the other hand, each Olympic Games is also utterly unique. We will review the standardised aspects later in this introduction, looking at the IOC rules and ideals for Olympic cities and the sense in which they can be said to construct a temporary 'Olympic event theme park'. As against this, Olympic Games events are also historically specific, uniquely dramatic, and memorable as such. They are unique not just in the changing casts of athletes and in their performances and achievements ('citius, altius, fortius', progression in world-level standards and records etc.), but also, obviously, in terms of their sites and locations.

In spite of occasional calls for a permanent site during the twentieth century (e.g. in the early and also post-war periods for a site in Greece, or, during the Nazi period, for the site of Nuremberg) the IOC and the Olympic movement has always required that the games be staged in different host cities, the city being decided by the IOC after an inter-city bidding processs and competition. The Olympic (de Coubertin) motto – which (to paraphrase it) is that 'the point is not to play to win but to take part, whether you win or lose'[18] – applies as much (if not more) to the competing cities (and to a certain extent to the competing nations, for whom presence at the Olympics is a badge of nationhood) as it does to the athletes. The development of the global inter-city competition to stage the modern Olympic Games event since its inception is summarised in Table 5.1. We discuss this 'game', in particular its problematic and questionable aspects in the late twentieth century, later in this chapter.

Table 5.1 Olympic Cities and bids 1896–2004

Period	Olympic year	Olympic City	Candidate Cities
Pre-1914	1896	Athens	None
	1900	Paris	None
	1904	St Louis	Chicago
	1908	London	Rome, Berlin
	1912	Stockholm	Berlin
World War	1916	Berlin (cancelled)	Budapest, Alexandria, Cleveland
Inter-war	1920	Antwerp	Amsterdam
	1924	Paris	Amsterdam, Rome, Los Angeles, Prague, Barcelona
	1928	Amsterdam	None
	1932	Los Angeles	None
	1936	Berlin	Barcelona
World war	1940	Tokyo/Helsinki (cancelled)	None
	1944	London (cancelled)	None
Post-war	1948	London	None
	1952	Helsinki	Detroit, Amsterdam, Los Angeles, Chicago, Philadelphia, Minneapolis
	1956	Melbourne	Detroit, Buenos Aires, Los Angeles, Vhicago, Philadelphia, Mexico City, Minneapolis, San Francisco
	1960	Rome	Detroit, Lausanne, Budapest, Brussels, Mexico City
	1964	Tokyo	Detroit, Vienna, Brussels
	1968	Mexico City	Detroit, Lyon, Buenos Aires
	1972	Munich	Montreal, Madrid, Detroit
	1976	Montreal	Moscow, Los Angeles
	1980	Moscow	Los Angeles
	1984	Los Angeles	None
	1988	Seoul	Nagoya
	1992	Barcelona	Paris, Brisbane, Belgrade, Birmingham, Amsterdam
	1996	Atlanta	Athens, Belgrade, Toronto, Manchester, Melbourne
	2000	Sydney	Berlin, Istanbul, Manchester, Beijing
	2004	Athens	Rio de Janeiro, Cape Town, Rome, Istanbul, St Petersburg, Buenos Aires, Lille, San Juan, Seville, Stockholm

Source: IOC 1996, p.84.

The idea that the 'Olympic movement' is a movement, and that it has a mission to spread its word around the world, is made tangible and real in the fact that the Olympics games event is a 'show' which is permanently 'on the road', taking its 'caravan' from nation to nation and city to city every four years. The Olympic event has rarely returned to the same city (i.e. only to Paris 1900 and 1924, London 1908 and 1948, Los Angeles 1932 and 1984, and Athens 1896 and 2004) without at least a generation having passed; usually it never returns to a host city. This means that each Olympic event is also a unique product of a unique configuration of power elites, always including the IOC in a dominant role, but also including the local Games organising committee, its national government sponsor, and particular combinations of large multinational media and corporate sponsors. Later, we review some important urban dimensions of late twentieth-century Olympic Games events, including aspects of their production and finance, as localised but simultaneously national and global events. In the course of this discussion we also consider their unique and variable contributions to the urban policies of their host cities in terms of their short-term economic impacts, their tangible long-term 'event legacies', such as sport, housing and transport facilities, and their other more intangible impacts in terms of tourism and city image.

In these respects, then, every Olympic Games event is inevitably unique. However, they are also, equally inevitably, and in many important respects, standardised and as identifiably and uniformly 'Olympic' as each other. Each host city's organising committee attends the preceding city's event and studies it in minute detail to learn lessons from its successes and failures. This process in itself is likely to promote a certain degree of uniformity of tried, tested and successful organisational features. But beyond this, of course, the uniformity ultimately derives from the control exercised by the IOC on the host city's production of the event. This control was tightened considerably after the local organising committee for the Los Angeles 1984 Games, operating with a considerable degree of licence, successfully demonstrated how the Games could be organised to maximise income from television, sponsorship and merchandising, and make a financial surplus over costs. The Olympic Charter's rules now define in detail the nature of the event and its organisation and financing, and control the use of such things as the Olympic symbols in the course of this.

Effectively, for every Olympic Games event the IOC, using local and national organisers, creates what we can refer to as the standard 'Olympic city' or more critically 'the Olympic Theme Park'. It does this in a number of ways. First, there is the very fact of using single cities as the frontline hosting and organising agency rather than, as in the case of FIFA's World Cup soccer mega-event, using the nation-state (even, in the case of the 2002 event, the two nations of Japan and Korea)[19] and a network of cities and their stadia within the host nation. The Olympic's single-city focus is emphasised through the sequence of national-level and international-level bidding competitions which cities are required to go through in order to win the right to stage the Games. We will discuss this bidding process further later.

Most of the numerous sports comprising the Olympic event must be sited in the host city. The key elements of the 'Olympic city-within-a-city' are the complex formed by the three key elements of the *athletes' accommodation* or *Olympic village*, the *main athletics stadium* (which is usually either newly built or refurbished for the games and is usually intended to represent a key part of the lasting Olympic 'legacy' to the city), and the media centre. In connection with the sport event there must be programmes of cultural events both in the Olympic village and also in the city more generally, which effectively makes central areas of the city and its transport infrastructure into elements of the 'Olympic city' for the duration of the event at least. Since the terrorist killings in the Olympic village at the Munich Olympics in 1972 all of the sport venues in the complex must have a high degree of security and entrance control. The main stadium and all sport sites, unusual for sports events in the late twentieth century and not the case for World Cup soccer for instance, must be 'clean' of advertising with only the Olympic symbols visible. The opening and closing ceremonies, while they may incorporate a lot of creative inputs from the city and national organisers, nonetheless have standardised and ritualistic features to them which we have discussed earlier. These include the national and IOC leaders opening and closing the event in the main stadium, together with key features of the opening ceremony (the entry of the Olympic symbols, flag, torch and anthem, the entry of the national teams, etc.) and of victory ceremonies (medal presentations, podia, anthems, flags, etc.)

Olympic cities: urban impacts and heritages[20]

We now need to review some important urban dimensions of late twentieth-century Olympic games events including their potential contribution to the broader urban social and economic policies of their host cities in more concrete terms. In this section we briefly review their financial outcomes and economic impacts, 'event legacies' in architecture, facilites and infrastructures in such areas as sport, communications, transport and housing, and tourism and city image impacts.

Economic impacts and architectural and facilities heritage

The Summer Olympic events, from the 1984 Games onwards, have derived their income from a number of sources. These are principally USA TV and other world regional (e.g. EU) TV (see Table 6.3 below), corporate sponsorship, ticket sales, merchandising and various other sources (e.g. public sectors, lotteries, etc.). The regional economic impacts include employment creation and the effects of improved infratructures and image. The costs include those of the event itself (including operational and sport facilities) and also of the broader urban infrastructure spending on transport, housing and communications which is involved in staging these events.

Generally in terms of spending, and with the exception of Los Angeles 1984, the Olympic Games of the 1980s and 1990s have required large-scale public spending on infrastructures, have generated high levels of income for the local organising committee, principally from the private sector (television and corporate sponsorship) and most have either generated surpluses of at least US$100 million. According to the organisers of the last four Olympics, no losses were made in the staging of these uniquely complex, risky and expensive events.

The building of the main Olympic stadium, the main swimming pool and the facilities complexes associated with these and other sports and sport venues created a substantial architectural heritage and an internationally recognised and relevant sport heritage for Berlin post-1936 and for most of the post-war Olympic cities (i.e. Helsinki, Melbourne, Tokyo, Montreal, Munich, Seoul, Atlanta and Sydney).[21] Major transport infrastructure improvements connected with Olympic Games events include the 'bullet train' inaugurated in the Tokyo Games in 1964; new metro systems introduced or extended for the Games of Rome, Tokyo, Montreal, Seoul, Barcelona and Athens (2004); major new urban road systems for Barcelona; and the creation of new international airports for the Barcelona and Athens Games.

We can illustrate some of these impacts briefly in relation to the 1996 Atlanta Olympics. Later we will look at economic and other impacts in more detail in the case of the 1992 Barcelona Olympics. In Atlanta, a new stadium with a planned baseball after-use was built for over $500 million, and other infrastructural and event-related spending amounted to $1.7 billion. The private sector provided the main sources of incomefor the event to cover these expenses. These included $425 million from spectator ticket sales to private individuals and corporations. However, the bulk of the income came from the private corporate sector. For example, $568 million came from the sale of TV rights, most of this coming from USA TV (i.e. NBC). This was matched by income from corporate sponsorship which generated $633 million (ACOG 1997: 280). The bulk of this came from the ten leading (TOP) corporate sponsors or 'partners' who were licensed to associate their brand with 'the Olympic brand' in marketing their products and services worldwide. These were Coca-Cola, Kodak, VISA, Xerox, TIme, IBM, Panasonic, UPS, Bausch and Lomb, and John Hancock, who each contributed $40 million (consisting of 50 per cent in cash and 50 per cent in services in kind) (Harrison 1995-P; ACOG 1997: 264). The economic impact of the event on the city, regional and Georgia state economies was significant. There was a boost of over 33,500 jobs in the preparation and event period in Georgia in 1995–6. Tax receipts to Georgia increased by $200 million in this period. The official economic impact study predicted a $5.1 billion impact on the Georgia state economy in the 1991–7 period.[22] An impact of $3.5 billion was recorded for the 1995/6 period, and as a result of the Games (but also no doubt as a result of other additional economic factors) the Georgia state economy grew 5 per cent per year in 1994 and 1995 (Harrison 1995-P). As a result of the Olympic mega-event overall, 77,000 full-time and part-time jobs were created in the state, 38 per cent of them in the hospitality industry (hotels etc.), together with $176 million additional tax revenue for the state government (ACOG 1997: 221).

The Olympic Games were perceived by Atlanta residents to be capable of leaving a positive legacy, including the revitalisation of certain downtown areas through the new stadium and the new 100-acre Centennial Park located near it, various urban renewals (including a $42 million Federal improvement grant and over 200 new homes in poor areas near the venues), new sports facilities for a number of colleges, additional employment and possible corporate relocations (Mihalik 1994). Overall, in spite of some image problems connected with their over-commercialisation and also some communications and transport problems, the Games event can be argued to have produced net benefits for the city of Atlanta, and in financial terms they were claimed to have broken even.

However, the staging of an Olympic Games event is obviously a complex and risky project carrying with it a range of potential social and political costs, in addition to potential economic costs. For instance, Hall and Hodges (1998) discuss some of these costs in their study of the 2000 Sydney Olympics. They address the theme of the urban politics of place and identity involved in staging such sport mega-events. Building on their previous research on 'hallmark events' in tourism policy-making and the social costs and benefits of 'hallmark events' (e.g. Hall 1989b, 1992, 1994a) they examine the case of the city of Sydney's preparations for its Olympic Games. In line with Hall's previous studies, they focus on the national and urban politics of this process and on the event's likely local impacts, particularly its planned and unplanned social impacts. They demonstrate the role of local growth coalitions and booster groups of politicians and leaders of business and the media in the creation and promotion of Sydney's original bid for the Olympics and its event prepartions. Global sport events like the Olympic Games evidently usually require new sport facilities to be built, together with the new urban transport infrastructures necessary to move and manage masses of people at and between the various event sites and facilities. We discuss and illustrate these issues in greater detail later in the case study of the urban impacts of the 1992 Barcelona Olympics.

Hall and Hodges are particularly concerned with the social impact of this new building in terms of its effects on the housing market and land values. These can involve housing relocation because of the compulsory purchase of land for clearance and building. It can also lead to a rise in rents and house prices, and generally to 'gentrification' processes in areas of previously low land values and low rents. Each of these processes, but particularly the latter, can cause serious problems of people living on low incomes in these areas. Hall and Hodges propose a new range of policy strategies which need to be seriously considered by urban politicians and planners if they are to adequately respond to these sorts of often very negative social impacts. These strategies include strengthening tenants' rights, developing relevant forms of rent control and generally developing and committing event organisers to undertaking social impact analysis as part of their approach to the staging of sport mega-events.

Tourism and image

One of the main impacts the Olympic Games and other mega-events are assumed to have on their host cities is in terms of the short- and long-term economic impact of the event on the flow of tourists into the city, and also the long-term cultural impact of the event on the image of the city nationally and internationally by potential tourists and private sector decision-makers and investors. Some of these assumed impacts are easier to measure and to establish than are others (Roche 1992, 1999d). Long-term impacts are always difficult to establish given the relative infrequency of and lack of funding for, systematic longitudinal studies. Also, even in relation to the short-term impacts, it is particularly difficult to estimate the *net* effect of the Olympic event, given that tourism to the city may have been increasing as a medium-term trend in the absence of it, and also given that such events can 'crowd out' normal tourism, raise accommodation and other tourist costs, and generally exert a 'stay-away' effect on potential visitors not interested in sport (Loventhal and Howarth 1985).

There are relatively few studies of the tourism impact of Olympic Games. In this section we review some of the key findings from the main studies. Pyo *et al.* (1988)

reviewed tourism impacts of the Olympic Games at Tokyo 1964, Mexico 1968, Munich 1972, Montreal 1976, Moscow 1980 and Los Angeles 1984. Most of the city experiences they reviewed were negative. There were not enough visitors and there was not enough spending by them to justify the event costs. This also confirms Hughes' review of Olympic Games impacts on urban tourism which we consider in a moment. Leibold and van Zyl, in their study of Capetown's bid for the 2004 Olympic Games, note that: 'It is likely that cities are becoming "products" of "brands" in their own right, more so than countries or regions, and a hallmark event such as the Olympic Games could be a major catalyst in this regard' (Leibold and van Zyl 1994: 142). Capetown failed in its bid, but is likely to bid again for the 2008 event. However, as with its former bid any new bid is likely to focus on long-term image-building and not short-term touristic economic returns.

Kang and Perdue, in their study of the 1988 Seoul Olympics, criticise the short-termism of most studies of and policy approaches to the touristic impacts of Olympic events. They try to take a longer-term view. They analyse the event's tourism impact in terms of a number of factors: mass media, awareness and image; event participation; short-term visitor impact; infrastructure and service improvements; visitor satisfaction and positive word-of-mouth; image decay and promotion to counter it; prices and final outcome (market share etc.). Their conceptual framework assumed that 'a long-term impact is generated primarily through improvement of facilities and services, [positive] media coverage, and word-of-mouth communication' (Kang and Perdue 1994: 222). Their findings appeared to confirm their theory. Their main focus is on the impact of the Seoul Olympics on national tourism to South Korea in the comparative context of demand for tourism to other Asian countries. They do not focus on tourism to the city of Seoul in particular. However, their study has implications for the tourism impact on the national capital city since Seoul's airport was the main international airport and entry point for international travellers to Korea. Also, at the time there were relatively few comparable complexes of hotels of equivalent scale to accommodate international visitors in other parts of the country. So it is fair to assume that the bulk of the international tourism into the 'nation' they discuss actually went to and/or through Seoul.

Their findings were that mega-events do have a long-term impact on international tourism to the host country; the impact is greatest in the year following the event and diminishes over time; and in the case of Korea the value of the benefit realised in a three-year period is estimated to be $1.3 billion.[23] Further general conclusions were that consumer reaction to a mega-event tends to be 'lagged and protracted' (i.e. positive visitor upturn occurs and peaks a year after the event); and 'international tourism is price sensitive' in general. A mega-event and its related media publicity 'alters the price-market share relationship, in effect shifting the demand curve for the host country' in an economically beneficial direction (ibid. pp. 222–3).

Hughes, in his study of 'Olympic tourism and urban regeneration', takes a more cautious view. This study was undertaken to provide background information for Manchester's ultimately unsuccessful bid for the 1996 Olympics. He is particularly concerned to evaluate the claim made in various political arenas, not least in national government circles in the 1980s and 1990s, that tourism per se, and particularly that stimulated by mega-events, can have positive economic impacts on deindustrialised and variously problematic inner cities. He believes that 'There can be no doubt . . . that substantial tourist flows result from the Olympics; the Olympics are a major tourist event' (Hughes 1993: 161). In general, Hughes believes that such an event can have positive impacts in cities which have an undeveloped sport infrastructure and which have high unemployment, less so in cities with a developed infrastructure and low unemployment.

However, Hughes also attempts to take account of mega-event costs as well as benefits. First, there is the 'stay away' factor, that is potential visitors' negative expectations of being crowded out of accommodation and tourist sites because of the pulling power of the event. This factor was identified in evaluations of the impact of the 1984 Los Angeles Olympic Games (Loventhal and Howarth 1985) and is part of more recent mega-event economic impact assessments (e.g. Dauncey and Hare 1999). Given this, Hughes believes that pre-event visitor number projections need to be cautious. Second, he also believes that large visitor numbers may be disruptive in relation to the city's 'carrying capacity'. Its hotel system, for instance, may be judged as not being able to cope with expected demand generated by the event. This in turn may lead urban planners to attempt to increase their city's hotel capacity. However, any permanent addition to hotel stock to satisfy a purely temporary peak in demand would need to be properly justified in terms of projections about its potential for being fully used post-event. This is also a reasonable concern. On the one hand, it is true that both Seoul and Barcelona experienced a permanent increase in tourism flows post-Olympics. However, on the other hand, over-optimistic projections about post-event demand, buoyed up by a urban policy-making culture of event 'boosterism', can lead to post-event financial problems and losses in the hotel sector. As we noted earlier, this problem was attested to, for instance, in the case of the 1992 Seville expo (Findling 1994b).

On the basis of considerations of this kind, Hughes believes that, for the purposes of urban regeneration, a programme of smaller-scale hallmark events is likely to be more effective and beneficial in cost-benefit terms than a one-off mega-event such as the Olympic Games. He argues that:

> The games could prove a distraction from the development and implement-ation of a firmly based long-term tourism strategy unless they are per-ceived as an opportunity to develop or strengthen such a strategy. . . . The full usage of roads, airports, housing etc. afterwards is as critical as it is for hotels and restaurants. The sporting facilities themselves may be little used after the hallmark event.
>
> (Hughes 1993: 161–2)

He suggests that while awareness of the host city may increase post-event, 'there is little evidence that visits increase' and 'It is unrealistic to expect tourism flows to stay at the Olympic level'. Hughes believes that the promotion of urban tourism can help in the regeneration of inner cities. By contrast the temporary flood of Olympic tourism is unlikely to be as beneficial for a city. This does not help much in the short term. It is based on hopes for the long-term in relation to increases in tourism and inward investment into a city because of factors such as improved urban environment and infrastructure, and improved awareness and city image. In general he believes that: 'The case for . . . [the beneficial effects of Olympic tourism] has . . . not yet been demonstrated' (Hughes 1993: 161–2). However, while this kind of assessment may have been appropriate for a city such as Manchester, more positive tourism impacts have been observed for other post-Olympic cities and we will consider this in relation to Barcelona next.

An 'Olympic city': Barcelona and the 1992 Olympics

In this section we will first consider some background information about the city of Barcelona; second, some genral points about the Olympic event; third, the economic and political impacts of the event; and finally, the event's tourism-related impacts

Background

Barcelona is the Catalan 'national capital'. It is an industrial port city, with an international orientation economically, culturally and politically. It staged expos in 1888 and 1929, and these events produced identifiable heritages for the city. Modernist art was a key theme in the 1888 expo and the advances made possible by the use of electricity was a key theme in the 1929 expo.[24] The Montjuic stadium was built for the 1929 expo, and a Workers' 'Olympic' Games event was planned for it in 1936, an event which was cancelled due to the onset of the Civil War.[25] It was subsequently upgraded and used as the Olympic stadium for the 1992 event. The city was an important base for Spanish republicanism and for resistance to Franco's fascism during the Spanish Civil War. In the post-war period the city tried and failed to create an expo in 1980. The city was always aspirational in relation to the Olympic Games. Before its successful bid for the 1992 Olympics, the city had bid unsuccessfully for a number of Olympic events over the years. In the inter-war period it had bid in 1922 for the 1924 event, in 1926 for the 1932 event, and in 1932 for the 1936 event. In the post-war period it had aimed to bid again for the 1960 Olympics, but it was hindered by the international image of Franco's Spain and withdrew (Verdaguer 1995: 202). It also aspired to be the Spanish candidate for the 1972 games, although the ultimate Spanish candidate was Madrid, which lost out to Munich. In 1981 it launched a campaign to win the 1992 games which was decided in 1986. The IOC president in the relevant period was Juan Samaranch, who is a Catalan and an ex-leading figure in Barcelona (albeit during the disgraced Franco period). It is not unreasonable to suppose, given the general influence of the President on the IOC, that this association had some influence on the IOC's decision to award the 1992 event to the city.[26]

The Olympic event: public investments and provisional assessments

Massive new infrastructural investments were made in the city which were connected with the Olympics. These included a new waterfront and residential area (which continues to be called 'the Olympic village'), a new international airport, two new spectacular skyline communications towers (the Colserolla tower at Tibidabo, designed by the notable architect Norman Foster, and the Calatrava tower near the Olympic Stadium on Mont Juic), six new sports stadia together with a major refurbishment of the main stadium, a new museum of contemporary art and a remodelled Catalonian arts museum, and various media facilities (which we consider separately and in more detail later). All of this cost at least $8 billion, significantly more than Montreal's legendary and 'excessive' $1billion, and indeed more than most Olympics have ever cost.[27]

In relation to the construction of new sports facilities, the local Olympic organising group (COOB) aimed to leave the city with a positive Olympic heritage for long-term post-event elite and mass sport uses, and to do so without risking excessive public spending. These aims were achieved in various ways. As noted earlier COOB used the recent precedent of the 1984 LA Olympic organisers and resisted IOC pressure to build a new large stadium, merely refurbishing the old expo and 'Worker's Olympics' stadium on Montjuic hill. Together with the city council they created two distinct organisations to manage the elite and mass sport after-uses of the facilities. The former organisation promoted large-scale elite sport and also non-sport events (trade exhibitions, political rallies, etc.) in the four main Olympic facilities (two large indoor arenas, the velodrome, and the main open-air stadium). The latter organisation operationalised the city council's 'Area of Sports' concept which involved a very decentralised distribution and location of many of the smaller-scale facilities used in the Olympic event. This decentralisation helped to popularise the Olympic event, to develop public–private sector partnerships in the post-event management of facilities and also to promote the after-use of the facilities by the mass public.

The local Olympic organising committee (COOB) naturally felt that they had created a great success; 'The . . . direct beneficiaries are the citizens of Barcelona whose surroundings have been immeasurably improved' (quoted in Thomas 1992-P). Many commentators also felt that the event was a great success. For instance, the architecture critic D. Sudjic judged that 'Olympic Barcelona is perhaps the only great success story of post-war planning on a city-wide scale' (Sudjic 1992-P; Milner 1998-P). Other commentators consider that there may be lessons to be learned from Barcelona's success, including the quality of its urban leadership under Mayor Pasquall Maragall. This is particularly relevant for cities in countries such as the UK, where national governments are considering reconstructing city leadership and recreating mayoral power (Nash 1996-P).

Garcia[28] observes that the city's Olympic Games project emerged from out of a period of economic crisis and industrial decline. A long-term strategy for modernisation, namely 'Barcelona 2000', aimed at regenerating the city's economy and its central urban fabric more generally, was undertaken from the mid-1980s. This provided the socio-economic and planning context for the Olympic event. In relation to the city's strategic modernisation process, there was a continuity of the developments connected with the Olympics. Many previous post-war plans for the city had also aimed at reconnecting it with its coastline, updating its economy and and upgrading socially deprived areas.

The developments undertaken in connection with the Olympics in the late 1980s enabled the city's strategic objectives to be more or less successfully achieved. The social policy aim was successfully achieved through, among other things, the new sports facilities, transport and housing built in the deprived city area of the Valle de Hebron and also in some of the areas adjacent to the Olympic village. The spatial and related economic aims of re-connecting the central city with its coastline and moving the city significantly towards the service sector and the international economy were boosted by the construction of the Olympic village and related developments such as the construction of new road systems and the remodelling of the old central harbour area.

The development of the Olympic village was initially controversial for local citizens and was debated as a process of unnecessary 'gentrification'. It involved the use of compulsory purchase powers and it changed the previous character of the area. New middle- and upper-income housing was created, together with high-density service industry office buildings and facilities, shops, clubs and renovated parks, waterfront and beach areas, which were intended to be attractive both to the local professional middle class and also to international tourists. Whatever the local debate, at least there was a clear strategy for the post-event use of this area, which has subsequently become part of the city's tourist attractions and, as such, seems to have had a positive effect on the city, at least in touristic terms, as we note later.

Economic and political impacts

In terms of general economic effects, Garcia notes the major public sector investments made in the city in connection with the event by the central, provincial and city levels of government, not least in major transport infrastructure development such as new roads to ease traffic congestion. At the local level the city council's attempt to fund event-related spending by raising local taxes was resisted by the citizens. This required a large increase in the city's borrowing, debt and interest repayments, and the public debt now exceeds the annual budget (Garcia 1993: 19). She concludes that 'Despite local public debt the benefits appear to outstrip the costs in very general terms' (ibid. p. 10). Also the economic growth effects connected with the event were significant, with foreign investment in the city continuously growing in the late 1980s and early 1990s after a period of stagnation. It is likely that the city leadership's strategic calculation was that the public debt could be reduced by the increased volume of local tax-take associated with sustained economic growth.

In terms of employment effects, Garcia concludes that the Games mainly benefited women and young people by accelerating service sector growth, which was probably an inevitable trend stemming from structural and global changes in modern economies. This development carries with it social costs in terms of social polarisation between the employed and unemployed, relevantly skilled and unskilled, and also in terms of the new flexibilisation of employment connected with service sector employment. In general the increase in foreign investment in the city also tends to drive up land values and housing costs in certain areas, leading to a further degree of spatial polarisation as well as social polarisation.

In terms of political effects, Garcia observes that undoubtedly the Olympic event was a product of a small political and planning elite, albeit a group which aimed to create a popular event and use it to produce positive socio-economic effects for the mass of Barcelona's citizens. The organisers correctly perceived that, as with many other events we have considered, popular support was essential for the practical success of the event, not least to enable it to achieve the necessary levels of volunteer labour and fee-paying spectators. However, in this case, the Olympics were also promoted as a vehicle of Catalan national identity and national pride. In order to achieve strong public support for the event, important developments such as the plans for new roads were debated with the public and modified as a result of their views. This helped to generate a sense of 'ownership' and participation amongst the general public, a sense of pride in the symbols of both Spain and Catalonia, and a trust in the city's leadership, a kind of 'civil religion' (ibid. p. 20).

Tourism-related impacts: internationalism and globalisation

In terms of tourism, Verdaguer observes that Barcelona has many natural assets: 'a sunbelt position, a rich architectural heritage, strong local and international culture, and a relatively developed socio-economic level' (Verdaguer 1995: 201). On this basis the city has created a successful tourism industry in the 1990s. However, as Verdaguer notes, the city's tourism success has been built on a long tradition which has periodically involved the hosting of mega-events. It has been internationalist in its outlook for decades. Its first tourist office was created in 1908, and its annual commercial fair was created in 1920. In terms of mega-event legacies the 1888 expo helped to inaugurate the city's first urban park, and the 1929 expo helped inaugurate a second park and additional cultural and architectural legacies. Each of these, particularly the latter, which is situated near to the Royal Palace and the Mont Juic facilities, is an attraction both for Barcelona citizens and tourists. In his analysis 'Mega-events: local strategies and global tourist attractions', Verdaguer takes a positive view of the impact of the Olympic event on Barcelona's tourism industry. He observes that international tourism in Barcelona has increased in recent years, particularly post-Olympics. He also observes that the city's economy has been significantly 'tertiarised' and internationalised as a result of the general urban planning and development process of which the Olympics was a part (ibid. p. 203).[29]

However, as a background to this assessment of the Olympic event's tourism impacts some other factors need to be taken into account when trying to understand Barcelona's evident contemporary success as an example of urban tourism. It is worth observing that the city is based in the Catalonian coastal region which, in the post-war period, has become one of the Spain's major tourist resort areas. It benefits from being close to one of the country's biggest contemporary mass tourist attractions, namely the Port Aventura theme park.[30] In addition, it is worth noting that Barcelona is the beneficiary of media-sport-related tourism unconnected with the Olympics. The city is the home of one of Europe's most powerful soccer clubs (Barcelona F.C.), which, in turn, possesses one of the Europe's greatest soccer stadia (the Nou Camp stadium). Like the cathedrals of old, this stadium has now become one of the city's major tourist attractions for foreign visitors.[31] The city's touristically-related economic development process and international image-construction is currently continuing with, among other things, the construction of a World Trade Centre in the central harbour area, and this is likely to stimulate business travel and related tourism.

For Verdaguer, Barcelona's touristic and economic development represents 'the resisting force of place' against international forces.[32] He concludes that cities can survive great civilisational crises such as globalisation, and that globalisation can in principle benefit cities (although in practice only certain cities may have the resources to reap this benefit). In general, Verdaguer emphasises 'the important role of tourist activities in the tertiarisation of cities.' He argues that 'cities are becoming more and more a stage, if not a final destination, as a cultural resource, alongside other new destinations . . . as well as the traditional products, like sun, sand and sex'. On the basis of his analysis of Barcelona's experience, he observes that, in relation to the challenges and opportunities presented by globalisation, 'Mega-events could be considered . . . one of the most visible elements of the current local strategies for [urban] survival'.[33]

Achieving the 'Global Olympic City': the Olympic 'media city' and global inter-city competition problems

We now need to consider some important aspects of cities' involvements with Olympic Games events and the Olympic movement, which (as distinct from the localist-orientation of much of the policy-making we have looked at so far) have more obvious and direct connections with globalisation processes in contemporary culture. First, we need to consider the fact that to enable the Olympic global media event (which we discuss in detail in the following chapter) to be achieved it is first necessary to construct an adequate material base for this. Thus to have any aspirations to becoming a 'global Olympic city' in the late twentieth century, contemporary cities must undertake to reconstruct and qualitatively upgrade their information and communications technology infrastructures to provide a uniquely large-scale and complex new city-wide system which we can refer to as the 'Olympic media city', capable of providing a platform from which the Olympic mega-event can be reliably broadcast to a global audience. Second, to become a 'global Olympic city', cities must bid to the IOC to become one, and thereby enter an inter-state and inter-city worldwide competition process. In this part of the section we consider some of the characteristics and problems of this particular version of the 'Olympic game', a game which has recently become highly controversial and which we return to in the discussion of Olympic movement problems later (Chapter 7).

Olympic cities as 'media cities'

The current IOC President views the relationship between the Olympics and media as follows: 'The media . . . are an integral part of the Olympic Movement and in every sense are a member of the Olympic family'.[34] The 'family' has been reproducing at a rapid rate in recent times, as can be seen in the growth of media personnel at successive Olympic Games since Los Angeles in 1984 (Table 5.2).

In the contemporary period, the connections between the Olympic mega-event and global culture, via the mediatisation and broadcasting of the Games as a 'global event', are evident enough. Equally evidently they carry important implications for the host city and host nation and for the imperatives which face them to provide the technological base appropriate to the scale of the task. The pace of technological advance in the information and telecommunications industries is rapid and thus the four-year Olympic cycle means that every city staging the event in the contemporary period has to face new challenges and use a new set of technologies each time. Researchers on contemporary Olympics point to the special and consequential character of the implications of tackling and solving

Table 5.2 Media personnel at Olympic Games: 1896–1996

Period	Year	City	Total personnel	Press personnel	TV and Radio personnel
Pre-1914	1896	Athens	12	12	0
	1900	Paris	(expo – no data)	(no data)	(no data)
	1904	St Louis	(expo – no data)	–	–
	1908	London	100	100	0
	1912	Stockholm	500	500	0
Inter-war	1920	Antwerp	200	(no data)	(no data)
	1924	Paris	(no data)	–	–
	1928	Amsterdam	614	–	–
	1932	Los Angeles	706	–	–
	1936	Berlin	1,800	–	–
Post-war	1948	London	(no data)	(no data)	(no data)
	1952	Helsinki	1,848	–	–
	1956	Melbourne	689	–	–
	1960	Rome	1,442	1,146	296
	1964	Tokyo	3,984	1,507	2,477
	1968	Mexico City	4,377	(no data)	(no data)
	1972	Munich	8,000	3,300	4,700
	1976	Montreal	8,500	(no data)	(no data)
	1980	Moscow	7,629	–	–
	1984	Los Angeles	8,200	4,000	4,200
	1988	Seoul	15,740	5,380	10,360
	1992	Barcelona	12,831	4,880	7,951
	1996	Atlanta	17,000	6,000	11,000

Sources: Spa *et al.* 1995, p. 40; Georgiadis 1996; Verdier 1996; ACOG 1997.

these problems when they refer to Olympic cities, by virtue of their preparation for the event, 'entering the Information Age' or becoming 'world cities'.[35]

In the case of the Barcelona and Seoul Olympics, at least as we will see in a moment, the Olympic event required the creation of the first stages of a new 'wired city' a new system of information and telecommunications technology insfrastuctures (or ITC technosystem) appropriate for the 'Information Age' and for participation in global society, particularly the global economy. This technosystem consists of microwave masts and towers, satellite communications centres, optic fibre underground cable systems, etc. The system is of great importance for the future economy of the city in areas like media and financial services (and beyond) and its linkage into the international economy. We can briefly illustrate these points in relation to the Olympic Games of Seoul 1988 and Barcelona 1992.

The Seoul 1988 Olympic media city[36]

The Seoul Olympics provides an example both of the technological transformation of the capital city, Seoul, into a 'media city' and also the nation more generally. The South Korean government, and the USA-educated military-bureaucratic-corporate 'establishment' elite at its heart, used the staging of the Olympic Games in the national capital Seoul instrumentally to achieve a number of nationalistic

political, economic and cultural goals. The gaining of international recognition as
a technologically modernised society was an important element among these goals.
Economically and technologically the elite used the Games event to qualitatively
develop the nation's (or at least the government's and big South Korean corporations') telecommunications infrastructures. The national development strategy
involved the promotion of telecoms-related industries both for domestic economic
purposes, and for the promotion of its electronics and technology exports and
generally to enhance its linkage into the global economy. A new satellite television
earth station at Poun was constructed for the event and also as part of this longer-
term national technology strategy. However, the peak demands on the system
during the event at times overloaded even the major additional capacity this
station provided.

The International Broadcast Centre (IBC) constructed for the Games was a
large-scale facility, located in Seoul city centre and designed for post-event use by
the national broadcaster KBS. The IBC represented Korea's first full-scale operational integration of computer systems and communication systems. A second-
order sport mega-event, the Asian Games, was used in 1986 to rehearse and
'reality-test' many of the new telecoms systems used in the Olympic Games. Larson
and Park argue that South Korea used the Olympic event 'to enter the Information
Age'. They suggest that the event 'gave impetus to the development of several
broadcast-specific technologies' produced by new Korean electronic industries,
which in turn can be shown to have fuelled the growth of Korean electronics
exports. This industry now represents the country's leading export industry,having
been developed in the 1980s in preparation for the Olympic event and overtaking
the previous leading export sector, textiles, in 1988 the year of the Games (Larson
and Park 1993: 145). They observe that 'Analysts have attributed such growth to
publicity associated with the Olympics and the promotion of technological growth
in electronics and telecommunications necessitated by the Olympics' (ibid. p. 145).

The Barcelona 1992 Olympic media city[37]

In their study of the Barcelona 1992 Olympics as a media event, Spa *et al.* comment
that: 'No event in the world is capable of generating such an effective information
and organizational system as found by international media upon arrival in an
Olympic city.' (Spa *et al.* 1995: 38). The numbers of media personnel in the
Olympic 'media city' typically outnumber the athletes at the event. At Barcelona
there were nearly 5,000 press personnel and nearly 8,000 TV/radio personnel.
Media personnel were accommodated in three Olympic villages, and facilities for
them were provided at the thirty-eight sports competition sites around the city.
The two major large-scale facilities for them consisted of the Main Press Center
(MPC) and the International Broadcasting Center (IBC), both of which were
located centrally in the 1929 expo area of Montjuic. Spa *et al.* comment that for
the duration of the Games, these complexes constituted 'a self-contained media
"world" only necessary to leave for sleep . . . since every sport event could be
viewed from the premises' (ibid.).

The MPC provided facilites for the text/photo-based media and the IPC provided facilities for the radio and TV broadcast media. To indicate the pace of
technological development and also the growth of demand, the MPC space

requirements at Barcelona were two and a half times greater than for the equivalent complex at the Los Angeles Olympics of 1984 and over half times greater than the equivalent at the Seoul Games four years earlier. Both complexes involved high-security access and continuous 24–hour operation. The MPC housed, among other things, a telecommunications centre, video library, TV monitors for all thirty-eight sport installations, sports results and news services and facilities, press rooms for interviews and press conferences (650 held during two weeks of event), and photo transmission systems. The IBC contained live studios, editing and post-production facilities for the main home broadcaster, RTO, and all rights-holding broadcasters, particularly the principal US, European and Japanese stakeholding media organisation (NBC, the EBU and NHK respectively).

The complexity of Barcelona's 'Olympic communication system' can be indicated by the fact that development work on it proceeded on five main fronts, namely signal development (picture, sound, text, data, etc.); media installations in the Olympic zones (the thirty-eight competition areas, the Olympic village); the acquisition and distribution of hardware (computer networks, terminals, printers, etc., mostly from IBM); user group communications systems and services (for athletes, journalists, police, spectators, VIPs, etc.); categories of information (transport, medical services, accreditation, accommodation, results, etc.). Determination of these five dimensions informed decision-making about the nature of the communications network (wide band, optical fibre, security circuits, etc.) and the communications infrastructure (communications towers, satellite link stations, etc.). IBM supplied most of the 'Olympic communications system's' computing requirements, and the Spanish telecoms state monopoly (Telefonica) supplied the city's telecoms network and infrastructures.

As noted earlier, two new telecommunication towers were constructed at Tibidabo on the hills overlooking the city, and at Montjuic, the latter being near to both the main Olympic stadium and the facilities housing the MPC and IBC. Microwave links in the city were thus both massively quantitatively extended and qualitatively improved. Also, optic fibre cable systems were also introduced into Barcelona for the first time in the form of a circuit linking all of the competition sites around the city. New teleports (satellite communications and broadcast centres) were created together with a new digital telephony centre in the Olympic village. Barcelona's 'Olympic media city' inevitably displayed many technological improvements over the Seoul version of the 'Olympic media city'. Nonetheless, it still did not represent a completely integrated and digitally-based information and telecommunications system. For instance, among other things, it used, as Seoul had done, a pragmatic mixture of analogue and digital television technologies rather than a fully digitally integrated approach.

The 'Olympic city bidding game': problems for the Olympic movement

This section looks at what can be called the global inter-city 'game' of bidding to become an Olympic city (see Table 5.1 above). This 'game' is conducted by the IOC. The IOC has a membership of over 100 elite individuals, who have been pointedly refered to as 'The Lords of the Rings' (Simson and Jennings 1992, Jennings 1996). This expression nicely refers not only to the the five-ring Olympic symbol and the aristocratic origins of the IOC, but also to the arrogance and decadence of some of its members. Members of the IOC need to be independently wealthy and privileged, since they contribute their time and services on an unpaid basis. They have to travel internationally on a regular basis as part of the role, and thus they expect at least their travel and accommodation expenses to be covered. They are received as quasi-diplomats around the world and, as such, expect to receive a high level of hospitality from their hosts, including, as is often the case in diplomatic circles, participating in a culture of gift-giving. They traditionally have the power to influence the decision on which city will win the right to host the Olympics. Finally, as individuals and as the IOC collectively, they can choose (and usually have chosen) to operate and exercise this power without any recognition of a need to publicly account to, and to be answerable to, anyone outside of the IOC about it. These four factors, among others, create conditions and temptations for corruption in relation to the inter-city bidding process. Increasingly, in recent years, city bid groups have assumed, reasonably as it has turned out, that they could get the support of IOC members for their bid by offering excessive expenses, or gifts, or services, or money.

In 1998/9 the IOC has attracted worldwide criticism because of revelations about the corruption and bribery which has developed in the inter-city bidding process in the 1980s and 1990s, the particular trigger for this being allegations connected with the successful bid of Salt Lake City to stage the 2002 Winter Olympics. These allegations led to an IOC inquiry in 1998/9, together with a number of other inquiries by relevant organisations.[38] The IOC's own findings and report (the Pound Report), together with the findings and reports of the other inquiries, led the IOC in 1999 to take the historically unprecedented step of expelling six of its members. In addition, at least another three resigned, a number were officially reprimanded and warned about future behaviour and some remain under investigation. The IOC produced a radical revision of their city selection process and have committed themselves to a process of major reform. We discuss these response to the problems further in the next chapter when considering a range of contemporary problems in the Olympic movement in relation to the idea and ideal of 'global citizenship'. In this section we provide the background for that later discussion.

The selection of Olympic cities is a process which requires interested NOCs, with the support of their national governments, to first organise an internal national inter-city competition to select a nationally representative candidate city. These cities then make bids to the IOC which assesses them, short-lists them and makes the final selection. Until the recent revisions in the selection procedure, the process involved much lobbying activity directed at the full IOC membership by candidate cities and governments, and a programme of visits to the cities by the IOC before the decision is made. This version of the selection process has long been criticised as being secretive, open to political influence and also open to more dubious forms of bribery and corruption.

It has been claimed that IOC members' support for particular city bids has been courted and won by various kinds of gifts by candidate cities. These charges relate in particular to the intensification of inter-city competition to be selected as host city which occurred from 1992 onwards, when the various potential economic and other benefits of performing this role had become evident and the event had become established as a global media-event. They do not apply in the same way to the preceding pre-war and early post-war periods when states' and cities' interest in the Olympics was variable and where they often had to be courted by the IOC rather than the other way around.

It is true (by definition) that most of the competitors in this global Olympic city bidding game must be losers, and it is also true that the competition can be expensive to enter. However, participation in this global inter-city game in the 1990s at least enables cities to achieve the status of being *potential* Olympic cities and thus to associate themselves with Olympic mythology and the (positive aspects of the) Olympic story. Usually, as we have seen, this, in and of itself, is understood to bring positive benefits in terms of city image, publicity and marketing. Ironically, it could be said that the traditional English/Olympic upper-class sport ethic – i.e. that 'it is not the winning but the taking part that counts' – perhaps applies most appropriately to this Olympic sport rather than in any other of the rest of the contemporary professionalised Olympic sports where, on the contrary, 'winning is everything'. In this section we first briefly review the bidding game in the early post-war period and then we consider the new situation in the 1990s and currently (see Table 5.1).

Selecting 'Olympic cities': the 1950s to 1970s

From the pre-First World War period to the mid-1920s there was a certain amount of inter-city competition to host the Olympic Games. However, this dried up in the late 1920s and 1930s, and the Second World War forced the cancellation of the 1940 and 1944 events. In 1948, the Olympic Games were staged in London, the devasted capital city of one of the 'victors'. The London event helped rescue the Olympic movement and its image from its disasterous involvement with fascism in the 1930s and early 1940s and implied that the Olympic movement could have a positive role to play in promoting internationalism and peace in the post-war reconstruction of European societies and in the world order more generally. There were no other competitor cities for the 1948 event. This situation changed in the 1950s and 1960s with many cities seeing the staging of the event as an opportunity to boost their international image and symbolise their status and modernity. The Helsinki (1952) and Rome (1960) events in particular heped to indicate that Europe was beginning to recover from the trauma of war, and the 1964 Tokyo event did so similarly for Japan.

However, in this period the event came to be used as a cultural and symbolic arena for Cold War and superpower conflict between the USA and the USSR in particular, and the costs and complexity of staging the event had begun to grow significantly. Thus the political risks (boycotts, terrorism, etc.) and the economic risks of staging the event began to rise and exert a braking effect on nations' and cities interests in bidding for it. Nonetheless, some cities persisted with bids in spite of lack of success, notably Detroit (in 1952, 1956, 1960, 1964 and 1968) and Los Angeles (see below). The late 1960s and 1970s was a bad period for the Olympic movement and its high-profile Games event. Mexico 1968 was associated with state violence and repression, Munich 1972 with terrorism and murder, Montreal 1976 with boycotts and massive debts, and Moscow 1980 with further boycotts. The net result of this was that there was effectively no competition for the staging of the 1984 Games. The only contender was Los Angeles, which had doggedly continued bidding for the event recurrently throughout the post-war period, losing the nomination for the 1952, 1956, 1976 and 1980 events.

The influence on global sport mega-event 'franchisers' – in particular the IOC but also FIFA – of sports good manufacturers, sport agents and sports marketing organisations,[39] and many other multinational corporations had been growing in the late 1970s. So too had the importance and value of sports programming to the major TV networks, particularly in the USA. The new level of the commercialisation of global sport mega-events was possibly realised first in FIFA's World Cup soccer competitions in 1978 and 1982, held in Argentina and Germany respectively.[40] It was the positive commercial result from these events, in addition to the strength of the US TV companies' interest, which helped the Los Angeles Olympic organisers to confirm that their commercialised approach was a viable one.

THE SUMMER OLYMPICS OF 1984

The bidding round for the 1984 event went on in a period of hangover from the debt-ridden 'billion dollar' Montreal Games (Auf der Maur 1976) and in the build up to the US boycott of the Moscow Games (Booker 1981). President of the IOC at the time, Lord Killanin, attempted unsuccessfully to drum up interest in the 1984 event from other cities (Killanin 1983). The Los Angeles organising committee (LAOOC), on its side, had failed to convince the citizens and public sector in the city to support the bid. So they promoted it as an independent bid which would have to involve commercial sponsorship and television company income on a major scale, or else it would simply not be viable. On this basis they were able to drive a hard bargain with the IOC and create the first substantially commercialised Olympic Games. The event turned out to be a great financial success, generating a large surplus, and this reignited interest around the international community in staging the Games.[41]

THE SUMMER OLYMPICS OF 1988

The competition for the 1988 event was decided in 1980, in the immediate hangover from the Moscow games, by the incoming IOC President Juan Samaranch. The choice was limited to a decision between the two Asian cities of Seoul and Nagano. The authoritarian anti-communist government of South Korea, with its strong US connections, lobbied the IOC more effectively and controversially, notably through the activities of its bid leader, ex-South Korean CIA man Kim Un Yong, than did Japan, and won the decision. Kim Un Yong subsequently rose through the ranks of the Olympic movement, being considered at one time to be in line for the presidency. However, in 1999 he was officially warned by the IOC in relation to corruption in relation to the Salt Lake Olympic Committee (SLOC) bid and its problems, and he remains under investigation by the FBI in respect of this case.[42]

The new bidding game: the 1980s and 1990s

THE 1992 SUMMER OLYMPICS AND THE 1992 AND 1994 WINTER OLYMPICS

The first opportunity to win the right to host an Olympic Games after the success of Los Angeles in 1984 was in the bidding round for the 1992 event. This got under way in the early 1980s and was decided in 1986 at an IOC meeting in Lausanne.

The competition was between Amsterdam, Barcelona, Belgrade, Birmingham, Brisbane and Paris. Paris, which had staged the event in 1900 and 1924, and Barcelona, which had formally bid for the event in 1924 and 1936, were acknowledged to be the front runners.

Unprecedented sums were spent by most of the bidding cities on promoting their case to the IOC. For instance, Birmingham spent £2.5 million ($4 million) and Barcelona spent £4.5 million ($7 million). Amsterdam is claimed to have lavished hospitality and gifts on various IOC members (including, it is alleged, the then head of FIFA, Joao Havelange). This increased the possibilities for candidate cities to attempt to outbid each other in 'buying' the votes of IOC members by means of gifts, hospitality and travel. The ex-British Sport Minister, Dennis Howell, who led the Birmingham bid, warned the IOC President 'about the cost of all this campaigning'. His obervation – 'Nothing like it had been seen before in the history of the Olympic movement. It is to be hoped that nothing like it will ever be seen again' – turned out to be optimistic.[43] The costs of bids for both the Summer and Winter Games has escalated further since the mid-1980s. New rules and policies were brought in by the IOC to control these problems periodically throughout the 1990s. These rules included the introduction of an $150 limit on the value of gifts which could be accepted by IOC members from potential host city bid groups. However, as is now evident, these rules were routinely ignored, remained unenforced and thus were rendered largely ineffective.

Ultimately, it is more likely that politics rather than economics was the influential factor in the selection of the host city for the 1992 Summer Olympics. This also goes for the selection of the venue for the 1992 Winter Olympics, which was decided at the same IOC meeting. France proposed Paris for the summer event and Albertville for the winter event. The summer event went to Barcelona, which was, not unconnectedly, the city favoured by the Catalan President of the IOC. Britain was compensated with the award of a meeting of the IOC in Birmingham in 1991. France was compensated with the award of the winter event and a major IOC conference in 1994. Swedish and American groups leading competitive bids for the winter event complained strongly about the political character of the decison in favour of Albertville (Jennings 1996, ch. 11).

In this period, the IOC moved the Winter Games cycle to the mid-cyle of the Summer Games, so that an Olympic event of one type or the other would occur every two years rather than every four years as previously. This was partly in order to generate a more continuous public profile for the Olympic movement and its events, and it was obviously also aimed at generating even more television interest and income. The next Winter Games would thus run in 1994. Lillehammer won the nomination and were alleged to have used very generous payments for IOC members' and their relatives' travel and services to help do so.[44]

THE SUMMER OLYMPICS OF 1996

The host city for the 1996 Olympic Games was decided in a bidding process which ran from 1988 to 1990. Since Athens in 1886 had inaugurated the modern Olympic event, it was assumed, not least by the Greek bid team, that Athens was the front-runner for the nomination. The other cities in the competition were Atlanta, Toronto, Manchester, Melbourne and Tokyo.

There have been some allegations of bribery in relation to the bidding process for the 1996 Games, but if there was it does not match with what was to follow in relation to bids for subsequent events. The Toronto team arranged for the employment of the husband of a Finnish IOC member (Mackay 1999A-P). Also, an Athenian businessman who was allegedly connected with the Greek bid team, attempted to buy the vote of an Australian IOC member with expensive gifts of jewelry for him and his wife (Mackay 1999J-P). Los Angeles had already possessed a sophisticated media infrastructure in 1984, and Seoul had created one specially for their event in 1988. However, Athens did not possess either the transport or the communications infrastructures necessary to stage a global sport event in the late twentieth century. Moreover, their bid team did not seem to appreciate the scale of these deficiencies or demonstrate the urgency that would be needed to resolve the problem. The complacency and lack of professionalism of the Greek bid made it unacceptable, a situation which was remedied in Athens' subsequent successful bid for the 2004 Olympics.

Whether Atlanta, which was eventually selected as the host for 1996, was indeed the 'best of the rest', given the strong and credible competition from Manchester and other cities, is debatable. Atlanta's bid might have appeared to have had advanced and credible plans for provision of the stadia and the transport and communications systems. However, ironically, as it turned out, there were problems with the latter two systems during the staging of the event which threatened to seriously undermine both the organisation of the event and the image of the city. However, what was undoubtedly in Atlanta's favour when the IOC took their decision was that the city was located in the USA, the most important and financially valuable TV environment in the world. Also the fact that the city was the headquarters of one of the Olympic movement's longest serving and biggest commercial sponsors, namely the Coca-Cola corporation, no doubt helped.

THE WINTER GAMES OF 1998

Nagano spent $10 million on its bid in 1990/91 for the Winter Olympics of 1998, a bid which was ultimately successful. The director of the bid team has acknowledged that, in spending on average $4,000 (£2,700) per IOC member on the sixty-two members who visited them, they exceeded the IOC's gifts value guidelines. Also, it is alleged that a wealthy Japanese businesman connected with the bid team contributed a subtantial sum towards the costs of setting up the IOC's $40 million Olympic Museum in Lausanne. Finally the Nagano bid team shredded their documents, including their financial documents and accounts, in 1992. This action made it extremely difficult to investigate further bribery allegations and did nothing to allay suspicions of the cultivation of a 'culture of luxury' between the IOC and city bid groups.[45]

THE SUMMER OLYMPICS OF 2000

The host city for the 2000 Summer Olympic Games was decided during a bidding competition in the 1992/3 period. The competitor cities included Beijing, Berlin, Brasilia, Istanbul, Sydney and, once again, Manchester. Beijing was assumed to be the front-runner because IOC President Juan Samaranch had for many years courted the Chinese government and the city's leadership to encourage them to submit a bid. In 1984 and 1985 he discussed this with the Chinese leader Deng Xiaoping. In 1989 he invited a Chinese government figure, He Zhenliang, to become a member of the IOC. In 1991 he presented Olympic awards to the Mayor and Deputy Mayor of Beijing. Jennings reasonably infers that it would have been unlikely that China would have risked the loss of face, as they would see it, attendant on a failed bid, if they had not be persuaded by the IOC President that he backed their bid and that their success was highly probable (Jennings 1996, ch. 16). However, the Tiannenman Square massacre in Beijing in 1989, for which the Mayor had considerable formal responsibility, the general repression of the democratic and human rights movement, and the objections of the US political leaders made a decision in favour of the Chinese bid for the 2000 Olympics politically unrealistic and likely to carry damaging implications for the IOC's international image and credibility. The Sydney bid was deemed 'the best of the rest' not least on the basis of the capacity of its current and planned communications infrastructures and resources. These involved facilities and personnel from organisations controlled by global media 'baron' Rupert Murdoch. Murdoch's organisations would be part of the complex of resources which would be used to project the Games as a global media event. China absented itself from the bid round in 1996/7 for 2004, which involved Athens, Capetown, Rome, Stockholm and Buenos Aires and in which Athens was successful. It remains to be seen whether China will be willing to risk loss of face again with a bid for the 2008 or 2012 games.

Given all of this, it is also the case that the bidding process for the 2000 games involved a considerable degree of unethical or corrupt practices. The Berlin bid team for the 2000 games spent roughly $45million (86 million DM or £30million) on their bid. Besides being unsuccessful, this bid was eventually revealed to have involved attempts to corruptly influence IOC members, for which the bid leader was sacked (Jennings 1996, ch.15). It is claimed that the Beijing and Manchester bid teams attempted to influence the votes of African IOC members by providing finance for sport training and related ventures in African countries. Finally, the bid team representing the ultimately successful city, Sydney, was also claimed to have at least 'bent' the IOC's rules against bribery. The Australian Olympic Committee provided $1.2 million to support sport programmes in African countries. The night before the IOC's vote to select the host city the Sydney bid team offered an extra $70,000 to Kenyan and Uganda IOC members, to be split equally between them, ostensibly for use in their countries' sports programmes. The following day, and against many obsevers' expectations, the Sydney bid won, by two votes (Mackay 1999E-P, I-P; Harverson *et al.* 1999).

THE WINTER OLYMPICS OF 2002

The Quebec bid team estimate that they spent around $660,000 on IOC hospitality (on the basis of sixty-six IOC members visiting them at an average cost of $10,000 per head). They also allege that some IOC members asked for free access to Canadian education for their relatives. However, it was the revelations about the Salt Lake City bid in the IOC's Pound Report and in other reports, which opened up the IOC's can of worms. and triggered the 1999 crisis in the Olympic movement. The SLOC were shown to have made a systematic effort to buy IOC members votes, paying out a total of $1.2 million in bribes to at least thirteen IOC members. Understandably, Quebec authories felt aggrieved and considered seeking compensation for their expenditures by suing the IOC for knowingly conducting a corrupt and thus fradulent competition.[46] In the 1999 crisis it became clear that elements of the Olympic movement had lost touch with Olympic values and with the ethics of sport, and we consider these issues further in Chapter 7.

Conclusion

In this chapter we have seen something of the important connections, in an urban context, between expo and Olympic mega-events, on the one hand, and touristic, urban and media culture, on the other. While the main concern has been to grasp the general significance and economic impacts of mega-events for cities, we have occasionally looked at political impacts, as for instance in the case of the issues touched on in the discussions of the Seoul, Barcelona and Sydney Olympics. As was suggested earlier, mega-events typically tend to be produced and imposed by urban elites who nonetheless need to attract the support of local citizens to legitimate, attend, work on, and help pay for them. Public responses can vary from the actively hostile, as in the case of the Seoul games, to the actively disinterested as in the case of the Los Angeles games, to the largely acquiescent as in the case of the Barcelona and Sydney games.

Sometimes, as in the case of the 1972 Montreal Olympics, and, on a smaller scale, the 1991 Sheffield World Student Games, citizens are saddled with long-term responsibilities for financing large-scale public debts. On other occasions, citizens can indicate at an early stage that they do not accept the urban leaderships' plans for an event, and will not finance any debts it may incur. Lack of local public support in general, together with lack of financial interest from the local business community, was behind the collapse of plans to stage a number of post-war expos, namely those planned for Paris in 1989 (which would have celebrated the bi-centenary of the French Revolution and the centenary of the city's 'Eiffel Tower' expo), Chicago in 1993 (which would have celebrated the centenary of the city's great 'White City' World's Columbian Exposition 1893), and Budapest in 1996. Lack of public support was also relevant to the organisation of the two American Olympics held in recent times. In both the Los Angeles and Atlanta Games projects, local citizens and their Mayoral representatives, after much public debate on this issue, held back from major local public sector involvement. This implied that the events would need to be organised by a private sector based group it they were to happen at all. They were organised largely on this private sector basis, and, as it turned out, largely successfully so in both cases.

Finally, we have discussed the presence of a significant amount of corruption of the Olympic city bidding process since the late 1980s. This raises issues about the 'global citizenship' role and responsibilities of the Olympic movement as a whole, and we consider these issues further in Chapter 7. However, it also evidently raises major questions about the quality of the urban leadership involved in many of these city bid projects, whether they were winners or losers in the global inter-city bidding 'game'. In some of these cases the political impact of the pursuit of 'Olympic city' mega-event projects and dreams was to normalise and institutionalise practices of unaccountability, bribery, and the cynically instrumental abuse of power among urban leadership groups, and thus to undermine the norms and practices of local democratic political community and urban citizenship in these cities. These were not the kind of 'mega-event legacies' that the Olympic movement typically appeared to promise, or that local citizens typically expected or deserved.

6 Mega-events and media culture

Sport and the Olympics

In this chapter we consider the relationship between mega-events and the media, principally through the event-based popular cultural forms (or, more emphatically, the event-based popular cultural 'social movements') of sport in general and of the Olympic Games in particular. There are three main steps in the discussion. The first section exemplifies the 'dramatological' dimension of mega-event analysis. Here we consider some of the most influential available perspectives on the relation between the media, mega-events, and sport – in particular 'media-event' analysis, 'multi-genre' event analysis, and 'media ritual' event analysis. The second section exemplifies intermediate and longer-term 'contextual', political and political economic dimensions of mega-event analysis. Here we consider the theme of 'media sport' and its regulation, looking in particular at sport in the corporate strategy of the Murdoch media organisation in the 1980s and 1990s. We also look at the implications of the development of this strategy for cultural citizenship and policy in the UK and European sporting and regulatory contexts in the contemporary period. Finally, in the third section we discuss the particular genre of media sport, namely the Olympics as a media event which, along with World Cup soccer, attracts the biggest global TV audience of viewers in the contemporary period. In this section we look in particular at some detailed studies of the 1988 Seoul Olympics and the 1992 Barcelona Olympics as case studies in the construction of the Olympics as media sport and and as media mega-events.

Background

In this chapter the emphasis is on the relatively recent period in which televison has transformed the nature, scale and resourcing of some major sport event cycles and the Olympic mega-event genre in particular. The pre-television period is not covered and nor is the relationship between the media and the expo mega-event genre. Television provided a crucial complement to the Olympics, adding to the scale and intensity of their dramatic appeal. By comparison, the rise of television, along with the rise of mass secondary and then tertiary education in the post-war period created powerful new competition for the expo genre. Television in particular undermined the attraction of the expos' periodic summations of 'modernity' and 'progress' in science, technology and art and their promotion of touristic consumerism through its weekly flow of informational, educational and advertising programming. While still a significant major event genre in international public culture, expos no longer have the historical cultural importance that they had for pre-television generations. However, to introduce this discussion it is worth briefly recalling pre-Second World War and pre-television periods, and the fact that both expos and Olympics often had an intimate connection with new developments in mass media from the turn of the century onwards.

Expos and the media

Expos were often used as stages on which new communications technologies destined to have an impact on mass society and popular culture were launched and previewed. Some of these are indicated in Table 6.1.

Media-related technologies launched and/or popularised at expos included photography, telegraphy and telephony, film, and radio as well as television.[1] For instance, telephones were first demonstrated to a mass public at the 1876 Philadelphia (Centennial) expo while television was first demonstrated as a potential medium for mass communication at the 1934 Chicago expo and later in a more highly developed form at the 1939/40 New York expo (Rydell 1993: 93).

Table 6.1. Expos and media-related technologies: 1862–1992

Periods and year	City	Media technologies
Pre-1914 period		
1862	London	Mechanical type-seting print process (re. mass press)
1876	Philadelphia	Telephone (Bell), typewriter (Bell), telegraph (Edison)
1878	Paris	Phonograph
1889	Paris	Electric light
1893	Chicago	Electric light bulb; kinetoscope (Edison)
1900	Paris	Large screen cinematography (Lumiere)
1901	Buffalo	Wireless
1904	St Louis	Long-distance wireless telegraph, radio tube
Inter-war period		
1933	Chicago	Experimental television
1939/40	New York	Mass television
Post-war period		
1962	Seattle	Wall-size television
1967	Montreal	Lasers; split screen film technology*
1986	Vancouver	Giant film screen technology**
1992	Seville	Computer-based information and communications technologies, holograms

Sources: Wachtel 1986; Nye 1994; Harvey 1996; Gunning 1996.

Notes:　*The Disney corporation had a pavilion at the Montreal expo and contributed to this exhibition of new film technology.
　**This was the forerunner of the now popular IMAC film technology. The Futuroscope theme park (European Park of the Moving Image) at Poitiers in France which was built in the same period and opened in 1987 is based around this kind of film experience.

From the 1880s and 1890s the new technology of photography generated images of expos, among many other 'newsworthy' events, for the new mass readership press together with postcard souvenirs from these events for the new mass tourism trade.

Commenting on the late nineteenth- and early twentieth-century American expos, Warren Susman argues that:

> world's fairs were 'media events'. Indeed they may have been among the first such events to deserve that modern name. Even those who did not attend them in person came to experience them secondhand through coverage in newspapers and magazines and eventually in radio, newsreels, and other media. Photographs of fairs (it is important to note that the photograph and international expositions developed in a sense simultaneously) brought the nature and possibly the significance of these events home to a vast audience. The fact that they were 'news' represents an important chapter in the story of fairs.
>
> (Susman 1983: 4)

Comparably MacKenzie argues that:

> It has been customary to see the age of the mass media as arriving with the cinema, the wireless, and television. But before the era of electrical and electronic media, printed and visual materials became available at prices so low as to place them in almost every home. It is perhaps difficult for us, jaded by the printed word and the omnipresent electronic image, to comprehend fully the impact of these materials. There seems to have been a craving for visual representations of the world, of events, and of the great and famous, which a large number of agencies and commercial companies sought to satisfy in the period from the 1870s to the First World War.
>
> (MacKenzie 1984: 16)

MacKenzie points out that the first displays of the achievements of the new technologies of film-making to a mass public were made at travelling fairs, and the series of imperial expos in Britain in this period and in the later inter-war period used short films as vehicles of imperial propaganda.[2] Newspapers often used expos to promote themselves by creating special souvenir editions of the great event. Unlike the advent of television which undermined them, the advent of radio complemented expo events in the inter-war period. The creation of a mass national-scale radio audience in the 1920s in the USA, the UK and other Western countries, was particularly important in conveying the drama of the opening ceremonies of the inter-war series of expos – (in particular, for instance, Wembley 1924/5, Philadelphia 1926, Chicago 1933 and New York 1939) – and in various ways enhancing their role in the construction of national/public and familial/private memories and narratives.[3]

Olympics and the media

From the 1890s the Olympic movement and the amateur and professional sports movements more generally, were intimately connected with the development of various forms of the press and journalism. This ranged from the elite to the mass press, from literate text-dominated formats to visual photographic formats, from the national to the local press, from the noticeboard/record-keeping function to the event-witness function, and from the generalist press to the sport specialist press. As far as the Olympic movement goes, regarding the revival of the Olympic Games in Athens in 1896 Georgiadis reports that, at the time, 'the support by the [Greek] press was universal' (Georgiadis 1996: 12). Although at times national presses have acted as fora for debate and critique in relation to the politics of hosting expos and Olympics, more often than not they have maintained this affirmative version of the 'Greek chorus' tradition in relation to mega-events. On the other hand, they rarely went to the lengths of being so supportive of these great events as to effectively finance them, or at least not to the extent that television currently does in relation to the Olympics.

The capacity of radio to enable a mass nationwide listening audience to imagine that they are present at a dramatic and important 'live' event received an early demonstration in the USA through broadcasts of the 1932 Los Angeles Olympics. In Britain, in this period, the BBC began to build its central role in British national elite and popular culture in part through its radio broadcasting of major national sport events.[4] The radio broadcasts of other big international sport events in the 1930s, such as heavyweight championship boxing matches between the American Joe Louis and the German Max Schmelling, helped to attest to the dramatic power and international scope of the medium of radio. This involvement of the media in major sport and other cultural events was supplemented by the distribution of news films of such events within the mass market for Hollywood films which had grown up in the 1930s.

These representations of major sport events helped prepare national publics in Western countries for the media and propaganda event of the 1936 Berlin Olympics. This was the first Olympic Games to be radio broadcast 'to the world' as a 'live' event at which international audience would feel as if they were 'present' as witnesses. It attracted an unprecedented scale of coverage in the press of participating countries and it was immortalised in the visual grammar of Nazi propaganda in Leni Reifenstahl's legendary film 'Olympia'. It was also the first major sport event to be televised, albeit on an experimental basis, via a limited local cable system only available in the city of Berlin.

Embryonic elements of the television culture of the post-war period, a mass popular culture that was to impact in different ways on the mega-event genres of expos and Olympics and on their international public cultural roles, were thus already visible in the mega-events of the late 1930s. Specifically, as we have suggested, they were visible in the 1936 Berlin Olympics and the 1939 New York expo. We can now turn to consider the nature and role of mega-events, particularly sport and Olympic mega-events in the post-war television era, and particularly in the contemporary late twentieth-century period.

Mega-events, sport and the media: dramatological perspectives

In this section some important concepts and perspectives for analysing mega-events, particularly sport mega-events, in relation to the media are outlined. They exemplify what I refer to in Chapter 1 as 'dramatological' perspectives. They derive mainly from American media and cultural studies and tend to explore, in different ways, the public ritual character of such events. Elihu Katz and Daniel Dayan's sociological analysis of 'media events' in general is the seminal work in this area, and we consider it first. We then look at American cultural studies analyses of mega sport events, in particular the Olympic Games, including John MacAloon's work on the multi-genre character of the Olympic Games as a cultural event. Finally we consider Michael Real's work on the ritual and mythic character of Olympic TV.

These American 'dramatological' perspectives, in spite of the evident differences between their media studies and sport studies fields of specialisation, nonetheless share some common intellectual resources and interconnections. An important resource is the work of the ethnographer and symbolic anthropologist Victor Turner, who, among other things, developed Van Gennep's (1960) classic analysis of the nature and role of ritual in human society. In his seminal study of ritual as process (Turner 1995) and in his later work, Turner emphasised the need to understand 'anti-structural' as well as structural dimensions of human social life, the importance of experiences of 'liminality' (marginality and transition) and of 'communitas' (open intersubjective encounter) to both dimensions, and the relevance of rituals and festivals in all societies as both structural and anti-structural processes. Turner's views on the theory of ritual and other related themes is an acknowledged influence on MacAloon's work in Olympic studies and the theory of 'the spectacle', Katz and Dayan's work in media-event studies, and, to a lesser extent, Real's 'ritual analysis' perspective in media and cultural studies.[5]

Mega-events, 'media events' and sport: Elihu Katz and Daniel Dayan

Mega-events such as the Olympic Games undoubtedly qualify as examples of 'media-events'. Television organisations typically consider that this kind of event requires a special type of production treatment; beyond the ordinary genres and categories of 'news' and 'entertainment'. A wide range of types of event, in addition to the great cultural, commercial and sporting events we have referred to as mega-events, also go beyond news and entertainment, and also can be said to 'make history'. Media-event analysis is, thus, concerned with the media's 'witness-to-history' role in relation to what Katz and Dayan typify as 'coronations, contests and conquests'. Such 'history-making' events can be exemplified by, in recent times, the death and funeral of Princess Diana, and generally by such things as great state ceremonies (such as Royal Weddings, state funerals, etc.), political/diplomatic events (such as the Pope's first visit to communist Poland, President Sadat's visit to Israel, etc.), and great technological events (such as the first Moon landing).

The theoretical frame of reference media-event analysts tend to use to interpret and explain these sorts of events and their social and political effects is one heavily angled towards neo-Durkheimian sociological theory. This is particularly concerned to identify and understand the periodic reproduction of social integration and solidarity in modern societies through public events (e.g. public ceremonies, rituals and festivities, etc.), regarded forms of (secular) 'civil religiosity' and celebrations of (secular) 'sacred' values and symbols (e.g. Rothenbuhler 1988). This has undoubtedly produced some rich and interesting research into the general culture and, in particular the political culture, of contemporary media-dominated societies. However, the generally functionalist cast of this perspective is open to criticism.[6] Later, in a case study of the 1988 Seoul Olympics as a media event, we will consider the need to counterweight this functionalist emphasis by building in political and critical dimensions to the media-event analytic perspective.

A criterion for qualifying as a media event is that people in many nations feel obliged to watch and feel privileged to be able to witness the event. Typically, these events are viewed in a ceremonial (ritualistic/civil religious) frame of reference. Where appropriate this is also often a festive or celebratory attitude and viewers typically make efforts to share their viewing with other people and/or to discuss their experience of the event and its significance with other people. In other words, viewers are 'mobilised' by the event. Media researchers in this field argue that people are not 'couch potatoes' in relation to media events. Rather they are typically active in response to the event coverage and experience participation of the event in a way which would not be true for routine TV viewing.

Some key empirical characteristics of media events (Dayan and Katz 1992, 1987, 1988) are that they are broadcast live, they are usually sponsored by an agency independent of the broadcasters, they are marked with a clear beginning and ending that interrupts normal social routines, they feature heroic personalities, they are highly dramatic or richly symbolic, and they are accompanied by social norms which relate to their special character (obligatory viewing, social viewing, etc.).

It is reasonable and useful to conceptualise this type of response to a mega-event – the reponse of media viewers of the event – as a particular type of popular/citizen mobilisation. This is one in which collective ceremonial and, here, festive characteristics of the event itself are participated in by being reproduced in miniature in the ceremonial, festive and social character of home-based viewing. Evidently, mass-media viewing of an event is not the same as 'being there', and the presentational and textual structures of event programming involve what Dayan and Katz refer to as 'an aesthetics of compensation'. This 'compensates' the viewer for 'not being there' by providing them with information, visual perspectives and commentary distinct from, and in many ways richer than, that available to 'in-person' participants (Dayan and Katz 1992: 92–100). Receiving this media-re-worked event in the apparently 'private' sphere of the home effectively transforms the home, temporarily, into a 'public' or quasi-public sphere, and the occasion is used to remember and reaffirm collective values and symbols (ibid. pp.127–34).

Dayan and Katz argue that for media events to occur successfully, an informal social contract and a consensus needs to have been, in some sense, 'negotiated' among three 'partners', namely the event organisers, television elites/organisations and the viewing public (ibid. ch.3). We might add – 'at least three'. In this formulation, Dayan and Katz appear to ignore other important potential 'partners' such as the state (i.e. the host politicians, whether at the civic, or the national level, or both), and the market (i.e. the world of corporate sponsors and advertisers willing to pay to use the event as their marketing vehicle). Given that mega-event projects occasionally fail, it is worth noting, *en passant*, that understanding the nature of the social contract among media-event partners provides us also with an understanding of the conditions of failure of event projects. Katz and Dayan (in functionalist vein) suggest that we see this as media-event 'pathology', when one or other of the partners fails to deliver on the informal social contract which usually underlies and supports media events and, we can add, mega-events more generally.

Katz and Dayan's work made only brief and passing reference to mega sport events such as the Olympics. However, it has been much cited in studies of Olympic TV, in particular those we consider below in section three. Indeed, as we will see, Larson and Park's study of the 1988 Seoul Olympics uses Katz and Dayan's analysis of media events as a key point of reference even as they also argue for its limitations and for the need for an approach to the study of the Olympic movement and Olympic TV which is more developed in terms of political sociology.

Mega sport events as multi-genre events: John MacAloon

Katz and Dayan's work on media events made only passing reference to media sport, but nonetheless carried implications for the latter which, as we will discuss later, have been taken up by Olympic TV researchers. Comparably, MacAloon's work, which has focused on the history and culture of the Olympic movement, has had relatively little to say about the Games as a media event. Nonetheless it carries implications for research in this area which have been recognised and responded to in the empirical Olympic TV research we discuss later (MacAloon 1984, 1989, 1992).

As we saw earlier (Chapters 3 and 5) MacAloon's history of de Coubertin and the early stage of development of the modern Olympics in the late nineteenth century provides valuable suggestions about the origins of the ceremonial and ritual character of the Olympic Games in the traditions and practices of inter-national expos. Also, MacAloon's perspective has been usefully applied to the analysis of the 1936 Berlin Olympics (Byrne 1987). In his later work, MacAloon analyses the contemporary Olympic Games as a complex cultural form of 'perfor-mance' or 'communication' involving a mixture of four analytically distinct genres simultaneously, namely 'festival', 'ritual', 'spectacle' and 'game' (or 'play' and 'sport'). These analytic distinctions and MacAloon's analysis in general were influential on Katz and Dayan (above) in their discussion of 'media events' which can be analysed as displaying various combinations of these features (Dayan and Katz 1992: 142–5).

As we have seen, the modern Olympic Games has always been a multi-genre event displaying spectacle, ritual and festival dimensions as well as the game dimension. However, this has always been a complex and at times contradictory mixture, and the advent of the television age and of the global Olympic TV media event can be argued to have changed the balance between these dimensions. In MacAloon's view the spectacle dimension now has a priority over the other dimen-sions, and also has an ambivalent relation with them. That is, the logic of 'the spectacle' – namely that stadia spectators and TV viewers are expected to be awestruck at the scale and grandeur of such elements of the Olympics as the opening ceremony – now predominates over the Olympic meanings and values associated with other dimensions.

One the one hand, this contemporary dominance of the spectacle dimension could be said to threaten the communicative potential of these other dimensions. However, on the other hand, the Olympics as global TV spectacle could be said to construct a special cultural space in which more people than ever before are convened together to experience the Olympic meanings and values, in particular those of peace and internationalism, available in the festive, ritual and game genres. The major institution of late twentieth-century international cooperation, the UN, outside of the high-level diplomatic arena it provides for the national governments and elites of the world, has little or no capacity to provide a public culture and public space for ordinary people to participate in. Noting this, and reflecting on the tragedy played out on a global TV stage of the killings of Israeli athletes by Palestinian terrorist militants at the 1972 Munich Olympics, and on the public responses of horror and mourning in relation to it, MacAloon observes: 'I would argue that the Games have become a sort of collective divination about the fate and condition of the world' (MacAloon 1984: 280, note 71). As such, it could be said that the Olympic Games events have a quasi-religious cultural significance for the new international public they convene, which is consistent with at least the Olympic values institutionalised in the ritual and ceremonial dimension of these events.

The spectacle dimension of the Olympics in the global television age, then, according to MacAloon's analysis, might be argued to carry positive as well as negative implications for their ritual dimension. However, in his view the implications of the Olympics as TV spectacle for the festive character of the Games event are more consistently negative. His main comparative points can be summarised as follows. As a cultural genre, participation in a festival is associated with such meanings and values as equality and democracy. But the Olympic TV spectacle celebrates the inequalities and hierarchies of sport 'stars'. People's participation in a festival is fragmentary, de-centred and perspectival involving a recognition of the multiplicity of experiences and narratives that they can generate of what only appears to be a unitary event with a unitary meaning. Olympic TV addresses itself to presenting just such a unitary event, prioritising some (dominant, official) perspectives and narratives over others. The experience of participation in a festival is one of being a 'flaneur', an experience of unhurried, unfocused unprogrammed, openness to the unfolding of the event. Olympic TV operates according to a logic of programming, sequential focus and pace which is at odds with this form of experience. MacAloon seems to imply that the TV medium *per se* is not incapable of communicating the festive experience but that this requires more creativity than sports-based broadcasting organisations typically seem to be capable of in their production of the Olympics as a global media event.

Media sport events as 'ritual and mythic events': Michael Real

Michael Real's work in media studies embraces a range of interpretive and analytic perspectives and has concerned itself interestingly with the understanding of the Olympics as a global media event (Real 1989, 1995, 1996a,b,c,d, 1998). Among the various perspectives he considers the most relevant to understanding contemporary Olympic TV are those which stress, on the one hand, the importance for it of myth and ritual, and, on the other hand, those which stress its 'post-modern' and/or 'consumer cultural' character. For Real, myth is analogical reasoning and ritual is patterned behaviour. When watching Olympic TV we participate as sports fans, or as otherwise involved and concerned viewers, both by behaving in patterned ways and also in being receptive to and active interpreters of the meanings and symbols communicated in the broadcasts. He regards sport culture and sport fandom in general in contemporary Western society as providing important forms and occasions, both through live events and TV spectatorship, through which many people, particularly males, attribute meaning to their lives. Within sport culture, the Olympic movement and its cycle of great events is particularly significant in terms of the additional meanings relating to peace and internationalism it seeks to promote. These transcend the world of sport and relate broadly to important historical traditions and life-relevant values in Western culture. As such, they offer sport fans a broad and rich inspirational and interpretive context to support the rituals of their participation, whether that takes the practical form of stadium spectatorship or TV spectatorship.

The culture of the Olympic movement and thus of Olympic TV is 'modernist', ostensibly a communication and celebration of peaceful nationalism and internationalism, of rationality (rules, training, technology, etc.) and individualism, etc. However, unlike MacAloon, Real suggests that Olympic TV, in spite of its efforts to communicate these overarching narrative themes, in practice presents something closer to a 'post-modern' cultural experience, which has more in common, if not with the experience of the festive flaneur, then at least of the hedonistic consumer. This arises from a combination of the commercialisation of the Olympics and of Olympic TV programming, which necessarily involves an overloaded mixture of images and messages, and also from the fact that the modernist themes can only be represented in a fragmented and superficial way through the 'information overloaded' coverage of the main ceremonies and the sporting action. As with MacAloon, in spite of his critical assessment of the current state of play and trends in Olympic TV, Real nonetheless implies that the situation while critical might be retrievable. As we noted earlier, MacAloon believes that the dominance of the spectacle and their associated ritualistic dimensions in Olympic TV can in principle be rebalanced by a more creative approach to the festive dimension. Comparably, Real implies that the current effectively post-modern fragmentation of modernist Olympic meanings and values in Olympic TV can be countered through a renewal of these intellectual justifications and rationales in ways appropriate to the contemporary period. From these dramatological perspectives we now need to consider more contextual political economic themes and issues in the analysis of media sport and mega-events.

Media sport: political economic and 'regulation' themes and issues

Background

Sport and popular culture in modernity

Marx's legendary dictum that religion is 'the opium of the people'[7] needs to be modified to apply to the ostensibly non-religious culture of late twentieth-century society. In this culture the mass of people claim to be disinterested in religion, but they also have virtually open access to the 'opium' of a vast range of mood-altering legal and illegal drugs. In this context, perhaps it is more appropriate to observe that 'sport is the religion of the people'. That is to say, it provides apparently secular, but (from a sociological perspective) quasi-religious experiences such as those of sacredness and transcendence, communal ritual and symbolism, and collective drama and emotionality. Sport is an important sector of popular culture in modern societies both as a quasi-religious institution and also as an industry. Particularly in its professional, spectatorial and media-sport forms, it provides one of the few significant arenas where collective identities, from the local to the national, can be publicly symbolised and emotionally expressed (Roche 1998). Sports calendars and cycles of controlled contests provide rich experiences and forms of participation for mass audiences. Major sport events have compelling dramatic, ceremonial and festive dimensions both as 'live events' in the cathedral-like structures of modern stadia and also as 'media-events', that is as a distinct, compelling and commercially important genre of television programming (Roche and Arundel 1998).

Modern sport has been increasingly globalised since the late nineteenth century, a process driven by, among other factors, the ideological agendas of European empires (Guttman 1994), the internationalist mission and values of the Olympic movement (Hoberman 1995; Houlihan 1994), the globalisation of consumer markets and the global reach of television.[8] However, it is worth noting, even allowing for the powerful influence of American commercial and media-sport models, that modern sport has a special relationship with Europe's cultures and identities. The cultural institutions of modern sport in most of its forms were largely created in Europe. This was most notably the case in nineteenth-century England where many modern games and the ideology of 'amateurism' were created, and also in late nineteenth- and early twentieth-century France where the Olympic movement and the international dimension of many sports was cultivated. The development of international sport in the late nineteenth and early twentieth centuries, as we have seen in Part 1, evidently provided a potent focus for the cultural mobilisation of the new urban middle classes and industrial working classes around the idea of nationalism and national identity. However, it also helped construct elements of a popular international awareness and helped give some form to ordinary people's conceptions of and interests in the social world beyond the nation-state.[9] In spite of the development of European-level governing bodies and sports industry markets and corporations, the development of the European Union in the late twentieth century has carried few implications for sport culture and media sport (Roche 1999b). However, recently this has begun to change and the EU is now a strategically important transnational public sphere and regulatory agency in relation to European sport culture and media sport as we discuss later.

Media sport and cultural globalisation

'Media sport' as a cultural form, and 'television sport' as a particular TV programming genre,[10] have long been seen as important to the construction of national cultural identity,[11] and thus as requiring full access by national publics. This access has traditionally been provided, in America and Europe in the post-war period, through different mixes of commercial and state-based broadcasting. The importance of the TV sport genre to the health, indeed the very survival of commercial TV networks has been particularly clear in the USA. Since the 1960s the competition between the big three networks for the TV rights to sport events seen as of national significance, such as major league baseball, American football and the

Olympic Games, has been increasingly intense over the years. It has been less well appreciated in European countries with state-based TV stations, such as the BBC in Britain, which have traditionally had relatively inexpensive and uncontested access to the broadcasting of such sports and events, and also where public access to 'key' sport events via TV may also have been protected in law.

With the advent of satellite and cable TV in Europe in the 1980s and with the simultaneous weakening of the previously central role of state-based broadcasting, there has been a greater recognition of the importance of TV sport. On the one hand, commercial TV recognises the capacity of media sport to 'capture' massive and/or committed audiences with class and consumption profiles attractive to advertisers and sponsors. On the other hand, public service TV recognises the capacity of media sport to provide opportunities for cultural inclusion and for bringing national and international publics together in the sharing of calendars of common events, and of sharable experiences in a common (mediated) space and time (Whannel 1992; Scannell 1996) – a common and recurrent national and international public culture in an increasingly fragmented and changing world (Roche and Arundel 1998).

State-based and commercially-based versions of wide-access terrestrial 'free to view' TV were competitive with each other, but they could also be compatible. They could even be complementary, in terms of sharing the broadcasting of a given year's major sport events. However, the advent of satellite and cable TV systems in the 1980s and their market penetration and growth in the 1990s has begun to shift the balance decisively and inexorably in favour of commercial television. This has raised major regulatory problems in relation to public access for all forms of programming, but in particular for sport TV.

These systems, and the further technological development they promise through digitalisation in the early twenty-first century, have enabled, and will increasingly enable, commercial TV to make profits by processes of 'intensification' of products and markets in ways notably different from, and additional to, the processes of 'extensification' involved in traditional 'broadcasting' to a wide audience. The process of extending mass market penetration in the British and European market, of course, continues in parallel with intensification, as satellite TV in particular attempts to use its buying power to control exclusive rights to attractive major sport events in order to sell receiver dishes. However, in the new generation of digitalised systems, profitability is made viable, to a greater extent than ever before, by attracting special-interest audiences. These audiences are willing to pay for access to channels specialising in intensive single-genre programming (pay-TV), and indeed are willing to go further and to pay extra fees, in addition, for one-off events, so-called 'pay-per-view' (PPV).

It is estimated that there is a very strong latent demand for PPV in Britain and Europe more generally. In Britain this latent demand is roughly estimated to be in the range of an extra $0.75 billion to $3.75 billion (£0.5 billion to £2.5 billion) annually in potential consumer expenditure across all programming genres, but particularly on sport programming.[12] In Europe generally it is estimated to be of the order of $40 billion by the year 2005 (Short 1997-P). To feed the bottomless programming needs of these systems, and in order to reap the profits that are available through both extension and also intensification processes, TV companies have risked taking on heavy debt exposure in order buy up exclusive rights to the transmission of many key national- and world-level sport events, because of their strategic importance and profitability Rowe 1996, 1999). This can be most clearly seen in recent years in the case of Rupert Murdoch's media companies' use of national and international spectator sport in their drive to dominate national and international media markets. We can now consider this case in a little more detail, both in general and also in terms of its implications for the European media-sport 'space', and the embryonic popular cultural rights to 'TV sport for all' within this space.

Media sport and media moguls: Rupert Murdoch

Media sport and media corporate strategy

Rupert Murdoch has always seen media sport as a key element in his corporate strategies and increasingly so in recent years as his companies have begun to create an international media network with truly global reach. For him they have always been a leading programming genre, along with films and live news. These three genres, with media sport prominent among them, are of great value to Murdoch in his efforts to enter and dominate national, international and global press and TV markets. Media sport in particular allows him to create profitable new synergies within his media complex between his press and TV companies, and more broadly between his media companies in general on the one hand, and the wider global corporate market place of advertising and sport sponsorship, on the other. In his own words, Murdoch uses sport as a 'battering ram' to break into new markets and promote his television companies.[13]

Murdoch's sport-led corporate strategies have been evident over a number of decades in his various media operations around the world – since the 1970s in Australia and Britain, since the 1980s in the USA, and in the 1990s in continental Europe and Asia. Within Murdoch's complex global network of press, TV and other types of media companies, his specifically television-oriented companies and interests, which have been most involved in developing his media sports-led global corporate strategy, include the following: Fox TV in the USA (including The Fox-Liberty local networks), Star TV in Asia, Phoenix TV in China, Channel 7 in Australia, the Vox and Kirsch media companies in Germany (in which he has stakes), and BSkyB in Britain and Europe.

Murdoch has had considerable success, particularly in the 1990s, in buying up many significant sports and sport events for his companies around the world (Barnett 1996-P) (see Table 6.2). The 'Murdoch – global media mogul' story began in Australia, and media sport was always an important part of it. Murdoch inherited from his father not only considerable holdings in the press of his native country, Australia, but also a talented, obsessive and restless interest in building and controlling media organisations (Shawcross 1993). He built energetically on the basis of his inheritance in the 1960s and 1970s to establish a powerful position in the Australian media, both press and TV, and sport was an important vehicle for him in this project. A measure of this position is the influence he had established on Australian media sport by the 1990s. For example, his Channel 7 is the home/ Australian broadcaster for the Sydney 2000 Olympics, and also for the Summer and Winter Olympic Games to be held in the 2002 to 2008 period. In addition he controls Australian TV rights for Australian-rules football, the Australian Open tournaments in golf and in tennis, and much of rugby league and rugby union, including the latter's 1999 World Cup. For the TV rights to the two rugby codes he paid $550 million in 1996 (Usborne 1997-P). We can now briefly review the broader international achievements of Murdoch's media sport-based strategies (that is, de facto, his sport event and mega-event strategies) in the key 'global regions' of the USA and Europe. Some key aspects of his media-sport 'empire' in the 1992–8 period are summarised in Table 6.2.

Table 6.2 A global media-sport empire: Rupert Murdoch 1992–1998

Mations and world regions	TV companies controlled	Type of sport influenced	Media-sport ownerships
UK and Europe	BSkyB	Soccer	English Premier League 1992–2001
		Rugby Union	England's home games The World Cup (1995, 1999)
		Rugby League	British + European League
		Test Cricket	The World Cup
		Golf	Ryder Cup (Europe v. USA)
USA	Fox TV (+ Fox-Liberty local networks)	American Football	NFL (50%) AFL (100%) The Super-Bowl
		Baseball	Major League (80%) The World Series (alternate years) The LA Dodgers
		Basketball	NBA (80%) NY Knicks (20%) LA Lakers (10%) Lakers' stadium (100%)
		Ice Hockey	NHL (100%) NY Rangers (20%)
		Various	Madison Square Gardens (20%)
Australia and other areas	Channel 7 TV (Australia) Star TV (Asia) Phoenix TV (China)	Olympic Games Rugby Union Rugby League Australian Football Tennis Golf	2000 to 2008 Australian RU Australian RL Australian league Australian Open Australian Open

Sources: Herman and McChesney 1997, ch. 3; McChesney 1998; Smith 1997-P; Usborne 1997–P; Cornwell 1998-P; Davison 1998-P; Tran 1998-P.

Murdoch and media sport in the USA[14]

Throughout the post-war period the USA has always contained the biggest, most technologically advanced and most potentially profitable media markets and media-sport markets in the world, and it continues to do so currently (Auletta 1997), in spite of increasing competition from the European nations grouped together in the European Union (Tunstall and Palmer 1991). Following his establishment of a foothold in the American media market in 1977 with his purchase of the *New York Post*, Murdoch energetically expanded his US media interests including the acquisition of the film-maker Twentieth Century Fox and the creation of the Fox TV network in 1985. By 1998 Fox TV transmitted his Fox News service and Fox Sport programming to 62 million US homes (and by definition, given multi-person households, to many more millions of US viewers).[15] Throughout this period he engaged in a relentless series of battles with the three major TV networks and some of the cable TV companies over control of the TV rights to US sport. In this war Murdoch has been prepared to take risks and also to drive up the price of US TV sports rights to unprecedented and even loss-making levels in order to drive his competitors out of the market. Murdoch is prepared to absorb high levels of relatively short-term losses (for instance $100 million per year on his American football TV rights) in order to promote the long-term strategic position and value of his companies.

Although the major networks won control of the US rights to the 1992, 1996 and 2000 Olympics, nonetheless in forfeiting these battles by 1998 Murdoch seemed to be well on his way to winning the war. By this time he had built up a formidable position of control of the TV rights for most of the prime quality American professional sports, and their leagues and competitions. This long-term strategy is currently continuing to roll out. However, by 1998 Murdoch had achieved the following position in US media sport. Fox TV controls most of the TV rights for NBA basketball (deals with 17 National Basketball Association clubs), NHL ice hockey (deals with 12 National Hockey League clubs), Major League baseball (deals with 22 clubs) and NFL and AFL American football (a deal for 50 per cent of National Football League and a deal for 100 per cent of the American Football League TV coverage). In addition, in terms of US sporting mega-events Murdoch has control of the TV rights, for alternate seasons, to the baseball World Series and to America's biggest and most lucrative media-sport TV event, the American football SuperBowl. In relation to the latter he acquired an interest in it for the 1995–9 period when he acquired a 50 per cent stake in one of the two major American football leagues, the NFL for a £1billion in 1995. In 1997 he consolidated his position in relation to the Superbowl and US TV sport in general with a huge competition-killing (even if tactical loss-making) $17.6 billion deal for the control of the TV rights to AFL American football events for the period 1998–2004.

In addition, Murdoch aims to control some of the most identifiable, attractive and televisualisable US sports teams, particularly those based in New York and Los Angeles, more directly either by buying them up and/or by buying up the stadia in which they play. On the West coast in 1997/8 Murdoch bought the legendary LA (ex-New York) Dodgers baseball club for $311 million (£168 million). The strategic significance of this move in relation to Murdoch's global operation as well as his

US operation is indicated in the fact that US baseball and the LA Dodgers in particular have strong followings in Latin America and Japan. In 1998 Murdoch was reported to have plans to build a new stadium for the Dodgers and, cashing in on 'brand recognition' and 'brand loyalty', to develop a Dodgers AFL American football club. In addition, he was reported to be planning a $150 million investment in East coast basketball through buying 10 per cent of the NBA's LA Lakers and buying control of the club's arena. On the East coast Fox TV controls 20 per cent of the legendary New York sport venue, Madison Square Garden. Besides giving Murdoch access to major boxing and other such events, this also gives him 20 per cent control of two of America's leading basketball and ice hockey clubs, namely the NBA's New York Knicks and the NHL's New York Rangers.

Murdoch and media sport in Britain and Europe

Murdoch has a long-proven ability to read and play media-cultural markets, and to take risks in order to dominate them (Shawcross 1993; Horsman 1997). Currently, for instance, the revolutionary new digital generation of massive capacity multi-channel and interactive TV systems, in both satellite and terrestrial versions, is being introduced in Britain and more broadly in Europe. The British terrestrial version of digital TV, in which Murdoch has a presence, began running 30 channels from 1999 while Murdoch's own satellite version of digital TV began running 200 channels to Britain and Europe in the same year. This in turn will provide for a much greater development of PPV in sport than already exists, for instance through single club-based channels, and also in other TV programme areas.

All of this being said, since it began operation in 1988, and particularly as it has grown in the 1990s, Sky has been enormously successful in buying up the rights to key British sporting events as well as international events of keen interest to the British sports fans. It has thus begun to exercise a major and growing influence on the nature and future of British sport. Sky controls the British rights for golf's 'world cup' (i.e. the USA v. Europe Ryder Cup competition), cricket's World Cup, rugby union's 1995 World Cup together with other rugby union and rugby league events which we will come to in a moment. In addition, although Sky may have had limited access to the 1998 soccer World Cup in France, it bought sole rights to the four-nation 'warm-up' tournament in France in 1997 involving the 1994 World Cup finalists Brazil and Italy (together with England and France). As far as future soccer World Cups go, Sky's part-owned German partner (Kirsch) has bought the rights to European transmission of the 2002 and 2006 World Cups and may be able to transmit them to Britain via Sky, possibly by-passing British media regulation and side-lining British terrestrial broadcasters.

The 'jewel in the crown' for Sky's British media-sport strategy has been the acquisition of TV rights to Premier League soccer, which in turn, for good or ill, has effectively revolutionised the professional soccer game in Britain. Since 1992 and the formation of the British Premier League (PL), Sky has paid unprecedented amounts (around $1.5 billion or £1 billion in total, i.e. £304 million 1992–7, and £640 million 1997–2001) for exclusive rights to live TV transmission of PL games, with the BBC restricted to subsidiary rights to highlights. This has both directly and indirectly (through sponsorship and other commercial spin-offs) produced unprecedented income flows into the top forty to fifty British soccer clubs, leading to the creation of new stadia, the acquisition of large numbers of foreign 'star' players, and the flotation of clubs as investment-worthy businesses on the London stock exchange. The global transmission of PL teams and their games through Murdoch's various TV operations, particularly in European and Asia, has led to the development of strong international 'brand' identities, public interest and even fan loyalties, for clubs such as Manchester United, and consequently for the merchandising operations and general profitability of individual clubs as multinational corporations in their own right.[16]

However, it may be that in promoting English PL soccer as a nationally-based but internationally popular media-sport phenomenon, Murdoch has opened up a Pandora's Box and created dynamics in the fields of popular culture and of the industries which serve it, which will be difficult to contain or to control in the future. Two 'Pandora's Box' possibilities are relevant to consider here. The first possibility is that in the new multi-channel television environment created by the digital revolution powerful soccer clubs will set up their own pay-per-view channels addressed to their national and international fans.[17] This would drain the advertising income pool from which Sky TV currently draws its funds to finance its control of Premiership soccer. In 1999 the UK's Restrictive Practices court affirmed the right of the Premier League to act collectively on behalf of its constituent clubs as it had previously done in securing its deals with Sky. However whether in future the major English clubs continue to be willing to give away all, or even part, of their ownership of the rights to broadcast their games to the Premier League to deal with on their behalf is doubtful and remains to be seen. The underlying and continuing potential for fragmentation of the UK's professional football media-sport market in the digital era caused Murdoch considerable anxiety. His response to this possibility was predictable given his track record in the USA. It was was to seek to buy a direct controlling interest in the Premiership's leading soccer club.

In 1998 Murdoch's BSkyB corporation announced a sensational and immediately controversial bid to buy Manchester United, Britain's leading soccer club, one of the leading clubs in Europe and probably the most commercially successful and internationally recognised sports club, and thus sports 'brand' name, in the world. The huge price he offered was £623 million ($1 biilion) which was, according to some estimates at the time, roughly equivalent to the market value of BSkyB itself. Vigorous objections were made to this bid locally and nationally by the club's many fans, and nationally by the non-Murdoch media and politicians including many involved in the New Labour government (176 MPs, including 131 Labour MPs). A successful purchase of the club would allow Murdoch to effectively sit on both sides of the table simultaneously in future negotiations over broadcast rights between Sky and the club and between Sky and the Premier League. This kind of issue was new to the British media-sport market, although it was familiar and not regarded as particularly problematic in American and other European media-sport markets. Because of its controversial character, the bid was refered to the relevant British competition authorities, initially the Office of Fair Trading (OFT) and subsequently the Competition Commission (previously the Monopolies and Mergers Commission (MMC)) for assessment. In 1999 the Commission recommended to the government that the bid should be rejected. The government was not bound to accept this recommendation, and there were political reasons (including currying favour with

Murdoch's politically influential mass tabloid newspaper *The Sun*) why it might have been tempted to not do so. However, it accepted the advice and blocked the deal.[18]

The second 'Pandora's Box' possibility is that some of the newly commercially empowered and newly internationally oriented leading English Premier League soccer clubs attempt to gain a bigger stage and a higher profile by joining with clubs of comparable status in the comparable national leagues of other European countries to create a new European 'super league'. The emergence of a such a trans-national league, probably with involvement of the European soccer governing body, UEFA, would obviously represent a threat to the standing and power of existing national leagues including the English Premier League, and thus might involve costs to the Murdoch organisation. However, on the other hand, new commercial opportunities are likely to be associated with a European super league, particularly in the new multi-channel digital television environment which is currently being created with its potential to expand and exploit the market for 'pay-per-view' (PPV). Given this, it is not surprising, notwithstanding his control of the TV rights to the English Premier League, that Murdoch's media operation has been involved in a consortium (called 'Media Partners') with German, Italian and other media corporations. This consortium aims to promote the concept of a European super league, even though the achievement of this would have profound and almost cetainly negative consequences for the Premier League and other comparable nationally-based soccer leagues in Europe.[19]

In 1998 this commercial pressure, coming in part from the leading European clubs and in part from multinational media companies, pushed UEFA towards an expansion of its European competion for national league champions and other high-placed teams. It also pushed them create bigger deals with Europe's TV companies in order to offer Europes' leading clubs bigger financial incentives for them to continue to participate in UEFA's competitions as against those planned by the 'Media Partners' group. However these developments work out for the status and influence of UEFA, they would appear to be the first of what is likely to be a series of steps on the road towards the consolidation of a Europe-wide soccer super league in the early twenty-first century. As such this development holds out the possibility of more integration in the field of European popular culture and greater popular identification with some concept of 'Europe' than the European Union has been able to achieve through its various initiatives in 'cultural policy' over nearly two generations (Roche 1999b).

This brief review of contemporary media sport has indicated something of the strategic commitment to the acquisition of major sports and sport event programming, both in general and also in the nationally and internationally important case of soccer, on the part of international media organisations, particularly those controlled by Rupert Murdoch. However, the media-sport 'industry', newly energised by the forces of globalisation and digitalisation, does not exist in a political vacuum. Some regulatory constraints on media sport exist in the UK and in other European nations which may possibly form foci for public debate both at the national and the EU levels. Such public debate may result in political and legal action at least to channel, if not more substantially control, the currently turbulent dynamic of sport organisations and media-sport corporations to reconstruct important sectors of public culture in the medium term in Europe. We now need to consider relevant aspects of the current regulatory environment in a little more detail.

Media sport: issues of regulation and cultural citizenship

In a European context, at least in principle, there appear to be constraints on the room for manouevre, in relation to British and European sport, of media organisations such as those of Rupert Murdoch deriving from media regulation and media policy. These constraints include the UK's 'listed events' legislation which requires key national- and international-level sport events deemed to be of national significance to be available on a free and widely available basis in the UK via traditional terrestrial broadcasters such as the BBC or ITV. There are versions of this kind of 'listed events' protection in other European countries' media legislation (Short 1997-P). 'Listed events' legislation could be said to be a media version of 'sport for all' policy, i.e. 'TV sport spectatorship for all' – a version of the cultural rights of national citizenship. In Britain the number of these listed events protected for 'free-to-view' TV was increased by the New Labour government in 1998. Some other European countries have similar media regulations, and currently there is some prospect of this kind of legislation being supported and complemented by EU-level media legislation. We first consider media-sport regulation at the British national level before turning to the EU level.

British media-sport regulation

In the UK the system of broadcasting regulation which has developed since the 1950s includes, as a part of its numerous provisions, the maintenance of mass public access to the viewing of a small set or 'list' of major sport events which are reserved for the major 'free-to-air' terrestrial TV networks (principally ITV and the BBC). A 'listed event' is defined as 'a sporting or other event of national interest' in the 1996 Broadcasting Act (para 97). Specific events are not explicitly mentioned in the legislation. The relevant government Minister (in a Ministry which, since 1997 has been known as the Ministry for 'Culture, Media and Sport') has authority to interpret and apply the legislation and to define and revise the 'list'.

Prior to 1998 there were eight 'listed events': the Wimbledon Tennis Championships, the English FA (soccer) Cup Final, the Scottish FA (soccer) Cup Final, England Cricket Test Matches in the UK, the Derby, the Grand National, the Olympic Games, and the FIFA World Cup (soccer) championships. Evidently there was a good deal of arbitrariness about this list in relation to British national culture and identity. The Scottish FA Cup Final was protected effectively for the 'nation' of Scotland and has never been an event of much interest to the majority of the English public, and vice versa for England's cricket matches as far as the Scottish public goes. Some events on the list had come to have less national cultural significance than they once had (e.g. the Derby), while others which continue to have great significance were not on the list (e.g. the Five Nations Rugby Union competition).

This state protection for access to the viewing of specific major sport events effectively amounts to a parallel policy to that of 'sport for all' in relation to the promotion of active participation which has developed since the 1960s. We can refer to it as a 'TV sport for all' policy. Just as the former effectively promoted sport as a cultural right of citizenship, so the latter does the same in relation to TV sport. This latter policy has been the subject of two Broadcasting Acts and numerous public debates in the 1990s. This intensification of political interest in 'TV sport for all' was occasioned largely by the development of off-shore (European-based) satellite 'pay TV' services, specifically Ruper Murdoch's British Sky Broadcasting (BSkyB, hereafter Sky) operation. As we saw earlier, since its launch in 1990, Murdoch has used the formidable buying power available to him from his international media empire to market Sky TV by buying up the TV rights to a number of important British sport events and leagues, most notably English First Division, or Premier League soccer.

Given Murdoch's proven record of interest and/or success in acquiring the TV rights to 'national sports' and also to the Olympics and the World Cup for Australia and other world regions, there appeared to be a clear threat to public access on 'free-to-air' terrestrial TV for at least some of the UK's 'listed events'. In the 1990 Broadcasting Act, the UK regulations surrounding the 'listed events' were updated with the intention of preventing the broadcasting rights being bought by 'pay-to-view' TV organisations. However, this could only apply to UK-based organisations such as the various cable TV operators. Technically this did not seem to prevent the sale of these rights to non-UK-based satellite TV operations such as Murdoch's Sky; a loophole he has not yet tested in practice.

Attempting to keep up with the rapid pace of technological and commercial change in the broadcasting industry in general, the British government felt, by the mid-1990s, that a new Broadcasting Act was needed to update and strengthen the regulatory system yet again. The 1996 Broadcasting Act was the subject of much debate, particularly given the growth of Sky TV and Murdoch's apparent threat to British terrestrial TV in general and its sport programming in particular, not least the 'listed events'. The 1996 Broadcasting Act bans 'pay-to-view TV' from obtaining sole control of the TV rights to live coverage of 'listed events'. However, in part to reward entrepreneurship in the TV sector and to maximise Event owners' TV income in this state controlled sphere, it promotes the concept of joint broadcasting deals. That is, the Act requires the owners of Listed Events to offer the TV rights to live coverage 'on fair and reasonable terms' to both 'free-to-view' terrestrial TV and to 'pay-to-view' TV. So, for instance, the rights to the televising of the FA Cup Final for the period 1997–2001 have been acquired jointly by ITV and Sky.

The New Labour government elected in early 1997 initially appeared willing to take further action to defend the 'TV sport for all' principle and to limit the market power of the Murdoch media. Thus in mid-1997 'Media' and 'Sport' were explicitly included in the title of the previous Heritage Ministry, which was now renamed the Ministry of Culture, Media and Sport. The new Minister promised yet another new Broadcasting Act and/or a new use of ministerial authority which, among other things, might involve an extension to the number of events protected for public access on the list, and might give terrestrial broadcasters rights to at least highlights programmes where 'pay-to-view' TV has already acquired rights to live coverage.

To begin to prepare the way for new use of Ministerial power in relation to 'listed events' and/or for new 'listed event' provisions in a new Broadcasting Act, in late 1997 the Minister set up an Advisory Group on 'listed events'. This took evidence and views from TV companies, sports governing bodies and event owners, and provided a focus for the current debate around the 'TV sport for all'. In their evidence the BBC argued for an extension of the list to cover four additional events, namely the Five Nations Rugby Union competition, the European Nations Soccer Cup competition, the Ryder Cup golf competition (USA v. Europe); and the Commonwealth Games staged in the UK (i.e. with a view particularly to the Games event to be staged in Manchester in 2002). Opinion polls suggest that British public opinion is very much in favour of this kind of extension of the List (60 per cent in favour of the BBC view) (Travis 1998-P). In their evidence to the Advisory Group, both Sky TV and some of the 'listed events' rights holders, particularly the governing body for English cricket, have argued either for the abolition of the list or for compensation for event owners' loss of income from their inability to sell their event for the highest market price available, whether or not from 'pay-to-view' TV.

In 1998 the New Labour government reconstructed the 'listed events' framework on a new 'A' and a 'B' list basis. 'Full protection', to maintain maximal free-to-view TV access for the public, was given to events in group A. These included an extended version of seven of the previous eight 'crown jewels' (namely the Olympic Games, all games in FIFA's World Cup, the English and Scottish FA Cup Finals, the Grand National and the Derby horse races, and the Wimbledon tennis finals. In addition, three new media-sport events were listed in group A for full protection, namely the final of UEFA's European Nations soccer competition, the Rugby Union World Cup final, and the Rugby League Challenge Cup final. A new category of 'partial protection' for public access was given to nine events in group B. This protection allowed sport authorities to sell exclusive rights to full event coverage to one broadcast organisation on condition that the contract ensured that such full coverage would be delayed and not 'live', that other television broadcasters would be allowed to buy the rights to transmit event 'highlights', and that other radio broadcasters would be allowed to buy the rights to full event coverage. Events in group B include all non-final matches in rugby union's international World Cup, the Five Nations Rugby Union competition, the Commonwealth Games, the athletics World Championships, the cricket international World Cup finals, Ryder Cup golf, British Open golf, and non-finals matches at the Wimbledon tennis tournament. They also include one of the original (and originally more fully protected) 'crown jewels', namely home-based Test Cricket matches involving England. This loosening of the regulations in relation to cricket was in response to the lobby by the sport's governing body that the future health of the game in England required that it increase its commercial income.[20]

Together with the government's blocking of Murdoch's bid to buy Manchester United in 1999, which we discussed earlier, the new List represents a significant effort to limit Murdoch's threats to British terrestrial TV programming in general and to ownership diversity and public accessibility in the strategically important sector of the televising of nationally important sports and major sport events.

European media-sport, regulation and cultural citizenship

The strategic use of media-sport programming, particularly in the form of 'flag-ship' media sport mega-events, by international media corporations such as Murdoch's stable of companies evidently can have a number of destabilising effects in relation to the organisation and identities of nationally- and/or regionally-based sports, and the communities from which they traditionally draw their support (Rowe 1996, 1999). On the one hand, the intervention of TV on this scale de-stabilises traditional relationships between organisers, players and fans within sports: important new flows of income are injected into sport governing bodies and their clubs, rendering them dependent on TV income rather than gate-receipts from fans and spectators, and leading to inflation and instability in the labour market for players (Bale and Maguire 1994). On the other hand, TV's intervention destabilises the public's access to nationally significant sport events by effectively privatising them.

In the late 1990s, particularly in Europe, we are seeing the development of complex power struggles in sports like soccer and rugby, over both of these issues, involving media companies, representative governments, sport organisations, and fans. These struggles are complicated by the trans-national character of some of the leading media companies, in particular Rupert Murdoch's stable of companies, and also of the system of governance emerging within the European Union (EU) as a result of the attempt both to create and to regulate the Single Market. In concluding this section of the chapter, and before we consider the global Olympic media event in some detail, it is useful to underscore the increasingly important trans-national dimension in the production, consumption and regulation of media sport with reference to Europe.

The European Broadcasting Union (EBU) alliance of EU nations' 'public service' broadcasters has been very effective in gaining European transmission rights to global mega-events such as the Olympics and soccer World Cups, and also the prestigious European Nations soccer competition. In particular, the EBU has long had a privileged relationship with the International Olympic Committee, receiving from them European TV rights to broadcast the Olympics at rates considerably lower than the comparable USA TV rights. Murdoch's European satellite TV operation, Sky, unlike the BBC, is not a member of the EBU and does not get access to the Olympics and other such media-sport mega-events.

There are problems and contradictions in the EU's regulatory approach in the field of telecommunications policy since, in this field as in many others (e.g. transport), the EU's Single Market project implies an undermining of nationally-based state-funded 'public service' organisations which have been developed, at least nominally, to protect national citizens' rights of access to these services. Questions are being raised, particularly by global media-sport corporations such as Murdoch's group of companies, about the 'cartel' and/or 'monopolistic' role of organisatons such as the EBU and also European-level sport governing bodies such as UEFA, and their allegedly anti-competitive, anti-Single Market character-istics. Interestingly, in this context, as we noted earlier, in 1999 the UK's com-petition authorities reaffirmed the right of a sports organisation, the Premier League, to act on behalf of its constituent clubs, not deeming this to be a cartel-type restriction of competion or against the public interest. It is possible that this judgement may have some influence on the approach of EU regulators to the relationship between sports organisations, the sale of broadcast rights and the public interest in Europe more widely.

Construction of the EU Single Market, now being accelerated by the creation of a common currency system through the Economic and Monetary Union (EMU) process, may ultimately benefit European citizens as consumers and create a common European public sphere in the form of a market and a consumer culture. But it remains unclear whether stronger and more substantial trans-national conceptions of European citizenship and the public sphere will be developed to compensate for the loss of national conceptions that this process seems to require (Roche 1997; Roche and van Berkel 1987). In the absence of this, and given the constitutional weakness of the European Parliament in the EU power system, organisations such as the IOC can claim to represent some version of the European public interest in acting to support the EBU's 'public service' 'free-to-air' approach in the area of Olympic media sport.

The IOC claims that its general approach to the televising of its Games events, as stated in its Olympic Charter (Rule 59.1, 1995 version), is to attempt to achieve 'the widest possible audience' for them. In the contemporary period this has usually meant support for large free-to-air TV networks, whether one of the private and commercial 'big three' networks in the USA, or the public networks in Europe. The growth of, on the one hand, the reach and power of private and commercial broadcasting in Europe and, on the other hand, of the EU as an agency of sport and media industry governance has begun to destabilise the status quo in the European sector of Olympic media sport and media sport more generally. In relation to this, it is notable that in recent years the International Olympic Committee has attempted to take a leading role in countering the growth of the EU's media-sport regulatory and policy roles. For instance, in 1998 the IOC convened European sport governing bodies together with the EBU, representing national public sector broadcasters, to review possible strategies and actions relating to this (O'Reilly 1998B-P).

In 1996 the European Parliament called on the European Commission: 'to work for the granting of transmission rights for big sports programmes to free television channels' (EP 1996-P). In response, the European Union Commissioner for competition policy, Karel Van Miert, recognised a responsibility to monitor, and if necessary control, the growth of exclusive TV rights arrangements in Europe (Short 1996B-P; Henderson 1996-P). The European Commission's (EC) general view is to attempt to strike a balance between public interests and commercial interests in media-sport events in Europe. This involves accepting that, in spite of market and competition rules, member states can impose 'public interest' rules on the market by creating lists of sport events the television rights to which are prevented from becoming the exclusive property of any single media corporation. For a number of years the EC's policy thinking on media sport has been evolving. Currently it seems to be moving towards a general position of support for the legitimacy of the principle of 'listed events'-type regulation at member-state level, together with a reluctance, at this stage in the development of Euuropean media sport, to engage with the problem of attempting to specify a common list of sport events for all of the EU which might be protected by regulation at EU-level (Short 1997-P).

In 1999 the EU officially limited the rights of sports governing bodies to control their own sports, clubs and players in the sphere of commercial activities. It advised them that where they act commercially they have no different status than any other commercial organisation and are subject to the EU's pro-competition and anti-monopoly laws and regulations.[21] This was particularly aimed at governing bodies using their power to enter into long-term, exclusive and exclusionary broadcasting contracts with a single media organisation. In 1997 the EU launched a preliminary investigation into anti-competitive practices by the governing body of Formula One Grand Prix motor-racing (the FIA). This investigation reported in 1999, finding evidence of serious infringements of EU competition rules, including abuse of monopoly in relation to the sale of TV broadcast rights to Grand Prix races. Since a prima facie case existed against the FIA in 1999 the EU launched a formal inquiry process which could result, in due course, in substantial fines for the FIA and the breaking of its various monopolistic powers and practices in the sport of motor-racing (Wolf and Finch 1999-P). In the same period, the EU challenged the German Bundesliga soccer league over its exclusive and exclusionary television deals. This effectively also implicitly issued a warning to English soccer's Premier League to expect that any attempt in 2001/2 to renew its collective and exclusionary deal with Murdoch's Sky TV company would be challenged and probably blocked by the EU. The implication of this is that sports clubs retain their rights to sell their own matches to broadcasters independently of any collective deal with a league or governing body.

This effectively protects the market and property rights of some citizens' (e.g. club owners') property rights, the rights of players to sell their labour[22] and some aspects of fans' and spectators' rights as consumers (i.e. giving them access to multiple broadcast sources). However, arguably this anti-collectivist EU stance risks running contrary to the EU's 1997 Amsterdam Treaty 'Declaration' on Sport. This Declaration can be read as implying that sports governing bodies have important rights as actors in EU civil society which need to be protected. For instance, they have a right to be consulted by the EU and to participate in a 'civil dialogue' comparable to the 'social dialogue' which is institutionalised in the sphere of EU socio-economic policy-making.[23]

In effect, these national-level and EU-level contradictions and struggles over access to media sport can be said to contribute to the development of new national and new 'post-national' conceptions of cultural identity (Morley and Robbins 1995) and 'cultural citizenship' and the rights of such citizenship in the contemporary period.[24] The development of these new forms of citizenship, and of the regulation needed to make the 'public space' and 'public culture' they imply, into a reality could in principle place important limitations on the grand designs of Murdoch and other media moguls in the popular cultural field of sport. Whether these principles and the current debates around them will result in significant action in relation to multinational media corporations of the scale and dynamism of those controlled by Rupert Murdoch remains to be seen.

So far we have considered dramatological and political economic dimensions of sport events, media-events, and their combination media sport and 'event'-driven TV programming. We now need to consider some aspects and implications of these dimensions in relation to the particular case of Olympic Games events as media sport and as mediated mega-events.

Olympic Games as media events

Understanding the Olympics as a media event, effectively as a TV genre (a 'TV show' or 'mini-series of shows'), means that, as with all media research, we need to explore the three core dimensions of all media processes and genres, namely production, content and audience reception. This is relatively readily achievable in relation to other more mainstream TV genres such as news, soap operas and more routine forms of sport coverage, which have attracted much research in all three of the core dimensions. However, perhaps understandably given the unusually large scale, complexity and rarity of the Olympic TV genre, relatively little substantial and credible research has been undertaken on it. What little research there is is relatively recent, having mainly been undertaken in the past decade and a half, beginning from studies of the Los Angeles Olympics in 1984.

The 1984 games was a turning point in what it revealed about the extent to which the American TV networks in particular were prepared to go in bidding up the price of the rights to transmit the Olympics, in terms of income to the Olympic movement and in terms of the threat of the Games being taken over by commercialism. The controversies and public debates that this has engendered around the world concerning the meaning and future of the Olympic Games event and the movement in general has meant that both the IOC, the TV networks and the main commercial sponsors since 1984 ought in principle to have an interest in supporting research on the Olympics as a media event, whether from the point of view of market research for sponsors or the movement, or as a contribution to wider public debates.

Consistent with this, and without necessarily carrying implications for their independence and objectivity, the few empirical case studies which have been made usually have some connnection with one or more of these interest groups. Substantial and systematic empirical media case studies were conducted on the Olympic Games of LA 1984, Seoul 1988 and Barcelona 1992. Less comprehensive and more specialist media studies were conducted on the 1994 Lillehammer Winter Olympics and the 1996 Atlanta Olympics. In addition, the IOC and UNESCO have supported research conferences and colloquia on the topic of the Olympics and the media (e.g. Jackson and McPhail 1989). Each of the main studies indicated has its strengths and weaknesses not least in terms of their coverage of the three main dimensions of media processes noted earlier. The LA study was mainly a piece of audience research into responses to Olympic TV, while the Seoul and Barcelona studies mainly focused on analyses of the production and content dimensions of Olympic TV, although the Barcelona study also contained a limited amount of audience research. Each of them, but particularly the Seoul study, generated some interesting theoretical interpretations and reflections.

In this section we mainly concentrate on exploring the Barcelona Olympics as a media event, as this was relatively recent and has attracted the most extensive and internationalised of these three research efforts, and much can be learned from a detailed case study such as this. Prior to this we review some of the findings from the other two main studies noted above, together with other relevant studies of Olympic TV. However, to introduce this topic it is necessary first to briefly review some of the main technical and financial features of the media's general involvement with contemporary Olympic Games.

TV and the financing of the Olympics

Television income is now crucial to underpinning the huge expenditures on facilities and infrastructures which, as we saw in Chapter 5, are needed for cities to be able to stage the Olympic Games in the contemporary period. Since the Los Angeles Olympics, media companies' payments for the rights to broadcast the Games have constituted at least a third of the total income of the event. In aggregate, they are usually the biggest single item as compared with the other main sources of, in descending order of magnitude, sponsorship, ticketing and merchandising.

TV income has regularly grown since Los Angeles, sometimes dramatically (see Table 6.3). In addition, by making the Olympics as a global media event possible, the involvement of television underpins the other main income sources. That is, by carrying advertising within the 'Olympic TV show' it indirectly encourages significant income from sponsorship, for instance through the TOPS programme (i.e. the licensing of the use of the Olympic symbols in international marketing by a select group of multinational companies). And it stimulates public interest internationally and thus encourages tourists and visitors to attend the event, thereby boosting ticketing income.

The biggest single source of TV fee income has always been one or other of the major USA TV networks. At Los Angeles this was ABC, but since Seoul it has been NBC. However, there are signs that this situation is beginning to change. The Atlanta Olympics showed the biggest ever total TV income, which was $900 million. It is worth noting that the local organisers, ACOG, kept $568 million of this to help cover event expenditures, while the rest went to the IOC to help fund the movement's global activities (see Chapter 7 below).

The $900 million represented a major increase from the $635 million total TV revenue at the Barcelona Games only four years earlier. The main reason for this overall TV income growth was the massive growth in the European Broadcasting Union's (EBU's) payments, namely a rise from $66 million at Barcelona to $250 million at Atlanta (or, including additional payments for technical services, from $90 million to $255 million). In 1996 the IOC introduced a new system of broadcast rights payments, in which the rights to the set of Summer and Winter

Table 6.3. TV rights income for Summer Olympics 1960–2000 (in $millions)*

Year	City	USA TV	Euro TV
1960	Rome	0.39 (CBS)	0.66 (EBU)
1964	Tokyo	1.5 (NBC)	no data
1968	Mexico City	4.5 (ABC)	1.0 (EBU)
1972	Munich	12.5 (ABC)	1.7 (EBU)
1976	Montreal	24.5 (ABC)	4.5 (EBU)
1980	Moscow	72.3 (NBC)	5.6 (EBU)
1984	Los Angeles	225.0 (ABC)	19.8 (EBU)
1988	Seoul	300.0 (NBC)	28.0 (EBU)
1992	Barcelona	416.0 (NBC)	90.0 (EBU)
1996	Atlanta	456.0 (NBC)	247.0 (EBU)
2000	Sydney	715.0 (NBC)**	(333.0) (EBU)***

Sources: *Adapted from Spa *et al.* 1995, p. 19 (NB figures include payments for technical services and other more minor payments); also IOC 1996a, pp. 170–3, ACOG 1997, p. 67, Rowe 1999, p. 71.
**Rowe 1999, p. 71.
***Author's rough estimate. The EBU's payment for the set of three Summer Games and two Winter Games 2000–2008 is $1.442 million (Culf 1996-P). Estimate is based on $221 million per Winter Games and $333 million per Summer Games.

Olympic Games, from 2000 to 2008 inclusive, were sold in one package. The EBU paid $1.442 billion for this package and NBC paid $3.57 billion. This system considerably increases the power of the IOC in relation to the national Olympic committees and the local organising committees of Games events it covers.[25]

Recent Olympics as media events

The 1984 Los Angeles Olympics as a media event

One of the most extensive research studies into an example of media event to date is the (USC) Annenberg School's study of American audience responses to the Los Angeles Olympics 1984, analysed and reported by Eric Rothenbuhler (Rothenbuhler 1988, 1989). This study involved a set of nationally representative telephone surveys pre-event, during the event and post-event, in the course of which a total of around 1,700 people were contacted nationwide. The study's expectations were that the American public would 'mark the occasion of the Olympic Games by looking forward to the event, seeking information about it, talking about the games (and) valuing them.' (Rothenbuhler 1988: 65). It was expected that audiences would be large and that individuals would watch a lot of the games coverage. It was also expected that individuals would rearrange their daily activities and routines to watch the games, that they would tend to watch 'in sociable gatherings marked by food, drink and talk in groups that resemble those that gather for other important events in the culture' (ibid.).

The study largely confirmed all of these expectations about viewer attitudes and activities. The study's hypothesis was that these findings would be best explained by the notion of the event being perceived by the public as a special event, involving special values and symbols they were prepared to affirm and to celebrate through the event (the 'Olympic celebration' hypothesis). Alternative potential explanations which were considered for the viewer response findings concerned the notions that either they might have been produced by any large sporting event (the 'just sport' hypothesis) or that they were produced by the unusually extensive and intensive media attention given to the games (the 'just hype' hypothesis).

The data gathered provided for the construction of a number of indicators to test these different candidate explanations. As against the 'just sport' hypothesis, viewer attitudes were found to be much more strongly inflected with Olympics-related ideology (idealism about sportsmanship, self-sacrifice, friendship between competitors, etc.) than is typically found among viewers of routine professional sport programmes. And the 'just hype' hypothesis failed because, among other reasons, the pre-event media attention was very mixed with a lot of negative news coverage (critical of the event's explicit commercialism, its possibilities for attracting boycotts and even terrorism, the likelihood of drug scandals, etc.) counterbalancing the positive Olympic images projected in the advertising campaigns of the event's major corporate sponsors (ABC, Coca-Cola, Budweiser, etc.). The overall result of the analysis strongly confirmed the 'Olympic celebration' hypothesis. In the pattern of viewer activities which the survey revealed, Rothenbuhler concluded that 'we find evidence of individuals enjoying themselves and a culture affirming its identity and values' (ibid. p. 78).

The 1988 Seoul Olympics as a media event

One of the most systematic studies of the Seoul 1988 Olympics as a media event was that of James Larson and Heung-Soo Park in association with Nancy Rivenburgh.[26] Their main theme is that of analysing the Olympic event as a form of political communication by the Korean hosts, addressing the world about their nation through 'global' TV. More generally, they used the Seoul case study to assess Katz and Dayan's media-event analysis. The research consists of a set of inter-related studies of the production, content and impacts of the event on the Korean public, introduced by an account of post-war Korean political history.

Their historical account rightly emphasises the Olympic event's role in the rapid economic modernisation of Korea in the 1980s and also, more questionably, emphasises its role in the often very fraught and conflict-ridden process of political modernisation and democratisation in the country over this time. To put the event in context it is important to briefly sketch this history. Recent revelations about Korea's politics (Higgins 1996A-P, B-P, C-P) and the IOC's sport politics [27] in this period casts more political shadows around the Seoul Games than Larson and Park found in their study.

Olympic Games events have always been capable of being used by national political elites to promote their own power and ideologies. This has been particularly so for authoritarian elites, as we saw with the Nazi's use of the 1936 Berlin Olympics (Chapter 5), and as also happened in the 1968 Mexico City Olympics and the 1980 Moscow Olympics. The Seoul Olympics to a certain extent can be said to have fitted this pattern. After the 1952 Korean War, partition of the country and US hegemony in the South, South Korea became an undemocratic military dictatorship in 1961, and effectively remained so until at least 1988, arguably until 1993. As assumed bulwarks against communism, South Korean leaderships were supported by the USA and by the presence of the US army throughout this period. South Korean leaders were changed, if at all, by assassination and coup d'etat, and the political system became increasingly corrupt, with politicians accepting huge bribes in exchange for contracts from some of the country's leading multinational companies.

The three presidents during the relevant period were Presidents Hee (1961–79), Chun (1980–8) and Roh (1988–93) all of whom were ex-generals. Chun and Roh were implicated in a massacre of protesters in 1980 after the coup which brought Chun to power. In 1996 both of them were convicted and jailed for accepting bribes throughout their careers (Chun £180 million/$280 million and Roh £240 million/$380 million). The dictator Hee had been impressed with Japan's use of the Tokyo Olympics in 1964 to mark its entry as a nation on to the world stage. He took the decision that Korea should bid for the 1988 Games in 1979 and assigned one of his secret service chiefs, Kim Un Yong, to assist with winning the bid from the IOC. Although Hee was assassinated later in 1979, Kim brought back the positive IOC decision to the new dictator Chun in 1981. In 1986 Kim led the Seoul organising committee, notably in pressuring the record price of $309 million out of NBC for the US TV rights, and in 1986 he also became a member of the IOC.

During the Games event itself, Korea's Olympic project may, ultimately, have been very popular with the huge international audience which watched it on global TV. However, like the dictators and 'strong men' who promoted it, it was not popular with the Korean people. Partly this was because Western sport culture was little known in the country in the early 1980s. Chun therefore created a new sport ministry to propagandise sport culture and the Olympics project and to build the necessary. sport facilities and telecommunications infrastructures in Seoul. As a result Larson and Park note that in this period, building up to and actually staging two sport mega-events, the Asian Games in 1986 and the Olympics in 1988, Korea's national image was often seen as being that of a 'Sports Republic'.[28] However, the unpopularity of Chun's dictatorship meant that a national political crisis built up in which the people (workers, students, new middle class) could exert pressure on government by threatening chaos during the Olympic event 'when the world would be watching'. This culminated in Chun's resignation shortly before the Games, with Roh taking over provisionally, getting an 'an Olympic truce' with his own citizens, and offering to hold presidential elections after the Games.

This background indicates why the Korean government, its media and the Korean people were all, for various reasons, very sensitive during the Games about the information and images conveyed in the world's media, particularly US TV. Koreans could receive US TV because of the presence of the US army and its broadcasting system. Two of the main stories carried to the world by Olympic TV, and by which the Seoul Olympics are remembered by the general public probably above all else, were the disqualification of the Canadian sprint star Ben Johnson for drug use and the 'riot' which occurred during a boxing match, both of them stories with a negative slant. Larson and Park, making reference also to Rivenburgh's content study, provide a substantial content analysis of those elements of the TV coverage which reflected most on Korea's national image. This included in particular the opening ceremony and also the boxing match incident.

The opening ceremony was watched by an estimated 1 billion peope worldwide, double the predicted audience and a new record for Olympic TV. Korean nationalism was built into the opening ceremony through the use of a veteran marathon runner as the torch bearer. The runner was the legendary Korean athlete and Olympian Sohn Kee Chung. In the 1930s Korea was dominated by Japan and was part of its Empire. As an outstanding athlete, Sohn Kee Chung had only been able to compete in international sport under the Japanese flag, and at the 1936 Berlin Olympics he become the Olympic marathon champion. Back in Korea, Chung had become a symbol of the anti-imperial, anti-Japanese struggle in this period. Generations later he remained a powerful symbol of national independence and this was the significance to be attached to his participation in the opening ceremony of the Seoul Olympic Games.

Korean–American relations suffered somewhat during the Games because of US TV's treatment of the opening ceremony and of the boxing match incident. On the one hand, there was NBC's apparent act of disrespect to the Korean hosts when it edited out much of the Korean culture section of the opening ceremony in its broadcast to the US audience. On the other hand, there was its allegedly 'anti-Korean' coverage of the boxing incident. In this case a Korean boxer had lost a dubious decision on points. Protesting against the decision Korean officials entered the ring and assaulted the referee, and the boxer staged a one-hour 'sit in' in the ring. The officials and the boxer were clearly guilty of a breach of the rules and were subsequently banned from the sport. However, at the time, NBC's negative news coverage of the event was deemed to be intrusive and arrogant to the host country, and led to a wave of anti-American feeling in the Korean media and public.

Larson and Park use the Seoul case to assess the overall soundness of Katz and Dayan's media-event analysis. They judge that the Seoul Olympics produced a wave of pro-Korean and anti-American nationalism together with apparently significant democratic concessions from the military dictatorship, namely post-Games presidential elections. As it happened, Chun's protégé Roh won in these elections. Larson and Park note that Katz and Dayan's view of media events was that they tended to be among other things, 'salutes to the status quo' and 'legitimations of elites' (quoted in Larson and Park 1993: 245). However, they feel that Korea's experience with the Olympics was 'a notable exception to the rule' and 'Political liberalization and democratization in South Korea quite literally framed or enveloped the Seoul Olympics'. The Olympic media event seemed 'to signal change...of the status quo' and 'delegitimation . . . of military dictatorship' (ibid.). However, this judgement seems to overestimate the reality of the political changes which accompanied President Roh's successful election. As it turned out, he was effectively little more than an acceptable face of rule by the same corrupt political, economic and military establishment which had ruled Korea since the 1970s. Katz and Dayan's 'status quo'-endorsing media-event analysis probably has more applicability to the Seoul case than Larson and Park suggest.

Beyond Katz and Dayan's analysis, Larson and Park argue for perspectives on media events which are more consistent with the approach taken in this book. Thus they propose that media-event analysis should take a long-term 'Socio-Political Process' view of media events rather than just a short-term event-centred view. In the Korean case, the Seoul Olympics was an eight-year project connected with economic and political processes and not just an isolated two-week event and TV show. Also they advocate a 'political' view of event production. That is, the Olympic Games event is effectively cultural 'theatre' in the world political system, and the Olympic movement is an important trans-national actor in its own right in this system.[29] Finally, given the evident and enduring inequalities in the world political system, they recommend that poor countries and world regions such as Africa should be provided with much improved access to global TV. In addition, they suggest that in the future the global cultural and political system could be interestingly represented using global TV technology to create multi-site global events, including a new multi-site version of the Olympics.

The 1992 Barcelona Olympics as media event

The main media research into the 1992 Barcelona Olympic event is reported in a study directed by Miguel de Moragas Spa, Nancy Rivenburgh and James Larson.[30] The research was significant not least for the fact that it was undertaken by a large interdisciplinary international team (hereafter the Spa team). In terms of comparability with the Seoul Olympics study discussed earlier, it is worth noting that there was an overlap in the core research personnel involved in these two studies.[31] The Barcelona research involved an interrelated set of production, content and audience studies. The Spa team offer a reasonable amount of insight into the production and reception dimensions of the Barcelona Olympics, probably more on the former than on the latter. But when assessing this it needs to be borne in mind that the main aim of the research was to explore the content dimension of Olympic TV rather than the other dimensions. However, as they observe: 'The Olympics as a television event is very much a constructed reality – virtually all is controlled except the moments of athletic endeavour' (ibid. p. 10). The content of the 'live event' of an Olympic Games is evidently the subject of a major planning effort by the organising group. So the content study necessarily revealed a lot, if a little indirectly, about the aims and nature of the production dimension.

PRODUCTION AND AUDIENCE DIMENSIONS OF BARCELONA OLYMPIC TV

The production dimension studies examined the financing, technology and televisual production of the Barcelona Olympics as a media event and as TV programming. Among other things they revealed how the unity of an apparently single event like the opening ceremony was opened up to very different and partial presentations in the Olympic TV programmes constructed and edited by each nation's broadcasters from the main telecast. In addition, a notable observation here was that the US network NBC's experimental joint venture with Cablevision, which offered the USA audience a daily repeated cycle of twelve hours of uninterrupted and effectively unedited 'live' coverage, albeit on a 'pay-per-view' basis, turned out to be a failure, losing NBC $150 million.

The reception dimension studies attempted, on the one hand to give some impressions of audience views from people in selected countries in the five continents, finding that in general 'local circumstances . . . greatly colour the experience of a global event like the Olympic games' (ibid. p.11). On the other hand, they also attempted to estimate the scale of the audience worldwide. A notable finding here was that the official estimate of 3.5 billion viewers for the opening ceremony was almost certainly a considerable overestimate, with the real figure probably being closer to 1 billion. There are evidently costs as well as benefits in this sort of research design for studying this sort of media event. In retrospect, the team themselves clearly felt that they had not been able to do enough work on the audience reception dimension. Thus they recommended that 'more systematic and cross-cultural reception analysis', particularly about differing national perceptions of the TV coverage and of the event, needed to be on the agenda in any future Olympic media research (ibid. p.249).

CONTENT DIMENSIONS OF BARCELONA OLYMPIC TV: THE OPENING CEREMONY

The content study involved a large-scale, systematic, and multinational set of studies of the content of twenty-four national broadcasts of the opening ceremony. This focus on content was justifiable given the fact of the importance of the opening ceremony in the profile of the Olympics as a media event. The opening ceremony is the first, most viewed and, along with the closing ceremony, the most theatrical element in the mix of TV programming generated by the event. Earlier we noted MacAloon's analysis of Olympic Games events as a multi-genre 'performance complex' including strong elements of the four key genres of spectacle, ritual, festival and game. The Barcelona opening ceremony certainly contained the genres of spectacle, ritual and festival, and the subsequent transmissions of the sport obviously contained, in addition, the game genre.

From the perspective of Olympic TV, and on the basis of this Barcelona study, a fifth genre needs to be added to MacAloon's list, namely advertising. This is in order to capture the fact that Olympic broadcasts of the opening and closing ceremonies in general, as in the case of Barcelona, are advertisments in two senses. First, from an audience perspective the programmes are normally interrupted frequently by the more mundane and familiar flow of commercial advertising images and messages. Second, the programmes are effectively extended advertisments for the Olympic movement, as well as for the host city, host nation and to a certain extent the competing nations. Spa *et al.* note: 'The hosting of global events is a well-known image management strategy. . . . much thought and planning went into the design of the Barcelona Opening Ceremony as a stage to present Catalonia as a distinct, yet complementary host with Spain' (ibid. p.10). This was known as the 'dual host strategy', although it is unclear whether it was universally understood and appreciated in the global TV coverage.[32]

From a media-event production perspective the organising group, COOB92, required its set of production companies to study videos of relevant aspects of the 1984 and 1988 Olympics, and it briefed them to create a dual 'spectacle', for the spectators in the stadium and for the TV medium (ibid. p.83). The opening ceremony aimed at being a universally comprehensible visual and musical experience that would hardly need commentary to give meaning. Spa *et al.* comment that 'There is little question that the ceremonies were conceived from the outset as major televised and musical super productions' (ibid. p.85). The opening ceremony cost $20 million and according to the Ceremony Director the aim was 'to create a spectacle more than a ceremony' (quoted in ibid. p.85).

The main elements of Olympic opening ceremonies, as we have seen previously, are the performance of the Olympic rituals, in particular the parade of the national teams of athletes, the institutional speeches and international diplomatic protocol, the enthronement of Olympic symbols (the torch relay and lighting the stadium flame, etc.). These rituals, as we have seen, are periodically capable of change and creative development. In the case of Barcelona a new ritual was created and enacted, namely the unravelling of a huge Olympic flag to cover the heads of all of the assembled athletes, symbolically enclosing them, whatever their national and individual differences, in the unity of the Olympic event. But before and after these ritual and ceremonial elements there was plenty of room for the creation of spectacle and of a festival atmosphere. In the case of this opening ceremony stars from the world of opera were used to focus and open the cultural performance. This developed into a large-scale theatrical presentation of ancient Mediterranean Sea myths and Greek myths including figures such as Hercules, themes of relevance both to the origins of the Olympics and also to Catalonian identity. As Olympic media analyst Rothenbuhler commented: 'Ultimately, it was charming to realize that Barcelona was portraying itself as at the centre of the origin of civilization – and doing it with convincing style' (ibid. p.185). The opening ceremony culminated, as many Olympics and expos have done since the late nineteenth century, with a large-scale and spectacular firework display over the stadium.

In their analysis of the various nation's TV presentations of the opening ceremony, and of the opening ceremony as TV genre, Spa *et al.* suggest that the main narrative aspects of the opening ceremony attended to in Olympic TV programmes were those of 'history', 'party' and 'show'. In conveying the meaning of the opening ceremony as an historic event, an occasion to review the previous period and say 'where we all are now', TV presenters, taking the role of witnesses to history, made reference to the end of the Cold War, and the fact that this was the first boycott-free Olympic Games. In conveying the meaning of the opening ceremony as a festive celebration or 'party', TV producers and presenters saw their role as that of being participants, and of expressing and communicating feelings of active participation in the event and cultivating these feeling among the TV audience. In conveying the meaning of the opening ceremony as a spectacular and entertaining 'show', TV commentators tended to take the role of an 'insider', warning of surprises to come. However, even though TV staff were given guide-books both by the organisers and also by the European Union to help with their presentation of the opening ceremony, their approaches were often richly descriptive but poorly interpretive. There were problems of cultural distance and a lack of understanding by TV presenters from outside Europe, for instance of the theatrical presentation of ancient European myths, and of the identity of Catalonia.

Olympic movement problems: nationalism and commercialism in Olympic TV

Two criticisms are often made of the Olympic movement and its main games event in the contemporary period. The idealistic meanings and values distinctive of the Olympic sport worldview are notionally internationalist rather than nationalist. Also, while the hightide of its 'amateurist' anti-commercial vision of sport is long gone, there remains at least an idealistic indifference to commercial gain in the meaning of 'Olympism'. On both of these fronts the contemporary Olympics can be argued to have lost touch with these values and even to be subverting them.

Whatever the Olympic movement can be said to have done for the cause of internationalism since their creation, the games have, in addition, also evidently provided a platform for competitive nationalisms. This was clear, for instance, in the Greek nationalism of the 1896 event, the American–British nationalist conflicts at the 1908 event, the German nationalism of the 1936 event, and the American–USSR conflicts of the post-war period which effectively turned the 1980 and 1984 games events into nationalistic celebrations of Soviet communism and American capitalism respectively. Such things as the IOC's formal recognition of participating athletes only as members of national teams and its rule that national flags and anthems are to be used as part of victory ceremonies underscores the nationalist reading of Olympic Games events. So too does the long-standing and informal but influential practice in the media of ranking and comparing national performance and success in winning medals.

The advent of the Games as a global media event arguably has only served to provide a bigger stage for competitive nationalisms. Also and equally evidently, the Olympic Games, particularly in its post-amateur global media-event incarnation, and particularly since the accession of Juan Samaranch to the IOC's Presidency in 1980, has become inextricably bound up with commerce. We consider the broader implications of these problems of nationalism and commercialism in Chapter 7. For the moment, we can take stock of them and consider their nature in a little more detail with reference to the findings of the Barcelona Olympic television study.

The nationalism problem in Olympic TV

Nationalism and nationalist messages have been found to characterise Olympic television broadcasts in each of the main studies of the Los Angeles and Seoul Olympics discussed earlier, and also in more recent studies, such as those of the Lillehammer Winter Olympics 1994 (Puijk 1996). The Barcelona research findings are largely consistent with these findings from other studies, with the interesting qualification, as we have noted, of the mixed messages relating to the technically 'sub-national' Catalan character of the production of the Games event.

The Barcelona study found that it was the 'local' (i.e. national) dimensions of the global event that meant most to the viewers around the world in terms of quality and interest of the viewing experience provided by Olympic TV. Thus they note that 'while certainly the global character (so many nationalities gathered together for elite-level sport) of the Games contribute to their attraction, it was the local [i.e. meaning mainly national] dimensions of the Olympic telecast that were critical to sustaining broadcaster and audience interest'. They found that viewership, after the opening ceremony and first few days, 'was most influenced by the participation of – and ability to view – one's own national athletes', and that audiences have a 'desire to see the local (self) as part of the the global (Olympics)' (Spa *et al.*: 248).

On this basis, one of the report's main recommendations to the IOC was to strengthen the national relevance of Olympic TV but within a strengthened 'Olympic' framework. So, on the one hand, 'opportunities should exist for all broadcasters to be able to customise the international signal for participating national and cultural groups so they may "see themselves" at the Olympics'. This could be assisted by the Olympic Solidarity programme in terms of providing some resources from poor countries to enable them to personalise their programming and show interviews with their athletes to their home audiences (ibid. pp. 248/9).

On the other hand, a more general and possibly controversial recommendation (given the current extent of the dependence of the Olympic movement on the televising of its major event), was that the Olympics needs to adapt even further than it already has to the requirements of television if it is to protect its (internationalist) Olympic message and communicate it better (ibid. pp. 247–8). Such things as the following should be considered: more timely information about the Olympics (beyond sport statistics) should be provided to broadcasters in media packages they can readily use; the structure of ceremonies and rituals should be altered to indicate when advertising breaks could be made without losing the narrative flow; cultural informants on the host nation and city, and also on the Olympic movement should be available to brief broadcast organisations well in advance of the event.; and more feature material could be produced, particularly for poor countries.

The commercialism problem in Olympic TV

The 1984 LA Olympics represented a first wave of intensive commercialisation of an Olympic event. However, less than a decade later, the Olympic movement was already beginning to get into difficulties in its new relationship with the consumer culture world of big corporate sponsors and global TV. The Los Angeles Olympic organising committee were the first to demonstrate the extent to which, and the practical ways in which, the Games event could attract income from sponsors. Drawing on that experience since that time, the IOC selects a special group of major corporate sponsors for its Games events (the TOPS programme), often including global multinationals like Coca-Cola and Kodak. For a high price this group is granted the sole rights to use the Olympic symbols in advertising their products, including in particular the five rings which appear on the Olympic flag.[33]

On its part, the Olympics, which Spa *et al.* call the 'world's largest athletic and media event' (ibid. p. 187), needs the finance provided by this group of sponsors and (because of them) by TV if it is to be staged on an appropriate scale. On their part, the sponsors need the prestige of association with the meanings and values of the Olympic movement, and the dramatic attraction of the Olympic event to keep an edge over their competitors in the marketplace. The relation between commercial and Olympic (non-commercial) meanings and values in Olympic TV is increasingly becoming as difficult a problem for the Olympic movement and the IOC as the issue of athlete's professionalism once was. The IOC insists on keeping the Olympic stadium, and thus TV images of it, clear of explicit advertising. The result of this is that, to achieve marketing value for the Olympic symbol advertising rights they have bought at high cost, and to prevent counter-advertising by their competitors, the main sponsors have to seek as much exposure as possible through multiple advertising breaks in the TV transmission of events like the opening ceremony. This in turn necessarily interrupts and intrudes upon the integrity of the Olympics images and messages the IOC is seeking to present through Olympic TV (ibid. p. 204, also IOC 1995b).

In the Barcelona case, the use of Olympic symbols and themes (by advertisers) by sponsors (e.g. rings) and also by non-sponsors (e.g. in the verbal use of word 'Olympic') risked hijacking the unique experience and special values associated with the Olympic Games event (ibid. pp.193–4). Coca-Cola adverts associated their drink with 'that special Olympic feeling'. Kodak inserted its advertising images and messages during the torch ritual in the US broadcast. Sponsors' logos were superimposed on TV screens and, more insidiously, were present on athletes clothing and equipment. 'Star' athletes who, outside of the Olympics, might appear in adverts and associate themselves with products and brands, whether they intend to or not, implicitly carry those associations with them in the context of an Olympic TV broadcast. As John Langer has observed: 'Select athletes themselves become corporate signs. They stand in for advertising' (quoted in ibid. p. 203). Spa *et al.* recommend that the IOC should at least seek to control the design and extent of advertising interruptions in relation to the key images and 'moments' they aim to communicate through the televising of events like the opening ceremony. However, they conclude that 'It is apparent from the evidence in this study that the mixing of commercial and Olympic messages' is a process at work in the contemporary Olympic movement and in Olympic TV in particular, and that this process is 'headed for increasingly murky waters' (ibid. p. 205).

Conclusion

As a counterpoint to the previous chapter which considered contemporary mega-events from a 'local/urban event' perspective, in this chapter we have seen something of the ways in which they are also, perhaps pre-eminently, media-events and thus non-local, indeed global events. In the terms of the perspectives outlined in Chapter 1, we considered the 'mega-events as media events' theme both from dramatological and political sociological perspectives. Dramatological points were touched on in the discussion of relevant theorists in the first section and the content analysis of the Barcelona Olympic opening ceremony in the third section. To put the development of the Olympics as a media event since the Los Angeles Olympics into a medium-term timeframe and a broader context, we also considered the development of media sport from political economic and political sociological perspectives in the second section.

In relation to these political aspects of mega-events as media events we considered the massive and growing power of media corporations, Murdoch's in particular, in the global promotion of media sport as a key element in their ambitions and strategies to take and make media markets at national and global levels. On the other hand, we also considered the possible limits and constraints on these ambitions provided by the growing interest in and alliance between 'public interest' and 'free market' themes in media-sport regulation. We considered these in the case of the British 'listed events' model and also as issues in the European Union's market and cultural policies. The two themes noted in the regulation of media sport embody citizens' expectations and demands for rights of access to major media-sport events on a 'free-to-view' mass access basis. Whether understood as an aspect of citizens' rights to information (public interest, civil rights) or as citizens' rights to choose (free market, consumption rights), the development of the politics of media-sport regulation in our period, whether at national or trans-national levels, can be interpreted as effectively the defence and promotion of cultural citizenship.

In this chapter we have also explored some of the reasons why the contemporary Olympic movement is in crisis. The advent of the Olympic Games as a global media event and effectively as a global cultural industry helps to explain the powerful motivations propelling urban leaderships to bid to host Games events. It helps to explain why, as we saw in Chapter 5, they are often prepared to bend or break the rules against bribery and corruption in their pursuit of this goal. These issues raise questions about the nature of the Olympic movement in relation to ideals of 'global citizenship', and we consider these questions next.

7 Mega-events and global citizenship

Olympic problems and responses

Introduction

The pre-eminent mega-event movement in our time, namely the Olympic movement, is evidently in a serious state of crisis as we enter the twenty-first century. This is clear from the issues raised in Chapters 5 and 6. In this chapter we aim to suggest some terms of reference for understanding and assessing the movement's problems and the adequacy of its responses to them. There are three main steps in the discussion. In the first section we review the Olympic movement's universalistic ideology, its global organisation and its operations in the contemporary global governance system, such as it is. In the second section we outline four key dimensions of the normative concept of global citizenship.[1] These are 'universal citizenship', which is connected with the theory and practice of 'human rights'; 'mediatised citizenship', which is connected with rights to participate in the mediatised world of trans-national media and information flows; 'movement citizenship', which is connected with rights of inclusion and democracy within trans-national movements, and 'corporate citizenship', which is connected with the responsibilities of corporate/collective actors in the systems of global governance and global civil society. In the third section we apply this citizenship frame of reference in an analysis and assessment of some of the main contemporary crises and problems of the Olympic movement.

The Olympic movement, global society and global governance

The Olympic movement: universalistic ideology and global organisation

Like the aristocratic British 'amateur' sport movement from which it derived so much initial inspiration, the 'modern Olympic movement', since the late nineteenth-century period of its creation by Pierre de Coubertin, has always taken the notion that sport culture has some kind of 'civilizing mission' in the modern world very seriously, and has seen itself as the leading voice of this culture. The movement's Charter was written, and has been periodically updated, by its ruling group the IOC, in large part to insulate and decorate the IOC's own power within the movement. The Charter suggests that the movement is founded on a set of values, ideology or 'philosophy of life', namely 'Olympism'.[2] This appears to seek to elevate sport into the leading edge of a broader idealistic and universalistic humanitarian mission in the modern world. On the one hand, this rhetoric and mission is compatible with key elements of the rhetoric and mission of post-war internationalism embodied in the United Nations and the Universal Declaration of Human Rights 1948 both as institutions and as the bases of movements and collective actions.[3] On the other hand, and also like the other examples of post-war internationalism, its idealistic and moralistic rhetoric has all too often been badly and sadly adrift both from its own practices and from the reality of world events.

Apparently, according to the Olympic Charter, 'The goal of Olympism is to place everywhere [sic] sport at the service of the harmonious development of man, with a view to encouraging the establishment of a peaceful society concerned with the preservation of human dignity' (Principle 3). It 'seeks to create a way of life' based on, among other things, 'respect for universal fundamental ethical principles' (Principle 2). The Olympic movement exists to implement the ideology of Olympism (Principle 4), and membership of the movement is, apparently, incompatible with 'any form of discrimination with regard to a country or a person on grounds of race, religion, politics, sex or otherwise' (Article 3.2). The idealistic goal of the Olympic movement is to use non-discriminatory sport to educate the world's young people in the values of peace, justice ('fair play'), mutual understanding and international friendship (Principle 6).

The IOC as a distinct organisation within the Olympic movement is the movement's 'supreme authority' (Rule 1.1, also 19–28). It usually consists of over 100 members who meet in plenary session on an annual basis. As an example of an international governing body it has, since its creation in 1894, had a distinctively 'trans-national' character. It is a self-recruiting and not a representative body. That is, its 'national' members are understood to be ambassador-like representatives or delegates of the IOC *to* their nations (and to their nations' national Olympic committees), rather than representatives *of* the nations (and of their national committees). Within the IOC, the bulk of power and patronage is centralised in the office of the President and the IOC Executive. The IOC's formal role is, among other things, to organise the 'regular celebration of Olympic Games' and to hold them in environmentally responsible ways. In the context of its responsibility for the Games event, but also more generally in terms of its self-appointed role as the leading organisation in modern international sport culture, the IOC declares itself to be dedicated to the promotion of 'sports ethics', to leading 'the fight against doping in sport', and to opposing the 'political and commercial abuse of sport' (Rule 2).

Besides the IOC, the Olympic movement formally is held to consist of the following (Rule 3.1): national Olympic committees (NOCs, Rules 31–35), international governing bodies and federations concerned with particular sport (IFs, also Rules 29, 30); the organising committees of current relevant Olympic Games events (OCOGs, Rule 39); together with any other organisation the IOC decides to recognise for this purpose (Rule 3.1).[4] It is worth noting (in spite of, it should be said, all appearances to the contrary at every Olympic Games event since 1896) that the Charter defines Olympic Games events as 'competitions between athletes . . . and not between countries' (Rule 9.1). In addition, and more generally, the Olympic movement is held to consist not only of national sports 'associations and clubs' but also of 'the persons belonging to them, particularly the athletes' (Rule 3.1). However, in spite of this, no distinct organisation or representative mechanism comparable to the others mentioned is indicated for the formal participation of grassroots sports people in the Olympic movement.

In addition to the organisations already mentioned, the sort of organisations which the IOC, in its Charter, authorises itself to recognise as members of the Olympic Movement include the five contintental associations of NOCs – that is, Africa (ANOCA), Asia (OCA), Europe (EOC), North and South America (PASO), and the Pacific region ('Oceania', ONOC) – representing the world regions which are symbolised in the five-ring Olympic flag and logo (Rule 4.2). They also include such related world-level organisations as the Assocation of all National Olympic Committees (ANOC), associations of IFs concerned with the Summer and the Winter Olympics, 'Olympic Solidarity' (which gives aid to the sports and Olympic programmes of poor countries), and any other NGO 'connected with sport' the IOC decides (Rules 4.2,4.3, 4.5, and 8). Interestingly, although they often feature large in OCOG and also in IOC discussions of Olympic affairs, particularly around the times of the Games events, the Charter does not mention the concept of 'the Olympic Family' which regularly appears in IOC discourse.[5] In this discourse this appears to refer to IOC members attending IOC missions, meetings and Games events (together with their relatives and friends), and the officials, relatives and friends of other recognised Olympic movement organisations. It also seems to be capable of being used to refer to the entourages of the multinational companies and organisations involved in the IOC's official Olympic sponsorship programme (TOPS) and media broadcasting programme

The IOC itself, besides its organisation into an Executive, is also organised into a number of Commissions concerned with such things as marketing, doping and other medical issues, 'sport for all' policies and programmes, Olympic education etc. (Rule 8, Bye-Law). The Executive is required to meet with the IFs and NOCs every two years (Rule 6). However, in terms of more general meetings of the movement beyond the IOC, all that is required is that the IOC convene an Olympic Congress 'in principle' every eight years (Rule 7.1). The most recent was held in Paris in 1994, in large part a centenary celebration of the creation of the IOC itself. Oddly, given the eight-year cycle indicated in the Charter rule, prior to this the next most recent had been held as far back as 1981 at Baden-Baden. The Congress is defined as consisting of delegates representing at least the IFs and the NOCs. However, this Congress remains very much a creature of the IOC rather than any serious representation of the Olympic movement. The IOC retains the right to recognise and invite any individual or organisation it decides on, the IOC Executive has the ultimately sole right to set the agenda; and the Congress is deemed to have a merely 'consultative' rather than decision-making status (Rule 7).

The Olympic movement in the international governance system

Clearly the Olympic movement in its various aspects and at its different levels is well integrated into the circuits of international diplomacy and cultural politics operated by nation-states, international governmental organisations (IGOs), and international non-governmental organisations (INGOs). The Olympic movement is the biggest and probably the most important cultural INGO in the world/ international system outside of world religions and scientific associations. FIFA is very important given its role in soccer, the world's most popular single sport, and also in terms of the scale of the World Cup mega-event it organises. Nonetheless, in terms of sport ideology it is better understood either as being an organisation which is a component part of the Olympic movement and of its sport ideology (FIFA is an IOC-recognised IF, and a member of the Olympic movement in this capacity, and FIFA's President is an IOC member) or as being politically overshadowed by it in terms of international cultural politics and policy-making.

There have always been, and there are currently, evident and often major gaps between the idealistic rhetoric of Oympism and the realities of international sport culture and political economy. In the 1980s and 1990s these gaps have widened as the Olympic Games event have become massively mediatised and commercialised. They have also widened, in the 1990s, as the IOC has sought to play a role with the UN in promoting the concept of an arguably unachievable and unenforcable 'Olympic Truce' between warring nations during the period of the Games. We discuss some of these gaps later. However, for the moment – and without committing ourselves to the proposition that its activity necessarily has much real effect – it is worth recording that in the 1990s the Olympic movement in its various organisational forms has become a fairly energetic player in the contemporary system, such as it is, of international governance.[6]

To illustrate this we can look at some of the international activities of the IOC in the single year of 1998. During the course of this year the IOC encouraged the UN to promote the Olympic Truce concept during the Winter Olympic Games held at Nagano in Japan. The IOC designed and hosted their own pavilion at the last international expo of the twentieth century at Lisbon, implicitly claiming a diplomatic parity as an organisation with the nation-states participating in the expo (Samaranch 1998). In the course of the expo the IOC contributed to two international conferences held under its auspices. It supported an international conference organised by Portugal and the UN on national and international policies for young people and their problems. It also supported the UN's World Youth Forum, which debated reports prepared by various UN-based or related agencies such as UNESCO, ILO (the International Labour Organisation),WHO (the World Health Organisation), and UNICEF on aspects of the situation and problems facing young people around the world (including drugs, health and other related problems) (Anon 1998d).

During the course of 1998 the IOC also held special meetings with the ILO and the WHO. Contacts between the ILO and the IOC date back to de Coubertin's interests in the work of Albert Thomas, the first Director General of the ILO in the early 1900s. At the 1998 IOC–ILO meeting, both organisations agreed to pursue joint efforts 'in promoting social justice and human dignity' and in encouraging activities 'which contribute to the elimination of poverty and child labour' (ibid.). These are particularly relevant concerns in the global sports goods industries which have often been shown to use cheap and child labour in the Third World. Whether this harmonisation of rhetorics will have any practical results remains to be seen.

The IOC's interest in being connected with the work of the WHO evidently stems from the assumption long prevalent in sports culture and ideology (although somewhat undermined in recent years by the rise of sports-injuries and sports drug abuse) that sport is positively correlated with health and is a means to the achievement and mraintenance of health (IOC 1996a: 140; Anon 1998c). Thus in 1998 the IOC supported the WHO's annual 'Day Against Smoking' campaign. In addition, it continued to participate in the WHO's International Working Group on Active Life. This group was created in 1996, and promotes a continuing world-wide campaign against smoking and against the interests of the powerful tobacco multinational companies. The Olympic Games have been smoke-free since Calgary 1988 and the IOC refuses to accept sponsorship from the tobacco industry. In this context it is also worth noting that, unlike soccer and most other sports worldwide, the IOC refuses to accept sponsorship from the alcohol industry, another area of concern for WHO. Finally, the Olympic movement, particularly in the form of the Olympic Solidarity organisation, held a number of international conferences to review the role it is aspiring to play in international civil society and global social policy. These conferences reviewed the problems facing the Olympic movement's activities in promoting sport in Africa, sport's role in developing societies and sport's role in anti-poverty strategies (Anon 1998b, 1998e).

Dimensions of global citizenship: normative criteria for the assessment of mega-events as cultural policies

As we saw earlier, in the late nineteenth and early twentieth centuries, in their association with nation-building, mega-events contributed to the development and promulgation among mass publics of notions of nation (national collective identity), nationality (membership or inclusion in the nation's tradition and destiny), and citizenship (the formal statuses, obligations and rights of participation associated with nationality). However, although they were usually largely dominated by the nationalism of the host country they also provided apparently 'international' stages and arenas for the display of current versions and ideals of international world order, that is of national identities and differences in a transient context of relatively peaceful coexistence and of common absorption in the ideals of the 'progress of 'Western civilization', and in the practices of touristic consumerism.

Contemporary expo and Olympic event movements continue this tradition, typically developing and promoting their events using an idealistic discourse of universalistic and humanitarian values. These values are ultimately derived from the Enlightenment and nineteenth-century 'progress' worldviews, and they are often currently expressed in terms of human rights and environmentalism. This event movement discourse, and its ideals, has in the past often been vulnerable to being undermined in various ways by its own practices, and it continues to be so in the present as we will see later in the case of the Olympic movement (section 3).

John Urry suggests that in the contemporary period various forms of widely experienced trans-national conditions, identities, rights and obligations have arisen which imply some, at least, informal concept of citizenship beyond the sphere of territorially-based and nation-state-based societies and their 'citizenship of stasis'. In contrast with this, Urry suggests that the contemporary period is characterised by the popular recognition of a number of 'citizenships of flows' connected with human mobility and/or the mobility of goods. In addition, he draws attention to the important role of the media in conveying and promoting images of the world in the contemporary period, and to the role of 'media events' (although notably not mega-events, whether in general or in sport culture in particular) (Urry 1998).

Urry proposes that participation in the complexities of modern society can be usefully conceptualised as the practice of 'global citizenship' and that this, in turn, should be understood in terms of the (unfortunately relatively unelaborated) concept of 'citizenship of flows'. In Urry's terms, global citizenship as 'citizenships of flows' are experienced in the form of popular understandings of status, rights and responsibilities connected with cultural participation, living in and off the earth's ecosphere, being a member of a minority, being a consumer, being a tourist, and having the potential to participate in cosmopolitan versions of democratic politics and polities.

In Chapter 8 we will outline some social theory perspectives which also make use of the image of 'flow' in helping to portray some of the characteristics of mega-events and the modernity that encompasses them. These perspectives are consistent with Urry's background social analysis. This might suggest that one way to proceed at this point is to develop the meaning of 'global citizenship' in terms of the 'citizenship of flows' concept. However, my discussion suggests that the concept of 'flow' (even if bolstered with the concept of 'network' – as in the concepts of 'network flows', or 'flows through a network' – as it is in both Urry's and in Manuel Castells' work[7]), is inadequate to the task in hand. For a more adequate analysis, we also need to recognise the role of new ordering and structuring processes in relation to 'flows' in modernity. That is, for instance, we can understand mega-events as social spatio-temporal 'hubs' and 'switches' that both channel, mix and re-route global flows, as well as being periodically 'overflowed' by them. Thus, besides the 'citizenship of flows' there may also be said to be various types of trans-national citizenship involved in the structuring processes which create global society's hubs and switches, whether in the form of mega-events, or key urban zones, or other such infrastructural phenomena.

In addition, the flows involved in the global-level activities of mega-event movements and media corporations are both constrained by and (increasingly) overflow the national and trans-national regulatory spheres within which they operate as publicly idenfitiable and legitimate legal and quasi-political entities. Thus, participation in them, whether as producers or consumers, involves people in conventional forms of legal and political citizenship at national and trans-national levels which are simply not referenced in the concept of 'citizenship of flows'. For these reasons the conception of global citizenship which will be outlined here and then applied to the assessment of the Olympic mega-event movement will be more conventionally legal, political and institutional than Urry's concept of the 'citizenship of flows' seems to imply.

For our purposes in this section, then, we focus on four dimensions or meanings of citizenship relevant to the characterisation and assessment of mega-events and their movements, namely what we can call 'universal', 'mediatised', 'movement' and 'corporate' dimensions of 'citizenship'. We briefly consider the meaning of each of these in turn.

Citizenship and mega-events: concepts and dimensions

'Universal citizenship'

In the modern period it has often been argued that all human beings possess individual human rights. The notion of 'universal citizenship' can be understood to be based on this argument. By inference, the notion refers to membership in the implicit and ideal global community constituted by the moral-ontological 'fact' of the common status of human being, and the possession, thereby, of these common rights. This idealisation can be understood to have normative force and moral authority whether or not, in reality, there exists any organised governance system with the political power and authority to implement and enforce such rights. Since the late eighteenth century, universal human rights ('natural rights', 'rights of man') have been inscribed in various versions in national constitutions (such as those of France and the USA in particular). However, in principle, human rights cannot be defined as, or confined to, rights conferred by citizenship in any particular territorially and/or ethnically defined and exclusive nation-state, and evidently they have often been denied in practice by states and national political systems and communities.

In the post-war period they have been inscribed in the United Nations Charter and other related documents. Human rights have only ever been implemented at best imperfectly and unevenly across the world's nations in the often violent and rights-abusing international history of the late twentieth century. Nonetheless, as we noted earlier, they have an increasing salience as a potential reference point for institution-building and constitution-building in the twenty-first century, as the various forces of globalisation increasingly challenge the contemporary international order to develop more explicitly trans-national forms of governance at world regional and global level. Such developments, if and when they occur, in principle are analysable as developments in the institutionalisation of 'global citizenship' (or 'cosmopolitan democratic citizenship' as Held refers to it in his notable theoretical analysis[8]), in this sense of 'universal citizenship'.

The relevance of these observations for mega-event movements, particularly the expo and Olympic movements, as has been indicated earlier, is that they have always tended to rationalise their production of their events and event cycles in terms of their relevance for universal, individualistic and humanistic values of a similar kind to those expressed in human rights codes. Mega-event movements are thus, in principle normatively assessable and accountable in terms of the degree to which they promote, or undermine, the maximal distribution and exercise of human rights and thus of the ideal 'universal citizenship' they imply.

The expo movement evidently claimed and still claims to promote public understanding of advances in science and technology, and thus it implicitly addresses human rights to information and education. The Olympic movement has always claimed to promote sport as a means to the promotion of such things as embodied freedom and achievement, a sense of 'fair play' (or more grandly 'ethics'), health, and peace. In more recent decades it has claimed to oppose various forms of discrimination, whether of race, gender or physical disability. As with expo movement ideals these ideals are also readily translatable into the language of human rights.

This involvement of the mega-event movements with human rights ideals and with the idealisation of the global governance of global citizenship has a general implication for them, together with a number more specific implications. The general implication is that it is intelligible and legitimate to assess the performance of, for instance, the Olympic movement in relation to the promotion or violation of human rights that it, or its various subsidiary organisational partners (particularly the nations involved in hosting its mega-events) is responsible for.

The Olympic movement often likes to claim a traditional, organisational and ideological 'independence' and 'self-government' vis-à-vis nation-states. However, this does not in principle involve any kind of exemption (as it does not for member states of the UN) from the requirement to honour the human rights ideals and thus to be answerable for the forms of universal citizenship that it claims to promote. We consider this later in relation to various human rights problems in recent Olympic history, among them those involving the strategic attempt to capitalise on China's opening to the West and involve the country in the movement by hosting an Olympic Games.

The more specific implications of any mega-event movement's involvement with 'universal citizenship' are those connected with its interaction with the media, its internal rules and democracy, and its activities as a corporate actor in international civil society. We can look at each of these briefly in turn.

'Mediatised citizenship'

In Chapter 6 we saw that the Olympics have become mediatised and thereby globalised as 'media events' in the late twentieth century. This process, and the problem of organising access to the Olympics via the media, raises issues about people's universal rights of access to information and also to inclusion and participation in contemporary global culture.[9] Various sorts of media problems affecting the nature of people's participation in the Olympics, which can be expressed in the language of citizenship, have been evident for a number of years and we will consider them in more detail later. The first media-related problem is the commercialisation of Olympic TV in which the problem for the IOC is the loss of public access to the special and traditional meaning of the event within programming formats which emphasise advertising and nationalist messages. The second media-related problem is what might be called the privatisation of the Olympics, namely the growing interest of global media corporations in obtaining exclusive broadcast rights to the Games in order to remove them from widely publicly accessible 'free-to-view' TV distribution systems and to create new markets in more inaccessible and conditional access 'pay-per-view' TV systems. Finally, there is the problem of the impact of the growth of the Internet on how the Olympic Games ought to be made available to the global public.

'Movement citizenship'

This refers to internal problems of democracy and exclusion within the mega-event movement, counting spectators as temporary members of the movement. First, as we have seen, there is a problem of social exclusion associated with mega-events which tends to undermine their claim to promote an inclusionary cultural citizenship. In the past, mega-events effectively tended to conceptualise the ideal visitor-citizen they aimed to address and culturally include as a host country ethnic national, as male, as white and as either middle class or upper working class – thus downgrading and/or excluding visitors who happened to be women, 'foreigners', blacks and the poor.

Second, there is a problem of democracy, of who controls the production of mega-events, which tends to undermine their claim to promote democratic empowerment.

In so far as the event movement discourse ever implied anything substantial about the notion of democracy, either through the ideal of the visitor-citizen or through the concept of human rights – this has tended to be undermined by the fact that to a significant extent event producers have typically excluded the public from decision-making and planning roles other than in the form of finance providers (via taxation and subsidies) or in token ways. It is consistent with this substantive democratic exclusion and disempowerment that mega-events can often also be presented as 'owned' by their host public and thus can be construed as a quasi-democratic exercise in cooperative cultural policy, a division of labour, between the activities of elite cultural producers, on the one hand, and the activities of the masses of consumers of popular culture, on the other. We will consider the problems of internal democracy in relation to the Olympic movement later, along with the problem of the quality of inclusion of sports people in the movement which are raised by drug abuse.

'Corporate citizenship'

Finally, there is the problem of the external behaviour of mega-event movements as corporate or collective actors in relation to global civil society and global governance. While this may appear to be distinct from individual human rights problems there are connections. These are not least that the control of collective actors is ultimately the responsibility of individual actors with authority in organisations. So, in this perpective much depends on the integrity, honesty and non-corruptibility of authoritative individuals in leadership positions and the degree to which they respect the human rights of others outside the movement with whom they have to deal on behalf of the movement.

The movement as a collective legal entity, and its officers, both as movement representatives and also as individuals, are in principle and in practice accountable for their actions under the national and international legal frameworks they have officially recognised and contracted into. No organisation or officers of an organisation, whatever their claimed 'independence' and 'self-government', have exemption from this context. Later we consider the contemporary problems of the Olympic movement as an actor in global society on terms of the problem of corruption in the process which in Chapter 5 we called 'the Olympic City Bidding Game'. In addition, we also consider 'corporate citizenship' problems connected with the Olympic movement's apparently laudable, if relatively recent, inter-national political strategy of attempting to arrange the cessation of war or 'Olympic truce' both between and within states during the periods in which its mega-events are held. We are now in a position to consider an outline analysis and assessment of the Olympics movement in terms of these dimensions of global citizenship.

The Olympic movement and global citizenship

The normative perspective on international mega-events which suggests that they might be seen as promoting contemporary and future forms of global cultural citizenship, in this all-too-imperfect world, is evidently a very idealistic one. This proposition might initially appear to be supported in the key case of the Olympic movement on the basis of what was suggested about its universalistic ideology and its participation in contemporary forms of global civil society and governance above. However, to assess this proposition more realistically it is necessary to consider the four aspects of the idea of 'global citizenship' outlined earlier and apply them to the Olympic case. These aspects are 'universal citizenship', which is connected with the universality of human rights, together with some areas in which these or related notions of rights could be said to apply. These areas of application of the universality of human rights are the 'mediatised citizenship' of people's rights of participation in the Olympics as media event, the 'movement citizenship' of people's rights of participation in the Olympic movement as a sports organisation and movement, and the 'corporate citizenship' of the movement as a collective actor in global civil society. We can now consider each of these in turn.

'Universal citizenship' and the Olympic movement

In spite of the idealistic universalism and political independence of its ideology the Olympic movement, as we have seen throughout this book, has evidently been periodically very vulnerable to political influences of various kinds throughout its history. This was most evident in the virtual 'capture' of the IOC by fascism in the late 1930s (Chapter 4), and it was also evident in the post-war Cold War period in its use as an international arena for the symbolic display of ideological superiority by the American and Soviet 'superpowers' (Booker 1981; Shaikin 1988). On the positive side, in the post-war period the Olympic movement (albeit after initial indifference and indecision) eventually provided substantial support to the UN-promoted cultural isolation of South Africa for the denial of human rights to its Black citizens from 1970 to 1992. During this time, South Africa was excluded from sending athletes to participate in the Olympic Games, an important denial of international recognition to a racist state.[10]

However, arguably the negatives outweigh the positives in the Olympic record. The IOC cannot be said to have ever taken a consistent and strong line on the human rights record of the nations which have hosted the Games. The regimes which won the right to stage the 1968 Mexico Olympics, the 1980 Moscow Olympics and the 1988 Seoul Olympics were all well known, when the events were awarded, for being highly repressive of the human rights of many sections of their own citizens. Furthermore, each of these states had to take specific additional repressive measures in the host cities in order to stage the Games. In Mexico and South Korea this involved brutal military crackdowns on political opposition, and in the Mexican case it notoriously involved the massacre of many demonstrators by the forces of the state a matter of days before the Games were due to start (Espy 1979; IOC 1996a).

More recently, and in spite of the 1989 Tiannenman Square massacre and the continuing record of suppression of dissidents and human rights abuses by the Chinese state, the IOC President encouraged Beijing's bid to stage the 2000 Olympics, a bid which only narrowly failed (Jennings 1996, ch. 16). Partly as a way of attempting to compensate for this very sorry record, in the 1990s the IOC and its President have promoted the idea of an 'Olympic truce' during the Games event, which in principle at least, aims to do something concrete towards peace and thus towards the most fundamental human right, namely the right to life. We consider this later as an example of the Olympic movement's 'corporate citizenship' in global civil society.

'Mediatised citizenship' and the Olympic movement

One aspect of the Olympic movement's global citizenship is the mediatised citizenship of the worldwide audience participating in Games events through television and other communication media, 'the globalization of the spectacle' (IOC 1996a, ch. 1,6). There are three main issues connected with this. Two of them relate to global television and the third relates to the Internet as a global information and communication system. They all relate to the notion that – since the Olympic Games events are supposed to be inclusive international events, and the technology exists to make them available worldwide – people around the world could be considered to have (human) rights of spectator participation and informational access in relation to them.

The two key television problems are, on the one hand, the commercialisation and also what we can call the 'nationalisation' of the content of Olympic TV programming and, on the other, the regulation of maximal public access to it. In Chapter 6 we considered some examples of these problems. In terms of the programming content problem these examples included analysis of broadcasts of the 1992 Barcelona Olympic Games. This research indicated that the internationalism and idealism of the Olympic message allegedly aimed for by the IOC was in reality subject to considerable interference and distortion both by the routine discursive and broadcast practices of nationally-oriented broadcasters and also by the intrusion of advertising messages and images. Processes of the mixing of commercial and Olympic messages were seen to be occurring, and these processes seemed to be out of the control of the IOC. Effectively, the Spa team's study can be read as implying that the IOC need to exert more influence on the actual delivery of the programming by national broadcasters if they are to protect people's rights to access the event as an international sport event (rather than as a different kind of event capable of being represented in mainly nationalistic and commercial terms), together with its specific symbolic and its ideological context and meanings (Spa *et al.* 1995: 204).

The public access issue has two aspects to it. One aspect relates to the fact that the inequalities between developed and undeveloped countries is reflected in the comparable inequalities between countries in the coverage and quality of their television systems. The unequal access to the Olympic media event in less developed countries has always been a problem in the post-war period, and, in spite of the rapid contemporary development of global television systems, continues to be so. The other aspect relates to the developed societies where the broadcast systems can in principle reach whole national populations and where broadcasters have a commercial interest in providing a mass audience platform for their advertisers to promote their products.

In this situation, and the USA is the major example here, the 'privatisation' of the broadcast rights has, at least up until now, not led to restriction of public access to participation in the Olympics as a media event, rather the contrary. In addition, in the UK and also in some European countries, public access to this particular sport mega-event, along with other 'listed events', is, at least notionally, protected by regulation in media law. Whether the 'listed events' system is, in reality, an effective guarantee of public access to the Olympics in the British case is unclear, as it has never had to be tested, a situation which could change in future. Also in the European case, until the 2008 Olympics, the IOC has continued to grant broadcast rights to the European Broadcasting Union (EBU), the association of national public broadcasting organisations.

However, future public access in Europe, at least, could be affected by the fact that the European Union (EU) is critical of the EBU in terms of its (the EU's) strategy of promoting a single commercial media industry market 'without frontiers' within the EU. From the EU's perspective, the EBU is effectively a cartel and thus is an interference with the free market, with the rights of market entry by other producers, and the rights of consumers to maximal choice. In addition, whether in the USA or in the EU, such regulatory obstacles as exist may not, when tested, prevent restrictive forms of transmission of Olympic TV programming if media corporations decisively come to the view that it is in their interests to go down this road. They may well do so, for instance, in relation to the commercial benefits to be derived from pay-per-view television. As we noted in Chapter 6, restrictive programming in relation to many major sport events and competitions, has occurred in recent times, particularly in Europe.

The IOC's Olympic Charter requires them to 'ensure the fullest news coverage by the different media and the widest possible audience for the Olympic Games' (Rule 59, IOC 1995b). This limited and pragmatically phrased rule can, at a stretch, be read as committing them to the protection of people's rights of access to the games media event worldwide. Consistent with this, the IOC has usually attempted to build in simple requirements about widespread 'free-to-view' access in its successive television rights arrangements with different media corporations and groupings. However, evidently the global media technology environment and the related global commercial environment are dynamic and subject to continuous change, not least in relation to the growth of the Internet, which we will come to in a moment. In relation to the changing technological demands and commercial opportunities of these environments, the IOC may come under pressure to license more complex and potentially restrictive television agreements as time goes by.

Finally, then, there is the issue of the Internet and people's notional rights of information access to the Olympics through this medium. In 1998 the Internet had 40 million users worldwide, most of them in the USA. This is predicted to grow exponentially through the early years of the twenty-first century in the USA, Europe and around the world as personal computer prices continue to decline and ownership becomes increasingly a mass phenomenon in the developed societies.[11] In the USA the major sport TV companies (CBS, CNN, ESPN, and more recently Fox), recognising the importance of the new medium, have also become major providers of information and access to the sport events they are concerned with through the Internet. They typically provide complementary perspectives on these events to those available through their live television broadcasts, including special camera angles and special commentary transcribed from major figures into Internet talk rooms (Wilson 1998-P). The *information, communication and interactive* resources of the Internet will, undoubtedly, add a new, qualitatively distinct, and culturally rich dimension to mega-events, like the Olympic Games, and mega-event movements, like the Olympic movement, in the future in many ways.

As we have seen in Chapter 5, a major new complex of state-of-the-art information and communication technologies needs to be created in order to successfully
broadcast each Olympic Games worldwide. This continues a tradition effectively
begun, as we saw in Chapter 4, with the limited local cable television transmission
of the Berlin Olympics in 1936. The Olympic movement, in this context, has thus
had to be connected with the leading wave of these technologies. This connection
with innovation also extends to the Internet. During the 1996 Atlanta Olympics
the event's netsite was accessed on 200 million occasions, and this 'hit-rate' rose to
600 million during the 1998 Nagano Winter Olympics (O'Reilly 1998C-P). This
'open' and publicly accessible Internet site carried such things as live results, radio
feeds, site pictures and relevant weather reports. Also during Nagano, a much
more ambitious service was provided on a closed (1,000 terminal) 'intranet' system
situated around the event site (IBM's Info98). This provided 'video on demand' for
users to access television coverage of sport action and also of press conferences,
together with events results and Olympic archival material (Wilson 1998C-P).

However, the running of live television broadcasts through the Internet, or
'netcasting', raises major problems for television broadcasting and for the control of
broadcast rights. This potential competition with television is currently limited
because computer-based picture quality is inferior and because of network-based
delays in picture reception. The competitive realities will undoubtedly emerge more
strongly as personal computer use and internet access continues to proliferate
around at least the developed world, and also as the technological problems are
progressively resolved. Anticipating the potential for the Internet to pirate, bypass
and subvert television companies' control of mega-event TV, mega-event organisations are currently treating the Internet very cautiously. FIFA withdrew from live
'netcasts' of the 1998 soccer World Cup stage in France and the IOC banned them
for the 2000 Olympics in Sydney (Wilson 1998-P, Mackay 1998B-P). Given the IOC's
alleged concerns for achieving 'the widest possible audience' for the Games, this
stance of denial of access to the event to people around the world using this powerful
new global medium may be achievable in the short-term, but it is unlikely to be
sustainable, whether politically or technologically, in the medium-term.

'Movement citizenship' and the Olympics

'Movement citizenship' refers to the practice of internal inclusiveness and democracy within the 'internal international civil society of sport culture' constituted by
the Olympic movement itself. The key problems of movement citizenship for sports
people involved in the Olympic movement are, first, those of the undemocratic,
unrepresentative and unaccountable nature of the IOC at the heart of the Olympic
movement and, second, those of drug abuse and related cheating against the 'fair
play' values of the Olympic movement and sport culture more generally.

Olympic democracy problems

The problems of lack of democracy and accountability in the Olympic movement
are long-standing, centre on the role of the IOC at the heart of the movement, and
are by now familiar enough to need no more than brief review here.[12] The IOC
had its origins, as we saw in Chapters 2 and 3, in late nineteenth-century aristo-

cratic elite groups of modernisers, humanists and internationalists, particularly in France and Britain, but also in their networks around Europe. Its social character as an aristocratic and upper middle-class male club was only marginally moderated over the early and mid-years of the twentieth century. Through the post-war period and up until the present day it has remained constitutionally and organisationally a self-recruiting and secretive elite international club, directly accountable and accessible to nobody but itself, and only weakly and symbolically accountable to the international organisations and movement that it has created, and that it funds and directs. Arguably, there may have once been some rationale for the nature of the IOC's self-appointed role in terms of its claim to independence from the influence of national governments. However, this rationale has long since evaporated given the evident vulnerability of the IOC to the pressure of powerful nations. The rationale has also evaporated given the internal problems of corruption within the IOC which lack of accountability generates.

As we saw in Chapter 5, a corruption crisis surrounding the IOC's global inter-city bid 'game' erupted in 1998, and we return to it later as a problem in the behaviour of the IOC as a 'corporate actor' in international civil society. However, one of its effects was to prompt strong calls from various sports ministers, national Olympic committees and even major corporate sponsors, for structural reform of the IOC. In particular, the 1999 report of US Senator George Mitchell, for the US Olympic Committee, into the Salt Lake City scandal, carried authority not least because of his internationally distinguished role in the peace process in Northern Ireland. The Mitchell Report called for radical new practices of openness and accountability within the IOC. It called for the election of IOC members from the NOCs and for an annual public financial audit of the IOC's operations (Kettle 1999-P).

The IOC's response to the worldwide waves of criticism of its activities and calls for reform which inundated it in early 1999 was to produce its first public financial account for four years, and to create an Ethics Commission and an IOC Olympics 2000 Commission. These bodies consist of non-IOC people as well as IOC members (the former group including two ex-UN Secretary Generals among others). The tasks of these bodies are to produce and monitor a new code of conduct for the IOC, to review the IOC's composition, organisation and role, and to create new processes for the selection of host cities. These responses could possibly have substance and credibility (Butcher 1999-P). Their aim is to put the IOC's house in order by the year 2000. However the architect and proprietor of the IOC's disorderly house for nearly a generation has been its President Juan Samaranch. He has admitted some responsibility for allowing the IOC's corruption problems to get out of control. For many observers the cause of long-delayed Olympic reform would have been best served by his resignation. However, he determined that he would remain in the post to control the reform process. What the consequences of his continued leadership are likely to be for the future of the Olympic movement remain to be seen. Given his track record there are evident grounds for concern.[13]

Olympic inclusion problems: 'fair play' ethics, drugs and cheating

Drug use by athletes and their coaches is a product of two interconnected factors. On the one hand, there is the intensification of competitiveness in the professional sports world produced in turn by mediatisation and commercialisation, increasing dramatically the monetary and status rewards for winners and 'stars', and increasing the absolute and opportunity costs for losers. This can create strong temptations and motivations to cheat, including drug use among other things to artificially increase the body's capacity to absorb and benefit from training regimes. On the other hand, there is the continuous acceleration of the drugs problem in sport. This is caused in part by the general phenomenon of the continuous progress of science, technology and information characteristic of society in modernity. There is a constantly changing context of new drugs, new distribution systems, and new test evasion procedures, which creates ever new opportunities and temptations for athletes and coaches to experiment and to cheat.

Apart from the high-profile drug abuses cases which have afflicted the Olympic Games event in recent years, and which we consider in a moment, it is worth noting that this is part of a much wider problem in contemporary sport culture. Drug use has proven to be extensive in international sport in general in the 1990s. Initial suspicions of drug use in many cases relate to things like very noticeable changes in body shape (re both men and women) and huge improvements in performance in relatively short timeframes. In many cases these suspicions were subsequently verified by scientific testing and were reaffirmed after athletes' legal and scientific challenges to the initial verdicts. We can take the year of 1998 as a recent example. During this single year, drug abuse cheating, together with the consequent threat to the public reputation of the major international sport events they occured in, was suspected and (at least initially, pre-challenge) scientifically demonstrated in the following cases: the Tour de France (Richard Virenque and the Festina team), Grand Prix Tennis (the Australian Open Champion, Petr Korda), the Swimming World Championships (the Chinese team), and the Boston Marathon for Women (Uta Pippig), among others.[14]

Throughout the post-war period there have periodically been waves of suspicion about drug use and cheating at the Olympic Games. It is to the discredit of the IOC and its regulatory regime and testing system that these suspicions have been allowed to accumulate to what is currently effectively a crisis situation.[15] Drug abuse cheating in the 1960s and 1970s was mainly a systematic and collectively organised practice generated by the state interests of communist bloc countries; East Germany, in particular, was desperate to gain international identity, recognition and status as a nation through the Olympic medal-winner tally of their sports men and women. More recently in the 1980s and 1990s, it has been generated by the commercialisation and professionalisation of athletics and sport in general, the consequent intensification of competition, and the greed of individual athletes and their coaches for the status and profits of sporting success.

In the 1960s and the 1970s there was much public and media debate and suspicion in the West about the systematic doping of athletes in East Germany, and attempts to explain their disproportionate success in the Olympics of the period. These suspicions were subsequently proved correct after the fall of the Berlin Wall in 1989 and the unification with West Germany in 1990, both in studies of East German government, medical and police records and archives and also in testimony by East German athletes (Butcher 1996-P). More individualistic and greed-based high-profile drug abuse cases in recent Olympic Games events include the following. In 1988 Seoul, there was the notorious and well-proven case of Ben Johnson (Canada) who, until his cheating was proven, appeared to be the sprint champion. In 1992 Barcelona, the women's sprint champion, Florence Joyner (US), was widely suspected to have taken drugs, but this was never proven – she died in 1998 amid renewed speculation on this issue.

In the 1996 Atlanta Olympics there were a number of cases (ACOG 1997, ch. 16). First, there was Michelle de Bruin (Ireland) who was the surprise winner of a number of swimming gold medals. There was a lot of speculation at the time and since that she had taken drugs to win these medals because of the scale and speed of the improvement in her performance pre-Atlanta. These suspicions were given some credibility when in 1998 she illegally interfered with a random test and was judged by the ISF to have taken drugs. Second, the Olympic shot put champion Randy Barnes (USA) was shown to have tested positive for drugs. Finally, there were also suspicions about Chinese swimmers (and athletes) which were not proven at the time. A US commentator mentioned this on air and produced a major sports diplomatic incident between China and the US. Subsequently the Chinese swimming team has been proven to have used illegal performance-enhancing drugs on a large scale at international events, and this strengthens suspicions that they used them to prepare for Atlanta.[16] Most recently, at the 1998 Nagano Winter Olympics, the snowboard slalom gold medal winner, Ross Rebagliati (Canada), tested positive for cannabis. However, this is not a substance which has been officially banned by the relevant international sport governing body (the International Ski Federation). As a result, he could not be disciplined and this indicates one of the many current problems for international regulatory regimes in this field, namely, in this case whether to include recreational as opposed to performance enhancing drugs in the lists of banned substances (Rowbotham 1998-P).

The drugs problem in international sport, including the Olympics, has been allowed to grow by inadequacies and confusions in the regulatory regimes and testing procedures used to detect and control the problem. Different governing bodies ban different substances, and they can often use very different testing and enforcement practices. The lists of banned substances and the testing and enforce-ment regimes need to be brought into line and made as standardised as possible between all sports and also between all nations which claim to support and promote participation in sport as being of positive health benefit for their citizens and which send teams to the Olympics in accordance with the Olympic Charter. The Olympic movement has been, and continues to be, in a position of special responsibility in this area, as the self-proclaimed leader of the international sport movement. However, its ruling group, the IOC, has been found wanting time and again in recent years, both in the cleaning up of its own act in the Games and also in leading and coordinating action more generally to clean up international sport.

The President of the IOC has been sending out mixed messages on this problem in the recent period. On the one hand, he has argued for a more liberal approach to drug use partly to recognise the problem of recreational drugs noted earlier, and partly to accommodate the apparent unenforceability of the current regulatory regime.[17] On the other hand, he convened a meeting in early 1999 of international sport governing bodies under IOC auspices to try to produce a more standardised approach to the problem. Although sport ministers from various countries were critical of the IOC's track record on testing for doping, attempts were initiated to create a new international agency to oversee and coordinate doping testing across the sports world.[18] All of this may, however, be a case of 'too little, too late'. The acid test for the effectiveness or not of any changes brought in here will be revealed in 2000 in the degree of success the IOC and the Sydney Organising Committee have in producing a drug-free Olympics, an achievement which has eluded the Olympic movement for at least the last decade or more.

'Corporate citizenship' and the Olympic movement

'Corporate citizenship' refers to the Olympic movement's activities as a corporate actor in the wider 'international civil society' and governance system external to it and within which it operates. There are two key problems of 'corporate citizenship' involving the Olympic movement. First, there is the potential for corruption in the way that it conducts the bidding process in relation to the nations and cities which make bids to it for the right to host the Olympic Games event. Second, there are the risks associated with the 'Olympic Truce' project launched by the IOC in 1990 and pursued by them since then. These are connected with the gulf between the movement's reach and its grasp, between its rhetoric and reality. The risk is that recurrent failure to achieve Olympic Truces will not only induce cynicism towards the aspirant, but also public distrust and fatalism with regard to the aspiration of peace itself.

Olympic city bidding problems

In Chapter 5 we considered the development of what can be called 'the Olympic City bidding game'. What was clear in that account was that while the right to host the Olympics had come to viewed as a dubious privilege in the 1970s, the great televisual and commercial success of the 1984 Los Angeles Olympic event changed the rules of the game. Since that time, city leaders and bid groups have tended to attach a very high priority to gaining the right to host what is now seen as the most prestigious sporting mega-event in the global cultural calendar. The city-bidding competitions have become intense and fierce, with cities prepared to spend on a grand scale to promote their cause. The motives of the competing cities are clear and familiar enough. To gain the prize guarantees that the televisual 'eyes of the world', and of potential future tourists and investors, will be focused on the city for the period of the Games. It guarantees that the city will contribute to the making of sporting history and will thereby have a permanent place in the international cultural record. It guarantees that the city will become a member of the select international club of current and ex-'Olympic cities' which have specific Olympic memories and architectural heritages and an enduring relationship with and place in the Olympic movement and its tradition.

However, this intensely competitive situation creates the potentials and temptations for bribery and corruption in the relation between IOC members and the representatives of the bidding cities. On the one hand, there are the lavish marketing efforts intended to impress visiting IOC members who alone have the power to make the decision, and on the other hand, there is the non-representative and unaccountable character of the IOC itself in which decison-making and voting is hidden in secrecy, with no public record of which IOC members voted for which city or why they did so.

Throughout the 1990s, claims had periodically been made in sport and media circles about corrupt practices during various Olympic bidding processes. These claims met with little effective response from the IOC other than the drawing up of new rules for the bidding competition in 1995. These new rules included the provision that no bidding city should offer IOC members or their relatives gifts or benefits worth more than $150.[19] The new rules may or may not have been adequate to address the problem, but their enforcement was evidently utterly inadequate.

In 1998, as we saw in Chapter 5, a corruption crisis enveloped the IOC. It was orginally triggered by Marc Hodler, a senior member of the IOC's Executive, a long-standing Austrian member of the IOC, who had for a period been the IOC's Deputy President. Hodler made a number of serious allegations about corruption in the IOC's Olympic city selection process.[20] First, he claimed that there had been financial mismanagement and possible bribery by the Salt Lake City organising group in the bidding competition for the 2002 Winter Games, a competition in which they were successful. Ironically, the bribery is likely to have occured after 1995, which, as was indicated earlier, was the year in which the IOC was supposed to have tightened up their rules in relation to such matters. Technically the new rules were intended to apply to the selection process, begun in 1996, for the 2004 event host, in which the winner turned out to be Athens. There have been no allegations, at least as yet, about instances of corruption in this particular bidding process. Second, and more broadly, Hodler claimed that over a 10–15-year period (1983/8–1998) four sports agents, including an IOC member, presented their services to bidding cities, stating that they could effectively 'buy' some of the available IOC votes for cities prepared to pay the price. They offered their services for up to $1 million to various cities bidding for various Olympic Games events, the events including those of 1996 Atlanta, 2000 Sydney, and 2002 Salt Lake City.

The IOC's response to these claims, although it initially attempted to downplay them, was to set up an inquiry, the Pound Inquiry, specifically into the Salt Lake City case.[21] This action avoided the issue, noted in Chapter 5, of possible corruption in previous rounds of bidding going back to the round for the 1992 Games event. The IOC claimed that there was a lack of documentary evidence in all of these other potential corruption cases and, thus, insufficient basis for any more searching inquiries. The Pound Report, as we have seen, in a judgement unprecedented in the history of the IOC, recommended the expulsion of six IOC members and the official reprimanding of a number of others. This was enacted at an IOC meeting in 1999. In addition, new rules were agreed to control the bidding and selection process which begins in 2000 for the 2008 Games and beyond. From 1999 onwards the system is that the IOC's Executive creates a 13-strong Selection Committee to conduct the selection process, reducing the candidate cities down to a short list of two. The full membership of the IOC then takes the final decision between these two; however, IOC members who are not on the Selection Committee are banned from visiting candidate cities, and city bid teams are banned from visiting them. Time will tell whether this new version of 'the bidding game' will work and will be effective in rooting out corruption in the Olympic movement and in its dealings with other actors in global civil society.

The 'Olympic Truce' project: ideals, realities and risks

Earlier, some indications were given of the role that the IOC in particular, and the Olympic movement in general, currently plays, or aspires to play, in the sphere of international civil society and governance. The most important and potentially substantial of these roles is that concerned with the so-called 'Olympic Truce' which relates to the fundamental value of the preservation of human life and the promotion of the ideal of peaceful coexistence. What the contemporary Olympic movement claims to offer is both a rationale and, through the organisation of its events, some definable periods of time, in terms of which nations that are at war with other nations (or through versions of civil wars, at war with themselves) might agree to suspend their hostilities at least temporarily. If anything might affirm the truly 'civilising mission' of the Olympic Movement in the midst of bloodthirsty modernity this would be it. Critics, with some justification, suspect the motives for developing the 'Truce' project, suggesting that it might also have something to do with the achievement of a Nobel prize for the President of the IOC.[22] However, without wishing to buy into current versions of 'Olympism', this seems to me to be, in the broader picture of things, an irrelevance. If the successful implementation of the idea of the 'Truce' can ever be judged to have saved one life, arguably it would have been worth it. If it ever creates any kind of a telling precedent and routinely enacted constraint on organised human aggression then it would have been even more worthwhile.

The historic precedent in the Western tradition for this idea of an Olympic Truce was the remarkable effectiveness of the temporary truces in the Hellenic world, which were called throughout much of the one thousand year history of the ancient Olympic Games.[23] This is an undoubtedly impressive precedent for the resuscitation of the idea in the context of the tradition of the modern Olympics. However, from the First World War to the nuclear standoff of the Cold War and beyond, modernity has relentlessly developed the scientific and technological capacities and motivations to create death and destruction on a 'total' scale in relation to nations, world regions and global human life as a whole. In the face of this, as we have seen in the course of this book, the modern Olympic movement, for many generations, has been able to do little more than allow the international community, such as it was and is, to gather together to lick the wounds of two world wars and to act as an arena in which the barely suppressed violence of the Cold War 'peace' between the so-called 'super-powers' could be symbolised and dramatised. Why should things be any different as we look into the cloudy and uncertain future of the twenty-first century?

The course of international conflict in the late 1990s does not bode well. The USA and UK were unwilling, in late 1998, to be influenced in their bombing of Iraq by the co-occurence of the great events in the calendar of world religions, namely Christmas, Ramadan and Hanukkah. In the face of contemporary evidence like this from nations allegedly long committed to the Olympic movement, why should it be assumed that modern nations are likely to have the slightest inclination to respect less established and more secular values and practices promulagated by modern Olympism?

The idea of a cessation of international conflict to observe the holding of modern Olympic Games is not a long-established tradition, whatever its echoes of the achievements of Hellenic civilisation. It was not seriously proposed by de Coubertin from the late nineteenth century through to the 1920s, and it was evidently not observed during the 1930s period in which the IOC sadly came under the baleful influence of fascism. Indeed the idea of an Olympic Truce did not come into focus as an explicit part of Olympic international politics and diplomacy in connection with the United Nations until the 1990s.

The Olympic movement and the United Nations have played something of a parallel role in the international sphere of the post-war and post-colonial period. New nations in particular have needed both political and cultural 'international arenas' or public spheres in which to display themselves, be recognised and be legitimated. Allowing for exaggeration there is some truth in the view that, albeit in different ways and with different implications, nations could be said to have needed recognition by the Olympic movement – particularly participation in the periodic ceremonies and sport of the Olympic Games events – almost as much as they have needed recognition by and participation in the United Nations organisation. However it is worth noting that the IOC, for much of the post-war period, had a fraught and unfruitful relationship with the UN and its system of organisations. In the 1970s in particular, UNESCO, under the influence of the USSR and its Third World allies in Africa and elsewhere, tried to take over the running of the Olympics, a move which was resisted by the then IOC President Lord Killanin.[24]

However, the Olympic Truce project has been a notable part of the IOC's activities in recent years, and this has been developed in cooperation with the UN.[25] The idea of pursuing the project of Olympic Truces without the support and participation of the United Nations organisation, with its vastly greater capacity to potentially broker, legitimate and enforce international peace arrangements, would, of course, have been entirely fanciful. The origins of this cooperation lie in the progressive and violent disintegration of the former Yugoslavia into its ethnic and religious elements during the course of the 1990s.

Initially, Croatia and Slovenia, and eventually Bosnia, sought independence and statehood, and were forcefully opposed by Serbia, the dominant player in the former Yugoslav state. In 1991 the UN Security Council declared a policy of international sanctions against Serbia/Yugoslavia in an attempt to constrain its aggression. In 1992 'sport' was included in these sanctions in UN resolution 757. This came on the eve of the 1992 Barcelona Olympics in which the de facto Serbian state had managed to gain entry under the banner of 'Yugoslavia'. This was a potential embarrassment for the IOC as it could have been construed as a breach of the UN sanctions policy. The IOC appealed to the UN and got an agreement that while Serbia/Yugoslavia should not be permitted to compete, nonetheless individual Serbians/Yugoslavs could compete under the Olympic flag, and also that Bosnia could compete as a nation. The potential for cooperation between the IOC and UN, which has begun to be explored more generally in recent years, was given a notable boost by understandings reached on these diplomatic problems of the Barcelona Olympics in the early 1990s.

In 1993 the general concept of a periodic voluntary Olympic Truce was developed by the ANOC and presented to the UN Secretary General by the IOC. The IOC requested that it be put to the General Assembly for support along with a proposal to declare 1994 the 'International Year of Sport and of the Olympic ideal'. The Secretary General agreed, providing the request could be shown to have the prior backing of a reasonable number of states. The IOC lobbied UN member states to achieve this and the Olympic Truce proposal received unanimous support from the General Assembly when it was presented to them.

The violence continued in the Balkans in 1994, with Serbia laying seige to the city of Sarajevo, the city which had hosted the Winter Olympics of 1984. Nineteen ninety-four was the year of the Lillehammer Winter Olympics, the first Winter Olympics to be run in a different year from the Summer Olympics on the new quadrennial cycle. With UN support, the IOC President visited Sarajevo and a temporary cessation of violence occurred. In 1995, during the 50th anniversary of UN, the IOC President addressed the UN General Assembly to ask for their voluntary support for the Olympic Truce during the 1996 Atlanta Olympic Games. This was agreed. In addition he proposed that, as a matter of its regular business cycle, the UN should automatically be asked to consider the Olympic Truce every two years, prior to each Winter and Summer Games, and to reaffirm it in relation to these events. This also was agreed. As a result of this as part of its regular agenda the UN reviewed the Olympic Truce in 1997 and reaffirmed it in relation to the upcoming Nagano Winter Olympics of 1998.

There is, then, some substantial evidence in this Olympic Truce project of a new and potentially positive level of cooperation between the Olympic movement and the United Nations. The IOC's interest in this cooperation, whether or not it includes the personal political ambitions of its President, no doubt at least includes the practical desire to reduce the risk of disruption to its Games events from international conflict. In addition the IOC could be said to need some such connection to the UN to add some diplomatic weight and international legitimacy to the aspirations and rhetoric of its ideology. On the UN's side, its interest in its current degree of cooperation with the Olympic movement is not clear.

It may be that the UN takes the view that, in the post-communist world of relatively small-scale and localised international conflicts and wars, temporary cessations of violence, of the kind called for by the Olympic Truce project, are more realistic and stand a greater chance of being taken seriously and being effective than they could ever have done in the Cold War era. Also, it may be that the UN sees its image in international public opinion and the media as being both abstract and negative. That is, the UN may take the view that, as an organisation, it is seen as a distant and formalistic body with little contact with ordinary people around the world, outside of the negative experiences of such things as wars and disasters. Thus, the UN may feel that, in terms of its public relations, it could benefit from allying itself with the Olympic Games and the Olympic movement, which, at least until recently, has been popularly perceived as being one of the most charismatic and idealist of the movements of twentieth-century international culture and civil society, a movement which is associated, via the global popularity of sport culture, with largely positive feelings and experiences among the international public and media. Relatedly, perhaps, the UN feels that by associating itself with the Olympic movement's commitment to sport culture and its global event cycle, it can thereby help to contribute a more cultural, active and engaged character to the practice of peaceful internationalism, than it could do in isolation.

Whatever the interests and potential benefits involved for each side in the IOC/UN cooperation on the Olympic Truce project, there are evidently also risks attached for each organisation. On the UN side, there are risks in being associated with an organisation which is as committed to commercialism, and thus to global capitalism and the consumer culture, as the Olympic movement currently is. This is not least because of the possible damage to the reputation and status of the Olympic movement's idealism – which may derive generally from its commercialism and more particularly from the problems of bribery and corruption associated with this – damage which could be passed on to the UN by association.

On the side of the Olympic movement there are risks in being associated with an organisation, the UN, which – particularly in the Cold War era, but also subsequently – has all too often proved to be ineffective in promoting international peace and justice, and, as yet, has not given much of a lead in the construction of a new system of global governance which the world needs as we enter the twenty-first century. In addition, if the Olympic Truce is regularly ignored or broken, the Olympic movement runs the risk of a loss of credibility and the very cause of peacemaking itself may be damaged. While in principle the Truce effort is worth the risk, in practice the IOC may not currently have sufficient credibility to carry the effort through effectively.

Conclusion

In this chapter we have considered the global cultural role of the main contemporary mega-event movement, the Olympic movement. Some of the problems and crises currently facing it have been analysed together with the IOC's responses to them in terms of the notion of 'global citizenship' and its various dimensions. We can summarise the implications of the discussion as follows. First, in relation to the 'universal citizenship' of human rights, the Olympic movement, in spite of its universalistic ideology, has always experienced problems in operationalising its interests, such as they are, in this field. It is likely that it will continue to face them as it negotiates its relationship with various nations and world regions in the early decades of the twenty-first century, not least among them China. China is rapidly emerging as one of the major global powers; it narrowly missed hosting the 2000 Olympics, and it is likely to bid again for 2008 or 2012. However, it has both a poor human rights record and also a poor record in terms of controlling drug abuse in its sport system. The Olympic movement is likely to be even more torn and compromised in future than it was in relation to the 2000 event between the political imperative to give the Olympic host role to China and the ethical imperative to refuse to do so.

Second, there is the issue of 'mediatised communities' and the related rights of public access to, and mediatised participation in, the experience of the Olympic event. The Olympic movement is committed to ensuring the maintenance and growth of mass worldwide public access to its events through its organisation of Olympic Games events as global television 'media events'. However, this project is facing problems and challenges, at least in relation to the commercialisation of the events. Commercialisation risks devaluing the meaning and value of the media event for its global audiences. Also, the exclusivity of the contracts between the IOC and particular world regional media organisations involves limiting the growth of global public access to the events through the Internet and its more personal and interactive forms of mediatised experience. The IOC currently seems to have little grasp of the importance of these problems and no strategies for dealing with them.

Third, in relation to 'movement citizenship' there are the well-known and long-standing problems of exclusion for ordinary sports people connected with the Olympic movement relating to, on the one hand, the notorious lack of democracy and accountability at the heart of the movement, and on the other, the movement's apparent inability to root out drug-use and cheating within in its sports and events. The IOC took a number of actions in 1999 to address these problems. These included attempting to set up, on the one hand, a semi-independent commission to advise on fundamental reforms of the IOC's and the Olympic movement's operations, and, on the other hand, a new international agency to control doping in collaboration with other national and international agencies and organisations. Time will tell whether these responses are adequate to the scale of the problem.

Finally, in relation to the 'corporate citizenship' of the actions of the movement in global civil society, there is a problem and a challenge. On the one hand, there is the current crisis of the IOC's interactions with nations and cities bidding to host the Games event, and the problem of bribery and corruption which seems to have become endemic this process. On the other hand, there is the challenge of maintaining and developing further the politically potentially important project of 'the Olympic Truce'. In 1999 the IOC reformed the city-selection process, restricting the involvement of the full IOC in the lobbying and decision-making processes. Although the new system is something of a compromise, in principle it is reasonable to assume that it has a good chance of squeezing many, even most, of the opportunities and temptations for bribery and corruption out of the process. However, this conclusion only holds true on the condition that the new system is implemented and policed rigorously. Unfortunately, in the case of an organisation with a dubious track record on self-regulation like the IOC, this condition may prove to be difficult to achieve. Even more unfortunately, until this condition is achieved, the IOC is likely to lack the credibility and legitimacy to be able to get much real international acquiescence in the 'Olympic Truce' project.

8 Mega-events, identity and global society

Theoretical reflections

Introduction

This book has presented a connected series of wide-ranging socio-historical explorations and accounts of the mega-event phenomenon in modernity. Based on these accounts, in this concluding chapter I now aim to focus some the general themes of my discussion by reflecting on some key questions. The aim in addressing large questions at this stage is not to provide definitive and exhaustive answers. Rather – in the spirit of my discussion as a whole, and revisiting some of the general themes and issues outlined in Chapter 1 en route – my aim is to illuminate the terrain of the political sociology and social theory of mega-events which this book has attempted to open up in its historical, descriptive and analytical accounts. Given that these accounts represent what is in effect a preliminary survey of the mega-event field, my aim is to suggest and illustrate some lines along which key questions might be explored further, beyond the reach of this particular study, in more extensive, intensive and systematic descriptive and theoretical research into mega-events. Also, given that these accounts have tended to give priority to the dramatological, political and economic dimensions of mega-events, my aim in this chapter is to attempt dig a bit deeper into the social theory of the sociological conditions and processes in modernity underlying and pervading these dimensions.

We need, then, to consider two key questions. First, what are some of the main personal and interpersonal meanings typically attributable to mega-events at the end of the twentieth century? Second, as we enter the early part of the twenty-first century, what are some of the main elements of the sociological role played by mega-events in the development of world society in our period? Addressing each of these questions offers different but related ways of reflecting on and understanding the relationship between mega-events and public culture in modernity, and the continuing relevance of the former for the latter in the contemporary period in which a global culture is developing.

The discussion in this chapter proceeds in two main steps. In the first section we address the first key question by considering the relevance of mega-events for 'personal identity' in modern society. Some of the main structures of meaning which continue to be associated with mega-events in modernity are outlined, and particularly those deriving from sport culture, in terms of the categories of identity, time and space, and agency. This section, then, aims to provide some elements of a phenomenology of the social world in late modernity relevant to the understanding of mega-events, particularly, but not exclusively, their dramato-logical features and appeal. In the second section we address the second key question by considering the relevance of mega-events for contemporary globalis-ation processes and the form of society and governance they are generating, namely 'global society'. A political sociology and social theory of mega-events and mega-event movements concerned with their actual and potential roles in contemporary global society is outlined. This analysis suggests that the periodic production of particular mega-events can be usefully understood as the production of 'hubs' and 'switches' in the flows and networks which help to constitute and develop global society. It is on this basis that, as we discussed in Chapter 7, mega-event movements can usefully be understood as playing important roles in the cultural aspects of institution-building at the global level and in the building, more generally, of systems of 'global governance' and global citizenship. Thus it is also on this basis that we can understand some of the political economic and contextual characteristics of mega-events.

Mega-events, identity and the lifeworld: elements of a phenomenology of the social world in late modernity

Mega-event genres in one form or another – and, at least apparently, independ-ently of the periodic seismic shifts and transformations in their societal environ-ments – seem to have an enduring popularity in modern society. As our review of the history in this book has indicated, this popularity is even greater now at the turn of the twentieth century than it was at the turn of the nineteenth century. Without underplaying expo-type mega-events this is particularly true in relation to international sport mega events such as the Olympics and FIFA's World Cup soccer tournament, which are but the tip of the iceberg of a host of other specialist and lower-level international sports events which have evolved in the last quarter of the twentieth century (Chapter 1, note 1). One way of attempting to understand this phenomenon is to try to relate cultural institutions and processes, such as people's interest in and their direct and/or vicarious participation in mega-events and sport culture, to fundamental features of personal and social life in modern society. That is, we should explore the possibility that mega-events and sport culture have played, and continue to play, a distinctive role in providing some significant cultural resources and opportunities for people in modern society to address their basic human needs for individual (and also group) identity and agency.

One important and relevant aspect of modernity and of the development of modern society since the Enlightenment has been the promotion of popular individualism and thus the continuous activation of people's awareness of their human needs for identity and agency. However, as is particularly evident outside of elite and middle-class groups and classes, the usually uneven and often contradictory development of society in modernity has often failed to satisfy these needs en masse. Often it has appeared to systematically threaten them. For instance, this threat or risk theme is a familiar one in the classical social theory concerns of Marx and Durkheim for the systemic and pervasive production, in modern society, of 'alienation' and 'anomie' among all social groups and classes. Arguably, other systemic aspects of modernity – for instance the industrialisation and scientisation of warfare and the organisation of state and inter-state militarism and violence, which were largely unanticipated in these classical analyses – became even more threatening to human identity and agency, not to mention social coexistence and individual existence itself, as the twentieth century unfolded.

Many additional and more contemporary social theory approaches no doubt can be deployed to explore identity and agency in the contemporary period. In the late twentieth century's 'risk society' (Beck 1992) the threats to human need satisfaction spinning out from both the intended and unintended consequences of modernity and its progress, have accumulated as rapidly as have the means of satisfying them. Some relevant social theory approaches include, among others, those deriving from phenomenology and related analyses of 'the lifeworld' (namely, typical interpersonal structures of meaning and experience relating to self, others, embodiement, time and space),[1] together with theories of human needs and human rights.[2] Without delving onto these analytic resources further here, we can summarise a line of argument, elements of which I have discussed further elsewhere, which is consistent with them in a number of steps which we can now consider further.[3]

Early modernity, identity needs and mega-events

People in all societies and periods, but particularly in the modern world, can be said to have basic needs for a lifelong and substantial experience of individual identity. Personal identity, in turn, is dependent, among other things, on socialisation into, and the everyday exercise of, a range of culturally recognised basic skills. These skills include those involved in autonomous action (agency) and in competent communication with others. They also include the skills involved in the everyday constitution of the socially shared spatial and temporal frameworks which all embodied action, communication and coexistence with others requires for its occurrence and its very intelligibility.

Early modernity (the late nineteenth and early twentieth centuries), as we saw in Part 1 of this book, can be said to have involved the building of the industrial capitalist nation-state on the basis of various socially constructed forms of embodiement, activity (work), space and time – forms such as a rigidly gendered division of labour, labour-intensive production technologies, employment-based time-structuring and a city-based structure of work and non-work space and social life. In the context of these forms, people generated class-related and nation-related cultures – both 'high' or effectively 'unpopular' versions of culture and 'low' or popular versions – through their activities, both in the public and the private spheres. People's individual and group identities and agency in early modernity can thus be said to have been significantly formed by the adaptations they made to, and the uses they made of, these structures of the emerging politico-economic societal environment.

In this politico-economic societal environment – which we explored in relation to mega-events in Part 1 – new dramatic cultural events and '*rites de passage*' of all kinds and at all societal levels grew. A modern 'event ecology' manifest in the cultures and spheres of family, neighbourhood, city, class and nation began to establish itself. This can be said to have helped to provide personal, interpersonal and cultural meaning contexts in which personal and group identities could be shaped through special patterns of embodied action, in special times and places.

This was particularly true of the male-dominated local, national and ultimately international sport cultures and their attendant event cycles which evolved in this period. International mega-events – particularly, as we have seen, expos but also increasingly including sport events – played a part in providing special non-work opportunities which people could use to review the agency (or lack of it) represented by their work, to review the space and time frameworks which structured their lives (into located destinies etc.) and to review their sameness and difference from their fellow citizens, from foreigners, and from 'Others', together with their capacity to coexist peacefully, and even possibly communicate, with them.

Late modernity, identity needs and mega-events

Social change, late modernity and identity

It can be claimed that social change in late twentieth-century modernity involves, among other things, the construction of a flexible, service-based and media/information technology-based economy at a global level. This has distinctive new features in terms of the way it generally influences the structures of the social world in terms of embodiement, activity (work), space and time. It produces a new generation of threats and problems in relation to the structures of the social world and the common forms of identity and agency developed in early modernity which had been sedimented and reproduced in the institutions and systems built around the nation-state and the industrial economy.

This is evident enough in people's everyday experiences of the substantive and symbolic political problems associated with the declining power and sovereignty of the nation-state in the late twentieth century. It is also evident in people's everyday experiences of the economic and gender relation changes and related problems associated with work. On the one hand, due to scientific and technological progress in production systems and labour productivity, there has been a long-term decline in the quantity and status of physically demanding (and thus strongly 'embodied') work roles in the industrial sector traditionally dominated by men since the nineteenth century. On the other hand, in the late twentieth century in particular, there has been a massive shift in economic organisation towards more sedantry (and, from that perspective, more 'disembodied') forms of employment in the service and information sectors. These changes, and the shift to more disembodied work roles in particular, has affected male work identities. In addition this shift has coincided with women's mass entry into the labour market, which has begun to carry with it the need to review the gendered nature of employment roles and to renegotiate the gender division of labour more generally in relation to socially necessary and traditionally unpaid childcare work.

In general terms, early modern personal identity forms are being required to change and to become qualitatively more reflective, disembodied, complex and flexible under late modern conditions.[4] Personal identities are required to be capable of continuously adapting to changes in the economy and the polity. In terms of the economy, there are new requirements to adapt, on the one hand to incessant technological and organisational change in employment systems and in the labour market, and, on the other, to the 'information overload' of advertising and the chaos of 'choice' in consumer markets and in mediatised 'consumer culture'.[5] In the polity there is the requirement to adapt to the continuous increments in the complexity of political community life associated with the growth of cultural and political pluralism within nations, and the growth of interdependence and trans-national governance between them. There are no doubt limits to the adaptations which are humanly possible in relation to these kinds of demands, limits which can be understood through such means as those of the human needs perspective we are considering here. Arguably, beyond these adaptive limits, the incessant demands of contemporary social change on personal identity and agency in late modernity can be argued to threaten new forms of 'alienation' and 'anomie', indeed even threaten the very possibility of achieving and sustaining coherent identity and agency altogether.[6]

From one perspective sport culture (from the local to the international), together with international sport mega-events and mega-events in general, can be argued to provide significant cultural resources for people in late modernity to use in order to adapt to the economic and political opportunities for life in the new social order. From another perspective they can also be argued to provide cultural resources for people to resist the threats which this contradictory new order can be said to pose to the very possibility of maintaining a coherent personal identity, and of exercising effective agency. Although both of these adaptation and resistance potentials are important, arguably the latter is currently more important, and we consider this further in a moment.[7]

To introduce this resistance-based interpretation of the popularity of mega-events and sport culture in late modernity, it is first necessary to briefly indicate the nature of the threats to identity and agency posed by the new social order a little further, as follows. It is often observed that late modernity's structural tendencies (globalisation, mediatisation, informationalisation, etc.) are capable of having some profound socio-psychological effects, many of which may ultimately be incompatible with development and maintenance of personal identity and agency to the degree that, as suggested earlier, these are dependent on, among other things, an investment in embodiement in activity and the maintenance of space-time frameworks. These potentially negative effects include the compression and de-structuring of people's experience of personal and social space and time, and, in various ways, the disembodiement of our experience of society, of others, and ultimately perhaps of ourselves. Partly as a result of the two preceding effects, an additional negative effect is that of a potential loss of personal and group agency (the capacity to plan projects and to take effective action to implement them) and fatalism in the face of the 'logics' and 'illogics' (the disempowering irrevocabilities, opaque complexities, and arbitrarinesses) of contemporary social and system change.

Late modernity, identity needs and mega-events

On the basis of the preceding outline analysis mega-events and sport culture, among other popular cultural forms, can be argued to provide distinctive cultural resources for resisting systemic threats to personal identity generated by the social order of late modernity. This can be seen in mega-events' and sport culture's roles in relation to the problems of time-space compression and effective agency. Special mega-events (particularly those connecting up with the familiar and accessible event worlds of local and national sport culture) and 'the mega-event world' of international event series, organisations and movements more generally, carry significant implications for people's lived understandings of embodiement, space, time and agency. Mega-events and sport culture provide people with enduring motivations and special opportunities to participate in collective projects which have the characteristics of, among other things, structuring social space and time, displaying the dramatic and symbolic possibilities of organised and effective social action, and reaffirming the embodied agency of people as individual actors.

TIME STRUCTURE AND MEGA-EVENTS

For the purposes of this discussion, the problem of the de-structuring of lived time can be abstracted from its otherwise important interconnection with the problem of the de-structuring of lived space (see below). The problem of the de-structuring of time is that of the degradation or loss of the lived experience of time structure which tends to be produced in late modernity's promulgation of an experience of time as (the structureless 'space' of) what Castells (below) refers to as a 'timeless present'.

The concept of 'time-structure' (Roche 1990) refers to an experience of time and a perspective upon the course of human life which allows people to recognise temporal difference and temporal distance. That is to say it refers to the experiencable difference between the present, the past and the future, and it involves the recognition of distance between the present and the further reaches, both in personal life and societal history, of the past and the future. It also refers to the capacity to experience the irreversibility and directional 'flow' of personal life from the past through the present to the future, the related capacity to understand personal life as flowing through youth, middle age and old age to death, and the capacity to situate the flow of personal life in broader experiences of communal and historical time.[8]

To a certain extent, as Anthony Giddens has argued, individual identity can be said to be both shaped by socialisation and integrated into the wider order of social institutions through the lived temporality of the repeated 'routines' of ordinary everyday life (Giddens 1984). However the achievement and reproduction of stabilised routines does not, of course, exhaust personal identity-formation nor people's identity-based needs for the kind of time-structures indicated here. Indeed, it is common observation that an experience of life which is reduced exclusively to the ordinary everyday routine (for instance long-term imprisonment) can in itself be de-structuring of time and threatening to identity and agency.[9] What is necessary to make a fuller time-structure, together with the wider temporal perspectives discussed here, recurrently available in personal life is the periodic interpersonal, communal and societal organisation of precisely non-routine, 'extraordinary' 'special events' , such as personal and/or collective *'rites de passage'* and other such charismatic and ritual celebrations. Among other things, these events are experienced as marking the passing of time and thereby generating time-structure among individuals and groups in more substantial ways than is possible with routine, and even than is possible with rituals.[10]

Participation in the contemporary mega-event world and/or sport culture offers people non-routine extraordinary and charismatic events, involving distinctive motivations and opportunities for dramatic experience, activity and performance, which can be used to recover and reanimate the time-structure dimensions of personal and social life in late modernity. This is so whether people participate in them in a direct and embodied way or in alternative less-embodied, but not thereby less-active, forms of engagement through the media and the event as 'media event', 'media sport', etc. That is, in the short term, the sphere of the present, participation in a mega-event and/or a sport event involves people in a culturally important and unique action project in which the present is experienced both as being dramatised in various ways and also as being evidently temporally bounded. In the medium term, involvement with mega-events and/or sport culture generates experiences of the distances between such events (and the distance of events from the present) created by their periodicities, the planning periods preceding them and the impact periods following them. Through the practices of memory and imaginative projection associated with them, involvement with mega-events and/or sport events, and with the mega-event world and/or sport culture more generally, has the capacity to generate and cultivate experiences of the longer-term temporal perspectives of tradition and futurity.

Time-structure involves the lived reality of 'generationality', that is, being a member of one particular 'generation' and not of other generations. The temporal structures of the lifeworld are experienced both intra-generationally and inter-generationally, they involve co-existence with other generations and they involve processes of inter-generational communication and influence. These features of time-structure in the lifeworld are important to understanding personal identity, selfhood and otherness. It is a common experience and observation that we tend to make our stongest identifications with, and differentiate ourselves as 'selves' and others in relation to, our peers (i.e. our immediate peer group in particular, and our wider peer generation more generally). We assume that we, at least, roughly share, or can reasonably expect to be able to access, the temporal perspective and temporal worldview of members of our own generation. Older and younger generations are experienced as being more radically 'other' than are the 'others' in our peer generation. We do not experience their temporal world-view as being directly accessible in the same way. Given these differences, as we know, there can be major communication problems, power conflicts and failures of 'recognition' and respect between generations. Mega-event projects provide opportunities for the organisation of their planning and production on a multi-generational basis (e.g. young people often perform alongside middle-aged managers and elderly politicians at mega-event opening and closing ceremonies). They can readily involve inter-generational and multi-generational communication and co-experience in the lived present of the event (all age groups can spectate at the site or on TV). They also involve the construction of collective memories which are accessible inter-generationally. We return to this generational aspect of the time-structure of the lifeworld when considering social structural issues later.

LIVED SPACE, IDENTITY AND MEGA-EVENTS

The threat to our sense of lived space and spatiality, and thus our identity in modernity, can be said to derive from a combination of the time-space compression problem and the disembodiment problem. First, it partly consists of the collapse of the experience of the world as involving great distance and inaccessible places through the continuous development of the capacity to access an increasing number of places around the world physically in a relatively short-term time period. Second, it partly consists of the belief that all places are becoming the same, a loss of the sense of the difference between places which is part of our sense of the spatiality of the world. Thirdly it partly consists in the problem of embodiment, namely that, on the one hand, the location and deployment of our bodies in particular places is of decreasing significance to what our lives are all about, and rather our visual and cognitive access to the world through the de-located spaces of the media, internet and communications technology are far more important in this respect.

Mega-events, particularly sport mega-events, provide resources to counter-balance these destructurations of lived space in late modernity. That is they offer possibilities for people to reanimate the sense of their world as involving spatial distances and differences. Mega-events promote the localisation of international/global event movement history in relation to host sites and cities, identifying them as unique places due to the fact that they staged unique events, and also identifying them as having the power to transform themselves from being mundane places, no different than others, into being these special 'host city' sites. Mega-events also promulgate the sense of the world as a knowable spatial world of spatially and historically distributed host sites and event-identifiable cities.

In addition, mega-events reanimate the importance of embodiment and place, together with the embodiment and proximity with others, involved in 'being there'. Sports events are particularly important in this respect because they also make the experience of embodiment a key focus and *raison d'être* of the event as such. To a certain extent, although to a lesser extent than in relation to time-structure, this also applies to those who participate in the event via the media – whether in their own homes (Rothenbuhler 1988), in sports bars (Eastman and Land 1995) or in public places (such as city squares during mega-events such as the soccer World Cup (Dauncey and Hare (eds) 1999; see also Chapter 6). However, in addition, there is the experience of embodiment and special place thereby conveyed by the practices of 'dressing up' and preparation for the public 'presentation of self', the active consumerism and sociability involved in eating and drinking at the event site, and the embodied responses to public perform-ances and displays. Thus participation in all types of mega-event has the potential to reaffirm the importance of embodied activity and embodiment in special places for an experience of personal and social life and identity in modernity which is otherwise threatened by disembodiment and the deconstruction of the spatial dimension of experience.[11]

LIVED AGENCY, MEGA-EVENTS AND MODERNITY

Involvement with mega-events, the mega-event world and/or the event world of sport culture provides opportunities for people to reanimate a sense of effective agency (and to defend against the threats to this which are present in the contradictory dynamics of social life in late modernity) in a number of ways. First, there is the experience of the producers of the events, the elite groups of international, national and local organisers. As we have seen in our various case studies of mega-events, these groups undoubtedly have a direct experience of personal and collective agency in the demanding processes of planning, bidding for, designing and managing the delivery of a hugely complex event. In ordinary life their actions and projects – whether as individuals or as leading members of organisations – may often be defeated or rendered ineffective by unforeseen circumstances, market competitors, or the blind logic of system change. However, in contrast to this, a mega-event represents a highly visible but bounded case study in potentially effective action. It represents the task of bringing a complex short-lived project through to fruition and completion by a deadline by means of a medium-term programme of plans and actions (whether or not the event ultimately turns out to be effective and manageable in its medium and long-term impacts).

Second, the (at least immanent) success of the staging of events can be an impressive model of effective collective action. For the masses of spectators who attend them, they can be understood to represent, among other things, the bringing of an order to an otherwise disorderly world – albeit a transitory order, and one predefined largely by the organisers and performers. Third, there are the various types of experience of agency associated with various types of event participation – that of people attending the event to participate in it through on-site spectatorship, that of people watching and participating in the event on TV, and that of people monitoring it via the press, radio or internet.

Events in general, and mega-events and sport events in particular, have a 'social order-creating' or 'cultural order-creating' character and potential.[12] They provide popular examples not only of controlled action and of the production of something distinctive, but also of the manifest production of something which is distinctively 'simple' (singular, ordered, etc.), a 'simplification out of complexity'. In all these respects mega-events in particular, and the sports world's event culture in general, offer high-profile arenas in which ordinary people can reclaim agency and order, arenas in which they claim to be part of great and enjoyable happenings, and arenas in which they can watch each other and also watch themselves doing this. This is compatible with people's ordinary understandings that outside of the special world of special events, back in everyday mundane 'reality', the social world is undoubtedly a more complex place and less amenable to agency than this.

Mega-events, global society and global governance

Elements of a sociology of 'meso-social' processes in late modernity

In the previous section we considered the argument that the popularity of mega-events and sport culture in the late twentieth century can be partly understood by seeing them as providing motivations, opportunities and cultural resources for defending and exercising identity and agency, and generally for constructing a meaningful social life in relation to a changing societal environment that has the potential to destabilise and threaten these things. This argument about the potentially positive and adaptive role of mega-events and sport culture, although it contains an understanding of societal structure and change, nevertheless develops its aims and points of reference from the priority it gives to the personal or phenomenological level of analysis and to the appeal of the dramatological features of mega-events.

We now need to consider societal structure and change more directly, in a way which is intended to be a complementary perspective to that of section one. In this section, then, we first need to briefly consider the general nature of the contemporary and changing societal environment, which we can refer to using the inevitably oversimplifying and shorthand expression of 'global society'.[13] This consists of distinct economic/cultural and political/governance aspects. Second, we need to consider the nature of the linkages between the personal level and this structural and systemic level. It is suggested that these can be usefully analysed in terms of the concept of the social spatio-temporal 'meso-sphere' and the 'networks', flows', 'hubs' and 'switches' which operate in this sphere. It will be suggested that generally mega-events are both important symbols of, and also substantive examples of, some of these mesosphere processes, in terms of the social hubs and switches for global society they provide through their movements and their calendar.

Global society, global governance and mega-events

Throughout this book we have attempted to take a systemic perspective in the accounts given of mega-events since the mid–late nineteenth century, through the early and mid-twentieth century to the post-war period and the late twentieth century. The concepts and periodisations of 'international', 'supranational' and 'global' have been used to attempt to characterise major long-term systemic changes in the modern social formation, particularly at the international level and in the international dimension of national societies. It has been argued that the main mega-event genres and movements, expos and Olympics, have played important roles in institution- and system-building both at the level of the nationstate and at the level of international society in the late nineteenth century and early–mid-twentieth century. This role is continuing in contemporary conditions of social change as we enter the twenty-first century and as the elements of a global society begin to emerge.

Economic and cultural globalisation and mega-events

Societies in general, and the societies of early modernity in particular, based as they were on nationally circumscribed states and civil societies, are composed of interconnected political, economic and cultural institutions, systems and processes. By contrast the emerging global society, although characterised by some 'governance' and 'civil society' aspects as we noted in Chapter 7, is currently less substantial institutionally and less organised than national societies have been in each of these dimensions of economics, politics and culture. As it has emerged in the late twentieth century global society is largely an economic space in which the capitalist economic order is dominant and is rapidly evolving. It is an economic space in which a relatively unregulated complex of markets and circuits of production, distribution and consumption operate in processes driven by multinational companies, by states acting as economic entities, and by consumers worldwide.

The economic space is made possible by global information, communication and transport technologies and systems.[14] To organise and regulate the operation of these technologies and systems, and also to provide a framework for planetary-wide environmental controls and peaceful international co-existence in a post-Cold War world, the political and legal dimension of global society has begun to develop, and become more institutionalised, both at the world level and also at the world regional level, such as the EU (Roche and Van Berkel (eds) 1997). As was observed in Chapter 7, and as we discuss further later in this chapter, mega-events can be argued to provide both symbols of, and also substantive working examples of, new intersectoral linkages in the modern economy, new techno-economic developments, and new needs for political economic regulation.

In this political and economic context it might seem that the cultural dimension[15] of the emerging international and trans-national social formation is not only less developed, but also less important. However, this view would be ill-founded. First, as we have seen, mega-events and movements such as the expos and Olympics, have been operating in, and thereby contributing to the reproduction and development of, an internationalised cultural sphere since the late nineteenth century. Second, the global economy which has developed, in many important respects amounts to what might be called a 'global cultural economy'. That is, it consists of a complex, evolving and interconnected set of mediatised markets linking the multinational production and worldwide mass consumption of popular cultural goods and services such as films, music, entertainment, news, sport and tourism. In turn, expos and Olympic mega-events, as we have see, together with their many mega-event clones and relatives, are evidently important elements in this evolving global cultural economy.

Global governance and mega-events[16]

In addition to the economic and cultural aspects of globalization, as was noted in Chapter 7, we also need to take account of globalisation's political aspects. The current 'global-level polity' which has developed in the post-war period – such as it is – can be said to consist of a 'global governance system' closely interconnected with a 'global civil society system'. The late twentieth-century global governance system is centred on the networks and institutions of international diplomacy, communication, cooperation and conflict-resolution surrounding the United Nations and its system of subsidiary international governmental organisations (IGOs), including institutions of international law, rights and peacekeeping. This governance system co-exists and links with what can be called the 'global civil society system' which consists, among other things, of the spheres of international non-governmental organisation (INGOS), multinational corporations (as legal and quasi-political entities) and nation-states and their bi-lateral and multi-lateral interrelations and alliances.

This global polity evidently currently lacks the coherence and power of conventional nation-states. Nation-states are slowly and irreversibly losing this coherence and power, but they still largely continue to possess enough of it within their own territories to make this comparison a telling one. In addition, the global polity also lacks the political culture – that is to say, such things as the collective identity and traditions, and the intensive ongoing internal communication – typically associated with nation-states and assiduously cultivated by them.[17] Nevertheless, the civil and political dimension of global society will continue to develop in response to the imperative need for the strengthening of governance and regulation in relation to endemic worldwide problems of, among other things, militarism, environmental damage, poverty and economic instability.[18] So the need for a global political culture – at least in the civil society terms of communication around regulatory policy-making, interest representation and litigation, and the minimalist state-like terms of recognisable symbolism of authority – will continue to grow in the early twenty-first century.[19]

In this context, international cultural institutions and processes – for instance, the leading mega-events and the organisations and movements which produce them, indeed the complex social ecology of events and event movements at the international level as a whole – are likely to be increasingly brought into alignment with the political dimension. Where possible, they are likely to be used as vehicles for the the ceremonialisation and celebration of the emerging global polity – as indeed they were used for generations, as we saw in Part 1, by the preceding international systems of nation-states and their empires. In relation to this, in Chapter 7 we considered something of the potential role of the Olympic Games and the Olympic movement in relation to the promotion of the political culture of the global polity.

We have, then, attempted to show that mega-events and mega-event movements, in particular in the forms of international sport politics and culture, have considerable importance in the contemporary international order. This field of issues has rarely seemed to catch the attention of academic social scientists, although the situation has improved somewhat since the mid-1990s. Some notable exceptions to the tradition of indifference to the importance of sport politics and culture for the international order are contained in the work of such analysts as Hoberman, Houlihan, Sugden and Tomlinson which we have referenced in previous chapters. Before we leave the theme of mega-events in relation to global governance, then, it is worth considering this work a little further, with a look at Barrie Houlihan's (1994) discussion of sport and international politics.

Houlihan's analysis provides support for some of the Olympic and sport-related themes explored in this book. He observes that in the post-war period in particular sport has been connected with many of the major political problems and movements. These include the Cold War struggle between capitalism and communism, with the differing versions of 'democracy' connected with each of them, and also the historic worldwide struggle against institutionalised racism in South Africa. Houlihan considers the development of international sport governing bodies and their interactions with international organisations like the United Nations, the European Union, and the Commonwealth. These sorts of international governmental organisations, as with nations, have often looked to sport to help build up their identity among mass publics. In relation to this it is worth noting that while there is a 'Commonwealth Games' sport mega-event, there is (at least as yet), no UN or EU equivalent. As Houlihan indicates, and as we have seen in Chapter 7, this has not been for the want of effort on the part of the UN and the EU, as each of these organisations has periodically attempted to create such sport mega-events. However, they failed due to their inability to get the necessary legitimation and cooperation from powerful international sport governing bodies, notably the IOC, which were of longer standing and were committed to defending their territory (Houlihan 1994, ch. 4, 5).

When considering the actual and potential role of sport in international politics, Houlihan suggests that a number of international relations theories and perspectives need to be taken into account. In particular, he considers the 'realist' perspective (sports policy as a tool of nation-states and national interests in the competition between nations) and the 'pluralist' perspective (sports policy as a product of the influence of various agencies including trans-national IGOs and INGOs as well as nations). In spite of his caution about the matter and his critical perspective on it, nonetheless a main thrust of Houlihan's discussion and an notable conclusion is that the last thirty years has seen the 'emergence of a global sports infrastructure' and that this is 'of major importance'. Now, he believes, national 'domestic sport is firmly embedded in a network of international organisational relations' (ibid. p. 208).

The role of the global media and its symbiotic relationship with the Olympic movement, as we noted in Chapter 6, strengthens the capacity of this and other international sport organisations both to act relatively independently of national sports organisations and of nation-states in the global arena, and also to promote processes of cultural and economic globalisation. In line with this, Houlihan observes that states treat sport INGOs as 'significant actors in the international system' and that the global sport structure has 'developed a capacity to facilitate the process of globalisation' (ibid. pp. 210, 208). Houlihan makes the point that the global sport infratructure has come to play an international political and diplomatic role beyond sport:

> The network of (sport) IGOs and INGOs reaches states and communities in parts of the world that are not part of the other major world institutions such as the UN. [International sport provides governments with an] elaborate but low-key network for contact and dialogue [and it is] significant in terms of its contribution to the establishment of a set of norms and values supportive of capitalist interests and of western diplomatic activity.
> (Houlihan 1994: 209)

To adapt Houlihan's terms, overall we can say that there is an ongoing dialectic in contemporary social reality between the processes refered to by the 'realist' and 'pluralist' perspectives on the role of sport in international politics. However, the upshot both of Houlihan's inquiries and also of the discussions undertaken throughout this book would seem to confirm the importance of a critical 'pluralist' approach. Both studies give support to the general theme of the sociological and political importance of the role of sport mega-events and mega-event movements in the sphere of contemporary international and global public culture

Global structuration, the 'meso-social' sphere and mega-events

PERSONAL AGENCY, SOCIAL STRUCTURE AND STRUCTURATION: GENERAL ISSUES

Understanding the fundamental nature of the relationship between individuals and society, the micro-social and the macro-social – and also understanding both the way in which society is a product of the 'structure-building' (or 'structuration', Giddens 1984) produced by people's actions, and in turn gives form and content (or structures) to those actions – has been a problem and an enigma for as long as people have given systematic thought to the matter. Part of the endemic problem of the individual–society relationship, is understanding the relationship between, on the one hand, individuals seen as conscious and choosing agents, and on the other, social systems seen as having an irreducible emergent reality, 'logic' and determining influence of their own. As we noted earlier, this problem was summed, although in no way resolved, by Marx in his well-known observation that 'men make history, but not in conditions of their own making'. For Marx, of course, it was important to be able to think dialectically and to take positions on both sides of this relationship as politics and history demanded – here arguing the need for a recognition of the power of the 'conditions', for instance in the form of 'laws of history', and there arguing for the need for working-class parties and collective action to 'make history' and 'change the world', for instance through the political (mega) event of a socialist revolution (Marx and Engels 1970: 96 and *passim*).

As we have seen, nationalist, liberal and capitalist middle-class and elite groups, trying to ride and guide the new 'conditions' (namely the material forces of science and technology-based mass production in the evolving industrial capitalist inter-national economy of the late nineteenth and early twentieth centuries) often liked to present themselves as 'makers of history', or at least 'makers of historic/ memorable events'. Thus they often used cultural and sport mega-events to help popularise, legitimate and institutionalise their versions of the nature and destiny of modern national and international society. As we have also seen, the major early twentieth century examples of revolutions against these class and elite groups, led by people seeking to mount and ride the new materal conditions of the modern economy in other directions, whether communist or fascist, also used (albeit explicitly politicised) cultural and sport mega-events as ideological tools to popularise, legitimate and institutionalise their alternative versions of the nature and destiny of modern national and international society.

Arguably, the fundamental individual and society relationship, and the structur-ation process in general, is becoming even more of an enigma in the contemporary (late modern) period, in which both the nature of human individuality and the nature of society are changing in major and irrevocable ways. On the one hand, advances in medicine, genetic and other sciences increasingly provide ways (both for individuals and for society) of intervening in and influencing the nature of human individuality. On the other, the nature of society is changing and becoming more complex as the traditional nation-state template for determining what a society is in modernity, is forced, in the new era of globalisation, to give way to and co-exist with various overlapping sub-national and trans-national templates for community, governance and collective identity.

In order to grasp the individual–society and agency–structure relationships present in late nineteenth- and early twentieth-century modernity as expressed through the production and consumption of mega-events, we have suggested (Chapter 1 and also above) that it is necessary to conceive of mega-events as having a three-dimensional character, where the dimensions are connected to aspects of time. The most evidently agentic dimension is the event understood as a short-term dramatic occurrence. By contrast, the most evidently 'conditions'-oriented or social systemic dimension is the event understood as an occurrence within a long-term time-horizon consisting of the underlying structural changes and causes/motivations of the event, together with the long-term effects and memories of the event. However, rather than presenting this as a simple juxtaposition, as much of the thinking in this area seems to assume, throughout this book we have attempted to provide some ways of thinking about the linkages between agency and conditions by considering a third dimension, namely that of the medium-term temporal horizon of the event. This is the horizon within which the event is planned and within which its major medium-term effects and event-heritages are managed. This sphere requires us to consider events as complex collective projects which involve event movements and networks both in their production and consumption. These considerations also point to the nature and role of mega-events in mediating and connecting 'micro' and 'macro' level processes in modernity. To explore this role further, it is first necessary to outline a time-structure-based conception of the form of the possible connection, namely in terms of an intermediary or 'meso-sphere' dimension of the social world.

CONCEPTS OF 'MESO-SOCIAL' PROCESSES 1: GENERATIONS AND TEMPORAL WORLD VIEWS

The concepts of generations, intra-generationalism and inter-generationalism noted in section 1 above are useful in helping to characterise the meso-sphere and structuration relationships between macro structures and micro-agency/agencies. Social structures are experienced in the lifeworld as those features of the social world which have some substantial continuity, and which are transmitted from generation to generation over a number of generations. It is against the background of such inter-generational continuities that we are able to identify and conceptualise social and structural changes, such as those that are involved in globalisation. This also allows us to characterise the meso-sphere as more ambiguous since it is an intermediate time sphere. As such, on the one hand, it is multi-generational and inter-generational. It thus consists of a variety of generational groups each representative of the elements of continuities and/or changes in the macro-social structure. These generational groups are differentiated by their chronological age, by their temporal worldview, and by the differing versions they have, and priorities they give to, the past, present and the future in their their life-projects and in the politics this generates.

The meso-sphere thus consists of the arena in which these groups express and communicate the inter-generational differences they represent in terms of the macro-order, in which they either reconcile, or fail to reconcile, these differences. In the inter-generational dimensions of the meso-sphere, people sense the limits of their lifespans. They (we) experience the macro-order, in its continuities and in its changes, as appearing to be more long-lived than them and in various ways to transcend their lives. On the other hand, the meso-sphere also contains an intra-generational dimension. Here, personal and collective agency appears to have priority over structure. People grow and change, and they believe that they can make differences through their projects. They tend to believe that the personal social problems they encounter in their lives and in their social worlds are either soluble in their lifetime or are likely to be more effectively managed if they are approached on this assumption. They can also believe that, in the course of their lifetime, structure-like features of their social world may turn out to be either young and still malleable, or declining and thus malleable. In the intra-generational dimension, agency has at least the belief that it has the time to affect what we can reflexively identify as being structural, and to make a difference to it before it becomes an unalterable and determinate fact of life. This analysis provides a basis on which we can now begin to formulate the meso-spheric location and social role of mega-events in modernity in terms of intermediary social processes. These can be conceptualised using metaphors such as those of 'flows', 'networks', 'hubs' and 'switches'.

CONCEPTS OF 'MESO-SOCIAL' PROCESSES 2: FLOWS AND NETWORKS

The perspective on mega-events which sees them as complex and fluid social processes is an instance of the more general concern with intermediate or meso-sphere processes in contemporary social theory.[20] This meso-sphere perspective has been used to understand agent-structure/micro-macro relationships more adequately, not just historically in relation to the late nineteenth and early twentieth centuries, but also in relation to the late twentieth and early twenty-first centuries. Late nineteenth- and early twentieth-century 'classical' social theory searched for its dominant theoretic metaphors and anologies for society and the social order in images derived from the industrial technology and science of its time, such as 'mechanism' and 'organism'. In the changed and changing times of the late twentieth century, contemporary social theory sometimes appears to have given up the search for equivalent analogies to grasp the new social order resorting to 'chaos' theory or 'post-modern' fragmentation and relativism, or, as against this, exaggerating the emergent orderliness in images of (artificially) intelligent self-regulating cybernetic systems. Where it continues to search for equivalents and relevant analogies its images often derive from the (essentially trans-national) transport infrastructures and information and communications technology systems of its time – images such as 'flows', 'movements' and 'networks', together with the 'spaces' in which these processes occur and/or which they constitute through their activity.[21]

Manuel Castells (1996, 1997, 1998), for instance, has recently provided a notable analysis of modernity as 'an information age' in which the dominant social form in a global social world is no longer the nation-state but rather 'the network'. Networks consist of a series of interconnected nodes and of flows between them. Power lies in the control of networks of networks (or what we can refer to as 'meta-networks') and with individuals and groups who can connect networks and act as switches between them.

In relation to space, Castells argues that elite power in the contemporary global capitalist economy, now takes shape in the global and electronic 'space of flows' (of goods, services, images, money, people, etc.) while ordinary people still retain an involvement with 'the space of places', namely such sings as local communities and cultures. Consistent with Lash and Urry's (1994) analysis, Castells argues that the 'space of flows' consists of three layers, electronic impulses, nodes (control centres) and hubs (communication centres), together with the globally distributed and interconnected spaces occupied by the dominant managerial elite (segregated urban/suburban residential and leisure areas, and also central cosmopolitian zones in cities, such places and spaces as international hotels and office service facilities in international airports).

Comparably, in relation to time, elite power also takes shape in the time of 'the timeless present' as opposed to ordinary people's boundedness to biological time and socially organised time.[22] In both spheres, Castells suggests that a new social polarisation and possible conflict between elites and peoples is developing, which can be characterised in terms of the current social organisation of space and time. This has implications for our analysis of mega-events and we return to this later. However, in his extensive accounts of late modernity in these terms (and rather surprisingly from the perspective of this book), Castells makes no substantial reference to World's Fairs, Olympic Games, or other such cultural and sporting mega-events.[23] This oversight does not undermine the general value of Castells' analysis. Extending this analysis, then, we can suggest that mega-events can be seen as important cultural networks and movements for characterising (late) modernity both in their own right and also in their role as variously multiple network movements and inter-network switches.[24]

Conclusion – mega-event 'hubs' and 'switches': mega-events as 'meso-social' processes in global society

As we have seen, expos and Olympic events are intrinsically complex processes. They typically involve combinations of political and economic elites, together with many types of cultural (including sport and media) elites and professionals, operating within and between urban, national and international levels, and working together in a medium-term time-horizon both to produce the events and to manage their effects.

The short-term drama of any given event can be pictured as a kind of socio-temporal node or 'hub' at which flows (of finance, information, people, goods, services, etc.) are targeted and assembled in the pre-event period for re-configuration and re-distribution during the event.[25] In his theory of global information society as 'network society', Castells, besides using the imagery of 'networks' and 'flows', also uses the imagery of 'hubs', particularly in relation to his characterisation of modern society as a 'space of flows'.[26] In both his and other relevant analysts' discussions, 'hubs' are in large part, and among other ways, visualised in the substantial and spatially located form of cities. 'Global cities' and the urban centres in which the world regional or the global headquarters of multinational corporations – coordinating worldwide operations throughout the global economy – tend to cluster are particularly important in this visualisation of the 'hubs' of global flows. In Castells' account of the contemporary dynamics of global social differentiation and polarisation (between the global elites and their 'spaces of flows' and ordinary peoples' 'spaces of places'), cities and other relevant spatial clusters assume a particular importance in providing at least for co-existence and possibly some communication between elites and publics.[27] Something of the same 'hub' functions which Castells' analysis proposes for cities can also be argued for understanding the role of mega-events in modernity.

Castells' analysis of social polarisation is that people and their localities and places become disempowered, cut off from where the real power is, in elites and in the 'spaces of flows' in terms of which they operate. He suggests that:

[There is a] structural schizophrenia between two spatial logics that threatens to break down communication channels in society. . . . Unless cultural and physical bridges are deliberately built between these two forms of space, we may be heading toward life in parallel universes whose times cannot meet because they are warped into different dimensions of a social hyperspace.

(Castells 1996: 428)

This is, perhaps, a basis for beginning to explain the contemporary role of mega-events. That is, they can be usefully conceived as temporary 'cultural and physical bridges' between these two forms of social space, between elites and the people. Indeed, as we have seen in Part 1, that is what they always were from the nineteenth century onwards, in one form or another.

The discussion in Chapter 5, exploring the importance of urban spatial locations for mega-events, is consistent with this analysis. Mega-event movements have evident needs to spatially locate events, usually in cities, and have a capacity to transform spaces into special places. However, it is also evident that this spatial dimension of the 'mega-event-as-hub' is only part of the picture. In addition, 'hub' imagery is also useful to understanding mega-events because it helps to clarify their temporal as well as spatial character. That is, as we have emphasised and illustrated throughout the discussion in this book, mega-events are also (and crucially) temporal hubs. They are both temporary intensive uses of space and place in the short term, and also they make reference to wider temporal and historical dimensions through their medium-term planning and impacts, and their location within periodic cycles and traditions.

The 'event-as-hub' – as both a temporary spatial hub and and a more broadly temporal-historic hub – can be argued to act as a 'switching centre' in a number of ways. First, various event producer groups and their associated political, economic and cultural networks meet to consume the event together (and thus constitute shared cultural memories and cultural capital together) and/or use the event for more instrumental sorts of meetings and interactions to further their individual, group or network interests.

Second, the 'event-as-hub' also acts as a 'switching centre' between the meaning-giving production project of the elite production groups and the meaning-making consumer activities of mass publics, both those present and those watching on TV or participating through some other medium. In the 'event-as-hub' on the one hand, masses of people are temporarily co-opted and mobilised into being active members of international cultural movements. On the other hand, during the event, the elite organisers of such movements see them temporarily take on some of the substance and scale of more explicitly political and enduring international social movements. As we saw in Part 1, mega-events were capable of transiently taking on the substantial ceremonial and ritual appearance of nationalist, imperialist, socialist and fascist movements in the earlier nineteenth–twentieth century periods. In a comparable fashion in the late twentieth century, mega-event organisers have attempted to connect them with liberal versions of multi-cultural-ist, environmentalist and, to a limited extent, feminist ideals and movements, projecting them in part as periodic mass festive ceremonials connected with these movements in contemporary consciousness.[28]

Third, the 'event-as-hub' and as transient 'switching centre' both symbolically represents and also in some small part contributes to contemporary understand-ings (both by producers and consumers in the global cultural industries in particular, but also in and between other industrial and post-industrial economic sectors) of possibilities for convergence, interconnection, cross-reference and synergy. This is evident enough in the interconnection between sport and the media in mega-events disussed in Chapters 5 and 6. It is also evident, as we saw, in the use of both of them in their interconnection, as advertising and promotional vehicles for a huge and diverse range of products.

Finally, the 'event-as-hub' and as 'switching centre' refers to the inter-generational communication they involve. This is the deeper significance of the idea that events like the Olympics or World Fairs are 'family' events, and that people of all generations participate in the drama of the live event whether as spectators or as TV viewers. Both as short-term events, but also in longer-term perspectives of memory and future calendars, mega-events provide inter-generational cultural reference points and thus relate to the identity problems facing people in contemporary society which were discussed earlier. Mega-events and their traditions and calendars provide inter-generational social space-time frameworks in relation to which, in part at least, some of the medium- and long-term processes of social reproduction and change in national societies and global society in the late twentieth and early twenty-first centuries can be ordered and reflected on in both personal and public ways. The lifeworld experience of inter-generationality – that is the currently lived, the remembered and the imaginatively projected aspects of inter-generational social relations – is the fluid temporal meso-sphere within which the meanings, ideals and realities of agency (produc-tion), on the one hand, and social structure (reproduction), on the other, can be understood to co-exist and interconnect.

In conclusion, then, mega-events – both in their particular organisation as unique events and also as the traditions and institutions, ideals and plans of the inter-event movements that sustain them – can be seen as important processes in the social meso-sphere in late twentieth-century society. We are likely to see much more of them, in both 'official' and 'alternative' forms, as 'global society' and its culture begin to take on a more patterned and institutionalised character in the early generations of the twenty-first century. To understand mega-events better is thus to understand something more broadly about the nature and fate of human agency and social structure, and of continuity and change, in modernity as we enter the new Millennium. In this book I have aimed to make a preliminary contribution to the agenda of research and analysis that this implies.

Notes

For full information on the sources cited in these Notes see the Bibliography.

1 Mega-events and modernity

1 The term expo will be used throughout this book to refer to what were known as 'International Exhibitions' in Britain, 'World's Fairs' in the USA and 'Expositions Universelles' in France. For relevant concepts and typologies of 'mega-events' (and related categories of 'hallmark events' and 'special events') see for instance Ritchie 1984; Hall 1989a, 1992; Getz 1991 ch.2; Roche 1992a; Rydell and Gwinn 1994; and contributions to Burns *et al.* (eds) 1986, AIEST 1987 and Syme *et al.* 1989.

2 The density of the contemporary international sport event calendar is discussed in IOC 1996a ch.1 and is evidenced in the half-yearly calendars produced by the GAISF (General Association of International Sports Federations). On the soccer World Cup mega-event, its governing body FIFA (the Federation Internationale de Football Association) and the politics of its organisation see Sugden and Tomlinson 1998. On rock music mega-events see Garofolo 1992.

3 On expo events as temporal markers, see, for instance, Rydell 1993 and Ley and Olds 1988, also semi-autobiographical writing such as Doctorow 1985. On sport events as temporal markers, see Real 1995, also autobiographical writing such as Hornby 1996. On the communal significance of urban mega-events see Chapter 5, also Roche 1999d. Generally on the subjective and intersubjective significance of mega-events see the discussion of lived time, space and agency in Chapter 8. Also see Gilbert 1994.

4 On invention of tradition (Hobsbawm 1992), imagined community (Anderson 1991), national commemorations, rituals and memories (Spillman 1997; Smith 1995; Mosse 1975; Lane 1981; Lukes 1975).

5 On the everyday life world see Schutz and Luckmann 1974, Berger and Luckmann 1967, and Roche 1973. On the problem of re-'enchanting' the everyday life world, against the forces of rationalisation and 'disenchantment' loose in modernity – a problem to which mega-events arguably have been one notable response – see Ritzer 1999 ch. 5, also see Chapter 8. See Weber 1947 for a seminal analysis of the relation between charisma and routine in modernity, also Debord 1973.

6 On the social theory of temporality and time-structures in relation to mega-events in modernity see Chapter 8.

7 Marx's formulation is: 'Men make their own history, but they do not make it just as they please; they do not make it under circumstances chosen by themselves, but under circumstances directly encountered, given and transmitted from the past' (Marx and Engels 1970: 96).

8 See Roche 1999a. The Olympics is the main 'perfomance' genre' (but also has important exhibitionary features); expos are the main 'exhibition' genre (but also require a rich complex of performances). Both genres are ultimately performance complexes. They are events in which, among other things, things are exhibited and also things are dramatised, and (via both of these aspects) events are transformed into spectacles.

9 See Chapter 2 in relation to cultural INGOs such as the IOC, BIE, FIFA, etc. In relation to international sport culture see Chapters 4 and 7, also Houlihan 1994 and Hoberman 1995. On cultural INGOs in general in the context of the contemporary world order and globalisation process see Boli and Thomas 1999.

10 Being a 'media event' refers to extraordinary events, and the simultaneous, or quasi-simultaneous, 'witness'-form of participation in them made possible through the media for media users (particularly radio and TV audiences, but also, to a certain extent via the popular press). See Dayan and Katz 1992, Roche and Arundel 1998 and Chapter 6.

11 This should be distinguished from various other uses of the 'drama' metaphor/model in social analysis such as those of Goffman 1959, Lyman and Scott 1970, Chaney 1993, Abercrombie and Longhurst 1998, and Hetherington 1998. The foci of most of these analyses tend to be on the micro and the everyday/the routine. My focus, in the sociology of mega-events, by contrast, is on the sociological significance of the large-scale, official, planned event which is extraordinary and non-routine.

12 See, for instance, Andersen and Gale 1992, also Kearns and Philo 1993. For relevant studies of public events from these fields see Jackson 1988, 1992 and Ley and Olds 1988.

13 See, for instance Huizinga 1971, Rojek 1995, Maffesoli 1996.

14 Benedict *et al.* 1983 pp.6,7,9; also generally Van Gennep (1960) on rituals.

15 The work of the anthropologists Victor Turner (Turner 1987, 1995) and Clifford Geertz (1975) on cultural events has been particularly influential on this and other aspects of the dramatological perspective. On Turner's influence see Chapter 6 section 1.

16 See, for instance, Benedict 1983, Falassi 1987, Falassi (ed.) 1987, Turner 1987, and Handelman 1998.

17 Rothenbuhler 1988, 1989. See also Duvignaud 1976, MacAloon 1984, and some of the perspectives discussed in Lukes 1975.

18 Examples of the applied economics approach are discussed and criticised in Roche 1992a, also see Ritchie 1984, Burns *et al.* 1986, AIEST 1987, Syme *et al.* 1989, Getz 1991, Hall 1992, Murphy 1994.

19 For instance, Espy 1979, Hill 1992, Larson and Park 1993, Houlihan 1994, Hoberman 1995, Simson and Jennings 1992, Jennings 1996, Sugden and Tomlinson 1998. Hoberman's notable analyses interpreting politics and power in national and international sport in terms of ideology connect political instrumentalism with critical functionalism, (see also Hoberman 1984, 1986).

20 Examples of critical analyses of non-rational aspects of power-elite production of mega-events can be found in Hall 1989a, 1989b, 1992, 1994a, 1994b; Hall and Hodges 1998; in critics of the Olympics, e.g. Gruneau 1984, Whannel 1992, and Simson and Jennings 1992, Jennings 1996, and also in Armstrong 1984 and Roche 1994, p.6.

21 See, for instance, Lavenda 1980, Hobsbawm and Ranger (eds) 1992, Horne 1986, Lukes 1975, Pred 1991, MacArthur 1986.

22 Mosse 1975, Lane 1981, Byrne 1987 and Chapter 4.

23 See for instance Gruneau 1984, Tomlinson and Whannel 1984, Simson and Jennings 1992, Jennings 1996; also Bourdieu 1998, 1999. Also see Chapter 7.

24 By the late twentieth century this dimension of national cultures in Western societies had grown from the toleration of the cosmopolitanism, multi-culturalism and international media attention implied by processes of media and market-based globalisation, to include increasing public recognition of the normative relevance and potentially instrusive constitutional influence of 'human rights' and of transnational legal and institutional frameworks embodying these things. See Boli and Thomas (eds) 1999, also discussions in Chapters 7 and 8.

25 For discussions of post-modern culture relevant to the themes of this book, see, for instance, Harvey 1989, Featherstone 1991, Rojek 1995 ch.7 and 8, Stevenson 1995 ch.5, Real 1996a ch.8, Harvey 1996 ch.5, Maffesoli 1996.

26 In terms of historical precedents and origins to help explain the contemporary meaning and role of mega-events in late modernity, in my view the late nineteenth century and inter-war period is far more important than the early post-war period of UN-oriented internationalism and 'superpower' supernationalism. For this reason, and also for reasons of space the development of expos and Olympics from the late 1940s to the late 1970s is largely bypassed in my account in this book. For sources on expos in this period see Allwood 1977, Schroeder-Gudehus and Rasmussen 1992, Rydell 1993,

Rydell and Gwinn (eds) 1994. For sources on Olympics in this period see Hoberman 1986, IOC 1995a, Guttman 1992, Hill 1992.

27 For notable recent analyses of globalisation processes which give appropriate weight to technological and economic dimensions and developments see for instance Castells 1996, 1997, 1998, and Held *et al.* 1999. Also see discussion in chapters 6 and 7, and discussion and notes in Chapter 8.

28 Since, for instance, Featherstone 1991, Robertson, R. 1992, Lash and Urry 1994, ch. 11.

2   Expos and cultural power

1 Anderson 1991 and Habermas 1989a, 1991. For an analysis of 'public culture', see Horne 1986. Also see Keane 1998 pp.157–90 for a relevant discussion of civil society and public spheres.

2 For instance, Rydell 1984, 1993; Greenhalgh 1988; Mosse 1975; Lane 1981; and Spillman 1997.

3 For relevant concepts of 'ruling class', class-based 'propaganda' and 'manipulation of the public', and discussions which deploy class-based concepts in the analysis of expos and other major cultural events, see MacKenzie 1984, Greenhalgh 1988 and Rydell 1984 and 1993. Also on class in expos see below and Chapter 3.

4 See Mosse 1975, Hoberman 1984, 1985; Guttman 1994, and Chapter 4.

5 The national cultural role of sport and physical education in the history of modern societies is well-worked territory. In relation to sport in British society, particularly in the late nineteenth century, see, for instance, Vamplew 1988, Holt 1992, Tranter 1998; on physical education in Britain in this period McIntosh 1968. On the international as opposed to the national dimension of sport culture see Houlihan 1994 and Hoberman 1995, also Chapter 4.

6 Hobsbawm 1992 p.305. On communist mass rituals, see Roche 1999c, also Lane 1981 and von Geldern 1993.

7 For relevant sociologically informed critical social histories of sport see John Hargreaves 1986, Jennifer Hargreaves 1994 and Jones 1988, and Chapter 4.

8 This is so, even in such minimal ways as observing dress codes and 'dressing to be seen', or promenading in order to be seen as well as to see (the flaneur). The point here is that people need to actively do or perform something; it is not a matter of people passively undergoing something. All of this is even more true of the concept of 'the people (particularly the Party) performing for itself' which underlay Bolshevik and Nazi mass festivals, see Roche 1999d, also Chapter 4.

9 This international dimension can be understood more empirically as the aggregate of all national publics' understandings of, images of, and attitudes to immigrants, to foreigners and to 'world society'. The latter can be conceptualised as including such things as media-generated and sustained conceptions of 'world public opinion', diplomatically sustained conceptions of 'international civil society' and 'global governance', and social movement-generated and sustained conceptions of 'human rights'. See also Chapter 7.

10 For analyses of the concepts of 'civil society' relevant to my discussion see Held 1995, Keane 1998, Boli and Thomas 1999 and Chapters 7 and 8.

11 On this common 'loss leader' characteristic of mega-events; - they can be compared to pre-modern inter-tribal 'potlatch' ritual event (Benedict 1983) and Roman 'bread and circuses' (Harvey 1996). On the pursuit of 'prestige' through (often loss-making) 'mega-projects', see Armstrong 1984, also Roche 1992a, 1994 and Chapter 5.

12 Or, perhaps, given the variety of types of experience they presented and the variety of types of performance they required from the public, it would be better to put it that 'the multi-media complex was the message'. On this multi-media aspect of mega-events see Chapter 6.

13 For further detail on the 1851 'Crystal Palace' expo see Auerbach 1999, also Luckhurst 1951 chs. 9–10, Allwood 1977 ch. 2, and Greenhalgh 1988 chs. 1–3.

14 Interestingly, given the subsequent cultural importance of Eiffel's tower produced for the 1889 expo, one of the more eccentric contemporary ideas for the relocation of the

Crystal Palace envisaged reassembling it as a monumental 1,000 feet glass tower (Rattenbury, 1997-P). Fortunately for the reputation of British engineering this idea did not get off the drawing board.

15 The profit at the time was £186,000 (roughly equivalent to £6 million or US$9 million at today's currency values).

16 London's 'expo heritage' includes, among other things, the Commonwealth (ex-Imperial) Institute, Wembley Stadium and the use of the names 'Crystal Palace' (by one of London's major soccer clubs) and the 'White City' (by a subway station), as well as the 'Albertopolis' complex.

17 For instance the national political crisis in France from 1897 onwards surrounding the Dreyfus affair had negative impacts on preparations for the great 1900 Paris expo and also on the image of France in competitor countries such as Britain and Germany (Mandell 1967), although the eventual success of the expo no doubt counterbalanced these impacts.

18 Besides expos' roles in providing vehicles for international political communication and networking among power elites, they also, of course, provided similar functions intra-nationally. For instance, mayors of towns and communities from all over France were invited to huge banquets at both the 1889 and 1900 Paris expos. At the 1900 expo, 20,000 mayors attended the banquet (Mandell 1967, p.86).

19 On Cole's role see Bonython 1995 and Auerbach 1999 *passim*, also Luckhurst 1951 and Allwood 1977.

20 See Allwood 1977, Rydell 1984 and 1993, also on American organisers see Findling 1994a and Susman 1983. Cultural and scientific organisations like the Smithsonian Institution and, in the inter-war period, also the National Research Council, provided focal points and continuities in the elite networks which produced most American expos.

21 On Kiralfy, see Greenhalgh 1988 pp. 40, 90, 91 and MacKenzie 1984 pp. 102–7; also see Knight 1978 p. 6.

22 See Luckhurst 1951, Allwood 1977, Bonython 1995 and Auerbach 1999

23 On the Smithsonian's role in the 1876 Philadelphia expos and the 1893 Chicago expo see Rydell 1984 pp. 22–7 and pp. 43–6; also on the links between American expos and museums, and between the elites involved in each, see Rydell 1993 pp. 31–5.

24 On Durkheim, see Lukes 1973 p. 350; on Weber, see Bendix 1962 p.3; on Einstein, see Rydell 1993, pp. 109, 111.

25 On the 1908 expo see Knight 1978, also Greenhalgh 1988 pp. 91–2 and MacKenzie 1984 p.105. For contemporary participants' views of the expo see Dumas ed. 1908. On the White City as a subsequent major event venue, see Knight 1978.

26 For studies of the 1889 and 1900 Paris expos in general, see Harriss 1975 and Mandell 1967 respectively. On the imperial theme in the 1900 Paris expo, Greenhalgh comments that 'the colonial sections' resembled 'a massive set for a silent epic film' and represented 'Europe at its presumptuous, confident peak' (Greenhalgh 1988 p.67) before the descent into the disaster of the First World War,

27 Greenhalgh 1988 pp.71–3. The Belgian King Leopold exercised an at times murder-ous colonial regime in the Congo in this period. His aim was to make profits from, among other things, the extraction of rubber for the booming and strategically important new technologies of electricity (insulation) and automobiles (tyres), tech-nologies which expos had a strategic role in popularising in the West in the 1870 - 1940 period. On this era of Belgian colonialism, see Hochschild's controversial critique (1999).

28 MacKenzie 1984 p.108, but also see Stallard 1996 for an alternative version of the event's finances.

29 The opening ceremony of the Wembley imperial expo was broadcast by the recently created BBC in 1924. The first Director-General of the BBC, John Reith, helped to illustrate his case for the national and public service role of the BBC in a presentation to the British government in 1925 by observing that the effect of this broadcast had been that of 'making the nation as one man' (quoted in Keane 1998, p.168; also see MacKenzie 1984 pp. 91–3).

3   Mega-events and cultural citizenship

1 On the connections between late nineteenth-century cultural developments, late twentieth-century consumer culture and post-modern culture, see, for instance, Featherstone 1991.

2 See Freud 1873. On the Vienna expo in general, see Allwood 1977 pp. 48–50,180.

3 On the sociology of tourism in modernity, see the classic analyses by McCannell 1989 and Urry 1990, also Hall 1994a, Apostolopoulos *et al*. 1996, Ryan 1997, Rojek and Urry 1997 and Wang 1999.

4 For instance, Featherstone 1991, Richards 1990, Pred 1991, de Cauter 1993, Zukin 1993 and Gunning 1994; also Williams 1982 on the influence of the French expos on the development of consumer culture.

5 On the 1893 Chicago expo in this context see Findling 1994a; also Lewis 1983, Rydell 1984, Hinsley 1991, and Susman 1983. For a relevant discussion of the 1904 St Louis expo in terms of touristic consumer culture see Gunning 1994.

6 On various linkages between expos and the institution of the modern urban museum see Rydell 1993, Macdonald 1996, Macdonald and Fyfe 1996. On equivalent linkages between expos and the institution of the modern urban department store, see Williams 1982, Lewis 1983 and Hinsley 1991. On linkages between expos and the touristic consumer culture institutionalised in the modern theme park see Chapter 5, and also Zukin 1993, 1995 and Smoodin 1994.

7 Expos influenced the form and content of the modern fair by providing high-profile opportunities for the introduction of new types of dramatic mechanised rides. This influence can be dated at least from the elevator ride and view offered by the Eiffel Tower at the 1889 Paris expo. This concept was copied by the tourist resort and fairground of Blackpool in 1894. Also there were failed attempts to build taller towers at the Chicago expo 1893 (Findling 1994a p.13) and Wembley, London in the late 1890s. The Eiffel Tower theme is echoed in the enduring proliferation of the construction of observation towers in contemporary cities worldwide. Expo influences on fairs also includes the classic 'Ferris wheel' constructed for the 1893 Chicago expo. This was subsequently copied at the Coney Island fairground in 1894 (Kasson 1978) and in Vienna's 'Riesenrad' in the Prater park fairground in 1897.

8 On the modernisation process as involving the construction and reconstruction of forms of 'national functionalism', see Roche 1996 ch.1 and 2.

9 Other examples of the involvement of leading politicians of the period with event production include, in France, the ex-prime minister Jules Ferry who was a leading planner of the Paris 1889 expo (Hoberman 1986), and, in the USA, Sol Bloom who was involved in both the 1893 and 1933 Chicago expos and was a leading Congressman in the inter-war period (Rydell 1984, 1993; Findling 1994a).

10 This is in spite of the fact that expos potentially represented major opportunities for workers to put pressure on employers operating under tight and demanding deadlines often involving innovative, complex and demanding construction work. Probably the most innovative and demanding expo construction, Eiffel's Tower for the 1889 Paris expo, was not disrupted by much labour unrest (Harriss 1975). However there was labour unrest and/or strike action at Chicago 1893 (Rydell 1984, also Findling 1994a), Wembley 1924/5 (in relation to women's working conditions, Greenhalgh 1988), Chicago 1933 and New York 1939. The generally inadequate black employment at these and other American expos, occasionally provoked controversy, and there were black trade-union pickets on the opening ceremony of the 1939 expo (Rydell 1993).

11 Benjamin 1973 p.166; Mehring 1966 pp. 319–21, 342; also Nicolaievsky and Maechen-Helfen 1976.

12 On gender, citizenship and civil society in the context of the modernisation process and the development of and reconstruction of 'national functionalist' forms of society in modernity, see Roche 1996 ch.2, ch.5 and *passim*.

13 The American fair tradition was modernised in this period by the creation of large scale travelling shows, in particular those of P.T. Barnum and 'Buffalo Bill' Cody, using the new reach of the railway system. Barnum's travelling circus included such things as

'ethnological congresses', which were renewed versions of traditional displays of 'freaks', 'primitives' and foreigners. Although he died in 1891, Barnum was an influence on the 1893 Chicago expo, on its 'orientalism' and its incorporation of the 'Midway' fairground zone. One of his biographers suggests that the success of the Barnum-influenced approach to expos led to 'the barnumization of subsequent U.S. world's fairs' (Adams 1997 p.195). Barnum was also an influence on British imperial expos through the expo impressario Imre Kiralfy who learned his showmanship with the Barnum organisation. Reciprocally, expos influenced the new generation of fairgrounds of the period, in particular Coney Island, with attractions from the 1893 and 1904 expos being relocated there when the expos closed (Kasson 1978, Gunning 1994).

14 For relevant discussions of Indians at American expos, see Rydell 1984, chapter 1, and Benedict 1994. On the history of North American Indians and their conflicts with the US authorities more generally, see Brown 1976.

15 Cody launched his 'Wild West' show in 1884. He toured it to England in 1887 (participating in events to celebrate Victoria's Jubilee); to France in 1889, (including participating in the Paris expo and visiting Spain and Italy); and to Germany in 1890 (also visiting Holland and Belgium). He toured Britain and European countries again in 1903 and 1904 (Blackstone 1986; Pegler and Rimer 1999). Also see Russell 1960.

16 Benedict 1994 p.39, Greenhalgh 1988 p.98, Rydell 1984 p.53.

17 A key analysis of the early expo-based Olympics is MacAloon 1981, which is the main source for this section; see also De Coubertin 1979. Other relevant sources include Meyer 1976, Lucas 1980, Mandell 1967, Rydell 1984 and IOC 1994.

18 Lucas 1980 suggests that de Coubertin had the support of the leading politician and expo supporter Jules Ferry who was education minister at the time, although MacAloon 1981, p.165, takes a different view. On the relationship between Ferry and de Coubertin, also see Hoberman 1986.

19 On the 1908 Olympics, see Killanin and Rodda 1976, p.37, Lucas 1980 ch.3, Guttman 1992 ch.2, and IOC 1994. On the 1908 expo see Knight 1978. On the BOA, see Anthony 1987 and on the AAA, see Lovesey 1979.

20 For other relevant 'theses' in the sociology of sport see Guttman 1978.

21 For a consideration of Le Play's significance for the sociological tradition, see Nisbet 1970 pp. 61–70.

22 In addition, Heinrich Schliemann the well-known German archaeologist responsible for excavating the site of the ancient city of Troy was an important participant in the international archaeological congress held at the 1889 expo (MacAloon 1981, p.145)

23 MacAloon suggests that de Coubertin became inspired with the idea of reviving the Olympic Games: 'between 1888–1892 when the European fascination with ancient Olympia was in full swing'. He notes that just two years prior to the 1889 expo a major history of ancient Greece was published in France. This contained information on the ancient Games and a site map of Curtius' excavations at Olympia, and it is likely that de Coubertin read it (MacAloon 1981 p.143).

24 Brookes was the founder and organiser of an Olympic event in Britain, at Much Wenlock, in the 1860s and 1870s. He had contacts with the Greek government and monarchy. He probably made de Coubertin aware at his meetings with him in 1890 of the Greeks' own periodic attempts to stage series of Olympic Games events (in 1859,1870,1875, and 1889) which were little known internationally (MacAloon 1981 p.151).

25 Crystal Palace expo organiser Henry Cole drew up an unofficial international memorandum to attempt to regulate international expos together with expo commissioners from five other nations at the Paris expo 1867 (Allwood 1977, p.179).

26 Dunning and Elias 1986, Dunning and Sheard 1979. Dunning and Elias see this as part of the 'civilizing process'. I prefer to refer to this as part of the development of cultural institutionalisation consistent with and characteristic of modernity. See also Guttman 1978, Hargreaves 1986 and Van der Merwe (ed.) 1996.

27 Also in relation to international sport INGOs, see Houlihan 1994, Hoberman 1995 and Sugden and Tomlinson 1998. On cultural INGOs in general, see Boli and Thomas (eds) 1998.

4 The Olympics, internationalism and supernationalism

1   On sport and empire in modern British and European history, see Mangan 1986, 1992; Holt 1992 chapter 4; Guttman 1994; Dine 1996 and Arnaud 1998. On cricket and empire, see Beckles and Stoddart 1995 and Guttman 1994, chapter 1.

2   Guttman 1994 ch. 1; James 1963, also Beckles and Stoddart 1995.

3   Guttman 1994 p.121, Moore 1986, Holt 1992 p.224. Also see Hoberman 1984 pp.91–93 on the views of John Astley Cooper, one of the main promoters of the idea of an 'Anglo-Saxon Olympiad'.

4   On Nazi sport ideology and state organisation, see, for instance, Mandell 1971; Hoberman 1984, 1986; Kruger 1986, 1998. On Soviet sport ideology and organisation, see, for instance, Riordan 1978, 1998; Hoberman 1984; and Gounot 1998

5   On this history, see, for instance, Lucas 1980, Kanin 1981 also Holt 1998b and Arnaud and Riordan (eds) 1998; on the Soviet use of sport internationally in the inter-war period, see Riordan 1998; on Nazi international sport policies, see Kruger 1998. On British sport and international policy in this period, see Holt 1998a, Beck 1999. On sport and international relations generally, see Taylor 1986, Houlihan 1994, Hoberman 1995, Mangan and Small (eds) 1986.

6   In his Olympic memoirs, de Coubertin noted the particularly moving character of the ecumenical religious service of rememberance for previous participants in the Olympics who had been killed in the war. The service was held in Antwerp Cathedral before the start of the Games (de Coubertin 1979, also his 1966 pp.80–7).

7   Riordan 1984. On inter-war socialist sport in West Europe and in the USSR, see Jones 1988, Gounot 1998, Riordan 1998 and Hoberman 1986.

8   On relationships between the IOC and the League of Nations in the inter-war period, see Kanin 1981, also IOC 1994. On comparable relations between the IOC and the United Nations in the post-war and contemporary periods, see Espy 1979, Hill 1992, Houlihan 1994, and Chapter 7.

9   IOC 1994; Lucas 1980; Hill 1992; Houlihan 1994; and Guttman 1992.

10   Unfortunately, whatever its post-war and contemporary ideology and cultural role, in the 1930s FIFA followed a comparable 'fascist fellow-traveller' road to that followed by the IOC in this period. For instance, Its first President, Jules Rimet, presided over a game between France and Germany in Berlin in 1933 and praised the new Germany (Hoberman 1995 p.18). He also organised the second World Cup competition in 1934 in Rome in collaboration with Mussolini's fascist sports authorities (Teja 1998).

11   Guttman 1994 pp.124–5; IOC 1994; Dine 1996.

12   IOC 1994 pp.234–43. Generally on the history of the conflicts around amateurism and professional principles and practices in international and Olympic sport see IOC1995a pp.89,155–64 and 1996a pp.236–54.

13   MacAloon 1981, also Chapter 3. See also de Coubertin's views on the athletes' oath (1906), and on the Olympic ceremonies (1910) (de Coubertin 1966, pp.15–16 and 34–6 respectively). He notes: 'It is primarily through the ceremonies that the Olympiad must distinguish itself from a mere series of world championships' (de Coubertin 1966 p.34).

14   Wilson 1976; Mandell 1971, Hart-Davis 1986.

15   On Lewald and Diem, see Mandell 1971, Guttman 1984 ch.6, IOC 1994 and Kruger 1998; also Hoberman 1984 pp.50–4 On the relevance of the concept of 'volk' underpinning German nationalism and its connections with sport ideologies and policies, see Mosse 1975 *passim*, and Hoberman 1986 pp.88–105 .

16   For discussions of the range and contradictions of Nazi views on sport, see Hoberman 1984 ch.6 and 1995 *passim*, and Kruger 1986, 1998.

17   Finley and Pleket 1976. In terms of the long-term character of Hitler's conception of the Olympics and the relevance of the Hellenic analogy, it is worth noting that Hitler held a meeting with the IOC in 1936 during the Berlin Games. At this meeting he announced that his Third Reich would finance the continuation and completion of the excavation of ceremonial and sporting sites at the ancient Hellenic site of the Games at Olympia. This work was undertaken from 1936 until the war interrupted it; it was ultimately was completed in the post-war period (IOC 1994 p. 271).

18 Interestingly, Speer, who in principle could well have been in this circle, later claimed that he only learned of the plan in early 1937, some months after the Berlin Olympics (Speer 1970 p.70, also see Serenyi 1995 p. 154 and Mandell 1971 pp.292–3).
19 For instance, Byrne 1987, in her account and critique of the Berlin Olympics, tends to overly focus on the short-term impacts.
20 Hart-Davis 1986 p.67; also Kruger 1986, 1998, and Hoberman 1986.
21 On the unsuccessful American boycott campaign see Guttman 1984 ch.6 on Avery Brundage who led the pro-Games opposition to the boycott, also Guttman 1992, ch.4, and 1998, and Hoberman pp. 50–7.
22 Guttman 1984, ch.6 and 1998; also Kruger 1986 and IOC 1994 pp. 266–7. Two members of the team, Helen Mayer a fencer and Rudi Ball, an ice hockey player, were part Jewish. However, they qualified as non-'Jewish' in terms of the law prevailing in Germany at the time. Their inclusion was based on the denial of their Jewishness. The most obvious discrimination against a Jewish German athlete was the exclusion of Gretel Bergmann, the leading high jumper in Germany at the time, from the German women's team (see Guttman 1984 ch.6).
23 On the sport systems in Italy, see Kruger 1986 and Teja 1996, 1998; on Spain, see Aja 1998; on Germany, see Kruger 1986 and 1998.
24 Von Halt was a Nazi Party member, stormtrooper, and Hitler's 'Reichssportfuhrer'. Von Reichenau commanded the 6th army at Kiev in 1941 and performed a massacre of Jews during this engagement. He died before he was able to be brought before a war crimes tribunal. However, he was Hitler's nominee for the IOC in the late1930s (see Jennings 1996, pp.37,38 and ch.6 *passim*; also see Hoberman 1995 p.29, and Kruger 1986 and 1998).
25 The radio broadcast 'The Philosophical Foundations of Modern Olympism' is reproduced in de Coubertin 1966 pp.130–4. In a speech which was produced for the closing ceremony of the Berlin Olympics, de Coubertin claimed that the event would leave: 'Memories of courage, for courage was necessary in order to face the difficulties . . . which the Fuhrer met from the outset with the fiat of his will . . .' (de Coubertin 1966 p.136). Also Guttman 1984, p.81.
26 Mandell 1971; also IOC 1994 and Hoberman 1984,1995.
27 With Mussolini's support, Rome had made failed bids, in 1929 for the 1936 Olympics, and at Berlin in 1936 for the 1940 Olympics (Teja 1998 pp.154/5 and *passim*, also IOC 1994).

5   Mega-events, cities and tourist culture

1 For a series of studies of the relationships between mega-events and touristic culture, particularly their relevance for urban tourism, urban policy and urban citizenship, see Roche 1992a, 1992b, 1994, 1999d and Roche and France 1998. On urban tourism and urban policy see Law 1993, Kearns and Philo 1993, Page 1995, Urry 1995, Williams 1997. On sport, urban culture and urban policy, see Bale 1992, Henry 1998, Henry *et al.* 1998, and Dauncey 1999. On the urban and communal significance of events such as festivals and parades see Falassi (ed.) 1987, Jarman 1997.
2 Harvey 1996 p.42; also see pp.167–9 and 182. The Welsh Garden Festival was staged in the Rhondda Valley in 1992 as part of a national government-sponsored biennial series of such large-scale festivals held around British cities as part of urban regeneration programmes in the 1980s. The 'Disney' reference is probably to the expo-like EPCOT centre in Disney World in Florida (see below).
3 On employment and production aspects of Disney theme parks, and also more general aspects, see Fjellman 1992, TPOD 1995 and Bryman 1995. On various aspects of the Disney corporation and the Disney theme park phenomenon in general with relevance to the analysis of mega-events and touristic consumerism, see Rojek 1993a; Eliot 1995; Zukin 1993 ch.8, 1995 ch.2; the papers in Smoodin 1994; Ritzer and Liska 1997; Ritzer 1999 ch.4, and Yoshimoto 1994.

4 Quoted in Ley and Olds 1988 p.202. In the context of this feedback relationship of the (expo-influenced) Disney theme parks on expo organisation, it is worth noting that the London Millennium expo 2000 organisers visited Disney World in Florida in 1998 in order to inform their thinking about the operational requirements of running a major international tourist and public attraction.

5 Davis 1996, p.399. Also see Davis' notable study of the San Diego 'Sea World' theme park, one of a number of such theme parks operated by the Anheuser-Busch corporation, a major competitor to the Disney corporation in the USA in this industry (Davis 1997).

6 On the development, in London, of permanent 'pleasure gardens' in the eighteenth century (e.g. at Vauxhall) and fairgrounds and exhibitions in the nineteenth century, see Altick 1978, and on New York's historically important turn-of-the-century fairground at Coney Island, see Kasson 1978. In Europe, important city fairgrounds such as Copenhagen's Tivoli (1843) and Vienna's Prater Park date from the mid/late nineteenth century period.

7 On the dimension of 'control' in the Disney theme park experience, see also Bryman 1995 ch.5.

8 On marketing linkages between film, TV, publications, music and merchandising in the Disney operation, see Fjellman 1992 pp.152–3. Universal Studios theme parks also exploit film linkages. In general, the concept of TV and film-linked urban tourism in the form of studio tours, which was pioneered in Hollywood, is now a familiar feature of many major cities around the world.

9 For accounts of visitor experiences and cultural meanings at Disney's Florida theme park in particular, see Fjellman 1992 and TPOD 1995. On the Tokyo Disney theme park see Yoshimoto 1994. On the Disney organisation, also see Rojek 1993, Lewis 1994, Bryman 1995 and Hiassen 1998.

10 On Disney and the 1964 New York expo see Eliot 2995 p.254. Sorkin 1992 argues strongly that 'The most direct ancestor . . . of Disney's theme parks) . . . is the World's Fair' genre (p.208), and implies that the 1939/40 New York expo gave Disney an image of what his future Disneyland might aspire to be (Sorkin 1992, p.224). Also, it is known that Disney's parents attended the 1934 Chicago expo (Eliot 1995 p.74 photograph).

11 Fjellman 1992 ch.7, also *passim*. On the impact of the development of Disney's and other theme parks in the Orlando area, Sorkin records the scale of the regional suburbanisation that they have engendered in that by 1992 the area had 'more hotel rooms than Chicago, Los Angeles, or New York' (Sorkin 1992 p.205).

12 For instance, Zukin observes that the organisational approaches involved in the creation and development of BID (Business Improvement District) areas in Manhattan, New York, have been influenced to a certain extent by lessons learned from the management of theme parks, (Zukin 1995 pp.65–69, chs.1 and 2 *passim*; also Sorkin 1992).

13 In the 1980s plans for a 1989 Paris expo and for a 1992 Chicago expo collapsed (Findling 1994a), and the 1984 New Orleans expo was a financial disaster (Dimanche 1994). However, the expo tradition was not completely dormant in the 1970s and 1980s. Other lower-level more nationally and/or world regionally significant expos, particularly in the Asia-Pacific region, were produced in this period, and these included 1975 Okinawa, Japan; 1982 Knoxville USA; 1985 Tsukuba, Japan; 1988 Brisbane, Australia. On Brisbane, see Bennett 1991, Spillman 1997 ch.4.

14 On the 1992 Seville expo, see Findling 1994b and Harvey 1996; on the 1993 Taejon expo, see Jeong and Faulkner 1996.

15 On the general impact of television on post-war expos see Gilbert 1994. On the contemporary role of expo-type events in urban policy and inter-city competition in Europe, see Rubalcaba-Bermejo and Cuadrado-Roura 1995.

16 On the Greenwich Millennium expo, see House of Commons 1997 and UK Government 1999, and Bayley's 1998 critique.

17 This area is next to the new and nationally very important 15-kilometre Vasco da Gama bridge which crosses the river Tagus and provides a vital new link between central and southern Portugal. From a national perspective, the expo effectively celebrated the opening of this important new element of national infrastructure.

18 There are various sources for this idea, which derives from the English sport tradition, in the modern Olympic tradition. De Coubertin's view that 'Dishonour would not lie in defeat, but in failure to take part', made in a lecture in Athens in 1894, is an early source (de Coubertin 1966 p.10).

19 For perspectives on the nationally distributed soccer World Cup mega-event, see Dauncey and Hare's collection of studies of the 'France 1998' event (Dauncey and Hare (eds) 1999).

20 Of course, seeing Olympic Games as urban events applies particularly to the Summer Games. Although, technically, Winter Olympics are also awarded to a host town or city, in fact they are usually, of necessity, distributed around mountainous and often inaccessible regions and they are typically used to attempt to develop the infrastructures and economies of these regions. Unlike Summer Olympic events Winter Olympic events, are regional policy rather than urban policy instruments.

21 Not, however, for London (1948), Rome (1960), Moscow (1980), Los Angeles (1984) and Barcelona (1992). London used Wembley Stadium, built for the 1924 Empire expo; Rome used the 1934 stadium Mussolini, built for Italy's bid for the 1936 Olympics; Moscow used the Lenin stadium, built for the World Student Games in 1957; Los Angeles refurbished the stadium built for the 1932 Olympics; and Barcelona refurbished the stadium built for the 1929 expo.

22 In addition to the contemporary economic data it provides, unfortunately this post-event report also continues to use economic impact assessments drawn from the official pre-event impact projections produced in 1992.

23 Kang and Perdue 1994, 'Summary' p. 205; on the general economic impact of the Olympics on Seoul and Korea, see Seh-Jik 1991 pp.130–6, also Larson and Park 1993 ch.5.

24 On the profiling of electricity at the 1929 Barcelona expo, see Allwood 1977, p.135. On the Montjuic area, central to the 1929 expo and the 1992 Olympics, see Eames (ed.) 1996 (chapter by Xavier Marti, pp.145–51).

25 For an account of the city of Barcelona's radical social, political and aesthetic movements and character in the late nineteenth century and through the inter-war period, see Kaplan 1993.

26 On the Barcelona bid and the 1986 IOC selection process for the 1992 host city, see Simson and Jennings 1992, and Hill 1992, ch.9.

27 On the financing of the Barcelona Olympics Games, see Garcia 1993, also Hooper 1992–P and Tsubota 1993.

28 Garcia (1993) provides a detailed account and assessment of the Barcelona's Olympic event production and impacts published in a German language version (see Bibliography). With the permission of the author, the discussion in the following paragraphs draws substantially from an unpublished English language version of this paper, which was presented at the 1994 ISA World Sociology Conference in Bielefeld.

29 On Barcelona's post-Olympic economic boom Milner notes that in 1998 a new tranche of £6.5billion ($10.5billion) of public and private sector finance was invested in more improvements to the city's port and transport infrastructure to encourage further tourism growth and further growth in inward investment by foreign multinational corporations (Milner 1998–P).

30 Port Aventura is the prefered location of Disney theme park competitor Universal Studios for its main expansion from the American market and into the European theme park industry.

31 On Barcelona FC, see Simpson 1998–P, and also Eames (ed.) 1996 (chapter by Lluis Permanyer pp. 89–91).

32 Verdaguer 1995 p. 203. The notion of 'the resisting force of place' resonates with Castells' general discussion of global–local dynamics; see Chapter 8 for comments and references.

33 Verdaguer 1995 p.204. For further aspects of the Barcelona Olympics as an urban mega-event, see the discussion of Barcelona's 'Olympic media city' in this chapter. Also see Chapter 6 for a discussion of the Barcelona Olympics as a media event.

34 J. Samaranch, quoted in Larson and Park 1993, p.123. On the Olympics as a media event and the increasing symbiosis between the Olympics and major media corpor-

ations, see Chapter 6. For the IOC's view of the development of this symbiosis, see IOC 1996a ch.1.

35 Larson and Park 1993, Wilson 1996, also Spa *et al.* 1995.

36 The following paragraphs draw substantially on the major study of the media aspects of the Seoul Olympics by James Larson and Heung-Soo Park. See Larson and Park 1993, ch.5 and *passim*.

37 The following paragraphs draw substantially on the major study of the media aspects of the Barcelona Olympics directed by Miquel de Morganas Spa, Nancy Rivenburgh and James Larson, (hereafter Spa *et al.*). See Spa *et al.* 1995 chs.3 and 4, and *passim*.

38 There were in all at least five main inquiries into these bribery problems, namely the IOC's own inquiry, directed by IOC member Richard Pound, the USA's National Olympic Committee inquiry, directed by Senator George Mitchell, and inquiries organised by the SLOC (the Salt Lake Olympic Committee), the state of Utah, and the FBI. See later notes (below) and Chapter 7 for sources.

39 The key figure from sports goods manufacturing was Horst Dassler (son of the founder of the sport shoe corporation Adidas), the key sport agent was Mark McCormack, and the key sport marketing organisation was ISL, half owned by Dassler. Each of these became extremely influential with the IOC, not least through the support of IOC President Samaranch. On ISL and Dassler, see Hill 1992 ch.4 and Simson and Jennings 1992, chs.2–4.

40 Sugden and Tomlinson 1998 (pp. 88, and ch.4 *passim*) argue that FIFA's sponsorship packages may have influenced Ueberroth's approach to Olympic sponsorship in 1984. The latter undoubtedly subsequently influenced the IOC's approach to Seoul 1988 and beyond. Also Simson and Jennings 1992 p.51 and ch.4 *passim*.

41 Ueberroth 1985; also Gratton and Taylor 1988a and Hill 1992 ch.7.

42 On Kim Un Yong see Simson and Jennings 1992 ch.11, Jennings 1996 ch.9 and *passim*, also Hoberman 1995. On Yong's involvement in the 1999 bribery inquiries, see, for instance, press coverage by Kettle 1999-P, Lashmar 1999-P, Mackay 1999E-P and Mackay 1999J-P.

43 Howell 1990, p.330, and ch.14 *passim*. On claims about problems with the Amsterdam bid, see Millward, D. 1999-P.

44 On problems with the Lillehammer decision, see Jennings 1996 ch.2, also Davison 1999B-P.

45 On allegations of problems with the the Nagano bid, see Daley 1999–P, Jordan and Sullivan 1999-P, Anon 1999-P.

46 On the Quebec bid team's experiences and views see Mackay 1999C-P; on the Salt Lake City bribery crisis in general, see, for instance, Mackay 1999A-P, 1999B-P, 1999D-P; Davison 1999A-P; Rodda 1999-P; and Calvert *et al.* 1999-P. Also see the discussion and notes to Chapter 7.

6 Mega-events and media culture

1 On the display and development, at successive expos from the late nineteenth century to the 1930s, of the key media-related technologies of electricity in general, on the one hand, and electrical light in particular, on the other, see respectively Nye 1994 and Schivelbusch 1988. Alexander Graham Bell's telephone was demonstrated at the 1876 Philadelphia expo (Allwood 1977 p.56; Rydell 1984 p.16) and long-distance wireless telegraphy at the 1904 St Louis expo (Gunning 1996). Early versions of film technology were demonstrated at various turn-of-the-century expos, including Thomas Edison's 'kinetoscope', the Lumiere company's large screen 'cinematograph' at Paris 1900, and 'biograph' films at St Louis 1904 (Gunning 1996).

2 Also see Toulmin 1994 on the early popularisation of film through travelling fairs in this period.

3 Rydell observes that the series of inter-war American expos 'took the nation by storm' and that huge audiences 'reveled in live radio broadcasts from the expositions' (Rydell 1993 p.1, and *passim*).

4 On the centrality of BBC radio broadcasting to the construction of a national and popular British sport culture and national identity from the 1920s to the 1950s, see Barnett 1990, Whannel 1992, and Scannell 1996. Scannell's 'phenomenological' discussion of the experience of radio broadcasts, particularly great sport events, illustrates the 'dramatological' character of media events and of sport mega-events as media events and generally the relevance of a phenomenological perspective in understanding them (Chapter 8).

5 See, respectively MacAloon (ed.) 1984 (a collection Turner contributed to), Dayan and Katz 1992, Handelman 1998; and Real 1989. Other relevant Turner-influenced ethnographic and anthropological work is contained in Falassi's studies of festivals (Falassi (ed.) 1987), Handelman's studies of 'public events' (some of it undertaken with Katz) (Handelman 1998) and Schechner's studies of play and ritual (Schechner 1995). On some of these intellectual connections, see MacAloon 1992 and also some of the discussions on Katz in Liebes and Curran 1998.

6 Katz and Dayan were by no means unaware of the gaps and problems in their analysis and of the strengths of alternative and more critical approaches, see Dayan and Katz 1992, Appendix. For a general critical review of Katz's contribution to the study of the media's address to ritual and identity, see Curran and Liebes 1998, and generally Liebes and Curran 1998. Also see Eastman and Riggs 1994.

7 Excerpt from 'Toward the Critique of Hegel's Philosophy of Right', in Marx and Engels 1969, p.303.

8 For relevant analyses of global television, see Barker 1997, Herman and McChesney 1997, also McChesney 1998. On the media globalisation of the Olympics, see Larson and Park 1993, and Spa *et al.* 1995. On the media globalisation of sport in this context, see Whannel 1992, Rowe *et al.* 1994, Sugden and Tomlinson 1998 ch.4, Whitson 1998, and Rowe 1999.

9 For instance, Houlihan 1994, Hoberman 1994, and Roche 1998.

10 See Wenner 1989 and (ed.) 1998; also Goldlust 1987, Wenner 1998, Whannel 1992 and 1997, Real 1996, Rowe *et al.* 1994, Rowe 1996, 1999, and Maguire 1999 ch.7.

11 On media sport in general and national identities, see, for instance, Chandler 1988, Klatell and Marcus 1988, Hargreaves 1986 ch.7, Whannel 1992, Blain *et al.* 1993, Bellamy 1998, and discussions by Whannel, and Blain and O'Donnell in Roche (ed.) 1998.

12 The higher figure is given in Gratton 1997. The more cautious assessment is given in Horsman 1998-P.

13 Murdoch made this statement in 1996 (quoted in Anon 1998B-P). On Murdoch and his media strategies more generally, see Barnett 1996-P, Horsman 1997 ch. 4, 9, Auletta 1997, ch. 14, McChesney 1998; and also Shawcross's biography (Shawcross 1993).

14 On Murdoch's US media-sport acquisitions and strategy, see Cornwell 1998-P, Davison 1998-P, Tran 1998-P, Smith 1997-P, Usborne 1997-P. The information in this section is derived mainly from these sources and relates to the period up to 1998.

15 The Fox/Liberty Network previously jointly owned by Murdoch and John Malone. It was taken over completely by Murdoch in 1999 (Teather 1999-P; Tran 1999-P). On Murdoch and Malone as 'media moguls', see Auletta 1997.

16 For instance, Manchester United have an estimated 20 million fans in China and sell club merchandise directly from their own outlet in the city of Guandong (Smith 1998-P).

17 This has begun to happen among the leading clubs in the English Premier League (PL). Media-based stakeholders and members of football club boards are likely to have a lot of influence on clubs' approaches both to the renegotiation of the PL's contract with Sky, which will be coming up in 2001, and also on the exploitation of their market position in the new digital TV age. Manchester United launched a subscription channel (MUTV) in mid-1998 to begin to test this market (Chaudhary1998-P) and leading English PL clubs are expected to develop PPV 'season ticket' access to coverage of their games (Cambell 1999-P; Ridley 1999-P).

18 For accounts of Sky's attempt to buy control of Manchester United FC, the OFT decision and the political debate which ensued, see Anon 1998B-P, Bell *et al.* 1999–P, Horsman 1999-P, Larsen 1999-P and Watt *et al.* 1999–P. When its bid was blocked Sky began to pursue a different strategy in mid-1999 aimed at acquiring minor stakes in a number of PL clubs (e.g. Chelsea FC and Leeds United FC). This would ensure a seat

on the boards of these clubs and a representation on the clubs' and PL's side of the table, as well as the broadcasters' side of the table, at future renegotiations cover TV rights in 2001 (McIntosh 1999-P).

19 The plans of the Media Partners group were revealed in early 1998 (O'Reilly 1998A-P) and confirmed later that year (O'Reilly 1998B-P, Bell 1998-P). For somethng of the debate that ensued, see Boggan 1998-P, Boggan and McCann 1998-P. UEFA responded with plans of its own in late 1998 for the 1999/2000 season, which have been temporarily accepted by the major clubs and leagues (Walker 1998-P).

20 A Ministerial statement outlining this new policy approach to 'listed events' was made from the Department of Culture, Media and Sport in 1998 (25th June).

21 Presenting the EC's position on the limits to the rights of sport bodies to control their own sports and players, EU Commissioner Van Miert commented: 'Sport is big business. . . . We have to live with it.' However 'If there is [broadcasting] exclusivity we would like others to have accesss to the competition. . . . Sports bodies should observe limits when they are exercising their power. If they are abusing their dominance or monopoly situation, this can fly in the face of EU commercial competition rules.' Quoted in Bates 1999-P.

22 The Bosman ruling in 1995 created the possibility of a new EU-wide freedom of movement for EU sport professionals and a new labour market in all sports (see Bates 1998-P and Taylor 1997-P; for relevant background issues on international 'sports labour migration', see Bale and Maguire 1994).

23 In 1998 the EC produced a working paper on 'the European model of sport'. recognising that 'there is a gap between the real world of sport and its regulatory framework'. In 1999 the Commission was still considering its position on sport policy (see EC 1999).

24 Rowe 1996 and 1999 pp. 87–91; Roche 1999b; also O'Keefe 1998.

25 See ACOG 1997 ch.7 on television in relation to the Atlanta Games and ch.12 on the event's finances. For information on broadcast rights fees for Sydney and subsequent Games, see Spa et al. 1995 ch.2, IOC 1996 ch.1 and 6, also Culf 1996-P. Within NBC's block deal for American broadcast rights to the 2000–2008 Winter and Summer Games it is claimed that the prices for the rights to the three Summer Games of Sydney 2000, Athens 2004 and the 2008 event were $715 million, $793 million, and $894 million respectively (Rowe 1999 p. 71).

26 See Larson and Park 1993, also Rivenburgh 1992. See also Gratton and Taylor 1988b and Seh-Jik 1991 ch.5 and *passim*.

27 For analyses of aspects of IOC politics in relation to the Seoul Olympics see Hill 1992 ch.8, Simson and Jennings 1992 ch.11, Hoberman 1995, Jennings 1996 ch.9.

28 Larson and Park 1993 p.3, also pp. 34–7; and Grayson 1993 on Korea's sport traditions and the background to this development.

29 On this theme, see also MacAloon 1984, Hill 1992, Hoberman 1986,1995, Houlihan 1994 and Chapter 7.

30 Herefter Spa et al. 1995. On media aspects of the Barcelona Olympics also see Blain et al. 1993, and Hargreaves 1996.

31 The discussion of the Barcelona Olympics as a media event in the rest of this section draws heavily from Spa et al.'s study.

32 See Spa et al.'s findings and analyses in 1995 ch.9. Communication of the Catalonian dimension of the Olympic host by national presenters varied from being substantial and effective (ibid. pp. 171–5), to being marginal (in the cases of Egyptian, Cuban, Indonesian, South African and South Korean broadcasts), to being largely absent (China) (ibid. pp.175–6). Also see Hargreaves 1996.

33 On the IOC's TOPS sponsorship programme, see Spa et al. 1995 pp.25–31; IOC 1996a, ch.7, also Simson and Jennings ch.2,8 and *passim*, Hill 1992, Sugden and Tomlinson 1998 ch.4.

7   Mega-events and global citizenship

1 On the contemporary social and political theory of citizenship in both national and transnational (global) terms see for instance, Turner 1993, Held 1995, van Steenbergen

1995, Roche 1996, Lister 1997 and Boli and Thomas 1999.
2 Olympic Charter IOC 1995b. (On the development of the Charter from the 1970s to the 1990s, see IOC 1996a p.143. For a slightly modified and updated version of the Charter, which does not affect the substance of the Rules and Principles discussed here see IOC 1996b.) On 'Olympism' as a moral worldview, see IOC 1996a ch.1 and ch.9, also McIntosh 1980 on sport ethics. For a critique of the 'amoral universalism' of 'Olympic internationalism', see Hoberman 1995.
3 Most of the main Human Rights documents are collected together in Council of Europe 1992.
4 On the structure and growth in recent decades of Olympic regional associations and other related organisations such as the Court of Sport Arbitration, see IOC 1996a chs.1 and 9.
5 For instance, the term 'Olympic Family' is used in such documents as IOC 1995c (Contents, III Annexes), in IOC 1996a *passim*, in the Atlanta Games report ACOG 1997, and also it is frequently used informally in the IOC's Olympic movement 'house' journal, *The Olympic Review.*
6 The IOC had a difficult relation with UN system in the form of UNESCO in the 1970s (see note 24 below). For an overview of relations between the IOC and WHO, UNICEF and other UN-system organisations, see IOC 1996a ch.5, Kidane 1995, 1996, 1998, also Anon 1998a,b,c,d. Also see Samaranch's statement in IOC 1996a p.419. For an analysis of the IOC's role in international relations, see Houlihan 1994 ch.5.
7 Castells 1996, 1997, 1998; Urry 1998; Lash and Urry 1994.
8 Held 1995 provides a normative theoretical argument for global citizenship derived from the principle of autonomy. He argues for a new set of institutions of global governance including, among other things, a reconstituted bi-cameral UN General Assembly and a new International Court of Human Rights which would have real authority in relation to nation-states. For a related but more empirically oriented analysis of the world order and the 'world citizenship it implies, see Boli and Thomas 1999 and also chapters in Boli and Thomas (eds) 1999. For relevant international human rights charters see Council of Europe 1992. On the connection between human rights and trans-national conceptions of citizenship see Roche 1987b and 1995b.
9 See O'Keefe 1998 on universal cultural rights including rights of access to media-sport, also Rowe 1999. On the IOC's version of sport as a human right and the relation of Olympism to human rights, see Samaranch 1999a and M'baye 1999, also Bhuvandendra 1999.
10 See IOC 1995a p.108, IOC 1996 ch.8, Espy 1979, Houlihan 1994 ch.5, also see Payne 1993. The IOC banned South Africa from the 1964 Tokyo Olympics. However, after the appearance of concessions in relation to its racist sports policies, the IOC initially readmitted South Africa to the 1968 Mexico Olympics, only reimposing the ban after a threat of boycott by African nations and the USSR. After a UN resolution proposing that countries cut sport contacts with South Africa, the country was expelled from the Olympic movement in 1970. On the often ambivalent policy pursued by the IOC in relation to South Africa and racism in sport, see IOC 1996a ch.8. pp.205–19.
11 On the Internet and social change, see Barrett 1997, Herman and McChesney 1997, and Coyle 1997; on the relevance of the internet for sport culture and media sport, see Rowe 1999 ch. 8.
12 For critiques, see Simson and Jennings 1992, and Jennings 1996; also see Hill 1992 and Hoberman 1986 and 1995. For a positive version of the IOC and the Olympic movement, see the IOC's centenary history (IOC 1994, 1995a, 1996a).
13 On the financial audit, see Mackay 1999I-P, J-P. On the Ethics Commission and the IOC Olympic 2000 Commission, see Anon 1999e and 1999f.
14 On the cases of Pippig, Virenque, de Bruin and Barnes, see Mackay 1998E-P. Korda tested positive for the use of anabolic steroids at the Wimbledon Tennis Championship in 1998 and retired from professional tennis in 1999 (Mackay 1999F-P).
15 For IOC perspectives and claims to leadership in fighting the drug problem, see IOC 1995a pp.165–7 and IOC 1996a ch.8 pp.255–73. For the IOC's attempt to renew its leadership in this field in 1999 see the 'Lausanne – Anti-Doping Declaration' (Anon 1999b) and Samaranch 1999b.

16 Four Chinese swimmers (Wang Luna, Cai Huijue, Zhang Yi and Wang Wei) tested positive for drugs at the World Swimming Championships in Perth in 1998. Chinese swimmers have given twenty-seven positive tests since 1990. See Mackay 1998A-P, Anon 1998A-P, Evans 1998-P.

17 In 1998 Samaranch controversially suggested that the lists of drugs banned by sport authorities like the IOC might be limited to only those drugs which actually damage the health of athletes and that non-damaging performance enhancing drugs might be legalised for use in sport. For criticisms of Samaranch's views, see Williams 1998–P; for a more supportive perspective on these views see Collier 1998-P.

18 On the debate for and against the IOC's record and role at the IOC-convened 'World Conference on Doping in Sport', see Mackay 1999G-P, Rowbotham 1999-P

19 The $150 limit is noted in IOC 1995c. In 1986 Dennis Howell, leader of the Birmingham Olympic bid for the 1992 Olympics, identified the corruption problem and made clear proposals to Samaranch for new IOC rules to eradicate it (Howell 1990 ch.14). The IOC's official history dates Samaranch's and the IOC Executive's alleged concerns about excessive gifts from 1986. However, it makes no reference at all to Howell or his proposals. On the slow evolution of IOC's largely, ineffective policy on gifts and bribery from 1986 to the early 1990s, see IOC 1996a, pp. 85–6 and pp. 80–7 *passim*. Also see Hill 1992, Simson and Jennings 1992, Rodda 1993-P, Jennings 1996 and the discussion in Chapter 5.

20 Hodler made his claims in December 1998, see Anon 1998C-P, Mackay 1998C-P, Mackay 1998D-P and Anon 1999c. Also see the discussion and notes in Chapter 5.

21 The Pound Report (produced by an IOC inquiry team chaired by Vice-President Richard Pound) was made public in January 1999. For a statement of the main findings, see IOC 1999; also see Samaranch 1999c and Anon 1999f. For press reports on the report and related issues, see Mackay 1999B-P, D-P, J-P; Mackay and Chaudhary 1999-P; Daley 1999-P; Davison 1999A-P, B-P; Calvert *et al.* 1999-P; also see discussion and notes in Chapter 5.

22 See Jennings 1996 ch.20. On de Coubertin's interest in the Nobel prize, his friendships with early Nobel prizewinners and his failure to win it himself, see Hoberman 1986 and 1995, also Chapter 4.

23 On the Olympic truce in ancient Greece, see Finley and Pleket 1976 p.98 and ch.8 *passim*. They point out that the truce was not intended to stop inter-state war (except against the state of Elis in which Olympia was located) and it did not do so. The aim was to stop wars (which might be ongoing during the Games) interfering with the Games and to ensure the safe inter-state travel of the athletes and spectators undertaking what was effectively a pilgrimage to Olympia.

24 On the IOC and UNESCO see Killanin 1983, IOC 1996 pp.130–3 and Stivachtis 1999. Also see Hill 1992 and Houlihan 1994 chs.4 and 5. On the IOC and the UN, see IOC 1996a ch.5. In terms of the continuing character of IOC–UN relationships it is worth noting the willingness of two ex-UN Secretary Generals to be involved in the 1999 Olympic reform process, and also the willingness of UN Secretary General Kofi Annan to receive an IOC award also in 1999 (Anon 1999a).

25 On the IOC's pursuit of the Truce project with the UN from 1992 to 1995, see IOC 1996a pp.136–9, and Kidane 1995. On more recent developments in the IOC–UN relationship, see Kidane 1996 (which includes the text of Samaranch's address to the UN in 1995 and of the UN's 'Olympic Truce' Resolution – UN Resolution A/50/L.15 'Building a peaceful and better world through sport and the Olympic ideal'), Kidane 1998, and Samaranch 1999d.

8 Mega-events, identity and global society

1 For instance, for discussions of 'the lifeworld', social constructionism and the theory of communicative rationality, see Berger and Luckmann 1967, Schutz and Luckmann 1974, Habermas 1989b, also Roche 1973. For relevant analyses of popular culture which also claim to use phenomenological and/or subjectivist approaches, but which

derive from an alternative, 'post-modern', perspective, see Rojek 1993b, 1995; Ritzer 1999; and Maffesoli 1996.

2 On the theory of human needs see the seminal study by Doyal and Gough 1991, on the theory of citizenship and human rights, see Turner 1993, also Roche 1987a and b, 1995b, and Marshall 1992.

3 On the relevance of phenomenological perspectives for sociology in general see Roche 1973 (also 1987a, 1988); on their relevance for the theory of citizenship see Roche1987b (also 1996), and of temporality, see 1990 (also 1989). On the meanings of sport and mega-events for identity and culture, see Roche 1992a and 1998.

4 For a relevant analysis, see, for instance, Giddens 1984, 1991, and for a discussion of Giddens' views, see Roche 1987a.

5 For relevant discussions of consumer culture, see, for instance, Featherstone 1991 and Rojek 1993b; also the debate around 'McDonaldisation', Ritzer 1996, 1998, 1999 and Smart 1999. On the importance of media and mediatisation in consitituting and re-constituting identity and the lived social world in modernity, see Scannell 1996 for a phenomenology of the lifeworld in relation to the media; also Thompson 1995 ch.1, 3, 4, and 7 and Stevenson 1995.

6 For an important and influential analysis of the 'lifeworld' and of the threats to it emanating from systemic features of the modern societal formation, threats which are formulated as processes of 'colonization of the lifeworld', see Habermas 1989.

7 For a review of general social theories and perspectives of the relation between sport culture and modernity see Jarvie and Maguire 1994 chs.9, 10 and *passim*, Houlihan 1994 ch.8, and Maguire 1999. Also see Binfield and Stevenson (eds) 1993.

8 For applications of the concepts of 'time structure' and de-structuring to the two life events and forms of experience of retirement and unemployment, see Roche 1989 and 1990 respectively. For relevant studies on the theory and experience of time in modern-ity, see Minkowski 1970, Toffler 1970, Rifkin 1987, and Young and Schuller 1988.

9 On temporality and routinisation in the experience of 'doing time' in long-term im-prisonment, see Cohen and Taylor 1972 ch.4. For a study of 'escape attempts' in relation to everyday routines, see Cohen and Taylor 1978 (also Rojek 1993b). For an analysis of the aestheticisation of everyday life in the contemporary period through people's interests in periodic rituals and temporary 'neo-tribal' gatherings, see Maffesoli 1996.

10 In Chapters 1 and 6, various perspectives concerned with the role of ritual in modernity were considered in terms of their relevance for understanding mega-events. Contem-porary studies of the importance of ritual, and its connections with the extra-ordinary, in social life (whether drawing inspiration and insights from the classic studies of van Gennep 1960 and Turner 1995 or from post-modern theory, as in the case of Rojek 1993b and Maffesoli 1996) provide useful counterweights to the overestimation of the role of routine in the lifeworld assumed by Giddens and others. Ritual in modernity can be said to provide mediations between everyday and 'unique' personal experiences and also between the personal and the communal. However from the 'time-structure' perspective outlined in this chapter, a fuller characterisation of the lifeworld and of the nature of temporality in it requires more than a new appreciation of the ritualistic in contemporary life. It also requires a serious address to and incorporation of notions of human needs, rights, life events and historicity (Roche 1987a, 1987b, 1988, 1996).

11 To understand 'body culture' more generally in contemporary modernity, the current role of the 'industries' and cultures of sport, sex, dress, dance, clubs, food, drink and drugs, the attractions of the athletic, the aesthetic and the anaesthetic, etc., would need to be explored in more of a coordinated and systematic way that has been attempted in much contemporary social science. On the concept of 'body culture' in social and ethnographic analysis, see Brownell 1995.

12 Handelman's discussion of the potentially order-creating and performative ('model-for' action) character of public events and rituals appears to offer insights (Handelman 1998). However, his approach requires him to focus on the 'logic' of events rather than the role of agency in them, and it is thus limited in terms of my concerns in this chapter.

13 For sociological accounts of the variously structurally uneven (e.g. economically advanced and political retarded) and normatively problematic reality of the emergence of an increasingly integrated global level and dimension in late twentieth-century modernity see for instance Sklair 1991, Robertson 1992, Waters 1995, Spybey 1996, Castells 1996, 1997, 1998; and Held *et al.* 1998. On political and economic aspects of globalisation see Ohmae 1995, Gamble and Payne 1996, Coyle 1997 (chs. 7 and 8). For critical contributions to the debate on globalisation, see Hirst and Thompson 1996, Martin and Schumann 1997 and Bauman 1998.

14 On the information technology and 'information age' aspects of contemporary globalisation, see, for instance, Castells 1996,1997, 1998. On the economic and social current and potential impact of the Internet, see, for instance, Barrett 1997, Coyle 1997 and Herman and McChesney 1997. Also more generally on the role of information and communication technology in the social history of modernity, see, for instance, Rogers 1986.

15 For general studies of culture and consumption at a global level see for instance Featherstone (ed.) 1990, Robertson 1990, 1992, Waters 1995 ch.6., Held *et al.* 1998 ch.7, Ritzer 1999, and Stevenson (ed.) 1999. For some useful analyses of cultural and consumerist phenomena of media and sport in particular at the global level, see, on the media, Thompson, 1995 ch.5, Morley and Robins 1995, Herman and McChesney 1997 ch.3 and *passim*; Barker 1997, Sreberny-Mohammadi *et al.* (eds) 1997; and on sport, Jarvie and Maguire 1994 ch.10, Houlihan 1994 ch.8, Hoberman 1998 and Maguire 1999.

16 See Chapter 7. On the emergence of a global level of politics, political order, and governance see for instance, Held 1995, Waters 1995 ch.5, Gamble and Payne 1996, Held *et al.* 1998. On global citizenship, civil society and human rights in relation to this global political order, see, for instance, Held 1995, Van Steenbergen 1995 (ed.) (chapters by van Steenbergen and Falk); Spybey 1996 ch.3, Deacon 1997, Urry 1998, Keane 1998, and Boli and Thomas 1999.

17 For a sociological analysis that asserts the continuing relevance of the nation-state and national cultures in an era of globalisation, see Smith 1995 and 1998.

18 For a discussion of these common problematic global social conditions, and one which is relevant to the notion of developing 'global citizenship', see Urry 1998, also see Chapter 7.

19 David Held makes one of the clearest and strongest normative cases for this (Held 1995, see also Keane 1998 and Boli and Thomas 1999). Part of Held's case is that the development of a global political culture is not only normatively consistent with the process of globalisation, but also is in fact likely to be impelled by the dynamics and problems of this process (see Held *et al.* 1998 *passim*).

20 Arguably, contemporary interests in meso- sphere perspectives in social theory in some respects re-play comparable interests in 'middle range' theory in the influential post-war social theory of Robert Merton and his associates (see Merton 1968).

21 Besides mass communication perspectives some origins of relevant socio-cultural conceptions of 'flow' include Toffler 1970 and Williams 1974. In contemporary social analysis, 'flow theory' has been developed by , among others, Appadurai 1990, Hannerz 1990, Lash and Urry 1994, and Urry 1998. The concept of 'social movements' has been well-worked in the last two decades; for recent relevant discussions see Touraine 1995, Roche 1995a, Maheu (ed.)1995. On the role of metaphor in theorising in general, see Lakoff and Johnson 1980.

22 On various comparable inter-group 'time wars' see Toffler 1970 and Rifkin 1987.

23 Castells does note, however, that in 1995 by electing a new mayor, the people of Tokyo rejected the possibility of staging an expo in 1997 (1996, pp. 425–8). He sees this as an example of localist resistance by ordinary people to the logic of international capitalism, apparently a rare triumph of the politics of the space of places over the space of flows. How this theoretical formula might be applied to the case of Barcelona is unclear (for his few passing references to it see Castells 1996, pp. 421–2). The city's economic fortunes, as discussed in Chapter 5, have, on any reasonable assessment, been consider-

ably improved by the investments undertaken for the 1992 Olympic mega-event with positive implications for local employment and thus for the quality of local social life.

24 The writings of David Held and his colleagues, on globalisation and related issues, which are otherwise of considerable relevance to the themes of this book, nevertheless also seem to ignore the role of expos and Olympics and other such mega-events, (see Held 1995 and Held *et al.* 1998).

25 A less useful concept than 'hub' (because of its post-modern theory context) for picturing related notions of inter-mixing of different streams and elements in contemporary society is that of 'de-differentiation'. See Crook *et al.* 1992 for a discussion in the context of an analysis of 'post-modernisation', and Harvey 1989 for an analysis of de-differentiation as an aspect of the contemporary 'post-modern condition'.

26 For Castells' analysis of 'the space of flows' and its 'layers' see ch.6 in Castells 1996. According to this the 'first layer' is the system of worldwide computerised linkages and is 'constituted by a circuit of electronic impulses'. (ibid. p.412). The 'second layer' 'is constituted by . . . nodes and hubs', it is 'place based' and it is illustrated by 'global cities' (ibid. pp. 413, 415).

27 Castells 1996 *passim*. Two other contemporary social analysts, Hannerz 1992 and Appadurai 1990, also focus on cities in their analyses of flows. Like Castells they also take cities both as the socio-spatial hubs between which flows operate and as themselves being places which are significantly constituted by the flows that they contain and in which the social fact of flows in modernity can be most readily observed and assessed in all of its diversity.

28 The IOC has attempted to make these connections in recent years and has attempted to use the discourse and rhetoric associated with these movements, increasingly so in relation to environmentalism, to promote its games events and to manipulate the worldwide public image of the Olympic movement in general.

Bibliography

Notes:

(i) The references for chapters by different authors in the same edited collection use the expression 'op. cit.' to refer to this collection. Full information about the collection can be located using the name(s) of the editor(s).

(ii) Multiple items by the same author in the same year in the main bibliography are indicated by a, b, c etc. after the name and the year, and are also referenced this way in the text and the Notes.

(iii) Relevant Press articles are included in separate list which follows the main bibliography. Items in the Press Articles List are indicated in the text and in the Notes by the letter P following the author's name and year of publication.

(iv) Multiple items in the Press Articles List by the same author are cited in the text or in the Notes by means of A, B, C, etc. after the author's name and year of publication.

Abercrombie, N. and Longhurst, B. (1998) *Audiences: A Sociological Theory of Performance and Imagination*, London: Sage.

Abrahams, H. (1976) 'London 1948', pp.60–64 in Killanin and Rodda (eds) *The Olympic Games*, New York: Macmillan.

ACOG (1997) *The Official Report on the Centennial Olympic Games*, Vol.1, Atlanta: ACOG

Adams, B. (1997) *E Pluribus Barnum: The Great Showman and the Making of U.S. Popular Culture*, Minneapolis: University of Minnesota Press.

AIEST (1987), *The Role and Impact of Mega-Events and attractions on Regional and National Tourism Development*, St Gall, Switzerland: AIEST (Association Internationale d'Experts Scientifique du Tourisme).

Aja, T. (1998) 'Spanish sport policy in Republican and Fascist Spain', in Arnaud and Riordan (eds) *Sport and International Politics: The impact of fascism and communism on sport*, London: E & FN Spon/Routledge.

Allan, D. (1981) 'The "Red Doctor" amongst the Virtuosi: Karl Marx and the Society', *Journal of the Royal Society of Arts*, 129, 259–61 and 309 – 311.

Allwood, J. (1977) *The Great Exhibitions*, London: Cassell and Collier.

Altick, R. (1978) *The Shows of London*, Cambridge, Mass.: Harvard University Press

Anderson,B (1991) *Imagined Communities*, London: Verso.

Anderson,K. and Gale,F. (eds) (1992) *Inventing Places*, Melbourne: Wiley.

Anderson, R. and Wachtel, E. (1986) 'Introduction' in Anderson and Wachtel (eds) *The Expo Story – 1986*, Vancouver: Harbour Publishing.

Anderson, R. and Wachtel, E. (eds) (1986) *The Expo Story – 1986*, Vancouver: Harbour Publishing.

Anthony, D. (1987) *Britain and the Olympic Games*, London: British Olympic Association.

Anon (1998a) 'Finding solutions to youth problems on the eve of the third millennium', *Olympic Review* 19, pp.25–6.

—— (1998b) 'Sport against poverty', *Olympic Review*, 19: 77–8.

—— (1998c) 'Health and sport' , *Olympic Review*, 20: 52.

—— (1998d) 'The IOC and ILO', *Olympic Review*, 20: 75.

—— (1998e) 'From Lisbon to Seville', *Olympic Review*, 21: 23–7.

—— (1999a) 'Jesse Owens Award to Kofi Annan' *Olympic Review* XXVI-24: 55.

—— (1999b) 'Lausanne – Anti-Doping Declaration' *Olympic Review* XXVI-25: 17–18.

—— (1999c) 'The Salt Lake City: Crisis' *Olympic Review* XXVI-25: 33.

—— (1999d) 'The 108th IOC Session', *Olympic Review* XXVI-26: 6–7.

—— (1999e) 'The Ethics Commission', *Olympic Review* XXVI-27: 5.

—— (1999f) 'IOC 2000 Commission', *Olympic Review* XXVI-27: 6–8.

Appadurai, A. (1990) 'Disjuncture and Difference in the Global Cultural Economy', in Featherstone (ed.) *Global Culture,* London: Sage.

Apostolopoulos, Y. *et al.* (eds) (1996) *The Sociology of Tourism: Theoretical and Empirical Investigations,* London: Routledge.

Armstrong, J. (1984), 'Contemporary Prestige Centres for Art, Culture, Exhibitions, Sports and Conferences: An International Survey' Unpublished Ph.D., University of Birmingham, Birmingham.

Arnaud, P. (1998) 'Sport and International relations before 1918', in Arnaud and Riordan (eds) *Sport and International Politics: The impact of fascism and communism on sport,* London: E & FN Spon/Routledge.

Arnaud, P. and Riordan, J. (eds) (1998) *Sport and International Politics: The impact of fascism and communism on sport,* London: E & FN Spon/Routledge.

Auf der Maur, N. (1976), *The Billion Dollar Game: Jean Drapeau and the 1976 Olympics,* Toronto: James Lorimer.

Auletta, K. (1997) *The Highwaymen: Warriors of the Information Superhighway,* New York: Random House.

Auerbach, J. (1999) *The Great Exhibition of 1851,* London: Yale University Press.

Bahktin, M. (1984) *Rabelais and his World,* Bloomington: Indiana University Press.

Bailey, P. (1978) *Leisure and Class in Victorian England: Rational Recreation and the Contest for Control,* London: Routledge & Kegan Paul.

Bale, J. (1992) *Sport, Space and the City,* London: Routledge.

Bale, J. and Maguire, J. (1994) 'Introduction: Sports Labour Migration in the Global Arena', in Bale, J. and Maguire, J. (eds) (1994) *The Global Sports Arena,* London: Frank Cass.

Barker, C. (1997) *Global Television,* Oxford: Blackwell.

Barnett, S. (1990) *Games and Sets: The Changing Face of Sport on Television,* London: BFI Publishing.

Barrett, N. (1997) *The State of Cybernation: Cultural, Political and Economic implications of the Internet,* London: Kogan Page.

Bauman, Z. (1998) *Globalization: The Human Consequences,* Cambridge: Polity Press

Bayley, S. (1998) *Labour Camp: The failure of style over substance,* London: B.T. Batsford.

Beck, U. (1992) *Risk Society: Towards a New Modernity,* London: Sage.

Beck, P. (1999) *Scoring for Britain: International football and international politics 1900–1939,* London: Frank Cass.

Beckles, H. and Stoddart, B. (1995) *Liberation Cricket: West Indian Cricket Culture,* Manchester: Manchester University Press

Bellamy, R. (1998) 'The Evolving Television sports Marketplace', in Wenner (ed.) *MediaSport,* London: Routledge.

Bendix, R. (1962) *Max Weber: An Intellectual Portrait,* New York: Anchor/Doubleday & Co.

Benedict, B. (1983) 'The Anthropology of World's Fairs', in Benedict, B. *et al. The Anthropology of World's Fairs* London: Scolar Press.

Benedict, B. (1994) 'Rituals of Representation: Ethnic Stereotypes and Colonized Peoples at World's Fairs', in Rydell and Gwinn (eds) *Fair Representations: World's Fairs and the Modern World,* Amsterdam: VU University Press.

Benjamin, W. (1973) 'Grandville or the World Exhibitions' (in Section III, 'Paris – the

Capital of the nineteenth century'), pp.164–6, in *Charles Baudelaire: A Lyric Poet in the Era of High Capitalism*, London: NLB.

Bennett, T. (1988) 'The Exhibitionary Complex', *New Formations*, 73–102.

—— (1991) 'The shape of things to come: Expo '88', *Cultural Studies* 5, 30–51.

Berger, P. and Luckmann, T. (1967) *The Social Construction of Reality*, New York: Anchor/ Doubleday & Co.

Bhuvandendra, T. (1999) 'Human rights in the realm of sport', *Olympic Review* XXVI-24: 15–25.

BIE (a) (undated), 'International Exhibitions Protocol', Paris:Bureau International des Expositions (BIE).

—— (b) (undated), ' Regulations respecting international exhibitions', Paris: BIE.

Binfield, C. and Stevenson, J. (eds) (1993) *Sport, Culture and Politics*, Sheffield: Sheffield Academic Press.

Blackstone, S. (1986) *Buckskins, Bullets and Business: A History of Buffalo Bill's Wild West*, New York: Greenwood Press.

Blain, N., Boyle, R., and O'Donnell, H. (1993) 'Centrality and Peripherality at the Barcelona Olympics', in Blain, N., Boyle, R., and O'Donnell, H. (eds) (1993) *Sport and National Identity in the European Media*, Leicester: Leicester University Press.

Boli, J. and Thomas, G. (1999) 'INGOs and the Organization of World Culture', in Boli and Thomas (eds) *Constructing World Culture: International Nongovernmental Organisations Since 1875*, Stanford: Stanford University Press.

Boli, J. and Thomas, G. (eds) (1999) *Constructing World Culture: International Nongovernmental Organisations Since 1875*, Stanford: Stanford University Press.

Bond, L. (1996) *Statue of Liberty*, Santa Barbara: Albion Publishing Group.

Bonython, L. (1995) 'The Planning of the Great Exhibition 1851', *Journal of the Royal Society of Arts*,143: 45–8.

Booker, C. (1981) *The Games War: A Moscow Journal*, London: Faber.

Bourdieu, P. (1998) 'The Olympics – an agenda for analysis', Appendix in his *On Television and Journalism*, London: Pluto Press.

—— (1999) 'The state, economics and sport', pp.15–21, in Dauncey and Hare (eds) *France and the 1998 World Cup*, London: Frank Cass

Bowles, S. and Gintis, H. (1976) *Schooling in Capitalist America*, London, Routledge.

Brown, D. (1976) *Bury My Heart at Wounded Knee: An Indian History of the American West*, New York: Bantam.

Brownell, S. (1995) *Training the Body for China*, London: University of Chicago Press.

Bryman, A. (1995) *Disney and his Worlds*, London: Routledge, London.

Burke, B. (1994) 'World's Fairs and International Expositions: Selected References 1987– 1993', in Rydell and Gwinn (eds) *Fair Representations: World's Fairs and the Modern World*, Amsterdam: VU University Press.

Burns, J., Hatch, J., and Mule, T. (eds) (1986) *The Adelaide Grand Prix: The impact of a Special Event*, Adelaide: Centre for South Australian Economic Studies.

Buzard, J. (1993) *The Beaten Track: European Tourism, Literature and Culture 1800–1918*, Oxford: Oxford University Press.

Byrne, M. (1987) 'Nazi Festival: The 1936 Berlin Olympics', in Falassi (ed.) *Time Out of Time: Essays on the Festival*, Albuquerque:University of New Mexico Press.

Castells, M. (1996) *The Information Age. Vol. I – The Rise of the Network Society*, Oxford: Blackwells.

—— (1997) *The Information Age. Vol. II – The Power of Identity*, Oxford: Blackwells.

—— (1998) *The Information Age. Vol. III – End of the MIllenium*, Oxford: Blackwells.

Chandler, J. (1988) *Television and National Sport: The United States and Britain*, Chicago: University of Illinois Press.

Chaney, D. (1986) 'The Symbolic Form of Ritual in Mass Communication' in P. Golding *et al. Communicating Politics*, New York: Holmes & Meier.

—— (1993) *Fictions of Collective Life*, London: Routledge.

Cohen, S. and Taylor, L. (1972) *Psychological Survival: The experience of long-term imprisonment*, London: Penguin.

—— (1978) *Escape Attempts*, London: Penguin.

Coyle, D. (1997) *The Weightless World: Strategies for Managing the Digital Economy*, London: Capstone.

Crook, S. *et al.* (1992) *Postmodernization; Change in Advanced Society*, London: Sage.

Council of Europe (1992) *Human Rights in International Law*, Strasbourg: Council of Europe Press.

Cunningham, H. (1980) *Leisure in the Industrial Revolution 1780–1880*, London: Croom Helm.

Curran, J. and Liebes, T. (1998) 'The intellectual legacy of Elihu Katz', in Liebes and Curran (eds) *Media, Ritual and Identity*, London: Routledge.

Dauncey. H. (1999) 'Building the Finals (France 1998): facilities and infrastructure', pp.98–120 in Dauncey and Hare (eds) *France and the 1998 World Cup*, London: Frank Cass

Dauncey, H. and Hare, G. (1999) 'The Impact of France 98' in Dauncey and Hare (eds) *France and the 1998 World Cup*, London: Frank Cass

Dauncey, H. and Hare, G. (eds) (1999) *France and the 1998 World Cup*, London: Frank Cass

Davis, S. (1996) ' The theme park: global industry and cultural form', *Media, Culture and Society*, 18: 399–422

—— (1997) *Spectacular Nature: Corporate Culture and the Sea World Experience*, London: University of California Press.

Dayan, D. and Katz, E. (1987) 'Performing media events', in Curran, J. *et al.* (eds.) *Impacts and Influences: Essays on media power in the twentieth century*, London: Methuen.

—— (1988) 'Articulating consensus: the ritual and rhetoric of media events', in J.Alexander ed. *Durkheimian Sociology*, Cambridge: Cambridge University.

—— (1992) *Media Events*, London: Harvard University.

De Cauter, L. (1993) 'The Panoramic Ecstasy: On World Exhibitions and the Disintegration of Experience' , *Theory, Culture and Society*, 10: 1–23.

De Coubertin, P. (1966) *The Olympic Idea: Discourse and Essays*, Cologne: Carl Diem Institute

De Coubertin, P. (1979) *Olympic Memoirs*, Lausanne:IOC.

Deacon, B. (1997) *Global Social Policy*, London: Sage.

Debord,G. (1973) *The Society of the Spectacle*, Detroit: Black and Red.

Dimanche, F. (1994) ' Ten Years After: The Louisiana World's Fair Legacy in New Orleans', in Murphy (ed.) *Mega-Event Legacies*, Victoria: Province of British Columbia.

Dine, P. (1996) 'Sport, imperial expansion and colonial consolidation: a comparison of the French and British experiences', in Van der Merwe (ed.) *Sport as Symbol, Symbols in Sport*, Augustin, Germany: Academia Verlag, Sankt Augustin.

Doctorow, E.L. (1985) *World's Fair*, New York: Random House.

Doyal, L. and Gough, I. (1991) *A Theory of Human Need*, London: Macmillan.

Dumas, F. (ed.) (1908) *The Franco-British Exhibition*, Chatto and Windus, London

Dunning, E. and Elias, N. (1986) *The Quest for Excitement: Sport and Leisure in the Civilizing Process*, Oxford: Blackwell

Dunning, E. and Sheard, K. (1979) *Gentlemen, Barbarians and Players*, Oxford: Blackwell

Duvignaud, J. (1976) 'Festivals: A Sociological Approach', in *Cultures*, III, 1:13–25.

Eames, A. (ed.) (1996) *Barcelona*, London: APA Publications (HK).

Eastman, S. and Land, A. (1995) 'The best of both worlds: sports fans find good seats at the bar', *Journal of Sport and Social Issues*.

Eastman, S. and Riggs, K. (1994) 'Televised sports and ritual: fan experiences', *Sociology of Sport Journal*, 11: 249–74.

EC (1999) 'Sport and the European Union: the European model of sport' EC (European Commission), DGX Consultation document, Brusssels. (also Internet publication: http://europa.eu.int/search97cgi/).

Eliot, M. (1995) *Walt Disney: Hollywood's Dark Prince,* London: André Deutsch.

Espy, R. (1979) *The Politics of the Olympic Games,* Berkeley: University of California Press.

Falassi, A. (1987) 'Festival: definition and morphology', in Falassi (ed.) *Time Out of Time: Essays on the Festival,* Albuquerque:University of New Mexico Press.

Falassi, A. (ed.) (1987) *Time Out of Time: Essays on the Festival,* Albuquerque:University of New Mexico Press.

Featherstone, M. (1991) *Consumer Culture and Postmodernism,* London: Sage.

Featherstone, M. (ed.) (1990) *Global Culture,* London: Sage.

Findling, J. (1994a) *Chicago's Great World's Fairs,* Manchester: Manchester University Press.

—— (1994b) 'Fair Legacies: Expo '92 and Cartuja '93', in Rydell and Gwinn (eds) *Fair Representations: World's Fairs and the Modern World,* Amsterdam: VU University Press.

Fiske,J. (1989a) *Understanding Popular Culture,* London: Unwin.

—— (1989b) *Reading Popular Culture,* London: Unwin.

Finley. M. and Pleket, H. (1976) *The Olympic Games:The First Thousand Years,* London: Chatto & Windus.

Fjellman, S. (1992) *Vinyl Leaves: Walt Disney World and America,* Boulder Co.: Westview Press.

Foner, P. (1976) 'Black Participation in the Centennial of 1876', *Negro History Bulletin,* 39, pp.532–8

Freedberg, C. (1986) *The Spanish Pavilion at the Paris World's Fair,* vol. 1, New York: Garland Publishing Inc.

Freud,S. (1873) Letter to Emil Fluss, (16th June, 1873), reproduced in *The Freud Museum Catalogue,* Vienna: Sigmund Freud Society, Vienna.

Gamble, A. and Payne, A. (eds) (1996) *Regionalism and World Order,* London, Macmillan.

Garcia,S. (1993) 'Barcelona und die Olympische Spiele' in Haubermann, H. and Siebel, W. (eds) *Festivalisierung der Stadpolitik,* Stuttgart: Leviathan-Westdeutcher Verlag. (English version: (1994) 'Big Events and Urban Politics: Barcelona and the Olympic Games', unpublished paper, ISA World Sociology Congress, Bielefeld, Germany)

Garofolo, R. (1992) 'Understanding mega-events: if we are the world, then how do we change it?' in Garofolo, R. (ed.) *Rockin' the Boat: Mass Music and Mass Movements,* Boston: South End Press

Geertz, C. (1975) *The Interpretation of Culture,* London: Hutchinson.

Gellner,E. (1983) *Nations and Nationalism,* Oxford: Blackwell.

Georgiadis, K. (1996) 'The press and the first Olympic Games in Athens', *Olympic Review* XXV-8, 11–12.

Getz, D. (1991) *Festivals, Special Events and Tourism,* New York: Van Nostrand Reinhold.

Gilbert, J. (1994) 'World's Fairs as Historical Events', in Rydell and Gwinn (eds) *Fair Representations: World's Fairs and the Modern World,* Amsterdam: VU University Press.

Giddens, A. (1984) *The Constitution of Society,* Cambridge: Polity.

Giddens, A. (1991) *Modernity and Self-Identity,* Cambridge: Polity.

Goffman, E. (1959) *The Presentation of Self in Everday Life,* London: Penguin.

Goldlust, J. (1987) *Playing for Keeps; Sport, The Media and Society,* Melbourne: Longman Cheshire.

Gounot, A. (1998) 'Between revolutionary demands and diplomatic necessity: Soviet and bourgeois sport in Europe 1920–1937', in Arnaud and Riordan (eds) *Sport and International Politics: The impact of fascism and communism on sport,* London: E & FN Spon/ Routledge.

Gratton, C. (1997) 'The economic and social significance of sport', unpublished paper, Leisure Industries Research Centre, Sheffield Hallam University, Sheffield

Gratton , C. and Taylor, P. (1988a) 'The Olympic Games: An economic analysis', (Los Angeles 1984), *Leisure Management,* 8, 3, pp.32–4.

Gratton, C. and Taylor, P. (1988b) 'The Seoul Olympics: Economic success or sporting failure?' *Leisure Management,* 8,12,54–8.

Grayson, J. (1993) 'Sport in Korea: tradition, modernization and the politics of a newly industrialized state', pp.151–67 in Binfield and Stevenson (eds) *Sport, Culture and Politics*, Sheffield: Sheffield Academic Press.

Greenhalgh, P. (1988) *Ephemeral Vistas: The Expositions Universelles; Great Exhibitions and World's Fairs, 1851–1939*, Manchester: Manchester University Press.

Grunberger, R. (1974) *A Social History of the Third Reich*, London: Penguin.

Gruneau, R. (1984) 'Commercialism and the modern Olympics' in Tomlinson and Whannel (eds) *Five Ring Circus: Money, Power and Politics at the Olympic Games*, London: Pluto Press.

Gunning, T. (1994) 'The world as object lesson: Cinema audiences, visual culture and the St. Louis world's fair, 1904', *Film History*, 6, 422–444.

Gutstein, D. (1986) 'Expo's Impact on the city' (expo 1986, Vancouver), in Andersen and Wachtel (eds) *The Expo Story – 1986*, Vancouver: Harbour Publishing.

Guttman, A. (1978) *From Ritual to Record: The Nature of Modern Sports*, New York: Columbia University Press, New York.

—— (1984) *The Games Must Go On: Avery Brundage and the Olympic Movement*, New York: Columbia University Press.

—— (1992) *The Olympics: A History of the Modern Games*, Chicago: University of Illinois.

—— (1994) *Games and Empires: Modern Sports and Cultural Imperialism*, New York: Columbia University Press.

—— (1998) 'The 'Nazi Olympics' and the American boycott controversy', in Arnaud and Riordan (eds) *Sport and International Politics: The impact of fascism and communism on sport*, London: E & FN Spon/Routledge.

Habermas, J. (1989a) 'The Public Sphere', in S.Bronner and D.Kellner (eds) *Critical Theory and Society*, London: Routledge.

—— (1989b) *The Theory of Communicative Action: Lifeworld and System*, Cambridge: Polity.

—— (1991) *The Structural Transformation of the Public Sphere* (original 1962) Cambridge: Polity.

—— (1994) 'Citizenship and National Identity' in B. van Steenbergen, (ed.) *The Condition of Citizenship*, Sage, London.

Hall, C.M. (1989a) 'The Definition and Analysis of Hallmark Tourist Events', *Geojournal*, 19, 3: 263–8

—— (1989b) 'The Politics of Hallmark Events', in Syme *et al.* (eds) *The Planning and Evaluation of Hallmark Events*, Aldershot: Avebury.

—— (1992) *Hallmark Tourist Events*, London: Bellhaven.

—— (1994a) *Tourism and Politics, Policy, Power and Place*, London: Bellhaven.

—— (1994b) 'Mega-Events and the Legacies' in Murphy (ed.) *Mega-Event Legacies*, Victoria: Province of British Columbia

Hall, C.M. and Hodges, J. (1998) 'The politics of place and identity in the Sydney 2000 Olympics: 'sharing the spirit of corporatism'', in Roche (ed.) *Sport, Popular Culture and Identity*, Aachen: Meyer and Meyer Verlag.

Handelman, D. (1998) *Models and Mirrors: Towards an Anthropology of Public Events*, 2nd ed. (original 1990), Cambridge: Cambridge University Press.

Hannerz, U. (1992) *Cultural Complexity*, New York: Columbia University Press.

Hargreaves, Jennifer, (1994) *Sporting Females: Critical Issues in the History and Sociology of Women's Sports*, London: Routledge.

Hargreaves, John, (1986) *Sport, Power and Culture*, Cambridge: Polity Press.

—— (1996) 'The Catalanization of the Barcelona Olympics' (unpublished paper), European Association conference 'Collective Identity and Symbolic Representation', Fondation Nationale des Sciences Politiques, Paris.

Harriss, J. (1975) *The Tallest Tower: Eiffel and the Belle Epoque*, Boston: Houghton Mifflin Co.

Hart-Davis, D. (1986) *Hitler's Games: the 1936 Olympics*, London: Century Hutchinson.

Harvey, D. (1989) *The Condition of Postmodernity*, Oxford: Blackwell.

Harvey, P. (1994) 'Nations on display: technology and culture in Expo 92', *Science as Culture*, 5,1: 85–105.

Harvey, P. (1996) *Hybrids of Modernity: Anthropology, the Nation State and the Universal Exhibition*, London: Routledge.

Held, D. (1995) *Democracy and the Global Order*, Cambridge: Polity.

Held, D. *et al.* (1999) *Global Transformations: Politics, Economics and Culture*, Cambridge: Polity.

Henry, I. (1998) 'Sport, symbolism and urban policy', in Roche (ed.) 1998 *Sport, Popular Culture and Identity*, Aachen: Meyer and Meyer Verlag.

Henry, I., Gratton, C., and Taylor, P. (eds) (1998) *Sport in the City*, vols.1 and 2, (international conference proceedings), Centre for Leisure Industries Research, Sheffield Hallam University, Sheffield.

Herman, E. and McChesney, R. (1997) *The Global Media: The New Missionaries of Global Capitalism*, London: Cassell.

Hetherington, K. (1998) *Expressions of Identity*, London: Sage.

Hiassen, C. (1998) *Team Rodent: How Disney Devours the World*, New York: Ballantine Publishing Group.

Hill, C. (1992) *Olympic Politics*, Manchester: Manchester University Press.

Hinsley, C. (1991) 'The world as marketplace: commodification of the exotic at the world's Columbian exhibition, Chicago, 1893', ch. 18 in I. Karp and S.Lavine (eds) *Exhibiting Cultures: The Poetics and Politics of Museum Display*, Washington: Smithsonian Institution Press.

Hirst, P. and Thompson, G. (1996) *Globalization in Question*, Cambridge: Polity Press

Hoberman, J. (1984) *Sport and Political Ideology*, London: Heinemann.

—— (1986) *The Olympic Crisis: Sports, Politics and the Moral Order*, New Rochelle: Aristide D. Caratzas.

—— (1995) 'Toward a theory of Olympic internationalism', *Journal of Sport History*, 22, 1:1–37

Hobsbawm, E. (1992) 'Mass-producing traditions: Europe, 1870–1914' in Hobsbawm and Ranger (eds) *The Invention of Tradition* (original 1983) Cambridge: Canto/Cambridge University Press.

Hobsbawm, E. and Ranger T. (eds) (1992) *The Invention of Tradition* (original 1983) Cambridge: Canto/Cambridge University Press.

Hochschild, A. (1999) *King Leopold's Ghost*, London: Macmillan.

Holt, R. (1992) *Sport and the British: A Modern History*, Oxford: Clarendon.

—— (1998a) 'The Foreign Office and the Football Association: British sport and appeasement, 1935–1938', in Arnaud and Riordan (ed.) *Sport and International Politics: The impact of fascism and communism on sport*, London: E & FN Spon/Routledge.

—— (1998b) 'Interwar sport and interwar relations', in Arnaud and Riordan (eds) *Sport and International Politics: The impact of fascism and communism on sport*, London: E & FN Spon/Routledge.

Hornby, N. (1996) *Fever Pitch*, London: Indigo.

Horne, D. (1986) *The Public Culture*, London: Pluto Press.

Horsman, M. (1997) *Sky High: The Inside Story of BSkyB*, London: Orion Business Books.

Houlihan, B. (1991) *The Government and Politics of Sport*, London: Routledge

—— (1994) *Sport and International Politics*, London: Harvester Wheatsheaf.

House of Commons, (1997) *The Millenium Dome*, (Second Report of the Culture, Media and Sport Committee, House of Commons), London: The Stationery Office

Howell, D. (1990) *Made in Birmigham: The Memoirs of Denis Howell*, London: Queen Anne Press/Macdonald.

Hughes, H. (1993) 'Olympic Tourism and Urban Regeneration', *Festival Management and Event Tourism*, 1:157–162.

Huizinga, J. (1971) *Homo Ludens*, London: Paladin.

IOC (1994) *The International Olympic Committee – One Hundred Years, Vol 1:1894 – 1942*, Lausanne: IOC (International Olympic Committee).

—— (1995a) *The International Olympic Committee – One Hundred Years, Vol 2: 1942-1972* Lausanne: IOC.

—— (1995b) *Olympic Charter,* Lausanne: IOC.

—— (1995c) *Manual for Candidate Cities for the the Games of the XXVIII Olympiad 2004,* Lausanne: IOC.

—— (1996a) *The International Olympic Committee – One Hundred Years, Vol 3:1972-1996,* (first printed September 1997) Lausanne: IOC

—— (1996b) *Olympic Charter,* Lausanne: IOC

—— (1999) 'The Inquiry' (Findings of the Pound Report) *Olympic Review* XXVI-25: 34

ITU (1996) 'The Olympic Games and the Media', in *Olympic Review* XXV-9: 57–66 (ITU, International Telecommunications Union).

Jackson, P. (1988) 'Street life; the politics of carnival', *Environment and Planning D: Society and Space,* 6: 213–27.

—— (1992) 'The politics of the streets: a geography of Caribana' , *Political Geography,* 11,2: 130–51.

Jackson, R. and McPhail, T. (eds) (1989) *The Olympic Movement and the Mass Media,* Calgary: Hurford Enterprises.

James, C.L.R. (1983) *Beyond a Boundary* (2nd edition), New York, Pantheon.

Jarman, N. (1997) *Material Conflicts: Parades and Visual Displays in Northern Ireland,* Oxford: Berg.

Jarvie, G. and Maguire, J. (1994) *Sport and Leisure in Social Thought,* London: Routledge.

Jennings, A. (1996) *The New Lords of the Rings,* London: Pocket Books,Simon and Schuster.

Jeong, G-H. and Faulkner, B. (1996) 'Resident perceptions of mega-event impacts: The Taejon International Exposition case', *Festival Management and Event Tourism,* 4: 3–11

Jones, S. (1988) *Sport, Politics and the Working Class,* Manchester: Mancheter University Press.

Kang, Y-S and Perdue, R. (1994) 'Long-term Impact of a mega-event on international tourism to the host country: A conceptual model and the case of the 1988 Seoul Olympics', *The Journal of International Consumer Marketing,* 6, 3/4: 205–25.

Kanin, D. (1981) *A Political History of the Olympic Games,* Boulder Colorado: Westview Press.

Kaplan, T. (1993) *Red City, Blue Period: Social Movements in Picasso's Barcelona,* London: University of California Press.

Kasson, J. (1978) *Amusing the Million: Coney Island at the Turn of the Century,* New York: Hill & Wang, New York.

Keane, J. (1998) *Civil Society: Old Images, New Visions,* Polity Press: Cambridge.

Kearns, G. and Philo,C. (eds) (1993) *Selling Places; The City as Cultural Capital, Past and Present* , Oxford: Pergamon.

Kidane, F. (1995) 'The IOC and the United Nations', *Olympic Review,* 25, 5.

—— (1996) Samaranch at the United Nations', *Olympic Review,* 25,6: 4–9.

—— (1998) 'The Olympic Truce', *Olympic Review,* 19:5–7.

Killanin, L. (1983) *My Olympic Years,* London: Secker and Warburg.

Killanin, L. and Rodda, J. (1976) *The Olympic Games,* New York: Macmillan.

Klatell, D. and Marcus, N. (1988) *Sports for Sale: Television, Money and the Fans,* Oxford: Oxford University Press.

Knight, D. (1978) *The Exhibitions: Great White City,* London: Barnard and Westwood.

Kruger, A. (1986) 'The influence of the state sport of fascist Italy on Nazi Germany 1928–1936', pp.145–64 in Mangan and Small (eds) *Sport, Culture, Society: International historical and sociological perspectives,* London: E. & F. Spon.

—— (1998) 'The role of sport in German international politics 1918–1945', in Arnaud and Riordan (eds) *Sport and International Politics: The impact of fascism and communism on sport,* London: E & FN Spon/Routledge.

Lakoff, G. and Johnson, M. (1980) *Metaphors We Live By,* Chicago: The University of Chicago Press.

Lane, C. (1981) *The Rites of Rulers: Ritual in Industrial Society – The Soviet Case*, Cambridge: Cambridge University Press.

Larson, J. and Park, H-S. (1993) *Global Television and the Politics of the Seoul Olympics*, Oxford: Westview Press.

Lash, S. and Urry, J. (1994) *Economies of Signs and Space*, London: Sage.

Lavenda, R. (1980) 'The festival of progress: the globalising world-system and the transformation of the Caracas carnival 1873', *Journal of Popular Culture*, 14: 465–75.

Law, C. (1993) *Urban Tourism*, London: Mansell.

Leibold, M. and Van Zyl, C. (1994) 'The Summer Olympic Games and its tourism marketing: with specifi reference to Cape Town, South Africa', in Murphy (ed.) *Mega-Event Legacies*, Victoria: Province of British Columbia.

Lekarska, N. (1976) 'Olympic Ceremonial', in Killanin and Rodda (eds) *The Olympic Games*, New York: Macmillan.

Lewis, J. (1994) 'Disney After Disney: family business and the business of family', in Smoodin (ed.) *Disney Discourse: Producing the Magic Kingdom*, London: Routledge.

Lewis, R. (1983) 'Everything under one roof: world's fairs and department stores in Paris and Chicago', *Chicago History*, 12, 3: 28–47.

Ley, D. and Olds, K. (1988) 'Landscape as spectacle: worlds fairs and the culture of heroic consumption' *Environment and Planning D: Space and Society* 6: 191–212.

Liebes, T. and Curran, J. (eds) (1998) *Media, Ritual and Identity*, London: Routledge.

Lister, R. (1997) *Citizenship: Feminist Perspectives*, London: Macmillan.

Loventhal and Howarth (1985) 'The impact of the 1984 Summer Olympic Games on the lodging and restaurant industry in Southern California', Sydney: Loventhal and Howarth.

Lovesey, P. (1979) *The Official Centenary History of the Amateur Athletic Assocation*, London: Guinness Superlatives Limited.

Lucas, J. (1980) *The Modern Olympic Games*, New York: A.S.Barnes & Co.

Luckhurst, K. (1951) *The Story of Exhibitions*, London: The Studio Publications.

Lukes, S. (1973) *Emile Durkheim: His Life and Work*, London: Penguin.

—— (1975) 'Political Ritual and Social Integration' *Sociology*, 9: 289–308.

Lyman, S. and Scott, M. (1970) *A Sociology of the Absurd*, New York: Appleton-Century-Crofts.

MacAloon, J. (1981) *This Great Symbol: Pierre de Coubertin and the Origins of the Modern Olympic Games*, Chicago: The University of Chicago Press.

—— (1984) 'Olympic Games and the theory of spectacle in modern societies', in MacAloon (ed.) *Rite, Drama, Festival, Spectacle*, Philadelphia: The Institute of Human Issues.

—— (1989) 'Festival, ritual and TV' (Los Angeles Olympics 1984), in Jackson and McPhail (eds) *The Olympic Movement and the Mass Media*, Calgary: Hurford Enterprises.

—— (1992) 'The ethnographic imperative in comparative Olympic research', *Sociology of Sport Journal*, 9: 104–130.

MacAloon, J. (ed.) (1984) *Rite, Drama, Festival, Spectacle*, Philadelphia: The Institute of Human Issues.

MacArthur, C. (1986) 'The Glasgow Empire Exhibition of 1938: the dialectics of national identity ' in Bennett,T. (ed.) *Popular Culture and Social Relations*, pp.117–34, Milton Keynes: Open University Press.

MacCannell, D. (1989) *The Tourist*, 2nd edition, London: Macmillan.

McChesney, R. (1998) 'Media convergence and globalisation', ch.2 in Thusu, A. (ed.) (1998) *Electronic Empires: Global Media and Local Resistance*, London: Arnold.

Macdonald, S. (1996) Introduction, in Macdonald and Fyfe *Theorizing Museums*, Oxford: Blackwell.

Macdonald, S. and Fyfe, G. (eds) (1996) *Theorizing Museums*, Oxford: Blackwell.

McGuigan, J. (1992) *Cultural Populism*, London: Routledge.

—— (1995) *Culture and the Public Sphere*, London: Routledge.

McIntosh, P. (1968) *Physical Education in England since 1800*, London: Bell & Hyman.
—— (1980) *Fair Play: Ethics in Sport and Education*, London: Heinemann.
MacKenzie, J. (1984) *Propaganda and Empire: The Manipulation of British Public opinion 1880–1960*, Manchester: Manchester University Press.
Maffesoli, M. (1996) *The Time of the Tribes*, London: Sage.
Maguire, J. (1999) *Global Sport: Identities, Societies, Civilizations*, Cambridge: Polity Press.
Maheu, R. (ed.) (1995) *Social Movements and Social Classes*, London: Sage.
Mandell, R. (1967) *Paris 1900: The Great World's Fair*, Toronto: University of Toronto Press.
—— (1971) *The Nazi Olympics*, New York: Macmillan.
Mangan, J. (ed.) (1986) *The Games Ethic and Imperialism*, New York: Viking Press.
—— (ed.) (1992) *The Cultural Bond: Sport, Empire and Society*, London: Frank Cass.
Mangan, J. and Park, R. (eds) (1987) *From 'Fair Sex' to Feminism: Sport and the Socialization of Women in the Industrial and Post-Industrial Eras*, London: Frank Cass.
Mangan, J. and Small, R. (eds) (1986) *Sport, Culture, Society: International Historical and Sociological Perspectives*, London: E. & F. Spon.
Marshall, T.H. (1992) 'Citizenship and social class' (original 1949), in T.H. Marshall and T. Bottomore, *Citizenship and Social Class*, London: Pluto.
Martin, H-P. and Schumann, H. 1997 *The Global Trap*, London: Pluto Press.
Marx, K and Engels, F. (1969) *Marx and Engels: Basic Writings on Politics and Philosophy*, Feuer, L. (ed.) London: Fontana.
—— (1970) *Karl Marx and Frederick Engels: Selected Works*, London: Lawrence and Wishart.
Mattie, E. (1998) *World's Fairs*, New York: Princeton Architectural.
M'baye, K. (1999) 'Sport and human rights', pp. 8–14, *Olympic Review* XXVI-24
Mehring, F. (1966) *Karl Marx: The Story of his Life*, London: Allen and Unwin.
Merton, R. (1968) *Social Theory and Social Structure*, Chicago: Free Press.
Meyer, G. (1976) 'The 1900 and 1904 Olympics', in Killanin and Rodda (eds) *The Olympic Games*, New York: Macmillan.
Mihalik, B. (1994) 'Mega-event legacies of the 1996 Atlanta Olympics' in Murphy (ed.) *Mega-Event Legacies*, Victoria: Province of British Columbia.
Minkowski, E. (1970) *Lived Time: Phenomenological and Pathological Studies*, Evanston: Northwestern University Press.
Moore, K. (1986) 'The 1911 Festival of Empire: A Final Fling?' pp. 84–90 in Mangan and Small (eds) *Sport, Culture, Society: International Historical and Sociological Perspectives*, London: E. & F. Spon.
Morley, D. and Robbins, K. (1995) *Spaces of Identity: Global media, electronic landscapes and cultural boundaries*, London: Routledge.
Morris, P. (ed.) (1994) *The Bakhtin Reader*, London: Edward Arnold.
Mosse, G. (1975) *The Nationalization of the Masses: Political Symbolism and Mass Movements in Germany*, New York: Howard Fertig.
Murphy, P. (ed.) (1994) *Mega-Event Legacies*, Victoria: Province of British Columbia (An edited version of some of these conference proceedings was subsequently published as Murphy, P. (ed.) 1995 *Quality Management in Urban Tourism*, New York: John Wiley and Sons).
Nicholaievsky, B. and Maechen-Helfen, O. (1976) *Karl Marx: Man and Fighter*, London: Penguin, London.
Nisbet, R. (1970) *The Sociological Tradition*, London: Heinemann.
Nye, D. (1994) 'Electrifying expositions: 1880–1939', in Rydell and Gwinn (eds) *Fair Representations: World's Fairs and the Modern World*, Amsterdam: VU University Press.
O'Keefe, R. (1998) 'The "Right to take part in cultural life" under Article 15 of the ICESCR', *International and Comparative Law Quarterly*, 47: 904–23.
Ohmae, K. (1995) *The End of the Nation State: The Rise of Regional Economies*, Harper Collins, New York.

Page, S. (1995) *Urban Tourism*, London: Routledge.

Payne, A. (1993) 'The Commonwealth and the Politics of Sporting Contacts with South Africa', in Binfield and Stevenson (eds.) *Sport, Culture and Politics*, Sheffield: Sheffield Academic Press.

Pegler, M. and Rimer, G. (1999) *Buffalo Bill's Wild West*, Leeds: The Royal Armouries Museum.

Phillips, G. and Oldham,T. (1994) *World Cup USA '94*, London: Collins Willow.

Pred, A. (1991) 'Spectacular articulations of modernity: the Stockholm exhibition of 1897', *Geografiska Annaler* , 73 B 1: 45–84.

Puijk, R. (ed.) (1996) *Global Spotlights on Lillehammer*, Luton: John Libbey Media.

Pyo, S., Cook, R. and Howell, R. (1988) 'Summer Olympic tourism market – learning from the past', *Tourism Management*, 9,2:137–44.

Real, M. (1989) *Super Media: A Cultural Studies Approach*, London: Sage.

—— (1995) 'Sport and the spectacle', in J.Downing, A. Mohammadi and A. Sreberny-Mohammadi (eds) *Questioning the Media*, 2nd ed. London: Sage.

—— (1996a) *Exploring Media Culture*, London: Sage.

—— (1996b) 'The Postmodern Olympics: Technology and the Commodification of the Olympic Movement', *Quest*, 48: 9–24.

—— (1996c) 'Is television corrupting the Olympics? Media and the (post) modern games at age 100', *Televion Quarterly*, Summer: 2–12.

—— (1996d) 'The Televised Olympics from Atlanta: a look back – and ahead', *Television Quarterly*, Autumn, 9–12.

—— (1998) 'Mediasport: technology and the commodification of postmodern sport', in Wenner (ed.) *MediaSport*, London: Routledge.

Richards, T. (1990) *The Commodity Culture of Victorian England: Advertising and spectacle 1851–1914*, Stanford : Stanford University Press.

Rifkin, J. (1987) *Time Wars: The Primary Conflict in Human History*, New York: Henry Holt & Co.

Riordan, J. (1978) 'Sport in the Soviet Union' in Riordan J. (ed.) *Sport under Communism*, London: Hurst.

—— (1984) 'The workers' Olympics', in Tomlinson and Whannel (eds) *Five Ring Circus: Money, Power and Politics at the Olympic Games*, London: Pluto Press.

—— (1998) 'The sports policy of the Soviet Union, 1917–1941', in Arnaud and Riordan (eds) *Sport and International Politics: The impact of fascism and communism on sport*, London: E. & FN Spon/Routledge.

Ritchie, B. (1984) 'Assessing the impacts of hallmark events', *Journal of Travel Research*, 23,2: 2–11.

Ritzer,G. (1996) *The McDonaldization of Society*, London: Sage.

—— (1998) *The McDonaldisation Thesis*, London: Sage.

—— (1999) *Enchanting a Disenchanted World: Revolutionizing the Means of Consumption*, London: Sage.

Ritzer, G. and Liska, A. (1997) ' "McDisneyization" and "Post-Tourism": complementary perspectives on contemporary tourism', in Rojek and Urry (eds) *Touring Cultures: Transformations of Travel and Theory*, London: Routledge.

Rivenburgh, N. (1992) 'National image richness in US-televised coverage of South Korea during the Seoul Olympics', *Asian Journal of Communication*, 2, 2: 1–39.

Robertson, M. (1992) 'Cultural hegemony goes to the fair', *American Studies* 33,1: 31–44.

Robertson, R. (1990) 'Mapping the global condition', in Featherstone (ed.) *Global Culture*, London: Sage.

—— (1992) *Globalization: Social Theory and Global Culture*, London: Sage.

Roche, M. (1973) *Phenomenology, Language and the Social Sciences*, London: Routledge and Kegan Paul.

—— (1987a) 'Social theory and the lifeworld ', *British Journal of Sociology*, 38: 283–6

—— (1987b) 'Citizenship, social theory and social change', *Theory and Society*, 16: 363–99

—— (1988) 'The political sociology of the lifeworld',*Philosophy of the Social Sciences*, 18: 259–63

—— (1989) 'Lived time, leisure and retirement', pp.54–79, in Winnifrith, T. and Barrett C. eds. *The Philosophy of Leisure*, London: Macmillan.

—— (1990) 'Time and unemployment', *Human Studies*, 13: 1–25.

—— (1992a) 'Mega-events and micro-modernization', *British Journal of Sociology*, 43: 563–600.

—— (1992b) 'Mega-events and citizenship', *Vrijtijd en Samenleving (Leisure and Society)*, 10, 4: 47–67.

—— (1993) 'Sport and community: rhetoric and reality in the development of British sport policy', pp.72–112 in Binfield and Stevenson (eds) *Sport, Culture and Politics*, Sheffield: Sheffield Academic Press.

—— (1994) 'Mega-events and urban policy', in *Annals of Tourism Research*, 21, 1, 1–19

—— (1995a) 'Rethinking citizenship and social movements', in Maheu (ed.) *Social Movements and Social Classes*, London: Sage.

—— (1995b) 'Citizenship and Modernity', *British Journal of Sociology*, 46, 4: 715–33.

—— (1996) *Rethinking Citizenship*, Polity Press, Cambridge.

—— (1997) 'Citizenship and exclusion: reconstructing the European Union', in Roche and van Berkel (eds) *European Citizenship and Social Exclusion*, Aldershot: Ashgate.

—— (1998) 'Sport, popular culture and identity' in Roche (ed.) *Sport, Popular Culture and Identity*, Aachen: Meyer and Meyer Verlag.

—— (1999a) 'Mega-events, culture and modernity: expos and the origins of public culture', *International Journal of Cultural Policy*, 5,1:1–31.

—— (1999b) 'Citizenship, popular culture and Europe', in Stevenson (ed.) *Citizenship and Culture*, London: Sage,

—— (1999c) 'Mega-events as theatres of power: mass festivals and cultural policy in the USSR and Nazi Germany', unpublished paper, Sociology Department, Sheffield University, Sheffield.

—— (1999d) ' "Event cities" and cultural citizenship', unpublished paper, Sociology Department, Sheffield University, Sheffield

Roche, M. (ed.) (1998) *Sport, Popular Culture and Identity*, Aachen: Meyer and Meyer Verlag.

Roche, M. and Arundel, J. (1998) 'Media sport and local identity: British Rugby League and Sky TV', in Roche (ed.) 1998 *Sport, Popular Culture and Identity*, Aachen: Meyer and Meyer Verlag.

Roche, M. and France, A. (1998) 'Sport mega-events, urban policy and youth identity: Issues of citizenship and exclusion in Sheffield', in Roche (ed.) *Sport, Popular Culture and Identity*, Aachen: Meyer and Meyer Verlag.

Roche, M. and van Berkel, R. (eds) (1997) *European Citizenship and Social Exclusion*, Aldershot: Ashgate.

Rogers, E. (1986) *Communicaton Technology: The New Media in Society*, New York: Free Press.

Rojek, C. (1993a) 'Disney Culture', *Leisure Studies*, 12: 121–35.

—— (1993b) *Ways of Escape: Modern Transformations in Leisure and Travel*, London: Macmillan.

—— (1995) *Decentering Leisure Theory*, London: Sage.

Rojek, C. and Urry, J. (eds) (1997) *Touring Cultures: Transformations of Travel and Theory*, London: Routledge.

Rothenbuhler, E. (1988) 'The living room celebration of the Olympic Games', *Journal of Communication*, 38, 4: 61–81.

—— (1989) 'Values and symbols in orientations to the Olympics', *Critical Studies in Mass Communication*, 6: 138–157.

Rowe, D. (1996) 'The global love-match: sport and television', *Media, Culture and Society*, 18: 565–82.

—— (1999) *Sport, Culture and the Media: The Unruly Trinity*, Buckingham: Open University Press.

Rowe, D. *et al.* (1994) 'Global Sport? Core concern and peripheral vision', *Media, Culture and Society*, 16: 661–75.

Rubalcaba-Bermejo, L. and Cuadrado-Roura, J. (1995) 'Urban heirarchies and teritorial competition in Europe: exploring the role of fairs and exhibitions', *Urban Studies*, vol.32, 2, 379–400

Russell, D. (1960) *The Lives and Legends of Buffalo Bill*, Norman: University of Oklahoma Press.

Ryan, C. (ed.) (1997) *The Tourist Experience*, London: Cassell.

Rydell, R. (1984) *All the World's a Fair: Visions of Empire at American International Expositions 1876–1916*, Chicago: University of Chicago Press.

—— (1993) *World of Fairs: the Century-of-Progress Expositions*, Chicago: Chicago University Press.

Rydell, R. and Gwinn, N. (1994) 'Introduction: fair representations – world's fairs and the modern world', in Rydell and Gwinn (eds) *Fair Representations: World's Fairs and the Modern World*, Amsterdam: VU University Press.

Rydell, R. and Gwinn, N. (eds) (1994) *Fair Representations: World's Fairs and the Modern World*, Amsterdam: VU University Press.

Samaranch, J. (1998) 'The IOC and the Exhibitions' Editorial, *Olympic Review*, 21.

—— (1999a) 'Human rights and Olympism', Editorial, *Olympic Review*, XXVI-24.

—— (1999b) 'Doping destroys health', Editorial, *Olympic Review*, XXVI-25 .

—— (1999c) 'A new horizon', Editorial, *Olympic Review*, XXVI-26.

—— (1999d) 'The culture of peace', Editorial, *Olympic Review*, XXVI-27.

Scannell, P. (1996) *Radio, Television and Modern Life*, Oxford: Blackwell.

Schechner, R. (1995) *The Future of Ritual; Writings on Culture and Performance*, London: Routledge.

Schivelbusch, W. (1988) *Disenchanted Night: The Industrialisation of Light in the nineteenth century*, Oxford, Berg.

Schroeder-Gudehus, B. and Rasmussen, A. (1992) *Les Fastes du Progres: Les Guides des Exposition Universelles 1851–1992*, Paris: L'Atelier d'Edition Europeen, Flammarion.

Schutz, A. and Luckmann,T. (1974) *The Structures of the Lifeworld*, London: Heinemann.

Scobey, D. (1994) 'What shall we do with our walls? The Philadelphia centennial and the meaning of household design', in Rydell and Gwinn (eds) *Fair Representations: World's Fairs and the Modern World*, Amsterdam: VU University Press.

Seh-Jik, P. (1991) *The Seoul Olympics: The Inside Story*, London: Bellew Publishing.

Sereny, G. (1995) *Albert Speer: His Battle with Truth*, London: Picador.

Shaikin, B. (1988) *Sport and Politics: the Olympics and the Los Angeles Games*, New York: Praeger.

Shawcross, W. (1993) *Rupert Murdoch: Ringmaster of the Information Circus*, London : Pan.

Sklair, L. (1991) *The Sociology of the Global System*, London: Harvester/Wheatsheaf.

Simson,V. and Jennings, A. (1992) *The Lords of the Rings: Power, Money and Drugs in the Modern Olympics*, London: Simon & Schuster.

Smart, B. (ed.) (1999) *Resisting McDonaldization*, London: Sage.

Smith, A. (1995) *Nations and Nationalism in a Global Era*, Cambridge: Polity Press.

—— (1998) *Nationalism and Modernism*, London: Routledge.

Smoodin, E. (ed.) (1994) *Disney Discourse: Producing the Magic Kingdom*, London: Routledge.

SOOC (1988) 'Olympics and the Korean Economy,' Seoul: SOOC (Seoul Olympic Organising Committee).

Sorkin, M. (1992) 'See you in Disneyland', in Sorkin, M. (ed.) *Variations on a Theme Park*, New York: Hill and Wang.

Spa, M de M., Rivenburgh, N., and Larson, J. (1995) *Television in the Olympics*, Luton: John Libbey Media.

Speer, A. (1970) *Inside the Third Reich*, London: Weidenfeld and Nicolson.

Spillman, L. (1997) *Nation and Commemoration: Creating National Identities in the United States and Australia*, Cambridge: Cambridge University Press.

Spybey, T. (1996) *Globalization and World Society*, Cambridge: Polity Press.

Sreberny-Mohammadi, A. *et al.* (eds) (1997) *Media in a Global Context: A Reader*, London, Arnold.

Stallard, P. (1996) 'A Fractured Vision; The World Fair comes to Wembley', unpublished paper, Geography Department, Sheffield University.

Stallybrass, P. and White, A. (1986) *The Politics and Poetics of Transgression*, London: Methuen.

Stevenson, N. (1995) *Understanding Media Cultures: Social Theory and Mass Communication*, London: Sage.

Stevenson, N. (ed.) (1999) *Citizenship and Culture*, London: Sage

Stivachtis, K. (1999) 'Cooperation between the IOC and UNESCO', *Olympic Review* XXVI-24: 47.

Sugden, J. and Tomlinson, A. (eds) (1994) *Hosts and Champions: Soccer Cultures, National Identities and the USA World Cup*, Aldershot: Arena/Ashgate.

Sugden, J. and Tomlinson, A. (1998) *FIFA and the Contest for World Football*, Cambridge: Polity Press.

Susman, W. (1983) 'Ritual Fairs', *Chicago History*, 12, 3: 4–7.

Syme, G., Shaw, B., Fenton, M. and Mueller,W. (eds) (1989) *The Planning and Evaluation of Hallmark Events*, Aldershot: Avebury.

Taylor, T. (1986) 'Sport and International relations', in Allison, L. (ed.) *The Politics of Sport*, Manchester : Manchester University Press.

Teja, A. (1996) 'The transformation of the national Italian Olympic Committee during the Fascist regime: Sport as a symbol of political power', in Van der Merwe (ed.) *Sport as Symbol, Symbols in Sport*, Augustin, Germany: Academia Verlag, Sankt Augustin.

—— (1998) 'Italian sport and international relations under fascism', in Arnaud and Riordan (eds) *Sport and International Politics: The impact of fascism and communism on sport*, London: E & FN Spon/Routledge.

Thompson, J. (1995) *The Media and Modernity: A Social Theory of the Media*, Cambridge: Polity Press.

Toffler, A. (1970) *Future Shock*, London: Pan Books.

Tomlinson, A. and Whannel, G. (eds) (1984) *Five Ring Circus: Money, Power and Politics at the Olympic Games*, London: Pluto Press.

Touraine, A. (1995) 'Democracy: From a politics of citizenship to a politics of recognition', in Maheu (ed.) *Social Movements and Social Classes*, London: Sage.

Toulmin, V. (1994) 'Telling the tale', *Film History*, 6: 219–37.

TPOD (1995) *Inside the Mouse; Work and Play at Disney World*, London: Rivers Oram Press. (the acronym TPOD refers to the collectively authored work of 'The Project on Disney' group).

Tranter, N. (1998) *Sport, Economy and Society in Britain 1750–1914*, Cambridge: Cambridge University Press.

Tsubota, R. (1993) 'A comparative analysis of the Summer and Winter Olympic Games 1992, Barcelona and Albertville' (unpublished M.A. thesis, Programme in European Leisure Studies (PELS), Tilburg University and Loughbourough University).

Tunstall, J. and Palmer, M. (1991) *Media Moguls*, London: Routledge.

Turner, B. (1993) 'Outline of a theory of human rights', in Turner, B. (ed.) *Citizenship and Social Theory*, London: Sage.

Turner, V. (1987) 'Carnival, ritual, and play in Rio de Janeiro' in Falassi (ed.) *Time Out of Time: Essays on the Festival*, Albuquerque:University of New Mexico Press.

Turner, V. (1995) *The Ritual Process: Structure and Anti-structure*, New York: Aldine de Gruyter (original 1969).

Ueberroth,P. (1985) *Made in America*, New York: William Morrow & Co. Inc.

UK Government (1996) *The Broadcasting Act*, London: The Stationery Office.

——(1999) 'Not only the Dome' (Government response to the 6th report of the Culture, Media and Sport Committee of the House of Commons), London: The Stationery Office.

Urry, J. (1990) *The Tourist Gaze*, London, Sage.

——(1995) *Consuming Places*, London: Routledge.

——(1998) 'Globalization, the media and new citizenships', unpublished paper, Department of Sociology, Lancaster University, Lancaster.

Vamplew, W. (1988) *Play Up and Play the Game: Professional Sport in Britain 1875–1914*, Cambridge: Cambridge University Press.

Van der Merwe, F. (ed.) (1996) *Sport as Symbol, Symbols in Sport*, Augustin, Germany: Academia Verlag, Sankt Augustin.

Van Gennep, A. (1960) *The Rites of Passage*, Chicago: The University of Chicao Press (original 1908).

Van Steenbergen, B. (1995) *The Condition of Citizenship*, London: Sage.

Varrasi, F. (1997) 'Creating Wembley: sport and suburbia', unpublished paper, School of Humanities, De Montfort University, Leicester.

Verdaguer, C. (1995) 'Mega-events: local strategies and global tourist attractions', in Montanari, A. and Williams, A. (eds) *European Tourism*, Chichester/New York: Wiley.

Verdier, M. (1996) 'The IOC and the press', *Olympic Review*, XXV-9: 65–6.

Von Geldern, J. (1993) *Bolshevik Festivals 1917–1920*, London: University of California Press.

Wachtel, E. (1986) 'Expo 86 and the World's Fairs', in Anderson and Wachtel (eds) *The Expo Story – 1986*, Vancouver: Harbour Publishing.

Wang, N. (1999) *Tourism and Modernity: A Sociological Analysis*, Oxford: Elsevier Science.

Walthew, K. (1981) 'The British Empire Exhibition of 1924' *History Today*, 34–39

Waters, M. (1995) *Globalization*, Routledge, London.

Weber, M . (1947) 'Charismatic authority' in his *The Theory of Social and Economic Organization* (Part III, sections IV-VI) (original 1920) London: Free Press, Collier-Macmillan.

Wenner, L. (1998) 'Playing the mediasport game', in Wenner (ed.) *MediaSport*, London: Routledge.

Wenner, L. (ed.) (1989) *Media, Sports, and Society*, London: Sage.

—— (1998) *MediaSport*, London: Routledge.

Whannel, G. (1992) *Fields in Vision: Television Sport and Cultural Transformation*, London: Routledge.

Whitson, D. (1998) 'Circuits of promotion: media, marketing and the globalization of sport', in Wenner (ed.) *MediaSport*, London: Routledge.

Williams, C. (1997) *Consumer Services and Economic Development*, London: Routledge.

Williams, R. (1974) *Television: Technology and Cultural Form*, London: Fontana/Collins.

Williams, R.H. (1982) *Dream Worlds: Mass Consumption in Late nineteenth century France*, Oxford: University of California Press.

Wilson, A. (1994) 'The betrayal of the future: Walt Disney's EPCOT centre', in Smoodin (ed.) *Disney Discourse: Producing the Magic Kingdom*, London: Routledge.

Wilson, H. (1996) 'What is an Olympic city? Visions of Sydney 2000', *Media, Culture and Society*, 18: 603–18.

Wilson, P. (1976) 'The 1936 Berlin Olympics', in Killanin and Rodda (eds) *The Olympic Games*, New York: Macmillan.

Yoshimoto, M. (1994) 'Images of empire: Tokyo Disneyland and Japanese cultural Imperialism', in Smoodin (ed.) op. cit.

Young, M. and Schuller, T. (1988) *The Rhythms of Society*, London: Routledge.

Zukin, S. (1993) *Landscapes of Power: From Detroit to Disney World*, Oxford: University of California Press.

Zukin, S. (1995) *The Cultures of Cities*, Oxford: Blackwell.

Press articles

The list contains news reports and commentary in UK newspapers of record particularly on professional sport, media sport and the Olympics in the 1996–9 period. Items in the list are indicated in the text and the Notes in the form: Name, Year-P.

Anon, 1998A 'World body trusts China to put its house in order', *Guardian* 19th January.

—— 1998B 'Murchester United? Sky must be resisted' *Guardian* 7th September.

—— 1998C 'IOC whistle-blower in "muzzling" claim', *Independent* 14th December.

—— 1999 'Nagano's 1998 bid prompts concern', *Independent* 18th January.

Barnett, S. 1996 'Turn on, pay up', *Guardian*, 26th July.

Bates, S. 1998 'Europe reaffirms Bosman ruling', *Guardian*, 7th January.

Bates, S. 1999 'Brussels gets tough on TV deals', *Guardian*, 25th February.

Bell, E., Cambell, D, and Honigsbaum, M. 1999 'How Murdoch was caught', *Observer* 11th April.

Bell, E. 1998 'Nothing super about this league for BSkyB – unless it's in the game', *The Observer*, 9th August.

Boggan, S. 1998 'Revealed: secret plan for football revolution', *Independent*, 6th August.

Boggan, S. and McCann, P. 1998 'Murdoch moves on superleague', *The Independent*, 5th August.

Butcher, M. 1996 'Police raids may rewrite Olympics', *The European* 27th June.

Butcher, M. 1999 'Delors on IOC wish list', *Observer*, 14th March.

Calvert, J. Connett, D. Gillard, M, MacKay, D. 1999 'There's all to pay for', *Observer* 24th January.

Cambell,D. 1999 'Armchair fans to have digital season tickets', *Guardian*, 2nd May.

Chaudhary, V. 1998 'United launch own TV channel', *The Guardian* 11th August.

Collier, J. 1998 'Injection of realism', *Guardian* 5th August.

Cornwell, R. 1998 'Rupert strikes out at Ted' *Independent* 20th March.

Culf, A. 1996 '£961m bid wins the Olympics for BBC' *Guardian* 31st January.

Daley, K. 1999 'IOC report shows "decades of bribery"', *Independent*, 21st January.

Davison, J. 1999 A 'IOC expels six as bribe row grows' *Independent*, 25th January.

Davison, J. 1999B 'Shameful story of how the games were won' *Independent*, 25th January.

Davison, P. 1998 'Baseball team owners allow Murdoch to swing their club', *Independent*, 20th March.

EP 1996 'TV -Challenge to satellite sports monopoly' EP (European Parliament), *EP News* 4.

Evans, G. 1998 'Medicine cabinet' *Guardian*, 30th January.

Harrison, B. 1995 'Atlanta counts its 1996 chickens', *Financial Times*, 3rd November.

Harverson, P. Robinson, G. and Jones, S. 1999 'Olympic games scandal officials refuse to quit', *Financial Times*, 26th January.

Henderson, J. 1996 'What big Games hunter is after', *Observer*, 14th January.

Higgins, A. 1996A 'Humbled Roh 'ready for punishment', *Guardian*, 16th January.

—— 1996B 'Politics exploits past sins' *Guardian*, 20th January.

—— 1996C 'Graft at the heart of Seoul miracle', *Guardian*, 24th January.

Hooper, J. 1992 'Barcelona goes for gold' *Observer*, 31st May.

Horsman, M. 1998 'They think its all over', *Guardian*, 1st June.

—— 1999 'Sky Blues', *Guardian*, 12th April.

Jordan, M and Sullivan, K. 1999 'Multi-million mystery as lid blows off Nagano', *Guardian*, 22nd January.

Kettle, M. 1999 'Corruption probe spares Samaranch', *Guardian*. 2nd March.

Larsen, P. 1999 ' "Damage to the quality of football" ', *Independent*, 10th April.

Lashmar, P. 1999 'Samaranch escapes the bloodletting', *Independent*, 18th March.

McIntosh, B. 1999 'BSkyB in talks to buy 9.9% of Chelsea', *Independent*, 16th August.

Mackay, D. 1998A 'Samaranch doubt over Beijing bid', *Guardian*, 16th January.

Mackay, D. 1998B 'Behind the screen', *Observer*, 31st May.

Mackay, D. 1998C 'Samaranch to act over bribes', *Guardian*, 15th December.

Mackay, D. 1998D 'Its the taking bribes that counts and the winning city that profits' *Guardian*, 19th December.

—— 1998E 'Plague pulls pedallers from their pedestal', *Guardian*, 30th December.

—— 1999A 'Salt Lake bribery scandal claims first victim', *Guardian*, 20th January.

—— 1999B 'Acrobats fall in five-ring circus', *Guardian*, 21 January.

—— 1999C 'Samaranch in the dock', *Guardian*, 23rd January.

—— 1999D 'Bribe claims dim the flame of sport', *Guardian*, 25th January.

—— 1999E 'Suave Samaranch facing angry backlash', *Guardian*, 26th January.

—— 1999F 'Korda sweats over court ruling' , *Guardian*, 29th January.

—— 1999G 'Samaranch to lead drug agency', *Guardian*, 2nd February.

—— 1999H 'Samaranch told by sponsors to reform', *Guardian*, 11th February.

—— 1999I 'Long live the king, says IOC, after six voted out', *Guardian*, 18th March.

—— 1999J 'Samaranch's expensive tastes revealed as IOC open its books', *Guardian*, 19th March.

Mackay, D. and Chaudhary, V. 1999 'Bribes scandal forces Olympics shake-up' *Guardian*, 25th January.

Millward, D. 1999 'IOC fights to rescue tarnished games', *Daily Telegraph*, 23rd January.

Milner, M. 1998 'Barcelona enjoys a post-Olympics boom', *Guardian*, 5th September.

Nash, E. 1996 'A capital vision – from Spain', *Independent*, 29th October.

O'Reilly, D. 1998A 'Football set for the great leap forward', *The European*, 30th March.

O'Reilly, D. 1998B 'Sports gang up against EU', *The European*, 30th March.

O'Reilly, D. 1998C 'Ban on computer games', *The European*, 27th April.

Rattenbury, K. 1997 'A Crystal Palace for the Millenium', *The Independent* (tabloid pp.6–7), 23rd May.

Ridley, I. 1999 'Passion will see our game survives latest fat-cat spat', *Observer*, 17th January.

Rodda, J. 1993 'How Sydney bought the winning votes', *Guardian*, September 25th.

Rodda, J. 1999 'How money made all the running', *Guardian*, 25th January.

Rowbotham, M. 1998 'Uncertainty leads to embarrassment', *Independent*, 12th December.

Rowbotham, M. 1999 'Banks leads attack on "sad, soured, sullied" IOC', *Independent*, 3rd February.

Short, D. 1996 'TV sports contenders get a new referee', *The European*, 25th July.

Short, D. 1997 'Brussels to back fans of TV sport', *European*, 13th February.

Simpson, A. 1998 'More than just a football club', *European*, 24th August .

Smith, A 1997 'Murdoch goes into bat for Dodgers', *Guardian*, 14th May .

Smith, D. 1998 'Why the best of British is big in China', *Sunday Express*, 9th August.

Sudjic, D. 1992 'Homage to Catalonian planning', *Guardian*, 16th July.

Taylor, R. 1997 'Bosman effect is spreading', *Independent*, 13th September.

Teather, D. 1999 'AT&T joins Murdoch register', *Guardian*, 7th April.

Thomas, T. 1992 'Olympic record as Spain wins gold', *European*, 25th June.

Tran, M. 1998 'Murdoch steps up his American game plan', *Guardian*, 4th April.

Tran, M. 1999 'Murdoch raises his TV sports game with share-swap deal', *Guardian*, 3rd April.

Travis, A. 1998 'Don't let Sky claim key sporting events, say viewers', *Guardian*, 7th April.

Usborne, D. 1997 'Murdoch scores a media double', *Guardian*, 6th June.

Walker, M. 1998 'UEFA to turn its own league super', *Guardian* , 7th October.

Watt, N., Wainwright, M., Finch,J., Gibson,J., Cowe, R. 1999 'Soccer decision leaves Murdoch's backing for New Labour in doubt', *Guardian* 10th April.

Williams, R. 1998 'No time for amnesty in war on drugs', *Independent*, 12th December.

Wilson, K. 1998 'The Web gets its skates on', *Guardian*, 5th February.

Wolf, J. and Finch, J. 1999 'F1 chief abused market power, says EC' *Guardian*, 1st July.

Author and name index

Macdonald, S. and Fyfe, G., 240
McGuigan, J., 16
McIntosh, B., 248
McIntosh, P. 107, 238, 249
Mackay, D., 155, 156, 206, 246, 249, 250
Mackay, D. and Chaudhary, V., 250
MacKenzie, J., 57, 58, 60, 61, 75, 84, 161, 238, 239
McKinley,W. President, 46
McLuhan, M., 45
Maffesoli, M., 237, 251
Maguire, J., 247, 251, 252
Maheu, R., 252
Malitz, B, 118
Mandela, N. xi
Mandell, R., 90, 118, 239, 241,242, 243
Mangan, J. , 242
Mangan, J. and Park, R., 107
Mangan, J. and Small, R., 242
Marshall, T.H., 251
Martin, H-P. and Schumann, H., 252
Marx, K., 8, 47, 77, 78, 167, 218, 230, 236
Marx, K. and Engels, F., 77, 230, 236, 247
Mattie, E. 43
M'baye, K., 249
Mecklenberg-Schwerin, Duc, 120
Mehring, F., 240
Merton, R., 252
Messersmith, G., 118
Meyer, G., 88, 89, 241
Mihalik,B., 139
Milliatt, A., 111
Millward, D., 246
Milner, M., 144, 245
Minkowski, E., 251
Mitchell, G., 246
Moore, K., 242
Morley, D. and Robbins, K., 252
Morris,P., 16
Mosse, G., 36, 115, 236, 237, 242
Munch, K. 118
Murdoch, R. 156, 170–181, 247 (and see Murdoch media corporation)
Murphy, P., 237
Mussolini, B., 121, 242, 243

Napoleon III, 76, 91, 48
Nash, E., 144
Nicholaievsky,B. and Maechen-Helfen, O., 240
Nye, D., 46, 160, 246

O'Keefe,R. 248, 249
Ohmae, K., 252
O'Reilly, D., 180, 248
Osten, H. v T. u., 118
Owens, J., 113

Page, S., 243
Paxton, J., 49
Payne, A. 249
Pegler, M. and Rimer, G., 241
Phillips, G. and Oldham,T., 101
Picard, A., 54, 88
Picasso, P. 99
Poincare, H., 55
Pound, R., 246, 250
Pred, A., 15, 237, 240
Puijk, R., 191
Pyo, S., Cook, R. and Howell, R., 140

Randolph, P., 86
Rattenbury, K., 239
Real, M., 29, 163, 166–7, 236, 237, 247
Reifenstahl, L. 99, 113, 116, 162
Reith, J., 239
Richards, T.,57, 69, 240
Ridley, I., 247
Rifkin, J., 251, 252
Rimet, J., 242
Riordan, J., 101, 104, 105, 106–7, 242
Ritchie, B., 18, 236
Ritzer,G., 251
Ritzer, G. and Liska, A.
Rivenburgh, N. 185, 186, 187
Robertson, M., 74
Robertson, R., 238, 252
Roche, M., 10, 15, 17, 18, 35, 36, 56, 168, 175, 180, 222, 236, 237, 238, 240, 243, 247, 248, 249, 250, 251, 252
Roche, M. and Arundel, J., 168, 169, 237
Roche, M. and France, A., 243
Roche, M. and van Berkel, R., 180, 227
Rodda, J. 119, 246, 250
Rogers, E., 252
Rojek, C., 4, 237, 243, 244, 251
Rojek, C. and Urry, J., 240
Roosevelt, F.D.R. President, 76, 77
Roosevelt,T. President, 76, 89
Rothenbuhler, E., 163, 184, 189, 224, 237
Rowe, D., 170, 179, 183, 247, 248, 249
Rowe, D. et al (Lawrence, G. Miller, T. and McKay, J.), 247,
Rowbotham, M., 209, 250
Rubalcaba-Bermejo, L. and Cuadrado-Roura, J., 244
Russell, D., 241
Ryan, C., 240
Rydell, R., 19, 46, 47, 48, 54, 63, 64, 73, 74, 75, 77, 80, 83, 85, 86, 130, 160, 236, 237, 238, 239, 240, 241, 246
Rydell, R. and Gwinn, N., 130, 236, 238

Samaranch, J., 147, 153, 155, 190, 203, 207, 209, 245, 246, 249, 250
Scannell, P., 169, 247, 251

Subject index

AAA (Amateur Athletics Association, Britain), 90, 109
ABC (American Broadcasting Corporation), 183, 184
AFL (American Football League), 172, 173
Africa, 58,63, 83–5, 110, 198
'Albertopolis' (exhibitionary area of London), 52, 55
America (see USA, and imperialism, American)
Argentina, 93
Asia, 73, 83, 110, 141
Australia, 58, 61, 63, 67,102
Austria, 65, 105, 108, 121

Bastille Day, 35,36
BBC (Britishing Broadcasting Corporation), 169, 173, 176
Belgium, 58 (and see imperialism, Belgian)
Berlin Olympic stadium, 113, 115
BIE (Bureau International des Expositions), 55, 56,95–6,
British Olympic Committee, 109
BOA (British Olympic Association), 90
'body culture' 39–40, 103, 107, 115, 116
  embodiement and identity needs, 221–225
Brazil, 93, 173
Britain, 34, 37, 42,44, 56, 60, 64, 169, 173–5, 204 (also see imperialism, British)
Burma, 63

Canada, 61, 63, 67, 103
capitalism, 70–78, and 33–98 passim
Ceylon, 63
China, 25, 73, 83, 201, 215
citizenship
  corporate (and Olympic movement), 194, 202, 210–216
  'cosmopolitan democratic', 200
  cultural, 65–98, 159, 176–181

European cultural (and access to media sport), 179–181
global, 151; and Olympic movement, 202–216,
mediatised (Olympic), 194, 201, 204–6
movement (Olympic), 194, 201–2, 206–210
'of flows', 198–9
universal (and Olympic movement), 194, 199–201, 203–4,
urban, 125–158
civil society, 41, 204, 226–7
class (social class), 65, 71–78, 102–3
Coney Island, 129
consumer culture (consumerism, consumption) in relation to expos, 65–98
'Crystal Palace' expo (see expos)
'Crystal Palace' (the Hyde Park building, see expos)
'Crystal Palace' (the Sydenham building), 52
cultural industries, 23
cultural institutions, 23, 64, 70–1
cultural policy, 35, (and see mega-events)

Disney (theme parks) 126–130, 134

EBU (European Broadcasting Union), 179, 180, 183–4, 205
Egypt, 83
Eiffel Tower, 36, 49, 93
Empire, (see imperialism)
EMU (Economic and Monetary Union, EU) 179
EP (European Parliament), 180
ethnicity (see racism and 'native villages')
Europe, 110, 121, 168, 169, 171, 172, 173–5, 179–181, 190, 204–5
EU (European Union), 179–181, 190, 193, 204–5, 227, 228 (and see Europe)

event analysis:

Lightning Source UK Ltd.
Milton Keynes UK
UKOW051915280612

195208UK00001B/39/A